Vegas 6 Editing Workshop

Douglas Spotted Eagle

DV EXPERT SERIES

CMP **Books**
San Francisco, CA

Published by CMP Books
an imprint of CMP Media LLC
600 Harrison Street, San Francisco, CA 94107 USA
Tel: 415-947-6615; Fax: 415-947-6015
www.cmpbooks.com
email: books@cmp.com

Managing editor: Gail Saari
Cover design: David Hamamoto

Distributed to the book trade in the U.S. by:
Publishers Group West
1700 Fourth Street
Berkeley, CA 94710
1-800-788-3123

Distributed in Canada by:
Jaguar Book Group
100 Armstrong Avenue
Georgetown, Ontario M6K 3E7 Canada
905-877-4483

For individual orders and for information on special discounts for quantity orders, please contact:
CMP Books Distribution Center, 6600 Silacci Way, Gilroy, CA 95020
Tel: 1-800-500-6875 or 408-848-3854; fax: 408-848-5784
Email: cmp@rushorder.com; Web: www.cmpbooks.com

Printed in the United States of America
05 06 07 08 09   5 4 3 2 1

ISBN: 1-57820-279-5

Contents

Foreword

In an age where there are so many heated debates and headlines focusing on the issues of illegal downloading and piracy, filmmakers and musicians have been quietly embracing and taking advantage of the digital revolution. Today's young independent filmmakers are honing their craft and creating visually exhilarating movies with inexpensive high-quality digital video cameras and affordable audio/video editing software, such as Vegas, on just about any consumer-level desktop or laptop.

These same tools are also available to any musician who wants to expand their visibility and level the playing field against artists who are signed to major record labels by creating professional-quality promotional videos and making them accessible as streaming videos on the Internet.

This book is a must-have tool for those who want to take full advantage of what Vegas, the most powerful and intuitive version of any digital audio/video editing software, has to offer. I've been using Vegas since its first version, and it's enabled me to create promotional videos of our band, Quiet Riot, by compiling live Jumbotron footage from a series of live shows and then digitizing them and editing it all in a few easy steps on my laptop while on the road. I've even been able to create my own instructional bass DVD with just my digital video camera and Vegas.

Even though Vegas has an extremely easy learning curve, I wouldn't have been able to create such professional-quality footage in such a short amount of time without the help of my Digital Guru, Douglas Spotted Eagle. Any time I have a question on how to improve my project, I phone Douglas, and he's always kind enough to take time from his busy schedule to answer my questions and give me insight into Vegas that goes beyond what the manual has to offer. I've learned more about Vegas in a five-minute phone conversation with Douglas than I have in a week's worth of reading the manual.

If you've had the opportunity to catch Douglas in action on one of the V.A.S.S.T. Tour seminars, then you've already experienced his ability to clearly explain step-by-step all the great features Vegas has to offer and to inspire you to take your creative vision to the extreme.

This book is the next best thing to having Douglas' phone number on your speed dial.

—Rudy Sarzo
Bassist
Quiet Riot, Whitesnake, Ronnie James Dio, Yngwie Malmsteen, and Ozzy Osbourne

Editor's Note

When I was asked if I would like to technically edit this book, I was pleasantly surprised, which became high excitement as the idea sank in. How many people get the opportunity to work professionally with someone of the stature and reputation as Douglas Spotted Eagle?

I had worked with Douglas before as a host on the Digital Media Net Vegas forums. We had also swapped many emails discussing everything under the sun from didgeridoos to prawns versus shrimps to the meaning of such Australianisms as arvo and Chrissy and to what a gorilla was. But we had never met—in fact at the time of writing, we still haven't and have only even spoken once on the phone, albeit for about 30 seconds when Douglas was walking down some obscure street in New York while I was firmly ensconced at home here in the northern beaches of Sydney, 12,000 miles away and half a day in the future!

Over this period though, I have come to know Douglas probably as well as I could know anyone under the same circumstances and have gained a huge respect for him and value him as a very close friend.

On the way through, one of the major traits I have learned about Douglas is the fact that he loves to impart to others the knowledge he has accumulated. You cannot stop him! In fact, so eager is he to get this information out to an waiting world that I have never come across someone with such a prodigious writing output!

I know you will enjoy this book and, more importantly, learn greatly from it and have fun in the process. Douglas is a truly great educator, and I am proud to have been able to work with him, even if in such a small way, and in the process learn more than I could ever have dreamed of!

Thanks Spot!
David Hague
Sydney, Australia

Acknowledgments

Although my name is the one that appears on the cover of this book, this book wouldn't exist without the assistance, advice, and help of many people, most of whom have no idea that they were a part. I bear responsibility for any errors contained within, but maybe by thanking them I can distribute the blame (or maybe not).

First and foremost, Linda deserves much credit for making sure that there are always cold beverages and clean clothes, because during the writing of this book, most of which took place in hotel rooms and airplanes, I forgot the normal responsibilities of life.

Special appreciation for my partner and friend at Sundance Media Group and V.A.S.S.T., Mannie Frances, for answering nearly every call that came my way and keeping the phones at bay, making sure I kept on schedule for the chapters, even though some of the chapters were outdated with each different build of Vegas. Mannie, we did it man....who'da thunk V.A.A.S.T. could grow so fast?

Of course, Dave Hill, Richard Kim, Dennis Adams, Caleb Pourchot, Brian Orr, Brad Reinke, Dave Chaimson, Bob, Steve, Andy, Leigh Herman, Craig Yanagi, Bob Ott and Curt, among so many more at Sony, too many to name, are tremendously appreciated for being patient with my constant requests for updates, answers, and readings for technical accuracy. I've also appreciated your friendships much over the years.

David Hague, the man who is half a world away from Utah, technically edited and vetted the entire book even in the midst of working on his own writings and suggested topics, rewrites, and repairs. Thank you David! Australia ROCKS!

Lonnie Bates of Thomson-Grass Valley has taught me a lot about the analog world and high definition as we traded information about DV and HD. He's forgotten more about calibration, scopes, and displays than most will ever know.

A lot of my editing tricks are inspired by requests, suggestions, questions, and arguments from folks in the various forums I've been a part of. There are literally hundreds, if not thousands, of people who have taught me a lot or forced me to find answers to difficult questions. Thanks to you this book was inspired. Without the folks at DMN, Sony, and the WWUG forums, this book never would have been. Lou, Frank, Michael, and DV.com, thank you for providing me a venue to meet new people and to see the questions that are hopefully answered in this book.

Of course, I can't forget to thank Windham Hill Records who refused to finance my first music video, causing me to start editing on my own many years ago. From those days of analog, I've been forced to learn to do things that I couldn't afford to have others do. That refusal was perhaps the best thing that ever happened to me. And the video went on to be a top video later that year.

Sterling Johnson, Brian Morris, Ric Burns, Ken Burns, Jeff Spitz, Andy Dillon, James Cameron, Steven Seagal, Jerry Lonn, and Tom Bee, you've all taught me to be better behind the camera and smarter at the editing console. Thank you.

Bruce Braunstein, Paul, Louise, Bill, and Amanda, thank you for loaning your images to this book as well. Mitch, T.J. and Cheno, thanks for the help with hundreds of screenshots. You guys are great, thanks for watching my back. Jeffrey P., you da MAN! Michelle, Trav, thanks for the encouragement when writing, touring, teaching, performing get to be too much.

Rudy Sarzo, you are the most awesome and humble rock star I've ever known or worked with. I wanna be just like you when I grow up. Thanks for the constant calls with words of encouragement. Your VAAST-ACID DVD rocks!

To all the manufacturers that have supported Sundance Media Group, V.A.S.S.T., and the endeavors, thank you. There are too many to mention; most are mentioned in this book and/or found on the included CD. I do have to mention Tim Wilson/Avid, Michael Feerer/Pixelan, Steve Pitzel/Intel, Tim and Mike at Canon, Phil Shaw at Matrox, Chris Hurd, and the VASST team. Phil, Bob, Julie, and the gang at Artbeats, your support is immense! (Nearly every image in this book comes from an Artbeats library.) Thank you. Appreciation to the guys at Canopus(and Kara) and ADS for providing me with immense knowledge and assistance.

Finally, many thanks to Dorothy, Paul, and the team at CMP for providing this opportunity to share my knowledge. We've now done several together, and it's been a great time so far!

Introduction

Interestingly enough, this book started out as a small guide to what became Vegas 2.0. The moniker of Vegas Video was dropped in the middle of the project, and the same happened with the Vegas Audio name, thereby creating a product known simply as Vegas.

As an audio engineer, I have used Vegas as my tool of choice for a long time, thus inspiring my audio-based tutorials for Vegas. In becoming a videographer/editor to further my musical vision many years ago, Vegas Video 2.0 soon became my application of choice when I had the opportunity to see it in an alpha version in Madison, Wisconsin, back in 1999. It became the perfect meld of my two favorite passions in one application.

Therefore, I wrote this book really intending to please two different groups of users: one being the audio user, and the other being the video user. Audio users rarely think of the video user, and that's fine. Video users, however, absolutely must become familiar with the tools of the audio user; hence, the fairly intense audio for video section in this book. Moreover, this book has many tips, tricks, and techniques that I've learned over the years as an audio engineer, compressionist, and videographer/editor, some of which I felt were critical to share. Others merely appear because I felt they were of interest.

The intent of this book is to teach and inform, yet also to provide reminders to professionals who have "done it all" and "heard it all" in the course of their years of experience. While I consider myself an experienced audio and video editor, nearly every engineer I've met has dropped some small golden nugget that I've been able to learn from. It is my hope that this book does the same for you.

The CD in this book contains video, VEG files, and test media I felt important for users to more completely grasp the concepts presented in this book. VEG files can also be found in-depth at http://www.vasst.com/login.htm. These files are for your educational use. If you use them as a significant part of what you create with your video project, please give credit where it's due, if it's due. That's part of the honor system of Vegas users. Scripts can also be found in this book as well and on the VAAST website.

If this book seems too technical, I suggest that you go back and re-read a passage. I've done my best to keep descriptions and explanations as simple as possible in this book, for the purpose of getting information across, not to demonstrate my technical skills or lack thereof. Multimedia is an articulate beast; anything combining the eye and ear are bound to sorely display any errors, whether you or others see them. Hopefully this book will teach you to avoid some of the pitfalls that you otherwise might step into. One of my favorite sayings is "I've screwed up more times than most people attempt to try." And I feel this is true. I've probably made every mistake that can be made in audio and video, multiple times. This book is a result of the knowledge that I've gleaned in the process of discovery.

Some of the information is necessarily technical and might be over the heads of some readers. If you sit with the book and read through a chapter once or twice, coupled with a little work in front of a computer, however, the information will make sense at some point. This book is absolutely not a white paper on any subject. It's a teaching tool for the uninitiated and a reminder/reference for the professional. A basic understanding of your camera, a computer, and general education are all that is needed to complete the tutorials found in this book. If I've missed something or you feel I didn't reach enough depth, I can be reached at dse@sundancemediagroup.com. My personal website, outlining some of my work, can be viewed at http://www.spottedeagle.com. Keeping my music career while expanding my video career has definitely been difficult, but pleasurable. One has benefited the other significantly. I hope this book does the same for you.

What's New in Vegas 6

What's New?

Welcome to the Vegas 6 segment of the Vegas Editing Workshop book.

Vegas, now in its sixth generation, has maintained a steady workflow throughout the growth of the application. In other words, techniques in earlier versions of Vegas are still applicable in the latest version of Sony Vegas software.

This book contains VEG files generated in various versions of Sony Vegas; this helps keep the projects applicable to users of older versions. You'll find Vegas 6 not only is the most efficient version of Vegas yet; it also holds many new tools for editing and creating as outlined in this first chapter.

Sony Vegas Version 6.0 was launched recently, and as this book was finished, Sony had released Build 115, or Version 6b. You'll want to be sure that you've installed Version 6b if you want to follow along with all the new features indicated in this chapter.

Before you install Vegas 6, it will require that you update Windows XP. You'll need to load up the .NET 1.1 update, and you'll also need to install DirectX 9. Vegas 6 will not install until you complete these two steps. Both are available from the Microsoft web site.

Once these files are installed, you'll be able to install either the Vegas 6 software application or the updates for Vegas 6. When installing Vegas 6, you'll note that by default Vegas 6 will install the Media Manager. You may or may not want to disable this; instructions for disabling the Media Manager and Microsoft SQL are found later in this chapter.

1.1   You'll find the .NET installer at http://www.microsoft.com/net, and the DirectX installer can be found at http://www.microsoft.com/directx.

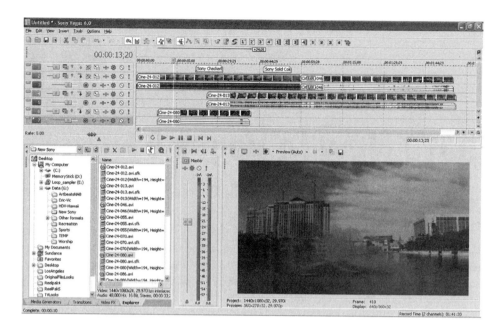

1.2   Vegas 6 hasn't changed dramatically on the face of things, but look under the hood and you'll be surprised!

The interface for Vegas 6 is little different than the interface for Vegas 5, with only slight cosmetic changes. However, the Preferences dialog in Vegas 6 has undergone significant changes in both look and features.

Preferences

There are new tabs found in the Preferences dialog, and a few options in various tabs have been moved to other locations. For example, the first tab that you might notice has changed is the Preview Device tab. Here is where you'll set up Vegas 6 for access to the Blackmagic Design DeckLink card, dual-head display, or OHCI FireWire access for previewing your video externally. The DeckLink card is an easy install; however you'll need to be sure your machine is up to the task of editing 4:2:2 uncompressed video. Finally, this is also

1.3   The new Preferences tabs offer many new choices. Notice that some preferences have been moved to the View menu.

where you'll select the OHCI/Firewire device as your output option. This is what you'll use if you're doing standard DV.

Next to that, you'll note the addition of the Print Device tab. This tab is where you'll select the device that you'd like Vegas to use when printing to tape. Again, note the Blackmagic DeckLink in this window. If you don't have a DeckLink installed, you won't be able to access this option.

Note the addition of the VST Effects tab. This is where you'll access VST plug-ins that you'd like to have accessible in Vegas. VST plug-ins significantly expand the number of tools that may be made available in Vegas 6. We'll cover the VST features later in this chapter.

Up to Speed

Another difference that isn't so visible is the multicore rendering engine. It's been reworked, rebuilt, and all I can say is, "WOW!" Working on some of the new VASST projects, as well as doing work for television stations, I've noticed a render-speed decrease of up to 60 percent. It's much, much faster than previous versions of Vegas. It's wonderful seeing the Sony engineers take on the render-speed issue, because this has always been a primary complaint about Vegas. The only thing keeping the previous versions in serious running is the quality of the render. Vegas has always enjoyed a reputation for superclean lines in titles, transitions, and overlays. Now users get the superclean renders while enjoying the speed increase.

If the machine being used for rendering is a single- or dual-processor HT machine, you likely won't see significant decreases in render time, and in fact, you may even see a slight increase in render time, depending entirely on how the computer system is configured.

In the Video tab, you'll notice a new field that allows for adjustment of threads for multi-threaded rendering. It's a good idea to leave this set to only 2 if you're using an HT processor, but if you've got a dual multicore along the lines of the new AMD 275 processor or the new Intel Multicore processor, you'll likely want to change this to its maximum allowable setting. In testing render times using one, two, three, and four multithread settings, I found that on a single HT processor machine, my renders actually ran slower than if the same machine was set to a value of one. Conversely, as this book was being finished, we acquired a dual AMD 275 processor machine on which shifting the multicore threads to a value of four decreased render time by approximately 10 percent.

1.4   The Video tab of the Preferences dialog contains a new field that allows for adjustment of threads for multithreaded rendering."

Nesting

Next in the lineup is the nested projects feature. This is a huge addition to Sony Vegas. What this does is allows users to take individual project files (VEG files) and drop them on a single Timeline. Why would you want to do this? For a number of reasons. One might be that you've got several scenes that you've built in various instances of Vegas. In earlier versions, you need to render each segment as a file, then compile the file in a master Timeline. Or, you'd have elaborate copy/paste schemes and risk losing any track motion or other track-based behaviors. With Vegas 6, you simply grab a VEG file from the Explorer window and drag it to the Timeline. Vegas then renders a small file very quickly, and that acts as a reference file. This saves the hassle of multiple renders. Further, it avoids rendering a file twice, once as a scene and again as a scene in a longer, completed project. If you've decided to modify a segment of the production, when you modify the VEG file in its own application, the master Timeline containing several VEG files, the master Timeline is automatically updated. Another use for this feature is that you might have several people working on various pieces of a project. As they each update their portions of the project, the master Timeline is also updated. You can even color-correct or match images in the master project!

To import a nested VEG is very simple. Open a new project in Vegas 6. In the Explorer window, locate VEG files from your project. You may find it helpful to name projects with project names and chapter numbers, but you'll likely find your own naming conventions once you start working with this feature.

Drag the VEG files from the Explorer window to the Timeline. Regardless of how many tracks of video and audio are included in the selected VEG file, it will show on the new Timeline as a single piece of media, much like an AVI, QuickTime, or other file format.

1.5   All the media on this Timeline except the audio and chapter headers is a VEG file. This is an assembled Timeline of chapters and scenes.

Before you can actually play the file back cleanly, the application will render a temporary file that carries the extension of .sfap0, and this file will be rendered to the location that you've specified in the Project Properties dialog. It's a good idea to render these temp files to a location other than the default C: drive. Rendering the file to the temp format will not take Vegas very long, depending on the contents of the VEG file being placed on the Timeline.

1.6   Drag VEG files from the Vegas Explorer to the Timeline, Vegas will treat them as though they were video files.

If you have auto-preview enabled, large uncompressed VEG files or files containing substantial numbers of tracks may appear to freeze when the VEG file is selected. Remember that the Explorer window is not buffered, and so you'll want to just leave Vegas alone when it appears to lock up. Eventually, it will play the file, but you may cause the application to lock up if you get impatient and start pressing buttons.

Vegas 6 provides an option in Options>Preferences, General pane, that allows users to "Ignore fact chunk" with nested VEG files. You'll want to enable this option only if you feel that the nested VEG file isn't playing the audio back properly. If you experience difficulty with audio files in nested projects, open the Preferences dialog, check this box, and restart Vegas. You'll want to delete the related SfapO file(s) as well, requiring Vegas to re-render the .sfap0 file(s).

Select another VEG file and repeat the process of dragging it to the Timeline.

Now that you've got two VEG files on the Timeline, drag them together to create a cross-fade just as you would with two video or audio files. Notice that the media behaves exactly as it would if it were a single video file. Add color-correction, special FX, or any other filter to the audio or video of the nested VEG file.

A good workflow in Vegas 6 for long-form projects is to:

1. Create intros, outtros, and any chapter headers separately as individual VEG files.

2. Create any stock or reusable lower-thirds or overlays as separate VEG files.

3. Edit each chapter as a separate VEG file, potentially without any titling or text. This can help ensure consistency from chapter to chapter and also allows a single process filter to be applied to any text you might want to process, such as using the Broadcast filter on all text events.

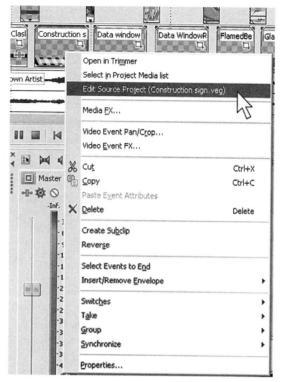

1.7 Right-click a VEG file on the Vegas Timeline to open a new instance of Vegas so that you can edit the VEG file.

4. Place all relevant VEG files on the Timeline, creating transitions from chapter headers, intros, or outtros on a master, nested Timeline.

One of the benefits of this workflow is also that all audio can be processed identically, helping to achieve a balanced, consistent audio output in Vegas. You can also drop your incident music in the chapter points, allowing it to fade from the chapter header into the file if you'd like to do so. Regardless, this is my personal workflow for most long-form projects in Vegas, as it allows me to have complete flexibility at all times.

Editing the VEG Files from a Nested Timeline

Files on a nested Timeline might require editing in place. For example, you might be working with stock lower-thirds that you've created for various projects in Vegas 6, or perhaps you're using the lower-thirds tool found in Ultimate S 2.0. This is very easy to do in Vegas 6.

Right-click the VEG file to be edited and choose Edit Source Project from the submenu that appears. This will open a new instance of Sony Vegas 6. When the new instance of Vegas opens, you'll edit the necessary areas and close the second instance of Vegas. When you close the second instance, Vegas will ask if you want to save the modified VEG file. Choose Yes from the options, and finish closing Vegas. The nested version of the VEG will be auto-updated.

One caveat to be aware of is that if you're using a file that you've designated as a "stock" file, such as a lower-third, teaser, or overlay, when you edit the original VEG, the original file is modified. One workaround for this is to do a Save As when you have finished editing the lower-third. Give the file a new name and continue. This will NOT update the VEG from the nested project. However, you can then go to the Project Media window and locate the original VEG file. Right-click the VEG file you'd like to replace with the newly named version of the same VEG, and choose Replace from the submenu that appears. This will keep the old version of the VEG in its current location and allow you to browse for the new version to be used in its place.

1.8 You can also choose Save As from the second instance of Vegas and then replace the VEG file in the Project Media window.

Track Flattening

Yet another use of this feature is to "flatten" intense composites or bring deep composites in as part of a bigger project without having to render out the composite. Personally, this is one of my favorite features. I've got a few lower-thirds that I've needed to render out in the past. Now, you can just drop the lower-thirds directly on the Timeline. Try this out by downloading some of the VEG files from the vasst.com site or by grabbing one of the lower-third VEG files found on the DVD in the back of this book. Drop them on top of existing projects. Import them one of three ways:

1. Choose File>Import>Media, and browse for the desired VEG file.

2. Drag a file from the Explorer window.

3. Double-click the file in the Explorer window.

1.9 These are all VEG files that have transparency or alpha channels. Notice that the Project Media folder displays the alpha channel when appropriate.

Notice them in the Project Media window, (which was called Project Media in previous versions). You'll see a thumbnail of your VEG file complete with any alpha channel that might exist.

Virtual Sound Technology

VST* is a plug-in format that often runs a little more smoothly than DirectX plug-ins but also offers a very wide array of access to various audio plug-ins that will benefit the audio user. In fact, there are a very large number of free VST plug-ins available on

1.11   The free versions of the Kjearhus audio plug-ins may be found on the DVD in the back of this book.

the web. I like the Kjaerhus audio plug-ins; they've got a Classic Series that are free, and they sound great.

To access the VST plugs, download or install them to a directory on your preferred hard drive. I install all my VST plug-ins to a folder on my C: drive labeled "VST" and that's it. Vegas searches for a default directory of C:\Program Files\Vstplugins\, so this is where you might prefer to install them.

Now, open Vegas, and go to Options>Preferences, VST Effects tab. Point the "Default VST search folder" to the folder you've installed or downloaded the files to if it's a location other than the default location indicated above, and then click the Refresh button. This will instruct Vegas to search for whatever plug-ins you've installed, and they'll show up in your Vegas Audio FX options in the folder marked "VST." This search could take a while if you've got a fair number of plug-ins installed. If you'd like to have alternative VST plug-ins, perhaps in the event that you'd like to sort them by manufacturer, Vegas 6 allows for up to two separate, alternative locations for search for FX. VST plug-ins (in the Windows format) are Dynamic Link Libraries (DLL), and the free versions of most VST plug-ins do not have an installer, but rather a zip file containing the DLL. As mentioned, you'll want to copy or install these DLL files to the C:\Program Files\ Vstplugins\ location. Find free VST plug-ins on the DVD found in the back of this book, along with demo versions of other VST plug-ins.

You'll apply VST FX just as you would other plug-ins. Double-click and click OK, or single click and select Add and then OK. Then adjust the parameters of the plug-in just as you would with any other plug-in. You can chain VST plug-ins right alongside DirectX plug-ins, and there are

1.12   VST plug-ins can be placed in a chain with DirectX plug-ins, and they operate much like a DirectX plug-in does.

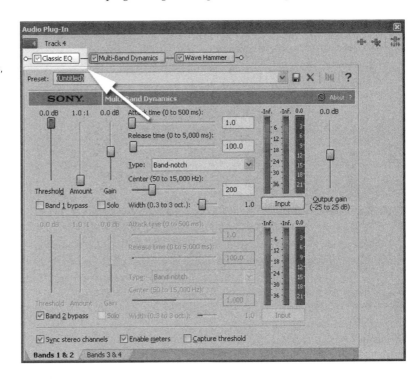

many automatable VST plug-ins available if you need to automate certain FX on the Timeline. Storing presets for VST plug-ins will be somewhat different, and these presets cannot be exported in the same manner as presets are exported using the Preset Manager.

One thing to note about VST plug-ins: If a manufacturer offers both VST and DirectX installations of their plug-ins (many do), then you should install both. The reasoning behind this is that some DirectX plug-ins occasionally cause audio to drift, while the same application in VST form might not. The opposite may also apply; a VST plug-in may incur drift where its DirectX counterpart might not.

*VST is a trademark of Steinberg Media Technologies GmbH.

1.13   Find the VST plug-ins in the VST folder for FX.

Broadcast Wave Format

Vegas now supports BWF files, or Broadcast Wave files. While the average user might not find these valuable, filmmakers, radio stations, television broadcasters, and users of high-end recording devices will appreciate this new feature. The Broadcast Wave file format was developed to foster a format of audio interchangeability by EBU Project Group P/DAPA (Digital Audio Production and Archiving), with significant input from the audio industry. An easy way to think about BWF files is as standard wave files with a metadata layer.

The BWF file metadata contains several parts not found as part of the standard wave file format. Included are:

- Broadcast Extension Chunk
- Compulsory Chunk defined by Microsoft
- The Broadcast Wave file
- Audio Data

Broadcast Wave Files are the same as WAV formats that you're likely already familiar with, except that a BWF file can contain metadata about the file, such as the author, the length of the file, and logging information that will allow the file to be logged for broadcast and copyright, or performance royalty needs. It also allows for timestamped files to be laid onto a Timeline in exact position. In order to add all this data to the file format, a new chunk, or layer of information is added to the wave file. BWF files also support the MPEG audio format, and an additional layer of information is added to the MPEG file where the BWF metadata resides. Only linear PCM and MPEG audio files may become BWF files. If the file is a not a PCM file, an additional chunk, known as a "fact chunk" will reside with the file.

The Broadcast Extension Chunk may contain:

- Description   Title information
- Originator   Name of the author or producer
- Reference   A reference number issued by the author or recordist
- Date and time   When the file was created
- Coding history   A record of the signal coding, e.g. linear PCM, MPEG, etc.

If you have BWF files, you can import them several different ways. Import them in alphabetical order, import them by timestamp, import files as a single Timeline track, or create a new track for each file imported. The latter is critical if you've got multitrack projects from recording devices that generate BWF files. You can find demo BWF files for import on the DVD in the back of this book.

To import a BWF file:

1. Choose File>Import>Broadcast Wave.

2. Browse to the device containing the Broadcast Wave or to the location that the Broadcast Wave is stored.

3. Determine whether you wish to add the file across tracks or across time.

4. Determine whether you wish to order tracks by timestamp or file name. (This applies only when you are adding across tracks, not adding across time.)

5. Determine whether you'd like to place the file based on where your cursor currently is placed or based on Ruler time.

> BWF file import in Vegas 6 is limited to stereo/two-channel only. You'll need to manually import multiple files if the project is a multitrack BWF file.

1.14   Import BWF files from File>Import.

Presets

Hallelujah! Track Motion presets have been restored; many users missed this feature in Vegas 5 software. These work just as they did in earlier versions of Vegas, except now Track Motion presets include 3D presets as well. This will aid users in creating their 3D masterpieces and allow the saving of the location of various settings.

AAF Import/Export

No, this isn't related to the band Alien Ant Farm. AAF, or Advanced Authoring Format, is one of a few current standards by which various DAWs and NLEs can share project files. Using AAF, basic project information may be shared. You can export a project from Vegas and open it in Final Cut Pro, Avid products, and a few other NLE systems via AAF, but it's not a perfect transport format tool. Don't expect things like composites,

I1.15   Choose the method you'd like to use to import BWF files and how you'd like them placed on the Timeline.

color-corrected video, or the majority of your transitions to open. It's primarily a means of getting the media onto a new Timeline in exact placement with a few additional granules of sugar thrown on top for sweetness, but it's not the total answer. We should see some improvements on this front at some near point from a variety of third parties.

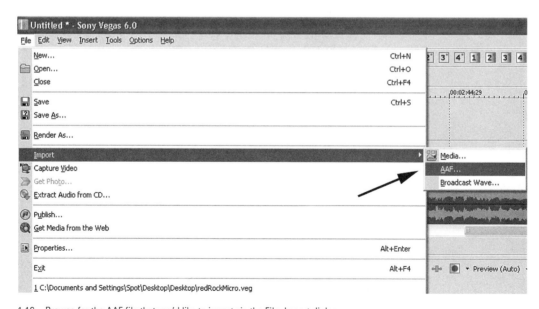

1.16   Browse for the AAF file that you'd like to import via the File>Import dialog.

To import an AAF project format, choose File>Import>AAF. Browse to the location of the AAF file that you'd like to import. This will import all media associated with that project file. Notice the use of the word "media." Any non-media file, such as generated titles or masks that are from a specific application that is not in graphic format, will not be imported. Bars and tones are also not imported if they have been generated by an application-specific process.

Transitions (other than crossfades), color-correction, any special filters, audio processors, and composites will also not be imported, as this is not part of the AAF format. Basically, AAF allows an application to locate assets *outside* of the application.

This is one of the drawbacks of the AAF format. AAF is a cuts-only transportation format from one application to another. While more robust than a typical CMX EDL export/import format, it doesn't provide perfect translation from one application to another. Let's hope that Vegas supports the more robust MXF, although somewhat complementary to AAF, in the very near future.

To export an AAF for import into After Effects, SaDiE, Final Cut Pro, Avid Express, Cakewalk, or other AAF-supported applications, choose File>Save As. From "Save as type," choose Edit Protocol Compliant AAF File." Use this format for most exports. You'll likely want to check the "Embed Wave/AIFC media" box for audio export in the Wave or AIFC codecs. You'll also note that there is an Avid Legacy AAF File option. Use that for exporting to older Avid software tools. The "Embed Wave/AIFC media" checkbox is not available for the Avid Legacy AAF File option.

Another option to check is that the default checkbox in Options>Preferences, General tab, is enabled for "AAF Export - Use frame unit for audio." Otherwise, audio is exported in sample units rather than frame units. Many NLE systems will not be able to read the AAF project file correctly if video is in frame units and audio is in sample units. Therefore, to ensure maximum compatibility, check this box.

1.17 Choose File>Save As to create the AAF file for export.

1.18 Find the "AAF Export - Use frame unit for audio" option in Options>Preferences, General tab. Use this as a default for exporting AAF files.

AV Sync Repair

Ever had video and audio drop out of sync? In previous versions of Sony Vegas, users needed to use the Trimmer or a scripting tool such as Ultimate S to resync audio or video that had lost its mate. Sony Vegas 6 offers a resync option to help users get frame-accurate audio to video (or video to audio).

What a *great* tool this is, in my opinion. Vegas will provide a display any time audio and video have become out of sync. You can resync by either slipping the audio back into place automatically or by telling the audio to be in sync from a particular point in the event or clip. Simply right-click and choose Synchronize.

Audio or video that has lost its synchronization is indicated by a red box in the event that will show how far out of sync the events are. If you don't see this, you'll need to choose View>Active Take (Ctrl+Shift+I).

Right-click the audio or video. Choose Synchronize, and you'll be presented with two choices. Generally you'll want to choose By Slipping, as this will slip the audio into place based on where the audio is. However, if you've looped or slip-edited the video file, you may want to select By Moving.

Choosing By Moving will move the right-clicked event to be synced with the other event related to the right-clicked event. Choosing By Slipping will slide the corresponding event to be synced with the right-clicked event. Files that have been slip-edited to the point that they're looping the end of the event to near the in-point of the event may find that choosing By Moving.

1.19 Right-click out-of-sync audio files to synchronize them with video.

1.20 Here, the audio has been resynced by slipping. Notice that the audio is in sync but that the end of the audio file extends beyond the video and is looped.

1.21 In this image, the audio has been resynced by moving rather than slipping. Notice that the audio is in line with the video clip.

Playhead Scrubbing

For those who like the way Adobe Premiere scrubs, Vegas now offers something similar, except it's better than frame-accurate. Grab the playhead on the top of the Timeline and scrub. You'll hear your audio scrub like an analog tape deck with no look-ahead or look-behind. This is most useful if you're after a very specific frame of audio or a particular sample point and don't want to drill in deep and visually locate it. The deeper you are zoomed in on the Vegas Timeline, the more detailed your audio scrubbing will be. You'll also notice that the deeper you zoom in, the more responsive the playhead scrub becomes. Although this is a very nice improvement to Sony Vegas, I personally find the Contour Shuttle Pro or Bella DV keyboard to be better suited for this sort of scrubbing. With the wheels on these two devices, it's quite easy to use the jog dial to scrub frame by frame.

Another addition is the slip-time indicator. This indicator will display any time value related to what you might be doing in Vegas 6. This display will indicate the length of time you're moving media down the Timeline, creating a transition, cross-fade, or other movement on the Timeline. It's a very useful visual display, particularly

1.22   In this image you can see how deeply you can zoom in to get sample-accurate scrubbing.

when rippling. The display will appear for selected and non-selected events, depending on what you might be editing. Although this is a small feature, it's one I've become quite addicted to.

Ripple Editing Changes

Users of previous versions of Sony Vegas will immediately notice the differences in ripple editing features. Earlier versions had a hole in the ripple process that confused some users as to what the ripple was actually doing or where it was taking place. In Version 6, Sony has created a workflow that whenever any piece of media is moved on its track, the events subsequent to the event being moved will move in tandem, immediately providing feedback as to where events will be moving. In this way, there should be no confusion as to where events are being moved. If two events are overlapped, the new ripple feature will display a cross-fade prior to the ripple edit actually taking place, allowing you to make decisions as to how you'd like the new ripple to function and where you'd like the overlap to take place.

You'll also notice the slip-time indicator showing the amount of time that the ripple will cover and indicating the length of the cross-fade being inserted. These two time indicators will help you immediately realize the effect the ripple edit will have on the project.

There are still three ripple modes, but the difference in the way the ripple works is just perfect, especially for long-form editing.

My personal workflow is to place all my media on the Timeline with slugs to indicate text or other overlays. Then, I play back the Timeline. Once I locate an undesirable area, I'll highlight that area as though a region was being created. With ripple enabled in All Tracks, Markers, and Regions, I'll then simply press Ctrl+X, (which is mapped to a button on my Shuttle Pro), and this deletes all media in the selected area. Ripple then automatically pulls all events that are downstream so that the next events butt up against the edit point just created by the deleted media/split point. This is a terrific means of working with HDV and rough-cutting either long-form .m2t files or CineForm files, and cutting them down to size. From here, it's an easy matter to export as an EDL, AAF, or finish edit inside of Sony Vegas.

1.23 Notice the slip-time indicator and the cross-fade indicated prior to releasing the mouse, causing the ripple to take place.

1.24 The area in the selection is to be deleted, and subsequent media or events will slide to the left, filling the deleted area.

Another workflow is to leave ripple off and simply make the cuts, leaving holes like you see in illustration V6.24. These holes can easily be cleared using either a scripting tool like Ultimate S 2.0, or you can double-click in the holes to create a region, enable ripple, and delete the hole. Ripple will fill the hole with the media that has slid down. If you intend on doing a lot of this style of cutting, you'll want to use a script, as a script can literally ripple hundreds of files in one shot, whereas you'd have to find every single hole and delete and ripple each hole manually.

Media Manager

You may have noticed that on launch of Vegas 6, a small window opens up that says "Starting Database" or "Opening Media Library." ACID 5 users have enjoyed this Media Manager format for several months now, so it was only logical that it would appear in Vegas at some near point in time. However, the Media Manager goes much deeper in Vegas. It displays thumbnails that Vegas auto-selects from the first frame of *visible* information, or you can set your own thumbnail. Sony engineers know that many video editors have black for the first frame or two of a video clip. Therefore, they built the system to look past the black for the first full frame of information, and the Media Manager displays that frame. To access a different frame that you'd prefer for

1.25 The new Media Manager in Sony Vegas 6. Notice the tags to the right that are associated with the file that is highlighted.

display, right-click the thumbnail and select Choose Thumbnail. From the Media Manager, you can actually start to build the project before placing anything on the Timeline!

More important, the Media Manager allows metadata, or file information to be embedded inside the video file. Tags that indicate the type of shot, angle of shot, panning/zooming/static, closeup, medium, wide, author, keywords, dates, length, and much more are all part of the media management. You can search your entire database for a clip and find it in seconds. Or search the database for a number of clips that contain the same attributes, such as searching for all clips labeled "B-roll," or "Closeup" or something similar. This does require some work at the capture and logging stage, but if you're working with several projects at once, working on a SAN, or sharing a number of project files with other editors, this tool is indispensable. You can also recapture media from here, and open files in Windows Media Player for a fast playback preview of the file.

To use the Media Manager, first open it up. Then click the Media Library Actions button. This provides the option to create a new media library. Of course, you can also open existing libraries if you have any already created. You can download a sample ACID library from the Sony web site. This will show you how the metadata structure functions, even though the sample library is for ACID and not Vegas. I strongly urge you to download this library, as Sony has gone through the trouble of cataloging hundreds of thousands of files. It will not only demonstrate how tagging can function but also save you hundreds of hours of cataloging and tagging effort.

Choose New Media Library from the drop-down menu, and this will offer a dialog to browse for the location of the folder(s) that you'd like to insert in the library. Browse to the location of the folder you want to be the new library, and give the media library a name. Click the Create button, and your new library will be created.

A window will open, looking like the illustration in Figure 1.28. This window will be where you'll set up most of the media library. Currently this library is empty, but we'll fill it up with new media.

You'll need to add files to this library, so select the Add Files to Media Library button. You'll see the dialog below, and here is where you'll add files to the library.

When the Add Files to Media Library window opens, you'll need to browse to the location that you'd like to add media files from. After you've pointed to the library, it's time to search the library. Notice you can choose a variety of file formats to either include or exclude. In this illustration, I've excluded the MIDI, Images, and Audio formats. Now click the Search button, and the Media Manager will begin searching the files you've got in the folder.

Depending on the number of files in the folder, this may take a few minutes, but it's usually quite fast.

When the Media Manager is finished scanning the files, you'll be able to view them in the new window that opens.

In this window, you'll first likely want to insert the descriptor tags to the video file. Do this by holding Ctrl and clicking on each tag attribute related to your file. In this shot, I've selected Closeup, Static, and Backgrounds as my preferred tags. (I created the Backgrounds tag myself.) You can now drag the tags to the media file, and on the right side of the screen, your selected tags will show up. In the Properties dialog, you can add all sorts of other search information and sorting or assets information, including keywords. The more you input, the more powerful the search and media management options become. This will assist you in finding any related media by using the search tool. In the future, I expect stock footage libraries from footage providers to come with metatags as part of the library structure. Of course, merely the library name becomes part of the metadata, and that alone is quite helpful in locating media.

> A standard Windows file system tree is single-rooted. It starts at one point and continues to split, but there is no cross-referencing. The Media Manager database allows you to cross-reference files, and cross-locate, ignore, or delimit searches. For example, pictures of animals can be classified by type (horse, bear, lion) or by country of origin (Australia, China, Africa) or by media type (B&W, color). This is virtually impossible to represent in a tree-type database structure without duplicating the asset. In this example, a single search could immediately locate B&W images of African animals. This is because during the tagging of media, you can cross-reference a bear that is in B&W and that comes from China.

Right-clicking in the Tags area allows you to create new tags. For example, I've added Backgrounds to my Media Manager system, since I do a lot of work with composites. This is very similar to the Photoshop browser that allows you to browse for images, except that Vegas' method can be a lot more intelligent, provided that you insert good descriptions.

At the bottom of the preview pane, which is illustrated as thumbnails in this window, you'll see a slider. This slider allows you to see the thumbnails at different sizes. Maybe you want to see more than eight images, or 10 images, or four images at time. Reducing the thumbnail size allows you to see more images. In Figure 1.33 you can see the entire Dolphins library in one view. Clicking on any asset or thumbnail will immediately show me all properties and metadata contents of that file. Hovering the cursor over a shot will temporarily zoom the shot to a larger view.

> It's strongly recommended that you download Sony's Media Manager library, as this library will save you hundreds of hours of cataloging files for use in Sony Vegas. Sony has already handily cataloged all their files. Once you install their Media Manager library, any ACID loop or video libraries you might install will be prepped for cataloging and searching.

The Details button allows the file name and extension to be viewed. Unchecking this will show only the thumbnail in thumbnail view mode.

You can insert metatags to multiple pieces of media at one time by holding Ctrl and clicking on all desired media, then clicking the tags you wish to use (again holding Ctrl to select multiple tags if desired), and dragging the tags to the media thumbnails. This

1.26   The first dialog in creating a new media library

adds the tags to multiple pieces of media at one shot, saving a lot of time, especially if you've got a group of similar shots or shots you'd like to make all B-roll or cutaways, or master shots,

1.27   For ease and speed when using Sony media libraries such as the Textures and Visions or Sony ACID libraries, be sure to download the Sony Media Manager library. It's well worth the effort.

or anything else. If you don't want to use keywords, create new metatags instead. It will still save you a lot of time.

One thing to note about the Media Manager: Because of the way it is implemented and uses Windows resources, it can slow down your initial boot time of Vegas. If you know you're not going to use it in a session, turn it off for faster boot speeds. Some system configurations do not do well with the Media Manager. Higher-end and better built systems will run the Media Manager with no challenges, but you'll want to be aware of your system limitations. The Media Manager uses the SQL database system, and you can learn more about SQL tools at www.microsoft.com/sql/default.mspx. Bear in mind that Sony has made the search utility simple, and although the SQL functionality can be confusing, the Media Manager interface keeps it very simple.

1.28   This is an empty media library, but it's easy and fast to add media to it.

1.29   Click the Add Files to Media Library button; a new dialog opens.

Performing the Search

There are two types of searches: Match Any and Match All. Match Any will match *any* of the search terms in the search window. Therefore, it's easy to have a huge list of found files, depending on what you might be searching for. The Match All search designation will locate only files matching the terms in the search window and will provide a smaller result in most cases.

Type in the word you'd like to search for, or check the tags that you'd like to limit the search to, and this will locate the files you're looking for. Be sure to remember to clear the search parameters prior to any new search, because if you don't, it's highly likely that you'll have legacy search parameters left in the search string, possibly returning more results than you bargained for, not to mention locating media that isn't related to the most recent search.

1.30 Allow the Media Manager a few minutes to search the files and catalog them.

1.31 If you don't click the small thumbtack in the upper right of the Properties window, the Properties window will open when the cursor is over its tab and close when the cursor moves away. This is a handy way to access Properties while still maintaining a full view of the Media Manager.

DVI Monitoring

This allows you to select a second, third, or other monitor to be used to monitor full-screen video, at a high resolution or full resolution (depending on your monitor's capabilities), just like an external broadcast monitor. This is particularly useful for editing HDV without an HD/SDI monitoring system.

In Options>Preferences (or right-click the track header), you'll notice a tab labeled Preview Devices. This allows you to decide if you'll be monitoring through a DeckLink card, OHCI/1394 card, or to a secondary monitor.

Vegas will allow you to identify which monitor is your display monitor. For viewing 1080i

You can drag tags to selected media, or you can drag media to the relevant tag. Either method accomplishes the same result, and which method you choose is dependent only on your workflow needs.

1.32   You can use this slider to resize the view size of thumbnails in the Media Manager.

1.33   Resizing the thumbnails allows you to see as many thumbnails as you can fit on a screen. It's great for being able to see lots of comparable images at once.

information, you'll need to have a monitor capable of 1900x1280 or more if you to see all the pixels in your image. However, if you don't have a monitor that meets these requirements, no fear. Vegas will display and compensate for whatever lower resolution you might have. Therefore, if you only have a 1280x768 monitor, Vegas will properly scale the frame to fit within that resolution space. Further, Vegas now offers a deinterlace feature on the display monitor, allowing you to view sharp, clean video on the second monitor. You can also use color management and select one of several profiles. There are calibration tools available from third parties that will allow you to calibrate your monitor for video, or your monitor may have come with a calibration disk or profile. Do the calibration, set your own properties, and save those properties as a color profile. Since Vegas can have its own color profile, you can also have a different color profile for your graphics, web, or other applications and use a specific profile just for Vegas. Be sure to leave the "Recompress edited frames" checkbox selected.

Insert still of my desktop setup. Notice that on the secondary monitor video is displayed full-screen. This is a great way to be able to display HDV without having an HD/SDI monitor.

Be aware that if you use a secondary display for DV, the entire screen will not be filled, simply because of the frame size being smaller than the secondary monitor will display. You wouldn't want the DV image to be scaled up, or it would be pixilated and look much like Vegas displays events in the Preview/Draft mode.

> It's a good practice to always clear the search by clicking the Clear button on the Media Manager search prior to any new searches. Otherwise, you might have data in the search parameters. Clearing the search parameters prior to any search will ensure a clean search.

Capture Tools and Hardware

Vegas 6 can now capture with total support from the DeckLink cards from Blackmagic Design as well as capturing HDV directly from the Vidcap application. Vidcap. Further, Vegas 6 comes with the CineForm codec installed, so you won't need to purchase this as a separate upgrade. However, keep in mind that the capture is capturing .m2t files, and you'll want to either convert to CineForm or use another method for conversion to edit such as the 4:2:2 YUV codec which

is what the DeckLink card will require, or perhaps you'll convert to straight DV for your edit and then replace the edits with the .m2t files for HD rendering later on. This will provide a high-quality editing experience, particularly those with slower computers. I'll submit that you might find the VASST Software tool named GearShift appropriately built for this conversion task. It can convert to a variety of codecs, frame rates, or a DV proxy for those editing on a slower computer, and with a one-button click, replace all media with the HD stream, saving a lot of time, effort, and potential headaches. We'll have a quick look at GearShift later in this chapter.

To capture DV in Vegas 6, choose File>Capture Video just as you've always done, or launch the capture utility just as you've always done.

This dialog opens up.

In this dialog, you'll want to select the external capture application. This will open the DV capture application that you're likely already familiar with. If you plan on using only this capture application, you might want to

---

👈 Tip_____

Every time you add files to a Media Manager library, a Scan tag is applied. You can rename this tag. In this particular instance, I've renamed the Scan tag to the Artbeats Lightwaves. This helps when sorting through multiple libraries in one search.

check the "Always use the selected method" box, and this will prevent this dialog from opening when you choose this capture option. You can always change this in Preferences later, should you start to work with HDV or HD/SDI or SD/SDI.

For this explanation, we'll be looking only at the new capture application. See the Capture Chapter for additional information on capturing DV in Sony Vegas.

In this new capture application, there are very few choices in the setup of the application. You'll note that in the Preferences for the new capture application, there are only two basic options with very few options beneath.

The first option, for a Device, allows for capture input from either a DeckLink HD/SDI or DeckLink SD/SDI card, or from an HDV device such as the Sony Z1, HVR M10U, or FX1 camcorders or decks. There is also a choice of "none."

Select the device that you'd like to use for capture. Sometimes, various HDV devices might not be seen immediately. You may need to cycle the device on/off/on in order for Vegas' video capture application to see it correctly.

1. In the Control Panel, choose System, click the Hardware tab, and click Device Manager.

2. Click on the AVC devices, where you'll see a connected device.

3. Right-click and choose Update Driver. You want to manually search for the new driver.

4. Browse to Sound, Video, Game controllers.

5. You want the SONY folder.

6. In the Sony folder, specify the DVHS driver.

7. Reboot the camera or HDV deck.

The other option in the setup of the HDV/SDI capture utility is to choose where you'll store files. When you select this option, a dialog will open up providing additional Preference choices.

In the General tab, there are four choices. If the computer being used to capture HDV is a slower machine (3.0GHz or slower), it's a good idea to disable all but the last choice in the dialog.

1.40   This is a new capture application found in Sony Vegas 6 and is used for capture of HDV or uncompressed footage via the Black Magic Design HDLink or SDLink cards.

This will task the machine with less processing horsepower, even though these preferences may not seem to be significant.

In the Disk Management tab, the only option available is to select a specific disk that you'd like to capture media to. The primary consideration here is to be certain that you're never capturing to your system disk. This is particularly important with HDV or SDI capture, as dropped frames would be a virtual certainty if media is captured to the system drive. For adequate SDI capture, you'll need a RAID 0 configuration. The RAID could be either SATA or SCSI, although SCSI is generally preferable, and a minimum of four drives, although a RAID of eight drives (10k speed) or more is a good idea. Blackmagic Design suggests you could possibly squeak by with only six 10k drives, but they don't recommend it. Hardware controllers for the SATA RAID are highly recommended, although there may be a software RAID controller available that will provide the necessary throughput. SDI and HD require a fairly significant amount of bandwidth, and so the drive array will need to be up to speed. One significant benefit of working with uncompressed media is that it actually requires less processor power than DV or transport streams require, as there is no compression taking place. The challenge in working with uncompressed files lies with throughput, not with processor speed. If you visit the www.blackmagic-design.com web site, you'll find a speed test utility that will let you know if your system is ready for processing uncompressed SD and uncompressed HD files. For SD file transfer and storage, 30MB per second is a safe benchmark data rate.

1.41

You'll need approximately 180GB of storage per hour of SD video. HD (without audio) is approximately 170MB per second, or roughly 600GB per hour of uncompressed HD storage. 1280x720p files require slightly less bandwidth and storage than 1920x1080 files, asking for an average of around 170MB per second. When working with uncompressed files on a marginal system, consider 24p as your frame rate, as this can significantly reduce throughput requirements, dropping the required data rate to just under 150MB per second. As you can see from these data rate requirements, you'll not be able to get into uncompressed SD or HD very inexpensively. Check the Blackmagic Design web site for additional details on supported and recommended motherboards, processors, and RAM configurations.

Finally, in the Device tab, you'll specify the default for capture, whether it's a DeckLink card or an HDV device captured via 1394. When an HDV device is selected, the connected device will display, such as you see in this illustration showing the Sony HVR Z1U camcorder.

If you plan on using one of the Blackmagic Design cards, you'll need the following:

i8You can download the system speed test software from the Blackmagic Design web site.

1.42   You can always change the capture options in Options>Preferences, Video tab.

The Blackmagic Design hardware cards that work in Vegas provide users with some options that previously weren't very easy to work into the Vegas workflow. Most importantly, rather than working with DV, users

Some loads of Windows XP may not see your HDV device immediately or may report missing drivers. You can install Windows XP Service Pack 2 (not recommended) or you can take the following steps to instruct Windows XP to recognize your camera.

can work with 4:2:2 uncompressed footage on the Timeline in Sony Vegas. Previously, to import uncompressed to the Vegas Timeline required capturing with a third-party application, importing to Vegas, rendering to the desired codec, then outputting via the third-party application. With the DeckLink card, you can import analog media or SDI media as uncompressed media. This means a deeper, richer picture, fewer artifacts, better color-correction processing, and a higher-quality output, depending on the originating camera or format.

Another benefit, especially for footage destined for broadcast, is that the signal can be transferred via SDI, or Serial Digital Interface. Coupled with a device like the Convergent Design SD Connect or HDV Connect, users can import uncompressed video directly from a BetaSP or HDCAM system and output right back to that same device via SDI.

If you aren't using BetaSP, SX, or HDCAM in your workflow and are primarily working with DV or HDV, you likely will find an SDI card to be unnecessary. If your only output format is MPEG-2 for DVD, SDI is of even lesser importance to most editors.

SDI requires a completely different setup on the equipment side than DV requires. For instance, most professional monitors don't come with SDI input and output, so you'll likely need to purchase an SDI plug-in card for the monitor. Additionally, you'll need a BetaSP or SX deck that has SDI input. Any switchers you might use also require SDI input and output. SDI-capable equipment isn't inexpensive and is really necessary for only a few areas of the video industry. Just being aware that Vegas can grow with you as your video skills and client base grows is a good thing.

1.43   Capture Preferences, General tab

1.44   DeckLink card

HDV in Sony Vegas

HDV is the "next big thing" in the video production industry, and just like DV changed the industry back in 1996, HDV is doing the same thing today. Computers and hardware that are plenty fast for DV aren't quite so optimal for HDV. HDV is to HD what DV is to SD. It's a lower-cost, extremely high-quality format that is accessible to most shooters and editors today.

HDV is another way of talking about MPEG files presented from the HDV camcorder as .m2t files. These are Transport Stream (TS) files and are not really optimal for editing. Aside from the fact that .m2t files require a lot of computer horsepower, these files also fall apart fairly quickly. One recompression of .m2t files is about all you can expect to get away with before noticing artifacts in the media. You'll see some marketing hype about "editing native HDV" and Vegas can do this too. But you won't want to.

Even on a very fast computer, native HDV (.m2t files) will at best offer a frame rate playback of around 18fps. This isn't suitable for editing by most standards, and so you'll likely want to consider other alternatives. This is related exclusively to the decode and processing of HDV in the MPEG-2 format. HDV itself carries the same data rate as DV.

HDV-Type 1: 19Mbps (720p camcorders)
HDV-Type 2: 25Mbps (1080i camcorders)

1.46   Capture Preferences, Disk Management tab

1.47   Capture Preferences, Device tab

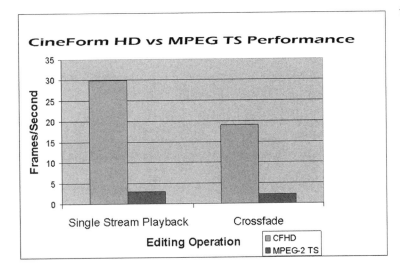

1.48 In this illustration, you can see how a DI, or Digital Intermediary can be a much more pleasant and efficient editing format than working with native HDV files.

Alternatives

Sony Vegas 6 comes with the CineForm codec as part of the application and HDV solution. This codec is one of the alternatives you'll want to consider for a significantly better editing experience. What this codec does is to convert the longer GOP (Group of Pictures) 4:2:0 file that the camcorder delivers into a short 2-GOP 4:2:2 file. Not only does this maintain the integrity of the picture, it also carries a lighter load on the processor, therefore allowing playback at frame rates of 29.97 or 25fps, depending on whether the project is 50i or 60i.

To use the CineForm codec in Vegas, users have a couple of options. The first option is to take

What can a Blackmagic Design card do for me? Should I be interested in using one?

all .m2t files as captured to a bin, and place them on the Vegas Timeline. With all files to be used on the Timeline, regions may be created, and the Vegas Batch Render tool may be employed to render to the CineForm codec template provided in Vegas. This can be time-consuming and offers several opportunities to make a mistake that will be even more costly to time or to the workflow, not to mention the potential to compromise the video quality.

Another option is to purchase the full HD Connect application from CineForm. This application will preclude the use of the Vegas capture tool, as you'll use the CineForm application to capture HDV. Currently the cost of the full application is $199.

What the application will do is to convert the .m2t files to .avi files on the fly, so rather than capturing and rendering, you'll simply capture, and the conversion is done during the capture process. The speed of the conversion will be dependent on the computer being used. On the dual AMD 275 system I recently built, conversion happens entirely in real time, so the capture process is identical to any other capture process. On a Sony VAIO 3.06 HT laptop, an hour of capture equals an hour of capture plus an additional 20 minutes for the conversion to take place. You can choose in the CineForm preferences whether you'll be keeping the original .m2t file or not. I highly recommend you do, just in case of any number of possible problems. Even on a 3.0GHz system, the CineForm codec will allow for full frame rate playback of HD files. This is helpful to the laptop editor or desktop editor on a slower system.

Another alternative to editing .m2t files involves a third-party tool from VASST called GearShift. GearShift is really quite simple in what it does, but there is nothing simple about the amount of

1.49 GearShift is a plug-in for Sony Vegas from VASST.

processing help and time-saving it brings to the HDV workflow.

GearShift is a plug-in to Sony Vegas 5 and Vegas 6, and is found in Tools>Scripting menu.

What GearShift does is allows users to import .m2t files to bins and convert them to several different formats. Users can also place long .m2t With GearShift, you can convert .m2t files to both DV Proxy and 4:2:2 YUV files. If you're working with the DeckLink card, you'll need to use the 4:2:2 YUV file format for export from Vegas via SDI. GearShift will also convert files to the CineForm codec if you'd like to do this.

The DV Proxy files allow users of very slow computers or computers that don't meet the Cine-Form spec to edit the HD files just as though they were DV files. GearShift applies the proper color-correction matrix to the DV files so that they are in the same ITU709 color space as the HD files, which allows users to work with the DV as though it was HD.

Note that the terms 50i and 60i are related to HD, not PAL or NTSC. This is because in the HD world, there is no difference between the color space and resolution of media played in the U.S. or overseas. The only difference between the continents and their media is the frame rate. With HD, televisions that support an HD signal can display either 50i or 60i, or the variants of these framerates. 24p, 25p, 30p, 50i, 50p, 60i, 60p are all frame rates and display formats that can be used in the HD space. When you see an image referred to as 1080 p30, this means it's a 1080 horizontal resolution file at 30 progressively scanned frames per second. Eventually, we'll get to the point of 1080 p60, which is technically the best display resolution and format that's been accepted by the ATSC.

During the editing stage, you may want to be able to compare the HDV footage to the DV footage. GearShift makes this quite simple. After opening the GearShift application, clicking the Shift Gears button will replace the DV files with the HDV files or with the .m2t files depending on what selections you've made in the GearShift application.

Another major benefit to the DV proxy format is that if you're working with an external HD and a laptop, you'll note that the requirement for file sizes is substantially smaller than if you're working with the CineForm or Sony YUV codec. Working with the CineForm codec HD files, you'll require approximately 40GB per hour. Working with the DV proxies, you'll need only 13GB per hour. This is good for the editor who doesn't want to convert the .m2t files and only wants to do a single render format.

1.50   When you shift gears in GearShift, the application offers choices between replacing the DV proxies with HD and replacing the HD with the DV proxy. This allows fast swapping of media formats.

As you can see, there are several workflows for HDV in Sony Vegas; it all boils down to what works best for you. Regardless of the final format, it's very likely you'll want to convert to some form of intermediary, whether it's using the CineForm codec or using DV proxies. The Sony YUV codec is great as well but involves very long conversions to a file format that while superior, is difficult to edit unless you've got a very fast RAID and very fast processor. Additionally, the 4:2:2 Sony YUV codec won't provide a lot of benefit for the DV editor, except as an archiving format.

Intermediary formats to consider relating to final output:

.m2t (MPEG 2)—Use this format for print back to HDV tape or for final render to DVD-destined MPEG 2. This keeps the finished media in the 4:2:0 sampling and color space of HDV all the way through to delivery.

CineForm codec—Use this for archiving or for stepping between the HDV media and going to HDCAM, or for rendering to SD for delivery in BetaSP, BetaSX, or DV.

Sony 4:2:2 YUV codec—This codec is the only choice if you're working with SD/SDI or HD/SDI files to be previewed via SDI. This codec is also used for printing to HDCAM from the Blackmagic Design DeckLink cards.

Getting Started with Vegas

Installing Vegas

Installing Vegas is no different from loading any application, but certain settings, steps, and habits can make operating Vegas more pleasant and efficient.

Before loading Vegas, make sure that any anti-virus software installed has been temporarily disabled. If a great deal of editing is to be done on this machine, it's worth considering building a separate user profile that keeps the anti-virus off at all times during the capture, editing, rendering, and printing-to-tape processes. Anti-virus applications are notorious for stealing system resources at will and for popping up when least wanted.

Vegas can be loaded either from a boxed-product CD or from a downloaded executable file. If Vegas is being loaded from a CD that came in a box, place the CD into the CD drive, close it, and follow the instructions as they appear on the computer screen. Vegas auto-starts unless this feature has been disabled in the Control Panel.

Complete the instructions given by Vegas' installation dialog. Vegas can be installed to any drive; it's generally best to install to the C:\ (or boot) drive, unless the application will be used on a network boot. (Special licensing is required to run Vegas on multiple machines at one time; with network rendering this will be important to observe.)

2.1 Vegas asks where it should be loaded/installed. In most cases, choose the boot drive.

2.2 Be sure to register Vegas so that Sony can notify you of updates and upgrades to the product and so that you gain access to the Get Media website.

Register Vegas when prompted to do so; by registering, you can access media for free that is on Sony's Get Media website, which is updated regularly for Vegas users. This media is generally royalty-free and worth having, particularly at the cost of registering the Sony software.

Registration can be accomplished via the Internet, telephone, or another computer. Registration also gives users 60 days of free technical support and special discounts.

Following the installation of Vegas, install the Boris Grafitti application and the Magic Bullet software plug-ins to Vegas in order to have access to these plug-ins. They will require separate registrations. At the time of this writing, Magic Bullet and Red Giant were offering additional presets as a reward for registering their software.

2.3 Vegas provides a successful registration screen after registration is completed.

The Basic Tools in Vegas

When Vegas launches for the first time, it's a blank screen with no media in it and makes no assumptions on how the user will be editing with Vegas.

The three primary levels at which audio, video, stills, and graphics are edited and processed are as follows:

- Event—can be viewed as individual pieces of media on a track. Many events can be on a single track.

- Track—is a single line on a project timeline, on which all events are placed. A project can have multiple tracks.

- Project—is a culmination of all tracks that contain events. (Filters may be inserted in the Project Media in addition to the above listed timeline options).

These terms shall be used throughout this book and the Vegas owner's manual.

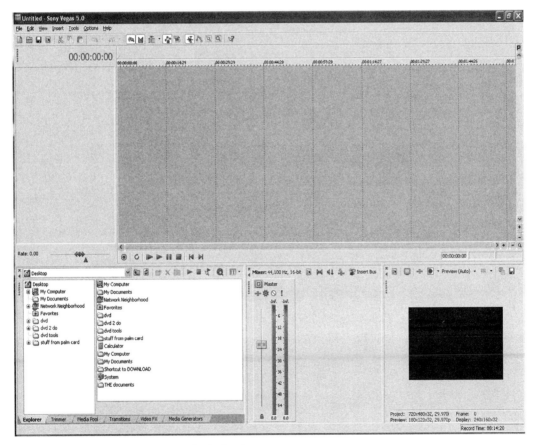

2.4   Opening the Main Window in Vegas for the first time.

Vegas is essentially broken up into three main workspaces:

- Track header/control
- Timeline/track view
- Docked windows

Track Control Pane

The Track Control pane is where track names are listed and track-focused effects are added. Users can also define special behaviors of the individual track, such as routing to external audio cards for sound control/mixing, and compositing behaviors for video. The Track Control pane is also where audio tracks and video tracks are inserted. Tracks can be inserted one of three different ways:

- Select INSERT | AUDIO TRACK or INSERT | VIDEO TRACK from the menu bar at the top of the screen
- Use a shortcut key: Ctrl+Q (audio tracks) or Ctrl+Shift+Q (video tracks)
- Drag media from the Explorer to the blank Timeline

The Track Control pane can be expanded or contracted, depending on the desired workspace and information space. This feature is particularly valuable on single-monitor systems where screen space is at a premium. Hovering the cursor over the line that divides the Track Control pane and the Timeline changes the cursor to a resize icon. Clicking the left mouse button when this icon appears allows the Track Control pane to be expanded or contracted.

The Track Control pane can be completely removed by using the shortcut keys Shift+F12. This step removes the control pane completely, so be aware that it's easy to forget that it's been hid-

2.5   Tracks can be inserted from the menu, as shown here, by dragging, or by using keyboard shortcuts.

2.6   The Track Control pane can be expanded or contracted, depending on the amount of space desired for viewing either the track pane or Timeline.

den. Using the Up Arrow and Down Arrow keys makes it fast and easy to move above or below a selected track. The currently selected track will be a darker shade than the tracks above or below. Multiple tracks can be selected by holding the Shift key and clicking each track chosen for selection. When multiple tracks are selected, any changes made to the controls on one track affects all tracks. This feature is useful when multiple audio tracks need to be raised or lowered in volume or for panning or bus routing. When multiple video tracks require changes to opacity or changes made in compositing modes, selecting multiple tracks is a fast way to affect all tracks simultaneously. Changes made to affect parameters will not affect multiple audio or video tracks, nor will track motion assigned to one track carry over to additional tracks when multiple tracks are selected.

Each track can be given a name for reference purposes. The track name becomes the default prefix name of the media stored on the Timeline when the audio is recorded.

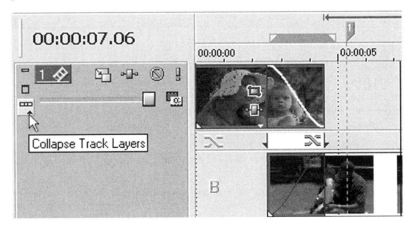

2.7   Track panes can also be expanded vertically, providing the traditional A/B roll view found in most other NLE systems. This feature uses twice the amount of screen space, which is the primary reason Vegas defaults to a collapsed track view. Expanding the view can help you become more familiar with editing in Vegas if you are coming from another NLE system. Simply right-click the track header, and choose Expand Track View from the submenu.

2.8   If a track is named before recording audio, the name on that track becomes part of the file naming process.

Adding a name value to a track after recording audio does not affect the filename properties of the audio. Adding a name value to a video track does not affect the name properties of the video on the named track. Adding a name value to audio ripped from a CD or imported does not change the name properties of the audio file.

✒ *Tip*

It's often said in the digital world that "if it ain't labeled, it don't exist." This is somewhat true in that cataloging media correctly at all levels is critical to locating and maintaining files. In today's digital world, files accumulate very quickly. Be sure to get in the habit of good track, file, and project management.

The Track Control pane is also where volume, panning, and bus controls take place in an audio track, as well as track-level audio processing. Each track has an FX button on it, where either default processing or custom plug-ins can be inserted. (See Chapter 5 for more details on plug-ins.)

Timeline/Track View

The Timeline/track view is where the majority of the work takes place. This location is where all audio and all video are displayed, edited, and viewed during the editing process. The Timeline can be expanded or contracted both horizontally and vertically to suit the preferences of the user. This area displays all media found in the project and can be zoomed in for sample accurate or frame accurate edits or out for overall views of the entire project regardless of length.

In addition, the controls for starting and stopping cursor movement and playback in Vegas are found in the Timeline/track view.

2.9   The Transport bar controls shuttling the cursor on the Timeline.

These controls can also be controlled by these shortcuts:

- Record—Ctrl+R
- Loop—Q
- Play from Start—Shift+Spacebar
- Play—Spacebar
- Pause—Enter
- Rewind—W
- Go to End—Ctrl+End

These controls can also be programmed in third-party hardware, such as the Contour ShuttlePro.

Next to the Transport bar control is a small yellow triangle that is used as a shuttle/scrub control. While playing media from the Timeline, this control can be slid to the right to scrub through audio/video during playback. The indicator will stay at the faster or slower speed until the yellow triangle is double-clicked. Double-clicking will restore the speed to the normal playback rate.

Scrub can also be achieved by pressing the J, K, or L keys during playback. J reverses audio and incrementally increases reverse speed if the key is continually held. K pauses playback, and L scrubs forward while incrementally increasing speed as the key is held. Speeds of up to 20x are possible within Vegas. To control the incremental speed adjustment and how fast it implements, choose OPTIONS | PREFERENCES | EDITING and select the JKL/Shuttle Speed option to suit personal preference.

The Contour ShuttlePRO, Space Station AV, and Bella Keyboard can all be used for incremental shuttle control. Setting the shuttle speed to High provides the greatest use of the shuttle wheels on these hardware tools.

2.10 The Scrub tool can be locked at forward or reverse speeds. Double-click to restore playback to its normal rate.

2.11 Setting the JKL/shuttle speed.

Above the Timeline is a series of tools on a toolbar that can be customized for individual use. These tools can be removed from the top of the toolbar by selecting OPTIONS | CUSTOMIZE TOOLBAR to add/remove them from the view. The toolbar space can also be double-clicked to call up the Customize Toolbar dialog.

2.12   The main toolbar in Vegas. Buttons can be added to this toolbar depending on editing needs.

2.13   Use this dialog to add or subtrack tools from the toolbar.

In the Add/Remove Tools view, select tools for display and click the Add button. Choose the tools to remove from the toolbar and click the Remove button. Audio editors might not wish to see tools related to video, just as video editors might or might not wish to see tools relating to audio. These tools are shortcuts to common editing tasks. All of these tools found on the toolbar can be accessed using keyboard shortcuts as well.

The dockable workspaces are found at the bottom of the screen in a default setting. Because these areas are dockable, they can be arranged to suit any specific need or desired appearance for efficient workflow. This feature greatly benefits users who have multiple monitors, as both the Timeline can be stretched across multiple monitors and the docking windows can be stripped off and placed on any monitor. Vegas supports multiple monitors.

Vegas Windows

The three primary windows used in Vegas are the Explorer window, the Mixer window, and the Video Preview window. Clicking the View menu at the top of the toolbar opens several dockable windows. A checked box next to the window name means that the window is open.

Dockable Windows

The exception to this rule is that the Timing window always defaults to the top-left of the Track View window. The Timing window can be docked or floated freely at any point, based on personal preference. As with all docking windows, the Time Display window can be expanded or contracted. Unlike other docking windows, however, the Time Display window can also be changed in background or number color by right-clicking the display and selecting Custom. This feature is significant in a dark studio where the time display needs to be large and not distracting.

Expanding a View of a Docking Window and Undocking Windows

Docking windows have always been a challenge to view when several windows are accessible, but Vegas offers a great solution to the issue. Not only may docking windows be torn off and their locations saved as templates, but for the single-monitor user of Vegas, each docking window now has a button that expands the selected docking window to the full width of the docking area. Click the horizontal triangle on the upper-left corner of the docking window and watch the window expand to fill the entire docking area.

2.14, 2.15   Clicking the Expand button found on every docking window will expand or compress the docking view.

For users of earlier versions of Vegas, tearing a docking window off has sometimes been a bit of a challenge if the small handle area of the docking window isn't accurately grasped. The most recent versions of Vegas make this much easier, with any area on the left hand side of a docking window being grasped, the docking window may be moved. Notice that in the new version of Vegas, the docking area has small indentations to better indicate the docking handle. To move a docking window into the docking window area without having the window actually dock, hold the Ctrl key while clicking on and moving the docking window. This will allow the docking window to rest wherever it's released.

2.16   The Time Display window can be undocked and moved around the screen but cannot be removed.

For video editors, some of these windows can be irrelevant. For audio-only studio use, many of the dockable windows might be superfluous as well, so it can be more visually efficient to hide the video-related windows. This feature is valuable to both, as it allows for custom views to be created for each individual.

The following is a list of the dockable windows, their shortcuts, and a brief description:

- The Explorer window (Alt+1) provides a view of all media on the computer system and network.

- The Trimmer window (Alt+2) allows media to be trimmed prior to placement on the Timeline.

- The Mixer window (Alt+3) mixes audio, FX buses, and Bus send/returns.

- The Edit Details window (Alt+4) displays all editing details pertaining to the current Timeline view. Resort, import, and view information in this window.

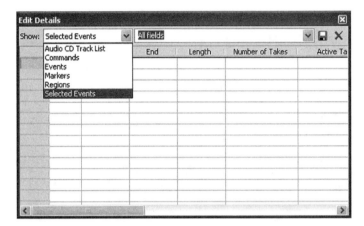

- The Project Media window (Alt+5) shows all media used in the current project, length of use, number of use, and allows for filters to be applied to large numbers of events.

- The Video Preview window (Alt+6) provides preview of video on the Timeline.

- The Transitions window (Alt+7) displays all transitions on the system, with motion thumbnail views of how the transition will function.

- The Video FX window (Alt+8) displays all filters on the system, with motion thumbnail views of how the filter will function.

- The Media Generators window (Alt+9) generates media as simple as a title, or as complex as gradient or noise generation. Test patterns are also found here.

- The Plug-ins Manager window (Ctrl+Alt+1) displays selected video or audio plug-ins that exist on the system, viewable by menu choice.

- Video displays and the Vectorscope may be opened from the Video Scopes window (Ctrl+Alt+2), providing color/luminance monitoring and matching tools.

- The Surround Panner window (Ctrl+Alt+3) is used to create surround sound keyframes and monitor the aural position of audio in a 5.1 mix. Right-clicking the Surround Panner window offers additional options.

To move a dockable window, grab the vertical bar on the left side of the window you want to move and click with the mouse. Hold the mouse button down and drag the window to the desired space. Release the mouse button.

2.29 Use the docking handle to undock a tool from the docking pane. Press and hold Ctrl down while moving the window back to the docking area to prevent the window from redocking.

2.30   Multiple windows can be floated on the workspace. This feature is useful when working with two monitors.

Windows can be stripped from the lower section of Vegas and dropped anywhere onto the Timeline, another monitor, or above the main work area. If a window is dropped too close to the lower section, however, the window will attempt to dock itself. Holding the Ctrl key prevents this problem and allows for precise placement of floating/dockable windows.

As many windows as desired can be docked. If space is limited, some windows can dock on top of others. Windows can float or stay left in place and then selected with the tabs at the bottom of the docking area. Dockable windows can also be expanded or reduced in size.

To place a dockable window in the lower section of Vegas, drag the dockable window to the lower part of the screen and release. The window will automatically dock and fit within the window docking area.

2.18   When multiple windows are docked in the docking area, each window has a tab for fast access.

The entire docking area can be hidden and recalled by pressing F12. This action will entirely remove the docking windows from view. To restore the docking area to view, press F11 again.

A useful feature in docking windows is that they can be automatically hidden. In the OPTIONS | PREFERENCES | GENERAL dialog, select "Automatically hide docking area." This action works the way Windows does when it auto-hides the taskbar while working within the desktop or an application. Just like Windows, moving the cursor to the lower area brings the docking windows back to view. This feature is exceptionally useful for audio editors who prefer to focus on the tracks during recording and only call up plug-ins or editing tools when desired. Video editors will also find this useful during in-depth compositing or when desiring maximum frame view for multiple tracks.

2.32 Hiding the window area mades more Timeline space visible. Audio editors will find this feature particularly useful.

Saving Templates/Layouts in Vegas

Vegas allows for new layouts to be created and preserved, permitting users to create their own layouts for single-, dual-, or even triple-head monitor configurations. Up to ten different templates may be restored/saved in Vegas for each editor's profile, or perhaps for each task. Each time Vegas opens, the saved layout will open as it was saved. Moreover, a template for each type of project may be created and opened, saving time. If various users are accessing Vegas 6 on the same computer, each user is capable of having their own personal layout template. To save a layout, create the layout appearance and save the template via the Ctrl+Alt+D then number keystrokes. This even allows for templates to be shifted during the editing process.

To save a workspace template in Vegas:

2.   Layout the workspace the way you'd like to have it look and feel.

2.   Press and hold Ctrl+Alt+D, then press a number key that you'd like to assign the layout to.

3.   Repeat up to ten times, saving up to ten layout templates.

4.   Recall layout templates by pressing Alt+number assigned to desired template.

Another power use of Vegas' template–saving feature is that a template might be saved for documentary work, a template for voice-overs, perhaps a template for surround mixes, templates for compositing, etc. This feature is one that has been long in coming.

2.33, 2.34   Vegas can save custom layouts that are recalled using Alt+D+ (assigned keyboard number).

Multiple windows may now be floating to various locations on the screen, so setting up a template is always a great idea if you'd like Vegas to open with the same views each time. Consider having a template layout for times when audio editing is the focus instead of video editing being the focus, or for times when deep composites and track views require more screen space, or even using a template during rough cutting and another template for finishing work. Whatever you prefer, Vegas now provides it.

 *Tip*_____

By modifying Vegas' internal preferences for Docking to TRUE, you can flip the docking area to the top of the computer monitor. This is great for situations where monitors sit high on a shelf, letting the Timeline be at the bottom of the monitor.

File Menu

Several choices under the File menu are available to help create a variety of settings, some of which are duplicates of the toolbar functions.

2.35   The File menu.

The Open dialog opens an existing Vegas project. Open can also be accessed by right-clicking the empty track window and selecting Open File or by pressing Ctrl+O. This step opens either a VEG file or media to go on the Timeline.

The Close dialog closes the current project. Vegas will prompt you to save, not save, or cancel. The Save dialog allows a project to be saved to a new name if it has not been named previously. The Save As dialog allows an existing project to be given a new name, which is useful for saving

2.36   The Timeline/project opens, and any media from the last project saved opens, unless
        this feature is disabled in the OPTIONS | PREFERENCES | GENERAL dialog.

Tip

Saving the same project with different names allows you to save various versions or stages of a project, which lets you instantly recall various mixes and edits. This feature is valuable when a producer wishes to hear/see comparisons between project settings. Save files by time, date, or a mix of time, date, and unique name, for example, "less bass mix-04-15-03."

a number of edits that may need to be recalled at a later date.

The Import Media dialog allows for import of single or multiple files of any nature compatible with Vegas. Files imported are placed in the Project Media for later use. This feature is useful for setting up entire projects before editing begins.

The Capture Video dialog opens up the Vegas capture utility, allowing for the transfer of DV from a camera or DV deck to a hard drive. This dialog launches a separate application.

The Get Photo dialog communicates with a scanner that is connected to the computer, allowing images to be directly scanned into Vegas' Project Media, saving users the time it takes to open a separate photo scanning or editing application. Vegas uses the scanning software found on the user's computer.

The Extract Audio from CD dialog is what its name implies: a means of ripping audio from an existing CD. Audio is then placed in the Project Media. This step only extracts audio from an audio CD, not a CD of WAV or MP3 files. Those file types are opened via the CD/drive selection in the Explorer window.

The Get Media from the Web dialog is a fantastic tool for Vegas users. It's a link to a website provided by Sony and their partners that gives users access to video, audio, and other media at no cost as a benefit for owning a registered copy of Vegas. Bed music and stock video files are regularly changed by Sony's partners.

2.37 Access video properties by selecting the Video Properties button found on the Preview Window toolbar.

The Project Properties dialog is a series of choices that allows a user to create project settings related to any number of workflows. Media that is going to be edited just for the web should have project properties that relate to web-oriented video or audio. Recording studio setups might want to adjust properties only for audio and never see any of the video tools. The CD with this book has projects already set up for you to use if you wish.

As with most options in Vegas, the Project Properties dialog can be opened from multiple places. Selecting FILE | PROPERTIES is one method of opening the dialog. The Project Properties button found in the Preview pane of the docking Video Preview window also opens the dialog, as does the Audio Properties button found in the Mixer dialog. Pressing Alt+Enter also opens the Project Properties dialog.

The default setting of the Project Properties is for an NTSC-DV project, which is used for projects captured from a DV camera to be edited and printed back to a DV camera or to another tape machine through a DV camera, DV-to-analog converter, or other DV device. This setting optimizes Vegas' preview and editing behaviors for the DV space. Other presets are there as well, including for PAL-DV, multimedia authoring, web-oriented editing, and MPEG-CD directed media projects. Any of these choices can be used as a starting point and then edited to suit specific needs.

 *Tip*_____

Be sure to set the timecode readout properties (right-click the time window) to PAL to see proper framerate playback.

Checking the "Start all new projects with these settings" box ensures that editors will have the same project settings each time they open Vegas for a new session. Having a series of project settings saved as templates is valuable, as it saves time and ensures correct settings in those hurried moments that are common in the studio, whether for audio or video work.

2.38   Using existing templates and creating new templates saves a lot of time when setting up an editing project.

⚓ Tip

Save VEG files for specific types of projects, such as a Timeline that opens with a station ID or corporate logo. Markers, chapter points, time counters, plug-ins, and other commonly used tools can be saved in a VEG file, ensuring that projects consistently open with all desired tools. This step also sets up a template that includes all consistent media. (See the DVD included with this book for VEG files.)

Setting Up Project Properties

Video project types are specified in the Video tab of the Project Properties. As a general rule, it's best to use the template settings to ensure that projects flow with ease and are trouble-free. Advanced users might want to edit the settings for specific results related to third-party tools or applications.

One major consideration with Vegas is to set the Prerendered Files folder to a new default. Vegas defaults to the `C:\Program Files\Sony\Vegas 6\` folder. Prerendered files will rapidly fill the `C:\` drive and are generally forgotten by most users, which can easily lead to problems. Click the Browse button, locate the second hard drive dedicated to media, and

2.39   Video properties can be accessed from the FILE | PROPERTIES | VIDEO dialog or from the Properties button on the Preview Window toolbar.

create a Prerendered Files folder on that drive. Point the default prerendered files to that folder on the media drive. This process will speed up prerenders and will ensure that media moved around from computer to computer (if the drive is external) will stay with the project at all times.

Properties for an audio-only project are also set up here. Engineers wanting to work with high bit rates and sample rates will want to adjust these in Vegas. Default settings are 16 bit/44.1KHz, which are standard CD quality settings. Vegas is capable of working with 24 bit/96KHz files, although for the most part, only professional sound cards can work with these higher sampling rates.

Take note of the Master Bus Mode, which defaults to Stereo. This setting is where Vegas is adjusted to author 5.1 surround sound files. If the applicable hardware is available to the system, anyone can now author 5.1 surround files in Vegas. (AC-3 encoding is not included in Vegas, as it's an additional purchase/plug-in package.) Vegas will output elementary linear pulse code modulation (LPCM) files, which are acceptable by most DVD authoring packages. Users that do not have 5.1-compatible hardware are able to select the 5.1 surround option and can output a 5.1 file. No ability to monitor/master the audio exists, however, which can result in a potentially unbalanced mix.

Up to 26 buses can be assigned in Vegas. (These correspond to the letters of the alphabet.) Buses can be used for inserting effects, such as reverbs, delays, exciters, and other audio plug-ins from Sony or other Direct X plug-in developers, such as WAVES or iZotope. Buses can also be used for submixing. Vegas offers bus-to-bus routing, discussed in the audio chapter.

Resample quality should generally be set to Best in the Project Properties Audio dialog. It defaults to Good.

This location is also where the default recording folder is specified in Vegas. Vegas sets the default audio recording

2.40 Audio project properties can be opened by clicking the Audio Properties button above the master volume controls.

2.41 This dialog sets preferences for how audio-time grids are displayed on the Timeline. This is valuable, even perhaps critical for users of ACID loops in Vegas.

to the `C:\ Program Files\Sony\Vegas 6\` directory. If recording long program material or multiple tracks, or audio is the primary use of Vegas, it is highly recommended that this setting be set to a secondary drive. Vegas will scan the specified drive and indicate how much memory is free on the identified drive.

 Tip_____

> Remember that it's important to have a second drive for media and that the drive controllers should be set to DMA in the Control Panel.

The Project Properties Ruler dialog box allows editors to specify how the Track View/Timeline appears. Audio editors will want SMPTE time for their house standard; DV editors can set this for 29.97 fps for grids defining their time space, and musicians can set this to beats or tempo.

 Tip_____

> Video editors will find the Beats grid valuable if the tempo of bed music is known. This ruler grid can mark the beat of the bed music and assist in placing edits so that they are in time with the beat of the music.

Time display formatting can also be selected by right-clicking the Time Display window and selecting the desired time format, which can be toggled between different time formats. Toggling between beat and SMPTE time won't change the timing of the audio or video; it merely allows for different grid views.

The Summary tab found in the Project Properties dialog allows users to log information about the overall project, such as engineer or copyrights. This information stays with the file in the event that the VEG is transferred to another system, user, or shared file so that the originator of the file is traceable. This data does not become part of the summary information embedded in streaming media, nor does it become part of Scott information embedded for radio play. Those summaries must be filled out separately.

The Audio CD tab in the Project Properties dialog has a form for inputting a Universal Product Code (UPC) or Media Catalog Numbers (MCN) that will be burned in the header of a Redbook-valid CD. Some compact disc players do not display this information, but the information is still embedded in the disc.

There is also an option for changing the first track number on a CD. This feature can potentially prevent a CD from playing on older or fewer-featured CD players even though the disc will be burned as a Redbook-valid CD. This option is only

2.42   The Summary tab allows copyright information, engineer information, and other important information about the project to be stored. This feature is particularly important when tracking a project.

supported as a Disc-at-Once (DAO) burn as specified by Redbook guidelines. Track-at-Once (TAO) authored CDs ignore this setting.

Edit Menu

Next on the menu bar is the Edit menu. It contains several options for editing media, some of which are duplicated on the toolbar. First on the list is Undo and Redo. Vegas is unlimited in the number of times that you can undo or redo actions. After a project is saved or closed and reopened, however, the project starts with a new list of undo/redo, so a project is not forever undoable. Be sure of your choices before closing. These tools are also found on the toolbar, identified by the Undo and Redo icons.

The shortcut key combination Ctrl+Z triggers the Undo function, and Ctrl+Shift+Z triggers the Redo function.

2.43 CD properties include the ability to insert a UPC code onto the disc for media cataloging.

 Tip_____

If you have a Contour ShuttlePro or Space Station, these two shortcuts are handy to have programmed as button strokes.

Next on the list are the Cut, Copy, and Paste actions. These are the same as nearly all Windows applications. Cut (Ctrl+X) removes media from the Timeline, and Copy (Ctrl+C) copies the media on the Timeline. Regardless of whether Cut or Copy is used, the media is copied to the board, so that the Paste (Ctrl+V) function can be used to place the clipboard-stored media to another location.

2.44 Undo can be accessed using the button or keyboard shortcut.

A feature found in Vegas 5 and 6, Paste Attributes, is useful for both audio and video editing. It allows you to copy switches, audio pitch shifting, playback rate, undersample rate, video event effects, and pan/crop settings from one event or media clip to others. As an example, suppose that there are ten tracks of audio, and in those tracks there are 40 events. A blur needs to be applied to half of those events randomly scattered throughout the Timeline. Rather than applying the blur to the entire track, click the event containing the correct blur settings and press Ctrl+C or go to the Copy button on the toolbar, (or right-click and select Copy or use the Edit/Copy function). Then select the event to which you wish to have the same blur settings applied. From the Edit menu, choose Paste Event Attributes. This step copies the blur and any other unique information contained in the media from which the attributes were copied and can be pasted on the next chosen event(s). Video editors find this method very efficient to pan/crop several still images at once or to copy effects settings to apply to several events at once. Paste Event Attributes can be applied to multiple events of the same type at the same time, so if one event contains the desired settings, those settings can be pasted over hundreds of similar events. Imagine being able to pan/crop 500 still images at once or being able to apply a unique reverb setting to 30 instances of a particular kind of event at once. This result can also be accomplished in the Project Media via applying a Media FX to all occurrences of video or audio in the Project Media. Very powerful and useful indeed!

There is no shortcut key for Paste Event Attributes.

Delete is next on the menu and is used to remove an event permanently. Select the event you wish to remove and press the Delete key or choose it from the menu.

Post Edit Ripple is the next item in the menu. This feature is a long-awaited upgrade in the Vegas series. Editors can now choose the behaviors of Vegas ripple features to suit their own style of editing. Ripple editing allows you to insert or delete events on the Timeline. At the same time, ripple editing keeps events in front of and behind the deleted or inserted event in the same order and time space that the events occupied before the insertion or deletion of an event.

An example would be a long-form documentary that has been edited, containing many tracks of video information. A piece of the documentary is determined to be incorrect and must be deleted. Deleting the piece, without filling in the exact amount of time occupied by the deleted events, leaves a hole in the Timeline. Deleting the hole causes all events occurring after the deletion to slide in place, with nothing lost. The new ripple modes allow Vegas users to decide how they want those inserts/deletions and movements of events to take place. There is a project file called `ripple.veg` contained in the DVD with this book.)

The Select All choice on the Edit menu allows for all media on the Timeline to be selected. This feature is invaluable for moving an entire project up or down the Timeline or for selecting an entire project to be copied and pasted into another instance of Vegas. Selecting either EDIT | SELECT ALL or pressing Ctrl+A selects or highlights all media.

The Select Event Start/Select Event End feature jumps the cursor to the beginning or end of a selected event. This feature can also be accessed by using the shortcut keys [(Select Event Start) or] (Select Event End).

From the numeric keypad, press the 7 key for Select Event Start or 9 for Select Event End. Use 4 and 6 to move or trim an event edge forward or backward in time, and use 1 or 3 to move the event forward or backward by frames. When not in Event Edge Edit mode, 4 and 6 move the event by one pixel, and 1 and 3 move by one frame. Use 8 and 2 to move the selected event up or down vertically to the next track. Pressing 5 exits the keyboard trimming mode.

2.45 Selecting EDIT | SELECT puts the dursor where it should be with frame accuracy; however, most editors find it faster and easier to use the ten numeric keypad shortcuts.

On a standard laptop, Num Lock needs to be enabled to use the numeric keypad. Targus manufactures a numeric keypad that is connected to the laptop via USB for the road warrior editor. This feature allows for rapid location of event edit points, which when coupled with the new ripple features, makes for efficient editing using the keyboard.

2.46 Using the Targus keypad with a laptop makes the laptop editing more efficient.

The Paste Repeat dialog allows an event or events that have been copied to the clipboard to be pasted multiple times.

To insert events at the cursor position on the Timeline and move media down the Timeline to accommodate the inserted events, copy (Ctrl+C) events to the clipboard, select the location that events are to be pasted, and press Ctrl+B or select EDIT | PASTE REPEAT. You will be prompted to input the number of times that the event should be pasted.

Events can be precisely separated in Paste Repeat mode, allowing for many elements, including images and video clips, to be spaced a prespecified distance. Input the length of time between events into this window. The spacing/length of time between pasted images can be determined in milliseconds, frames, seconds, minutes, hours, beats, or musical note values.

2.47 Use EDIT | PASTE INSERT to paste an event on the Timeline, while moving everything subsequent to the paste down the Timeline.

 Tip

Use the Musical Note Values feature when you want a repeating instance of an instrument. For instance, a fast way of building a rhythm would be to insert a sample of a kick drum on every downbeat and third beat and a snare drum on a different track hitting every second and fourth beat. Use the Tempo dialog found in the Project Properties to set the tempo and grid for the project. ACID Loops that match the tempo can also be inserted, making a fast music bed for either editors or musicians to work with. Video editors will find this method a visually and aurally compelling way to edit quickly, if bed music has not been completed but a tempo is known. This process is often called tempo-mapping and allows video editors to build rough video comps while a composer finishes a musical cue for the project.

The Trim feature is another excellent feature in Vegas. To delete all portions of the event outside the selected area, select a portion of an event by scrolling the mouse over the event(s), hold the right-click button down, and select EDIT | TRIM or press Ctrl+T.

This feature can be used on an individual event or on all events across the Timeline.

The Split tool splits a selected event/events at the point where the cursor is parked. If a selection is made on an event, only that event is split. If no selection is made, the split occurs across all events that fall under the cursor. Park the cursor at the desired point and select EDIT | SPLIT or press S. The event on the right side of the split is selected automatically, in the event that it should be deleted.

The Editing Tool dialog specifies what type of editing behavior the cursor shall have.

2.48 Repeating a copied image is definable in the EDIT | PASTE REPEAT dialog.

These same choices are found on the toolbar mentioned earlier. Pressing Ctrl+D returns the cursor to the normal Selection Edit cursor mode, which is generally the most commonly used cursor mode. None of the other cursor editing modes have shortcut keys.

Before CTRL+T   After CTRL+T

2.49 The Ctrl+T edit command deletes all events not inside the selected area. Coupled with the Ripple feature, this feature is very powerful.

   Using the Switches dialog, users that have been using Vegas in earlier revisions will find that several right-click dialogs have been augmented by shortcut keys and by selecting EDIT | SWITCHES. Mute, Lock, Loop, Invert Phase, Normalize, Aspect Ratio, Reduce Interlace Flicker, and Resample have all been made accessible through the EDIT | SWITCHES menu selection. A Smart Resample, Force Resample, and Disable Resample selection have also been added. Smart Resample instructs Vegas to seek media that has been time-stretched, is a graphic-based event, or does not match the frame rate and the frame rate of the event is greater than 24 fps. Vegas then resamples media meeting those parameters. Force Resample instructs Vegas to resample all events regardless of their format or frame rate. Disable Resample prevents Vegas from resampling any events, regardless of whether they have been selected for resampling or not.

2.50 Although the new take being dragged to the existing event is longer or shorter than the event over which it is being laid, adding as a take trims the new media to fit the existing media. Shuffle through takes during playback by pressing T.

 Tip_____

If you are coming to Vegas from the AVID world, you can download a free tool from the www.vasst.com site that will permit you to do Overwrite edits.

Vegas' Take feature allows you to place several takes on top of each other and allows those takes to be switched to view during playback in real time. For example, perhaps a multicamera shoot occurred, and the director or producer would like to see the scene with the different camera angles that were shot. Either multiple tracks must be used with muting on the fly, or takes are used, having all of the shots living in one event and switching on the fly. This workflow is more efficient in most instances. This process is also useful when a musician wants to perfect a particular part of a song and plays the piece over and over again. Each take can be placed, and different versions can be toggled through in real time by pressing T. Any event that has filters, effects, or other edits made to it can apply those filters, effects, or edits to the take.

The Group menu allows you to create a group of clips that are temporarily locked together so that when they are moved, they can be moved together without having to select multiple events

➤ Tip

Video editors that work with a formula-based editing situation, such as a wedding video editor, can build a template of empty events marking locations of where media should go, complete with transitions and filters. Video is then dropped onto the empty events as a take, and within minutes, a finished video is ready to print to tape. Studios doing preset-time voice-over work can find this useful as well, fitting 30-second or 60-second radio spots, complete with compression, EQ, and other filtering into an empty event to be replaced by new dialog. For recurring-format editing projects, this method is terrific for cutting repetitive actions to a minimum and keeping projects/productions in a consistent appearance or sound.

each time. To implement this feature, select a number of events and press G or select EDIT | GROUP | CREATE NEW. This option locks the selected events together, so that when one is moved, all are moved. To remove an event from the group, select the event and press U. The event can also be removed from the group by selecting EDIT | GROUP | REMOVE FROM. All grouped items can be selected at once by using Select All. This option allows for an entire group to be deleted as a whole or to have other processing applied. Grouping is a very powerful tool, and one that is worth the time to get familiar with.

One great use of the Grouping feature is to select a number of events and group them.

Now hold Ctrl while dragging the left edge of the left-most event. Notice that all events stretch or shrink at equal values. If you need to match video or stills to a music selection, this is a fast way to accomplish this task.

View Menu

The View menu is a series of check boxes that determines what dockable windows are available for immediate view.

Place a check mark in the box next to the name of each view to turn the view on or off.

The Mixer Preview Fader option adds another set of sliders to the menu and allows the previewing volume to be changed regardless of what level the Master Volume is set at. The Mixer Preview Fader option only affects media in the Trimmer and Explorer. This slider set does not affect the level of rendered files, whereas moving the master slider does affect the level of audio mixed from the Timeline.

The Show Bus Tracks option is a feature in Vegas 6. Buses can now be viewed as tracks, including volume and panning automation control. This feature provides much greater control over mixed tracks that use bus mixes, while also providing a visual reference for mix controls. Buses can now be automated to increase/decrease volume of an effect on the bus or to control panning. Coupled with the Automated Effects now found in Vegas, Vegas feels more like an actual hardware mixer.

The Show Audio Envelopes option hides or shows volume control views, depending on the current view state of the control. This new feature allows volume controls on all audio tracks to be hidden at once, cleaning up the screen view substantially in the event of a large mix.

The Show Video Envelopes option has the same control over the video envelopes: composite, track fade-to-color, track keyframes, and velocity envelopes.

The Minimize All Tracks option reduces all track views to a minimum size, immediately freeing up space for users to see previews, add full size tracks, or make a large number of tracks fit into a small area.

This option can be accessed via the ~ key. Pressing ~ again restores tracks to the previous view.

The Rebuild Audio Peaks option redraws/refreshes the wave file views on the Timeline. Vegas uses 16-bit peak samples, and on slower machines, you can speed up the system by turning off peak drawing in the OPTIONS | PREFERENCES | GENERAL dialog. This option, also accessed via the F5 key, causes all views to be redrawn.

2.51 Set the Vegas workspace to appear exactly as you would like it to appear.

2.52   View bus behavior in Vegas 6, allowing full automation attributes in a mix.

2.53   View bus behavior with the Minimize All Traccks option turned on.

Vegas stores graphic representations of wave files as .sfk files. These small files may be deleted at any time; however if they are deleted, Vegas will redraw the graphics, creating a new .sfk file. Delete .sfk files when deleting projects.

 Tip

If screen views will not be vertically zoomed in-depth, instruct Vegas to draw 8-bit file views. This option allows the process to become faster and increases responsiveness in Vegas. Change the screen draw by going to the OPTIONS | PREFERENCES | GENERAL dialog and scrolling down to the "Build 8-bit peak files."

2.54   Instructing Vegas to draw 8-bit file views.   2.55   The Insert menu.

If you are struggling with your video preview edges, sometimes it's easier to see the edges if you change the background color of the Preview window from the default gray to either black or white, depending on the video you are previewing. To do this, right-click in the Preview window and select Black or White from the menu. You can also simulate device aspect ratios in this dialog. This is very handy for knowing how your image will appear on a specific display such as a television or webstream.

Also, you can double-click the header bar of the Preview window to ensure that the Preview window is showing at the project property size. This is a quick method of ensuring that you aren't working in lower resolutions than the project, and that you are seeing everything at accurate resolution in the Preview window.

Insert Menu

The Audio Envelopes option in the Insert menu has two submenus: Volume (Shift+V) and Pan (Shift+P). These place volume lines and pan lines on the Timeline on selected tracks.

 *Tip*_____

Select all audio tracks before using Shift+V or the menu. This option places volume controls on all audio tracks, saving time. You can select all tracks by pressing Ctrl+A

The Video Envelopes option has three submenus: Composite Level, Fade to Color, and Velocity Envelope. Composite Level allows users to set the opacity of a track over time, by adding nodes or handles to the composite envelope and moving the envelope up or down on the Timeline at desired fade points. This feature reduces the opacity of the track, allowing video events below the affected track to become visible. Fade to Color adds an envelope to the selected track, giving control to the color to which a track will fade. The default color is black; however, any color can be selected in the OPTIONS | PREFERENCES | VIDEO dialog.

2.56   One great feature of Vegas allows users to define envelop colors.

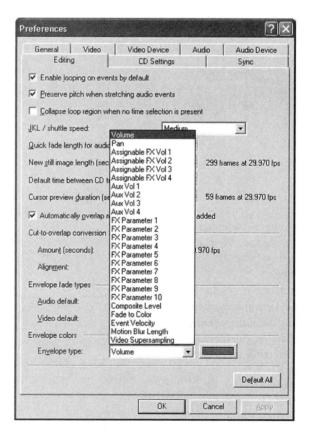

The Velocity Envelopes option allows users to create an envelope that causes a video event to speed up or slow down. Inserting an envelope and creating handles on the envelope, and then either dragging the envelope upward speeds up the event or dragging the envelope downward slows down the event. If an envelope is dragged past the 0 percent speed point, the event reverses itself.

 Tip

> For the surreal speed effect that looks natural but slightly dreamy, slow files to 80 percent of the original speed. The event won't appear to be slow but will have a natural, dreamy slow motion applied to it. This feature is great for slowing down high-speed events.

An event that has the Velocity Envelope it set to -100 percent will play at normal speed, but in reverse. An event that has it set to +300 percent will play at three times normal speed.

 Tip

> If you want speeds of greater than three times normal speed, right-click the event and select Properties. Input the additional speed in the Playback Rate window. Insert a Velocity Envelope. Files can be sped up to 12 times their normal speed by using a combination of the Velocity Envelope and the Playback Rate dialog!

2.57   Velocity can be sped up incrementally and significantly in Vegas via the Velocity Envelope.

2.58   Velocity can also be slowed down over time. This sort of effect is extremely popular in modern editing.

Always use either the Smart Resample or Force Resample feature with speed-altered events. The Reduce Interlace Flicker feature can be valuable with speed-altered media when flickers are seen in the previewed image.

Selecting the Audio Track option (Ctrl+Q) in the Insert menu inserts a new audio track on the Timeline beneath any audio track that is already in place. Dragging audio to a blank space in the Timeline workspace where no audio tracks currently exist creates a new audio track. Dragging an audio event to the Timeline allows an audio track to be created above or below existing audio or video events depending on where it is dropped.

Selecting the Video Track option (Ctrl+Shift+Q) in the Insert menu inserts a new video track on the empty Timeline or above existing video tracks. Dragging non-audio events to the Timeline also accomplishes the same task by creating a new video track for the non-audio event. Dragging a non-audio event to the Timeline allows you to create a new video track above or below an existing audio or video track, depending on where it is dropped.

The Audio Bus option (B) accesses the audio control or destination tracks. A hardware mixer has assignable buses, allowing the audio signal flow to be routed to a number of places before leaving the mixer. During this routing, the audio signal flow can be processed through a variety of tools, such as delays, reverbs, chorusing, flanging, or other processes. Buses can also be used as routing tools to hardware outputs. If a multichannel sound card is used, bus assignments are required to monitor the audio for multiple outputs beyond a simple stereo monitoring system. Up to 26 buses can be inserted in Vegas. Buses can also be used for submixing, assigning all mixes of a group to one location for final leveling. Automated muting or muting envelopes are now available in Vegas as well.

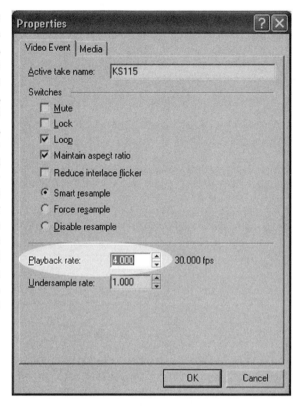

2.59 Adjust the rate of an entire clip with the Playback Rate list box found in the Properties Video Event dialog.

 Tip

Use bus assignments to route together all harmonies, all guitars, all basses, all drums, and all sound effects for submixing.

The Video Bus Track option (Ctrl+Shift+B) allows specific effects and processes to be controlled by envelope on the master video bus. Supersampling, MotionBlur, and Master Fade out to Transparent Black are all possible with envelope control in this window.

Selecting the Empty Event option in the Insert menu inserts a blank event on the Timeline. Empty events can be used as markers for specified lengths of time in current projects or used as placeholders for takes in projects requiring a consistent edit and workflow, allowing video or audio takes to be dropped on the empty event. Empty events can have filters, effects, or other attributes assigned to them that are maintained when a new event is dropped on the empty event as a take. Empty events can also be inserted by right-clicking an audio or video track and choosing the Empty Event dialog.

Selecting the Text Media option opens the titling dialog.

2.60   Select generated media types in this dialog.

2.61, 2.62   Creating color bars is one of the functions of the Generated Media tool.

Selecting the Generated Media option in the Insert menu opens a dialog allowing users to create a variety of different forms of media appearances.

Gradients, solid colors, credit rolls, test patterns, and text can all be inserted via this dialog.

Selecting the Insert Time option in the Insert menu inserts time across the entire Timeline. If a cursor is placed in the middle of an event, that event is split and the portion of the event to the right, or later in time than the cursor, is moved according to the amount of time specified in the Insert Time dialog box.

2.62 Insert blank time with the Time menu option.

Inserting a marker is possible by selecting Marker from the Insert menu; most users, however, find that inserting a marker is more efficient by pressing M. This option drops a vertical line at whatever point in time the cursor happens to be at when M is pressed or the menu option is selected.

Regions can be defined as a space between two markers or a selection created by dragging the mouse across the Timeline. Pressing R also activates the Regions option in the Insert menu.

2.64 Regions can be created via a selection on the Timeline and pressing R.

CD regions/track numbers can be assigned via the Audio CD Track Region option on the Insert menu. CD regions, however, are also assignable by pressing N when a selected event or time frame is on the Timeline. This feature is how Vegas creates track numbers for compact audio discs.

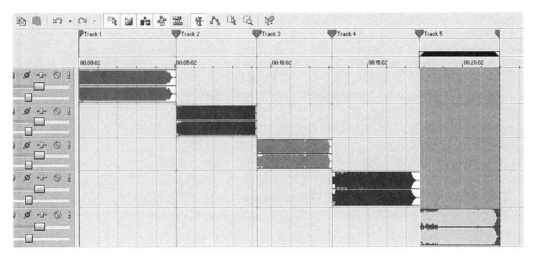

2.65   Using the regions in a CD Project makes for fast track indexing.

Selecting the Audio CD Track Index option (Shift+N) allows for separations between a track number and an index in a track, similar to a chapter and subchapters in a book.

Selecting the Command option in the Insert menu creates metadata commands for streaming media. This menu selection brings up the Command Properties dialog box that gives a selection of different forms of metadata to be inserted into the Timeline for authoring of metadata-rich streaming media.

2.66   The Command tools allow for the insertion of metadata that create a more interactive experience for streaming media or distributed disc viewers/listners.

Tools Menu

The Tools menu contains tools for rapidly creating final products, quick renders of edited media, and other highly useful tools. This menu is where the majority of work is done within Vegas outside of the trimming tools and actions.

2.67   The Tools menu.

The Audio option in the Tools menu has a number of subchoices within it. These choices are also accessible via a right-click an audio event. The first choice, Open in Sound Forge, opens the actual event—audio, video, or both—in Sound Forge where destructive/permanent edits can be applied to the file. Open Copy in Sound Forge opens a copy of the audio event in Sound Forge, where a take is created that exactly replaces the original event on the Timeline. Pressing T lets users toggle back and forth between the original and edited audio. Any audio editor can be chosen as the preferred audio editor; however, the unique relationship between Sony products makes Sound Forge a worthwhile application to have in partnership with Vegas 6. To set the preferred audio editor, select OPTIONS | PREFERENCES | AUDIO and browse to the .EXE of the preferred audio editor. Audio opened in any audio editing application is replaced in Vegas as a take.

 Tip

> Always open audio from AVI files as a copy rather than as a destructive file. This option generates a take and does not affect the original. As a result, you can always go back to the original. It also speeds up the save process, as Vegas isn't generating a new video file for the original AVI.

The Apply Non-Real-Time Event FX option is great for slower computers or for applying processes that don't work well in real time, such as Noise Reduction and Acoustic Mirror processes. These processes are so resource-intensive that only the fastest machines can carry the load. They also take resources away from other actions taking place on the Timeline.

When using the Apply Non-Real-Time Event FX option, remember that these effects are destructively assigned to the event, allowing the processor to be free of having to deal with the load of real-time effects. Users with slower computers or with little RAM in their machines generally find this feature beneficial as well, as it frees up system resources for processing more audio, video, or mixed events. When working with non–real-time effects, you'll be prompted to provide a new name for the audio file so that the original is preserved. Vegas does not allow you to use the original filename, as the original file is currently open on the Timeline. The file with a new name is added as a take to the Timeline and can be compared against the original sound by pressing T. Users can toggle back and forth between the original and newly affected sound during playback.

While not readily evident, effects are broken down into various folders, including a folder called \ALL\. This folder allows for all Direct X plug-ins to be viewed at once. Other folders, however, show third-party effects, Sony-only effects, and FX chains, found in a folder labeled \FX Packages\. There is also an Automatable FX folder in which access to all FX that can be controlled with the FX automation envelopes are found. Only a limited number of Direct X FX can be automated. The folder \Track Optimized\ contains a select group of FX, which are optimized for maximum processor performance.

Choosing the Track FX option in the Tools menu opens the effects found on the Track Control pane in Vegas. A Noise Gate, Equalizer, and Compressor are assigned by default to every audio track on the Timeline. These can be accessed via the Tools menu (TOOLS | TRACK FX) or by clicking the Track Effects button on the Track Control pane. These effects can be deleted, replaced, or augmented, depending on the user's preference.

The Insert Assignable FX option automatically inserts a new bus in the mixer section of Vegas. Selecting this option calls a list of all available plug-ins, where as many as needed can be chosen as a chain of effects.

2.68 Each event has an FX button on it unless the button is removed in the OPTIONS | PREFERENCES dialog.

2.69 FX can be sequenced in any way desired.

2.70 FX can be removed at any time. FX can also be A/B compared by checking and un-checking the box next to the effect name.

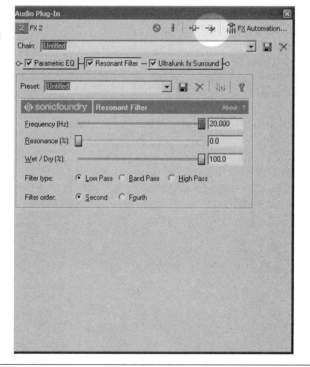

👍 *Tip*

Use the Options>Bypass All Audio Effects to disable all audio effects on buses, tracks, and events.

Effects in the chain can be re-ordered by clicking and holding an effect on the chain, dragging it to the desired priority in the chain, and dropping it. Also, right-clicking any effect and selecting the Move Left or Move Right pop-up menu option reorders effects. Effects in the chain can be removed by selecting the Remove Assignable FX option from the Tools menu or by clicking the Remove button in the upper-right corner of the FX dialog box.

Inserting video effects works exactly the same as inserting an audio event effect, except that it is always non-destructive to insert a video event effect.

When the Video Effects option in the Tools menu is selected, all video effects are shown in a dialog box, allowing the user to choose multiple video effects. Effects in the chain can be re-ordered by clicking and holding an effect on the chain, dragging it to the desired priority in the chain, and dropping it. Also, right-clicking any effect and selecting the Move Left or Move Right pop-up menu option reorders effects.

2.71   Video FX are selected the same way audio FX are. Chains of FX are stored in the Filter Packages folder.

2.72   Reording video FX is a single button selection.

Clicking an effect on the Video FX chain and then clicking the FX Help button pops up a screen that demonstrates how the selected effect affects the video image. A short explanation of how each slider or button on the effect will behave is also included.

2.73   All aspects of Vegas 6 have a Help Icon or button associated with them.

2.74   Calling up help by selecting the FX Help button opens a brief tutorial explaining how effects work.

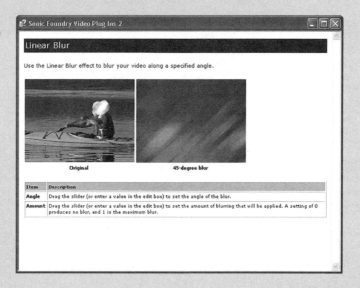

This feature allows users to preview the event effect as a static image before it is applied to the event on the Timeline. It's also a great way to learn the attributes of each video effect.

Effects in the chain can be removed by selecting the Remove pop-up menu option or by clicking the Remove button in the upper-right corner of the FX dialog box.

The Video FX dialog can also be accessed by right-clicking the event on the Timeline or by pressing the Video FX button found on each non-audio event.

2.75   Select the effect requiring removal of adjustment.

2.76   Right-clicking an event accesses a pop-up menu in which you can open the FX dialogs if the FX button has been removed from the event.

The Pan/Crop tool can be opened by selecting TOOLS | PAN/ CROP. This tool is one of the most powerful and oft-used tools found in Vegas, particularly by users of still imagery. Selecting the Pan/Crop option opens a dialog on the Timeline, in which the event image can be cropped to meet the screen size, forced to match the aspect ratio of the project settings, or have zooms, pans, and other movements applied to otherwise static images. Images facing right or left, up or down can be reversed in view easily by right-clicking the Pan/Crop tool.

Video FX button

2.77 FX button found by default on all events.

2.78 Open the Pan/Crop dialog either by right-clicking the video event or by selecting the Pan/Crop button.

Right-clicking inside the Pan/Crop tool brings up a secondary dialog. Choosing Restore restores an event image to its prepanned/cropped status. Choosing Center centers the image around the small dot or center indicator found in the middle of the Pan/Crop tool. Moving the dot to another location in a cropped image, right-clicking, and choosing the Center option moves the cropped selection to a point where the dot will re-center itself.

Choosing the Flip Horizontal option in the Pan/Crop pop-up menu reverses the horizontal image. This option is indicated by the "F" (focus) in the middle of the event image in the Pan/Crop dialog. The "F" is backward if this choice is made.

2.79 Before cropping.

2.80 After cropping.

2.81　In Preview window, preview image is reversed horizontally.

2.82　In Preview window. Preview image is reversed vertically.

2.83　Image before matched aspect ratio is applied.

2.84   Image after match aspect ratio is applied.

2.85   The source aspec t ratio can also be applied to a pan/crop.

Choosing the Flip Vertical option turns the image upside down in the Preview window.

Choosing the Match Output Aspect option assigns the aspect ratio of the Project Properties to the image, regardless of the original aspect ratio of the event before panning or cropping the image.

The original aspect ratio of the image in the figure is 16:9 and does not match the project properties of this project. Choosing Match Output Aspect crops the image to match the 4:3 aspect ratio of the DV-NTSC Project Properties defined in the FILE | PROJECT PROPERTIES dialog.

Choosing the Match Source Aspect option matches the aspect ratio of the source, while maintaining any cropped status applied to the event image.

The Pan/Crop tool can be accessed by right-clicking the media or by choosing the Pan/Crop icon found on each non-audio event on the Timeline. (See the advanced editing and still image in Chapter 4 for more information about the Pan/Crop tool.)

Selecting TOOLS | VIDEO | TRACK FX opens the Video FX dialog box and allows the assignment of FX to an entire track of video on the Timeline, rather than just a video event on the Timeline. This action can also be chosen on the Track Control pane of the desired track.

2.86 The Pan/Crop button is found on all video/graphic events.

Choosing the Track Motion option in the Video Tools submenu opens the Track Motion dialog box. This dialog box allows users to create picture-in-picture imagery, motion of multiple layers of video, divided video screens, moving titles, and other motion imagery. This feature is another of Vegas' most powerful and oft-used tools for the creation of composited media, in-depth motion, and other creative motion.

This tool is used to create the popular *Brady Bunch* screen format with multiple motion images applied to grids on a screen. A *Brady Bunch*-like VEG file is included on the CD accompanying this book.

2.87   The Track FX button is found on all Track Control panes. If this button is not shown, drag the Track Control pane to the right into the Timeline. The button will become visible.

2.88   The Track Motion button is found on all video Track Control panes. If this button is not shown, drag the Track Control pane to the right into the Timeline. The button will become visible.

 Tip

Try using Pan/Crop to create overlays and Picture in Picture rather than Track Motion, as the image may be cleaner. Rather than cropping inward on an image, pull the crop indicators outward so they are larger than the image.

2.89   Selecting TOOLS | VIDEO also opens the Video Tools submenu.

2.90   Track motion is a fast way to split screens, build multiple video views, or move a picture in picture.

Two layers of video are placed in the Preview window with the Track Motion tool. By moving event images to grid points, exactly one-quarter of the screen can be filled with a video image. Shadows or glows can be applied to the event image. The Track Motion tool affects all media on the track to which it is applied. Motion can be keyframed for motion/movement. Shadows and glows can also be keyframed. (See Chapter 4 for more information on keyframing.)

Right-clicking in the Track Motion dialog opens several menus. Selecting Restore restores the Track Motion settings to a null position, removing any track motion applied, and thus restoring any event image to the original settings.

Choosing the Center option centers event imaging on the dot found in the middle of the Track Motion dialog with the same behavior as the Pan/Crop dialog. Moving the dot to the point that is desired as the center focus and then choosing the Center option moves the track motion box to so that it is centered over the dot.

Choosing the Flip Horizontal option reverses the horizontal image. This option is indicated by the "F" in the middle of the event image in the Track Motion dialog. The "F" is shown backward if this choice is made.

Choosing the Flip Vertical option turns an image upside down in the Preview window.

This option is indicated in the Track Motion window by the direction of the "F" shown in the window.

2.91   Right-clicking the Track Motion dialog opens several pop-up menus.

Choosing the Match Output Aspect option assigns the aspect ratio of the Project Properties to the image, regardless of the original aspect ratio of the event image.

Choosing the Match Source Aspect option matches the aspect ratio of the source, while maintaining any cropped or reduced-size status applied to the event image.

Selecting TOOLS | VIDEO OUTPUT FX applies effects to the entire project. This step is the final one in the event/track/project opportunity to apply effects to the video imagery. Regardless of how many effects are placed on an event or track, applying effects at the project level causes effects to be applied over the top of existing effects. Effects can also be applied at the project level by dragging an effect to the Preview window or by clicking the Video Output FX button in the Preview window.

2.92 FX can be applied at the project level, affecting all media in the project.

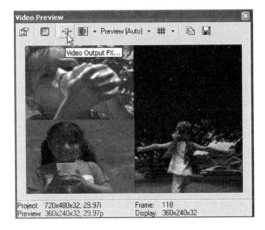

The Render to New Track option (Ctrl+M) in the Tools menu is a valuable feature in Vegas. This feature allows edited media, regardless of the number of tracks, to be rendered to a new file that is placed on a new track at the top of the Timeline. Because the media is rendered, it plays back at full frame rate, full resolution at all times until it is filtered, edited, or has new media placed above it. This feature is useful when large composites are made and playback is slow, yet the events are finished in the editing process and the user doesn't want to have it consistently slowing down the rest of the project. At the same time, if edits to the composited or filtered media beneath the new track might be needed in the future, the events are still in place beneath the newly rendered track, making it accessible at all times.

The Preview in Player option in the Tools menu is a necessary tool for streaming media authors. This feature allows authors to preview selectable sections on the Timeline in a Windows Media Player, a REAL Media Player, or a QuickTime player complete with metadata embedded in the media stream. Files can be previewed at any speed, using templates or custom settings. In the past, authors of streaming media needed to render out entire files, and if dissatisfied with file quality, re-encode the file. Sony set the pace with this tool in their 2.0 version of Vegas, and the

2.93 View streaming media (or other media formats) in their related players, complete with metadata.

⤷ Tip

You can bypass all video effects in the Preview Window.

2.95   Prerendered video.

encode quality has only gotten better with time. This feature saves enormous amounts of time and effort as encoders can see exactly how the stream will appear in a player from any place in the Timeline.

The Preview in Player tool isn't limited to streaming media. AVI, MPEG, MP3, Ogg Vorbis, and other file formats can be previewed in any of the major players complete with any applicable embedded metadata. Synchronized multimedia integration language (SMIL) embedded in REAL media is viewable in the REAL player, along with URL flips, text information, or other call-outs.

The Selectively Prerender Video option (Shift+M) in the Tools menu is used to prerender video sections so that the user can see exactly what the rendered video will look like. When a section of video is prerendered, a new temp file is written to the hard drive/folder specified in the FILE | PROJECT PROPERTIES dialog. This drive should be the second hard drive on the system for maximum efficiency.

After a file has been prerendered, a small blue bar is displayed above the Timeline, indicating that the time section covered by the bar has a temporary prerendered file associated with it.

After an event time selection has been prerendered, moving, editing, removing, or any other edit applied to that time section invalidates the temporary file/prerender, as the temp file is no longer accurate as to what is contained in the time/event selection.

Be sure prerendered video is going to the folder you specified in Project Properties. Otherwise temp files are being written to the default `C:\Program Files\Sony\Vegas 6\`, and your boot drive will rapidly become filled with temp files that aren't readily apparent. This issue significantly affects per-

2.95   Prerendered section.

formance in a generally undesirable manner, slowing down the entire application and system.

This tip is a great shortcut to program on a Contour Shuttle Pro or other hardware device, as it is typically used fairly often.

Selecting the Clean Up Prerendered Video option presents a dialog box asking which prerendered files should be cleaned up or deleted.

The default of "Delete inactive prerendered video files" is the most often required choice, but in the event that all prerendered files should be deleted or if a section has been prerendered several times,

2.96   Remove unused prerenders with the Clean Up Prerendered Video dialog.

it might be best to clean up files related to a specific time selection only. After files are cleaned up/deleted, they cannot be recalled.

The Build Dynamic RAM Preview option (Shift+B) in the Tools menu works much the same as Selectively Prerender Video option, except that it does not write a temp file to a hard drive. Instead, it uses available RAM for the temp file. This render is faster and is deleted as soon as another prerender is called on or when an event is moved or edited. The amount of RAM available for a prerender is specified in the OPTIONS | PREFERENCES | VIDEO dialog. Approximately 60 percent of RAM installed in the machine can be made available for Vegas to prerender files with. The entire RAM space cannot be used, as the operating system, applications, and services require a minimal amount. This issue is why Vegas does not show all RAM installed in the machine as available.

The Print Video to DV Tape option is just as it implies. This option prints the project on the Timeline to videotape without rendering the entire project as a new AVI. When Print Video to DV Tape is selected, Vegas renders all edited portions of the file to a temp prerendered track. It can

2.97   Print-to-tape presents faster options for placing media on a DV tape. This option renders only the modified sections of a project, preparing them to be printed to DV or analog tape faster than completing an entire render.

give a warning that over 80 percent of the Timeline needs to be rendered. This issue is expected in longer or more intense projects with lots of filters, edits, transitions, or color correction.

The dialog box asks for preferred black leader and tail at the end of the print-to-tape. A minimum of three seconds of black at the beginning and end of the print are recommended to compensate for any camera compatibility issues. It also provides an option to print an SMPTE color bar pattern and test tone at the head of the file and provides options for length of color bar and test tones. Forty seconds or greater of color bar and test tone are considered standard. Check with your replicator or broadcaster for their requirements.

Selecting the Lay Out Audio CD From Events option instructs Vegas to look at audio events on the Timeline, insert index markers, and create necessary information to burn a successful audio CD. Make sure audio events are not touching on the Timeline, or Vegas will see the touching events as a single event.

Vegas auto-inserts two seconds at the head of the audio and two-second index spaces in order to create a Redbook-compliant CD master. This issue only applies to disc at once (DAO).

Selecting the Burn CD option opens a submenu that lays out either audio or video CDs for burning, displaying the following options:

- Track at Once Audio CD—burns one song at a time to an audio disc.

- Disc at Once Audio CD—burns an entire project at a time, including index markers. This option is the Redbook standard.

- Video CD—burns an MPEG-1 video CD. MPEG-1 is the VCD standard.

- Multimedia CD—burns an MPEG, REAL, WMV, QuickTime, or other multi-media form of CD. MPEG-1 files are not compliant.

Both of the video formats can be burned from a template, existing file, or Timeline-based file. Files not previously rendered require rendering before burning to disc, so Vegas prompts you through the required steps.

2.98   Vegas can automatically lay out a CD for burning. Using scripts can make this even faster. See the related scripts in the Tools>scripting menu.

Selecting the Clean Project Media option removes from the Project Media media references that are not active on the Timeline. This step should be done before saving a project with media. If files have been placed on the Timeline, they do not appear in the Project Media whether they were kept on the Timeline or not.

The Run Script option is a feature in Vegas that allows users to write custom macro scripts for batch processing events in nearly any way that a user can imagine or require. Need a script that tells Vegas to render an AVI, use the AVI as a master to render a QuickTime, Windows Media Video, and REAL file, beep twice, then render an MPEG-2 file with AC-3 audio? The Run Script option can make this happen if the scripting code is written correctly. An example of a script in Vegas looks like the following listing:

```
**
 * This script will remove all effects of a particular type from items
 * in the project's Project Media.
 *
 * Revision Date: Jan. 30, 2005
 **/
import System.Windows.Forms;
import Sony.Vegas;

// This is the full name of the plug-in associated with the effects
// you want to remove.
var plugInName = "Sony Timecode";

try {
    var mediaEnum = new Enumerator(Vegas.Project.MediaPool);
    while (!mediaEnum.atEnd()) {
        var media = mediaEnum.item();
        var effectsEnum = new Enumerator(media.Effects);
        while (!effectsEnum.atEnd()) {
            var effect = effectsEnum.item();
            if (plugInName == effect.PlugIn.Name) {
                media.Effects.Remove(effect);
            }
            effectsEnum.moveNext();
        }
        mediaEnum.moveNext();
    }
} catch (e) {
    MessageBox.Show(e);
}
```

Custom scripts are found on the disc included with this book.

A button can be created on the toolbar making scripts immediately accessible. To insert a button, select TOOLS | SCRIPTS and locate the script for assignment to a button. Assign the script to one of the ten script location points.

A

2.100 Assign a script to a shortcut (a) which can be assigned to a button on the toolbar (b).

⟐ Tip
_____

Scripting can save hundreds if not thousands of keystrokes. Experiment with the scripting tools found on the disk in this book, and you'll quickly see how time-saving scripting tools can be.

Using the Customize toolbar dialog, assign a key shortcut to a button on the toolbar. The script is now a one-button operation. Up to ten scripts can be loaded on the Timeline at one moment.

Ultimate S 2.0 is a scripting interface that may be purchased from a third party. Ultimate S 2.0 enables as many as 200 plus scripts to be accessed from the toolbar, including multicamera switching, automated lower thirds, audit tools, and other important functions. A trial version is found on the disk in the back of this book.

2.101 Loading scripts to a toolbar button makes running scripts fast and easy.

2.102 Ultimate S is a scripting tool that can enable real-time multicamera editing, create photo montages of up to 9,999 images complete with motion and matched to music beats, project setup, media management, compositing tools, automated lower thirds, and much, much more. Scripting tools such as this one are made for broadcast and event editors, and will not only save time, buy you'll likely find them inspirational as well.

Options Menu

This series of menus are predominantly for setting behaviors and functions of Vegas to specific needs. Many are related to video-centric, and others are not.

The Quantize to Frames option generally should be checked for most video editing situations; it should be unchecked if Vegas is being used as an audio-only tool. This option forces video in an event to snap to a frame boundary, preventing a trim from occurring in the middle of a frame, regardless of the grid or time settings. Pressing Alt+F8 turns the Quantize to Frames action on or off.

Selecting the Enable Snapping option causes events to line up or snap to grid markers, other events, cursor positions, or inserted markers. This feature is useful when a user wants to ensure that timing is correct in the recording studio environment, that no frames are missed in the video editing environment, and that timing is accurate in placing events on the Timeline. Snapping can be enabled via the menu or by pressing F8 to turn this feature on or off. Turning Snapping off allows media to be slid around in time if necessary. Snapping is typically left on, except in instances where sound effects or video events should not fall on a marker, grid line, or inaccurate cursor placement.

The Snap to Grid (Ctrl+F8) and Snap to Markers (Shift+F8) choices are dependent on whether Enable Snapping (F8) is on or off. If snapping is turned on and either of these selections are enabled, events will snap to the marker or grid line to which they are dragged closest. If no grid line or marker is present, an event will snap to the closest event to its release point when dropped or moved on the Timeline.

2.103 Notice the events snapped to frame-level grid lines.

Snapping can be enabled to music tempo, video frames at selectable frame rates, or absolute times.

2.104 Assign grid spacing to personal preference or to a house standard.

Grid Spacing options allow for a variety of gridlines to be selected, which is dependent on the user's working methods. This selection controls how tightly or closely spaced gridlines are placed on the Timeline.

Recording studios or musicians might want to use musically based timings, such as tempos and beats, to lay out a grid. Video editors might desire the grid to be frame-based at whatever frame rate they can be editing at, such as 25 fps for PAL or 29.97 drop-frame for NTSC DV. Musical grids can be laid out as tightly as 32nd note triplets, while video grids can be laid out as tightly as single frames. Grid layouts are very important if you intend on using ACID loops in Vegas, as they'll assist in lining up audio files on the Timeline.

2.105 Set rulers for the manner in which the grid is viewed for snapping, alignment, or time selection.

Different from the Grid Spacing options, the Ruler Format options determine how grids are laid out. If different forms of ruler formats are chosen from the selection of grid spacing, such as choosing a frame-based ruler while a beat-mapped grid is selected, the grid lines disappear from the Timeline. Vegas cannot make a distinction between incompatible ruler and grid formats, leaving it to the user to define these settings. Studios recording music to picture will probably want to use the more common beat maps but can switch back and forth between grid forms, helping calculate tempo to time for musical cues.

The Automatic Crossfades option, selectable by menu or the X key, defaults to on. When two events cross over each other, Vegas creates a cross-fade, indicated by an "X" in the middle of the space in which they are crossed.

Automatic cross-fades are generally left on. Events crossed over each other with automatic cross-fades turned off become hard cuts.

Auto Ripple (Ctrl+L) is a powerful feature found in Vegas. This feature allows the trimming of an event edge. Subsequent

2.106 Crossfades are indicated by the "X" between events.

events snap into place to fill the hole left by the trim, or if the event is pulled longer, Vegas auto-moves all events down the Timeline for the same duration as the pulled event's time addition. If media is pasted in place and auto ripple is turned on, Vegas moves all subsequent events down the Timeline to accommodate the inserted event. By the same behavior, if an event is deleted, auto ripple slides all events forward in time to fill the space left by the deleted media, ensuring that whatever amount of time is added or deleted, it ripples in or out events following the changes.

This new feature also exhibits other behaviors, in that it can be track-dependent or project-dependent. Further, events can be shuffled on the Timeline, with all events moving with shuffled events.

👍 **Tip**_____

Be aware that if inserting media underneath existing events with auto ripple enabled, all events are shifted in time for the length of the media event insert. If video events are on the Timeline, disable auto ripple before inserting media. Press Ctrl+L to enable/disable auto ripple.

2.108 Layout of media before a ripple is executed.

2.108 Layout of media after a ripple is executed.

Notice that when "A" is moved down the Timeline with auto-ripple turned on, "C" stays snapped to "A" and moves down the Timeline for the same duration as "A" was moved down the Timeline.

Selecting the Lock Envelopes to Event option causes volume controls, panning envelopes, bus envelopes, compositing envelopes, and velocity envelopes to move on the Timeline with their corresponding events. If 80 audio events are on the Timeline with 200 envelope changes, if this feature is disabled, and if any one of the events is moved, the audio fades will be incorrectly timed.

The Loop tool is another one of Vegas' most-used tools and can be accessed through the menu or pressing Q. This feature allows users to draw a selection on the Marker bar and have the cursor loop over that selection over and over, while edits are being performed. Using this tool is an excellent way to tweak transitions, color correction, panning, track motion, and other edit effects and tools, while seeing the events change in real time on either the internal or external monitor.

👍 **Tip**_____

Use the Loop tool during editing of critical spaces while watching video on the computer monitor rather than the external monitor. As Vegas loops through the selection, it draws a RAM render automatically, increasing the resolution and frame rate as it loops. Let a section loop while having a cup of coffee or on a phone call, and within a few short moments, the entire section will be playing smoothly and clearly. Be sure to have enough RAM specified in the OPTIONS | PREFERENCES | VIDEO dialog.

The Simultaneous Play & Record option, if enabled, allows audio to be recorded at the same time as audio is being monitored. This feature is critical for a recording studio. The majority of sound cards are full-duplex, which means that they allow audio to pass in both directions at the same time. Most laptop sound cards are half-duplex, not allowing audio to be bi-directional. In this case, the feature requires disabling to avoid error messages. If a laptop is used for monitoring and recording, an external sound card/device is usually required via FireWire, USB, or CardBus.

2.110 Original envelope

2.110 An event that is not locked to envelopes moves
without affecting the position of volume/pan/FX.

2.111 A locked envelope moves all markers; volume/pan/
FX changes with it.

The Metronome feature is an audio metronome that can count time at the tempo and beat settings specified in the FILE | PROPERTIES | AUDIO dialog. This tool is handy for both musicians and video editors. The metronome is not recorded to hard disk if used during the recording process.

The Mute All Audio option is exactly as its name implies. All audio on the Timeline is muted/silenced. Deselect this feature or select a track directly to unmute audio.

Selecting the Mute All Video option has the same effect, with the exception that it causes all video tracks on the Timeline to go dark. Individual tracks can be unmuted and viewed or deselect this menu to bring video back to the screen.

Selecting the Timecode option calls up a submenu, asking what and where timecode is to be read/generated.

Timecode can be generated for MIDI devices. MIDI time code (MTC) is read by nearly all software applications and many hardware tools. MTC is used for synchronizing software applications together or synchronizing hardware and software together.

Vegas generates MTC each time playback is started.

2.112 Select timecode options to fit hardware or house requirements.

Vegas also has the ability to generate Midi clock. The MIDI clock feature is different from MTC in that it also contains song pointer position (SPP) and carries tempo information as well. Musicians will want to use this feature, as it allows Vegas to carry increasing or decreasing tempos and the slaved application or hardware will then increase or decrease in tempo according to the tempo map laid out in Vegas.

 Tip_____

Registered users of Vegas can access Sony's website and download the virtual MIDI router (VMR) utility at no cost or get it from the Vegas installation disk. The VMR utility allows VEgas to drive other timecode-capable applications such as ACID or triggering Sound Forge. This option is great for syncing a music bed that isn't completed in ACID to the Vegas video Timeline.

Vegas can also be started/stopped via the Triggering option from timecode. An external device that generates timecode, or that feeds a generating device that can accept SMPTE timecode and convert it to MTC, can be a master device, and Vegas can be its slave.

Vegas users can customize the toolbar to suit their specific needs and desires for Vegas' appearance with this toolbar. Video editors might wish to hide audio-only tools, just as audio-only studios might desire to hide the video tools found on the toolbar in Vegas. In any event, Vegas can be set up to look and feel the way any user chooses.

The OPTIONS | PREFERENCES dialog is the primary place in which the look and feel of Vegas can be set to individual preference.

2.113 Adding a custom tool to the toolbar is the same for all tools as shown in the Scripting section.

Select preferences that suit your workflow. Experiment with settings that work best for you. Each tab has several options relating to General, Video, Audio, CD, Editing, Sync, Video Device, and a tab for Audio Hardware.

 Tip_____

Make sure that volume and pan envelopes are of greatly differing colors if the default colors are not used, so that they can be differentiated at a glance when mixing in Vegas. Applying color schemes that are similar in style, such as making all EQ gain envelopes varying colors of green, bandwidth envelopes varying colors of blue, and so on help in rapidly assessing a mix and determining what envelopes are performing various functions.

2.114 Set Vegas to feel the way you'd like it to feel in there Preferences dialog box.

Preferences in Vegas 5 were expanded significantly, including options for keymapping, human interface devices (HUI), and draggable cursors.

In the preferences dialogs, you'll want to take note of the External control features, requiring a MIDI card, and the new scrubbable cursor features. We'll look more closely at the External Control preferences in the Mixing section of Chapter 4.

Cursors and Selections

In Vegas versions 2-4, dragging the cursor on the Timeline created a selection. For most users, this has been a satisfactory workflow, while for others coming from various NLE workspaces, this has been confusing. Vegas 5 and 6 allow the cursor and playhead to be dragged across the Timeline without creating a selection.

To enable cursor dragging on the Timeline:

2. Open the Options>Preferences dialog box.

2. Check the Allow Edit Cursor to be Dragged check box at the bottom of the General dialog box.

3. Select Apply and close the Preferences dialog box.

 *Tip*_____

In Vegas 6, not only is creating a selection easier, but also arrows and a time indicator will display, showing the amount of space an event is moved, time of a crossfade or fade in, and amount of ripple action as well.

This allows the cursor to be dragged about the Timeline without creating a selection. Selections may still be created by clicking twice and dragging. One sure way to know if a selection will be created is to left-click on the cursor. If a double-ended arrow appears beneath the cursor, it's a draggable cursor or playhead. If the double-ended arrow does not appear, it's going to create a selection on the Timeline. This new function may take some getting used to, as it isn't entirely intuitive like most of Vegas' functions are.

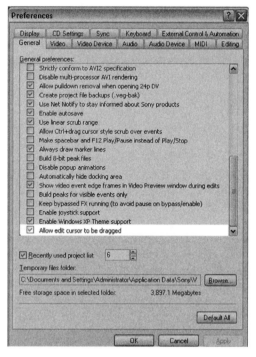

2.115 Select this check box if you wish to be able to drag the cursor across the Timeline without creating a selection. Leave it unchecked if you are satisfied with the method in which Vegas has worked in previous versions. It is checked by default in Vegas 6.

2.116 When you see this indicator, the cursor may be dragged across the Timeline without creating a selection.

Say You'll be MINE!

One of the power tools of Vegas is to allow users as much customization as possible with the application. Layouts, appearances, key commands, and docking are just a few of the user-defined settings that may be customized by users. In the General preferences, click on the Keyboard tab. This dialog allows you to input a series of keystrokes, and on the right side of the tab, you can choose what actions you'd like that specific series of custom keystrokes to take.

XP Themes in Vegas

Vegas now allows for themes chosen in the XP Themes dialog to determine how Vegas appears. This allows users to create their own appearances for Vegas, suited best to their editing environment.

To modify an XP theme, open the Control Panel and select Display from the options. In the Display dialog you will find a Themes tab. In this tab are dropdown menus that will allow you to select pre-built themes for XP or view online themes that you can download. Generally, most editors prefer darker themes that are easier on the eyes in dimly lit editing rooms. A web site at http://www.themedoctor.com has a number of downloadable themes to create custom appearances for XP that will also affect how Vegas appears. You can also obtain more themes by purchasing Microsoft's Microsoft Plus add-on for Windows XP.

In order to have Vegas accept custom themes for Windows XP, you'll need to go to Options>Preferences, and tick the checkbox for Enable Windows XP Theme Support. Without this box ticked, Vegas will use it's default colors. Notice that the icons in Vegas 5 and 6 are softer, a little larger, and less sharp in appearance from earlier versions of Vegas.

The icons will not change appearance with different themes applied to Vegas, only the colors, backgrounds, display and header fonts will change in appearance. Keep in mind that changing themes will often affect how some applications may appear, so choose your themes carefully if your editing system is also used for email or other common functions. Themes may be stored/saved and recalled for specific tasks when needed. To create a theme in Windows, right-click the desktop and choose Properties, and then select the Appearance tab. Choose Advanced, and use the drop down menu choices to select your system's appearance settings. Save a theme after creating your custom settings by clicking the Themes tab at the far left of the Display Properties dialog, naming the Theme, and choosing Save As. This will store your theme in the Documents folder unless you choose a new location in which the theme should be stored.

2.117 The Windows display properties may be accessed from Control Panel or right-clicking the desktop.

2.118 Save the theme, close Vegas and restart Vegas to see the new appearance.

Key Features!

Vegas also provides custom keyboard mapping.

This feature allows users to create their own custom keyboard shortcuts to increase efficiency in editing.

One of the hints that you are a Vegas power user is how much you use a keyboard instead of a mouse. You'll nearly always be faster with a keyboard than a mouse, given the fewer number of hand movements. This is true with nearly any application, since both hands remain on the keyboard most of the time.

To unlock the power of Vegas' customizable keyboard commands, open the Options>Preferences dialog. You'll notice the Keyboard tab in the Preferences dialog. Select it.

When the dialog opens, the existing keyboard shortcuts are displayed. These may be changed to fit your particular needs.

To change a shortcut or to create a new one, place the cursor in the "press new shortcut key" box. If there is another command in the box, press the Shift, Ctrl, or Alt key and release the key. This will clear the box. Now press and hold the Shift, Ctrl, or Alt key while pressing it's companion key desired for the shortcut. This will set the shortcut in the dialog box. However, the

2.119 Vegas allows for cusltomized keyboard shortcuts. In this instance, Ctrl+E have been assigned to rip music from a CD.

2.119 In this example, Alt+G has been assigned to open the Render As dialog.

2.120 The "Key is Also Assigned To" box will light up and display any shared key commands as your only warning that you are about to change an existing keyboard command.

shortcut is not assigned to an action until an action is located in the Available Commands and selected.

If a command does not appear in the Available Command window, then the option of assigning a keyboard shortcut is not available.

If a newly created shortcut is sharing a command with an existing shortcut, the Key is Also Assigned To box will indicate the shared command.

For those who operate Vegas on multiple computers such as a desktop and laptop system and who would like to share the key commands without having to take the time required to set up the second computer, Vegas allows a .ini file to be used to export the customized keyboard settings.

Select the Export button in the Keyboard dialog, and an export dialog box opens. Create a name for the .ini file, and save the file to a location where it can be later located. This can also be saved over a network to a different machine on the network.

2.121 Key commands may be exported to another computer, saving time and matching the workflow of a desktop machine to a laptop or other computer on the network.

To import a customized key command set, select the Import button in the Keyboard dialog. Browse to the folder the .ini file was saved in, and select it. Press the Open button, and the custom key commands will be installed as part of Vegas 6 on the second machine.

Key commands may be returned to Default settings by selecting the Default All button in the Options>Preferences>Keyboard dialog. Keep in mind that selecting the Default All button will wipe out all customized key commands, and if they have not been saved to another location, any commands you've created will be gone.

Color My World

In Display Preferences for Vegas, you'll find a dialog that allows the color of track headers, saturation of icon colors, bus or FX envelopes, and icon color tinting, further offering a custom look for your particular Vegas style. In the General preferences dialog, check the tickbox for Windows Theme support, and any theme you create for Windows XP will then be part of the Vegas color scheme. This is the means by which you can create a dark, smoked look for Vegas should you like that sort of appearance.

Flashy Titles

Titling is extremely important in any video production. Some would argue that titling sets up the viewer for what they are about to see, and therefore makes the difference between a good film and a great film. Titles can take a lot of artistic development time, and a lot of creative energy as well, and therefore titles are often farmed off to editors or artists that specialize in nothing but titling sequences. On of the formats for titling in video is Macromedia's Flash format.

When importing Flash files into Vegas, they must be from Flash 5 or earlier. Flash MX files contain metadata types that Vegas cannot correctly read and import to the Timeline.

Vegas now supports Flash import, and .swf or .fla files may be dropped directly on the Vegas Timeline. While these files don't always play back at full framerate, they provide unique opportunities for users to import powerful sequences of images. Flash files containing ActionScripts, audio, or motion video may not be inserted to the Timeline, nor may Flash files created in Flash MX. Only files created in Flash 5 or older may be loaded on to the Timeline.

Flash is also a powerful animation tool for product presentation, lower thirds, or for portray-

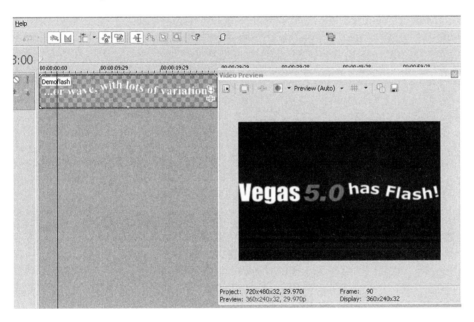

2.122 With Flash now importable to Vegas, the titling and animation possibilities are greatly expanded.

ing a specific type of image from a website or other multimedia presentation. Many companies have Flash introductions or menus on their websites. These may now be set up and used with productions created in Vegas. Graphs, charts, and spectacular titles are all part of the Flash graphic format that may be imported to Vegas. Interactivity with Flash files will not carry over into Vegas.

Flash is often being used for creating instructional media, giving an added edge when combined with video presentations. However, CoffeeCup Software and Swish are both available for creating excellent Flash files, and are substantially easier to learn and use. Learn more about these products at http://www.swishzone.com and http://www.wildform.com. You can also download demo files from these sites to practice working with the Vegas Timeline. Find the demoflash.swf

At the time of this writing, Vegas was not scaling Flash media cleanly when the Pan/Crop tool is used to zoom in on the Flash file, suggesting that the vector information in Flash may be ignored. Create your Flash projects at full size and resolution for best results. Vegas will properly scale them to project resolution. In summary, this is only a problem when zooming in on the Flash file with the Pan/Crop or Track Motion tools.

file on the DVD in the back of this book. Drop it on the Timeline, laid over an existing video file, and you'll see how clean the Flash file can be. If you are unsure of whether the Flash is showing at the project property size (it should always scale to the project property size) then double-click the header or title bar of the Preview window to set the Preview window display to the project properties. To get a better understanding of how this function works, reset the project properties to a new setting, such as changing the project properties to a PAL setting, and you'll see the Flash project scale to the new project property settings.

Capturing Video

Getting Media from the Camera to the Hard Drive

Capturing media from a camera is the first step in the video editing process. Vegas has a unique application that functions from within Vegas but can also function outside of Vegas as a separately accessible tool. A separate capture icon can be placed on the desktop if so desired. Browse for the `VideoCap50.exe` application or find it directly at `C:\Program Files\Sony\Vegas 6\` for most installations. (You might need to search for the `Vegas40.exe` file if Vegas was not installed to the `C:\` drive.) It is highly recommended that you launch the capture tool from within Vegas. If launched from Vegas, media captured in Video Capture is added automatically to the Media Pool in Vegas.

Transferring video from tape to a hard drive is called *capturing*. In the OHCI world, this process is different from the hardware-assisted capture card world as no compression or altering of the video takes place in the transfer. With M-JPEG cards or hardware-assisted cards, media is compressed or has header information that some editing applications can't read. Fortunately, while Vegas can't read every form of video file captured in the Microsoft Windows environments, it can read nearly every form of video file captured in the Windows environment if the proper video for Windows (VfW) codec is installed on the machine. For M-JPEG AVIs, you might need to download and install an M-JPEG codec. Matrox and Main Concept are good sources for these codecs. However, the Video Capture utility only controls cameras through the OHCI cards. Vegas cannot take advantage of hardware-assisted codecs, such as those offered by Matrox, Pinnacle, and Canopus, although Vegas can edit media captured with the capture utilities that come with those cards.

Video capture enables media from the camera to be placed on the hard drive. This process works with live or pre-recorded media. Vegas uses a standard called open host controller interface (OHCI) to control cameras and to facilitate the transfer of video from the camera to the hard drive. Vegas functions with some analog capture cards but consult your owners' manual for more information. To control the start, stop, rewind, fast-forward, and record functions of a digital camera, however, the only card Vegas functions with is the OHCI standard. Cards manufactured by ADS, SIIG, Unibrain, as well as the new OHCI-compliant card from Canopus, the ADVC1394 card, are all compliant examples. Analog or non-OHCI cards do not have the ability to control a DV camera from within Vegas.

Vegas automatically senses the frame rate, image size, and any other information that might be part of the DV stream. No special settings are required for capturing DV from a DV camera via an OHCI card. Whether the media is PAL, NTSC, 24p, 16:9 anamorphic, or other supported format, it is captured, or transferred, from the camera with those attributes recognized.

Manual Capturing/Capturing Entire Tape

Connect the camera to the OHCI/FireWire card installed in the back of the computer. If a shortcut is not on the desktop, open Vegas and select FILE | CAPTURE VIDEO, which opens the Vegas Video Capture utility. The capture utility can also be opened from the Media Pool by clicking the Capture Video button.

3.1 Opening the Video Capture utility from theMedia Pool. You may want to place the capture tool icon on the main Vegas toolbar if you need to access capture regularly

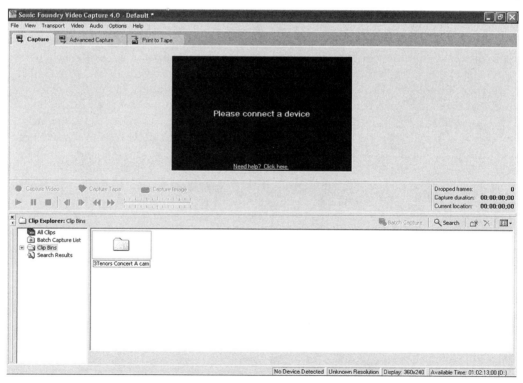

3.2   First capture window when the utility opens.

In some systems, the camera is not auto-detected. If this happens to you, go to CONTROL PANEL | SYSTEM | HARDWARE and look for the 1394 Bus Host controllers device line. Double-click the line, and the properties of the bus will open, showing the installed drivers. In some instances, a Microsoft driver and another driver, such as a TI, Lucent, or VIA driver will be present. Right-click any driver that is not a Microsoft driver and uninstall it. Repeat for all non-Microsoft drivers.

Some 1394 cards are installed as network cards, which can cause conflicts with the camera and bus operations. If this becomes an issue, open the network adapter hardware and disable the 1394 NIC/Network card. This process should not affect other networking tasks or abilities.

3.3 Open the M | HARDWARE tab to adjust 1394 and Network properties.

When Video Capture launches, select OPTIONS | PREFERENCES. Select the Disk Management tab. The default capture location for captured files is `C:\Documents and Settings\username\My Documents\`.

If the camera is turned off, Video Capture will prompt you to turn it on.

When the camera is turned on, Windows will automatically open screens asking what it should do with the camera. Cancel the Windows screens, as Video Capture is already open. If you select anything else, it may override the Video Capture drivers, and then you'll need to start again by shutting down the newly launched application and recycling the camera power. If Video Capture and/or Windows doesn't auto-sense the camera when it is turned on, be sure the camera is in videotape recorder (VTR) mode.

3.4 Windows automatically senses most DV cameras.

If a capture drive has not been specified, Video Capture will ask for a drive to be specified. Unless absolutely necessary, never capture media to the same hard drive as the operating system. Specify a hard drive and specify a disk overflow size that is at least three percent less than the overall drive size. This option will allow room for defragging drives and will prevent a drive from filling to total capacity, possibly rendering the drive incapable of being recovered in the event of a drive or system crash. Default overflow is 360MB. Larger drives can require a slightly larger overflow, such as 500MB.

Video Capture will prompt for a tape name with the Verify Tape Name dialog. This step is the first in proficient media asset management (MAM) or digital asset management (DAM). Enter the name of the tape you wish to capture. This tape name will be appended to filenames as they are captured, so be sure it's correct. You will have one more opportunity to correct this easily later on. This process is known as *logging*.

3.5 Specify capture drive. Notice that Vegas indicates capture time available based on selected hard space.

 Tip

Enter the name of the tape exactly as it's written on the tape spine in the event that you want go back and recapture the media. This process avoids errors in logging and locating tape.

The Verify Tape Name dialog also provides choices as follows:

- "Don't capture any clips right now"
- "Start capturing all clips from the current tape position"
- "Start capturing all clips from the beginning of the tape"

For the moment, select "Don't capture any clips right now" and click OK. Video Capture is now ready to capture video. Clicking the Play button or pressing the

3.6 Be sure to label tapes correctly at capture to assure quick location of clips during editing.

spacebar causes the camera to begin playing. Video is not captured until you click the Capture Video button or press Ctrl+R.

Video Capture can capture video from the camera/tape in several ways, including:

- Manual capture by starting and stopping (labor/time intensive)

- Capture from a specific location and detect or not detect scenes, starting and stopping with the control (users' preference, can be labor/time intensive)

- Capture entire tape with scene detection (little effort)

- Batch capture logged clips (fair amount of effort to log clips; time saving/disk space saving in end view).

 *Tip*_____

For a rapid-start capture:

1. Connect camera to OHCI card.

3. Turn camera on.

3. Launch Video Capture.

4. Choose Capture Entire Tape.

Scene detection is a feature in which Video Capture sees breaks in the date and time stamps created when the camera is started and stopped during the recording process. Each time the camera is stopped, Video Capture sees the change in the date and time stamp and starts a new file. So if you've started and stopped the camera ten times while videotaping at an event and then connected the camera to the computer and opened Video Capture, Video Capture creates ten files in the media pool when it is activated. (Files are stored in the folder/drive specified in Disk Management. Media Pool creates a pointer to that file; files are not actually stored in Media Pool.)

 *Tip*_____

When using DV tape, be certain that timecode isn't broken on the tape. Broken timecode often happens when re-using old videotape or when cameras aren't allowed to run for a moment following shooting. This problem also happens when tape is viewed in the field and allowed to play past the end of timecode. Avoid this problem by:

- Always recording blank time completely over previously used videotape by recording with the lens cap on for the length of the tape.

- Allowing 5–10 seconds of tape to roll by when recording in the field, if you know you will be reviewing tape in the field.

Video Capture is capable of batch capturing an entire tape while left unattended. Click the Capture Entire Tape button. Video Capture will rewind the tape to its beginning/top and then start to capture the tape to the folders/drives specified in the Disk Management preferences. If the specified hard drive does not have enough space to store an entire tape, be certain to specify more than one drive. Video Capture will automatically roll files over to the next specified drive.

Tip_____

Hard drives formatted as FAT 32 drives may not have files larger than 4GB, or about 18 minutes in tape time. Video Capture will automatically find the best point to divide files in the event of FAT 32 drives. NTFS drives have a file size limitation of 4TB, which is roughly 330 hours of DV.

Begin capturing tape by either pressing Ctrl+R or clicking the Capture button in the capture tool. Video Capture will start capturing from the moment you click the button. If the camera or tape deck is OHCI/1394 standard, the device will start playing and transferring media from the tape to the hard drive. Clicking the Capture Entire Tape button instructs Video Capture to rewind to the beginning of the tape and start recording. Video Capture will auto-detect scenes in the tape and create new files for each scene. (Enable Scene Detection is enabled by default in the OPTIONS | PREFERENCES | CAPTURE dialog.)

In the Video Capture OPTIONS | PREFERENCES | CAPTURE tab, set the minimum clip length to 5 or 10 seconds. This instructs Video Capture to ignore the OOPS!-type of files, in which a camera was inadvertently started and stopped, leaving small video clips on the tape. Of course, if working with animations or other projects that require short shots, you might wish to leave this set unchecked, which is the default setting.

3.7 Setting the minimum clip length.

Animation-type capture is also possible by selecting a maximum capture length of only one or two frames. Experiment with clay models or action figures to get the hang of editing this type of captured media.

Analog camera

Analog to DV converter box

Computer

Analog tape deck

3.8   An analog camera or video deck, such as a VHS or Beta SP machine, uses composite S-Video, or component video output to a DVC, which converts the analog video to digital video so that the computer can see the video signal as data.

In the analog tape world, such as a VHS or Beta SP, a digital video converter (DVC) is required to convert analog to DV. Several converters are available in the market today, from the very high-end Laird Blue Flame to the Canopus ADVC 1394 card. YUV input, composite input, and S-Video input are all common input features, making it fairly simple to find a converter that meets your specifications.

If an analog machine is used with a converter or analog card, the machine must be turned on and play enabled before capturing video. Scene detection does not take place with analog tape machines passed through a converter. Machine control is not possible with analog machines, with the exception of some high-end converters that read DV control signals and translate them to RS-422 control signals to which some analog decks will respond. DV control can be disabled in the OPTIONS | PREFERENCES | GENERAL dialog. Typically, leaving DV control enabled does not affect a DV capture but can create some confusion if shifting between DV and non-DV sources.

When Video Capture has captured the entire tape or when you have manually captured all clips desired from the tape, Video Capture will prompt you to save the capture session. This feature is useful if there is any possibility that you will be going back to the tape to recapture at some future point. Lost video, accidentally

3.9   Disable the DV control when working with non-DV decks or analog capture cards.

deleted video, and failed hard drives are all reasons to recapture tape, so it is generally good practice to save the capture session.

3.10 The post-capture dialog pvovides information about clip length, dropped frames (if any), location of media storage, frame and data rate, and check boxes to place media in the Vegas Media Pool. Unchecking the "Show after every video capture session" option will prevent this dialog from popping up after each capture.

3.11 Store the capture session if any likelihood exists that the same tape will need to be recaptured later or if the session needs to be shared on a network.

After capturing video and closing the Video Capture application, the captured media will appear in the Media Pool in Vegas 6.

Video Capture has other tools available for logging and capturing in Vegas. Click the Advanced Capture tab. This tab opens a different view of Video Capture. Comments, ratings, length of clip, and in/out information can all be logged and added in this view. Use this feature to keep track of media and how it appears for rapid editing decisions later in the editing process. These comments appear in the Media Pool and can assist in making editing choices.

 Tip

See the Vegas 6 chapter for information on how to capture HDV media or media via the Black Magic Design Decklink hardware.

Advanced Capture Tools

The Advanced Capture tab has dialogs that allow for more advanced file management. Open the Advanced Capture tab at the upper left of the capture utility. Detailed capture logging tools are located on the right side of the capture screen.

Using Batch Capture

Batch capture only functions with OHCI devices. To use the Batch Capture tools in Video Capture, click the Advanced Capture tab. Begin playing tape via the control seen on screen.

To mark the point on the tape where you want capture to begin, click the Mark In button.

To mark the place on the tape where capture should end, click the Mark Out button.

Video Capture will note the in/out times in the windows next to the Mark In/Out icons and will show the clip length in the Clip Length field.

3.12 Advanced capture tools offer efficient capture logging and automated capture tools, saving tremendous time in the editing/capturing process, in addition to saving disk space.

The Mark In/Mark Out dialogs contain two buttons for returning the tape to the in or out point. Selecting the "Cue To In" (shift+I) or "Cue To Out" (shift+O) buttons will cause the tape deck or camera (T/C) to auto-locate to the selected in or out points indicated in the In/Out dialog boxes.

To log the clip, click the Log In/Out button under the Length field. Video Capture creates a note based on the tape deck or camera in/out markers and displays the clip in the current bin in the right pane of the Clip Explorer. Change in/out markers as many times as necessary to correctly mark the clip. The clip is not logged until you click the Log In/Out button. Only the displayed time in the T/C in and T/C out fields are used to mark the clip for batching later on.

Mark as many clips as necessary. Multiple tapes can be logged at once. Be sure that tape names are changed in the logging dialog so that Video Capture knows when to prompt for a new tape to be put in the deck.

As clips are marked for batch capture, an icon of the capture will appear in the list view/bin window. These icons have a red dot in the center, indicating that they are marked for capture. When all clips are logged, click the Batch Capture button found above the list view/bin window. Clips can be automatically marked for batch capture by selecting the OPTIONS | ADVANCED CAPTURE check box.

3.13 Use the Mark In (|) and Mark Out (O) buttons to mark timecode points for a batch capture of selective clips

In this same dialog box, clips can be commented on and rated. Comments assigned to an individual clip can be viewed in the media pool after the clip is identified in Vegas. The Media Pool search tool allows Vegas to search for keywords based on these comments, so while this feature is convenient, it's fairly indispensable for long-form work where rapid searches for specific clips are needed. It's also good media management, even if it takes a bit of time to do.

Video can be graded on the quality of shot, helping to assign the priority clips for later identification and location.

The Capture and Advanced Capture dialogs provide the ability to create and use Clip Bins. Each master tape or B-Roll might have its own bin, and clips can be sorted in any fashion that makes sense to the project editor or producer. Remember how Radar O'Reilly stored the maps to the minefields on M.A.S.H. under "B" for "BOOM"? Each person has their own method of sorting and storing files. Media bins accommodate this. Right-click the Clip Bins folder, select Create New Bin, and name the bin with the filename information that relates to the part that the clips will play in the project. If the "Add Clips to Media Bin" check box is selected in the post-capture dialog, clips are auto-added to the media pool bins in Vegas, and bins from Video Capture can be dragged to the Media Pool in Vegas as well.

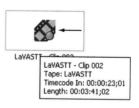

3.14 The red dot on the clip indicates that a clip is marked for batch capture.

3.16 When video is lost, is moved to a different folder, or is corrupted, but is associated with an event on the Timeline, the event will provide a placeholder on the Timeline that can be replaced with a take or recaptured from the DV tape.

3.15 Right-click the Media Bin to create a new bin to aid in locating, managing, and logging media.

Bins from the Video Capture utility can be imported to the Media Pool in Vegas by creating the bin in Vegas before capturing media.

In the NLE world, if a clip is on the hard drive, it is considered to be online. If the clip disappears from the hard drive but is part of a project, it is considered to be offline, and Vegas shows the file as offline in the Media Pool, shown as grayed out or missing media with the text "Offline Media" in the lower-left corner of the Media Pool. Vegas provides the opportunity to recapture offline media by right-clicking the offline media and selecting "Recapture Offline DV Media."

Recapturing media from the Media Pool launches the Video Capture application automatically, and you will be prompted to place the correct tape in the deck/camera if you have not already done so. This point is where careful logging/labeling is invaluable. Video Capture will seek out the timecode related to the clip that is marked for recapture and start the capture process with no assistance. The recaptured media will need to be directed to a folder on one of the drives.

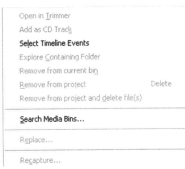

3.17 To recapture DV media with Video Capture, right-click in the Media Pool in Vegas and select "Recapture All Offline Media

Capturing Stills with Video Capture

The Video Capture tool allows stills to be captured and cataloged during the capture process. To capture stills, click the Capture Still button. Still images by default are stored as JPEG files unless otherwise specified in the OPTIONS | PREFERENCES | CAPTURE dialog. In this same dialog, Video Capture can be instructed to de-interlace video images and can be instructed to apply correct aspect ratio to still images. If the "Saved Captured Stills as JPEG" box is left unchecked, images are stored as uncompressed Bitmaps.

Stills captured to the clipboard can be opened in any photo editor for color correction, image correction, resizing, or other manipulation.

Many video cameras have the ability to capture stills as well. Still images are generally captured to videotape and can be narrated during the still capture on the video camera. Video Capture treats these still images as video because the tape is moving and the still image generation is created by the video camera. Default still-image length on most DV cameras is five seconds. If Scene Detection is enabled, Video Capture creates a new file for each still photo taken with the camera.

3.18   Still images can be captured directly with Video Capture 5.

Changes in Video Capture

In the very near future, most DV cameras in the consumer and semi-professional markets will sport not only IEEE-1394 and S-Video connectors but will also have USB mini connectors (Type B) as well. This option will occur because of increased manufacturer support of USB2 as a data transfer protocol. All DV cameras currently have a FireWire/IEEE-1394 connector on them. Sony cameras label this output as an i.Link connection. Having both USB2 (Type B) connectors and 1394 connectors means that cameras will be able to connect to any type of computer, regardless of hardware configuration. Both formats operate reasonably the same as the other.

3.19 Specify preferences for managing still images in Video Capture and about viewing formats.

3.20 USB Type B connector and FireWire/1394 four-pin connector. Soon, all cameras will have both types of connectors.

 Tip

Never use USB 2 when FireWire is present. Vegas Capture doesn't do very well with USB 2 camera dialogs. USB 2 uses more system resources than does iLink/IEEE1394.

Another major change coming in digital video is the advent of portable, battery-powered hard drives that will eventually be built directly into cameras. For the time being, these drives are belt-worn and have rechargeable batteries. Many of the units use the IBM TravelStar drives found in laptops. As drive speeds and sizes increase, these drives or similar storage mechanisms will be stored in the cameras themselves. The ADS Technology belt-clip drive is capable of holding up to five hours of DV media, with a built-in rechargeable battery. The drive housing has a built-in six-pin 1394 connector, which is connected to the FireWire output of the DV camera.

3.21 The ADS 3.5 drive kit has a self-powered housing with a six-pin FireWire connection.

3.22 The four-pin FireWire output from the DV camera plugs directly into the FireWire input on the drive kit. Video captured directly to the drive kit will not require capture, as it is already in digital format on the drive and merely needs to be plugged into the computer/electric system.

3.23 The Nnovia A2D can not only capture from a DV camera, but it also can capture video and audio directly from an analog camera, converting it to DV on the fly, removing the process of capture

Editing Tools, Transitions, Filters, and Other Basic Video Tools

Importing Media to the Timeline

Aside from capturing media, many methods can be used to bring media into Vegas. Vegas is format agnostic and resolution independent, meaning that nearly any form of media recognized by the Microsoft Windows-operating system can be imported to the Vegas timeline as an event.

Vegas has an Explorer that by default opens in the lower-left corner of the dockable tool space. This Explorer can be dismissed from view and recalled at any time by pressing ALT+1. The Explorer is a dockable tool that can be sent to a second monitor to preserve space on the timeline.

Open and view the Explorer. Any form of media that can be imported is shown in the Explorer. Media files, such as GIF, TGA, JPEG, BMP, PNG, TIFF, MOV, AVI, WMV, and MPG are all media file formats that can be opened in Vegas.

4.1   In this picture of the Media Pool, different media formats are placed as events on the Vegas timeline.

Tip

If QuickTime files are to be viewed and edited within Vegas, the QuickTime full install is required. Visit www.quicktime.com and download the current player. When installing, three choices are presented: Full Install (recommended), Custom Install, and Minimal Install. Choose full installation so that Vegas is able to access authoring tools for the QuickTime MOV file type. Without this installation, Vegas won't be able to access or edit QuickTime files or TIFF files.

All media formats may be placed on the same track, which means that an AVI file might be next to a JPEG file, which in turn might be next to a QuickTime file, which might be next to a WMV file, and so on. About the only Windows-recognized media format that cannot be opened inside of Vegas is the REAL (rm.ram) file format, as this format is protected by Real's protection algorithms.

To place media on the timeline, drag the media from the Explorer to the timeline, where the media becomes an event. If a track is not present, Vegas automatically creates one for the media that has been dragged and dropped. Double-clicking a file in the Explorer window automatically adds the file to the timeline as an event and creates a track for the file if a video track isn't already present.

To manually insert a new video track, right-click the track control pane and select INSERT | VIDEO TRACK or press CTRL+SHIFT+Q.

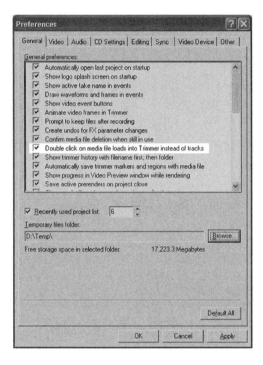

4.2 Selecting **preferences** for loading media in Trimmer.

Media can also be opened in the Trimmer window. For those familiar with other NLE systems, the Trimmer window is much like a source window where media can be previewed and trimmed to the desired length/information before being placed on the timeline. To accomplish this task, right-click the media and select Open in Trimmer. Vegas can be set to open files directly in Trimmer, by going to the OPTIONS | PREFERENCES | GENERAL dialog and checking the "Double-click on media file loads into Trimmer instead of tracks" check box.

Media can also be dragged directly into the Media Pool, which is where Vegas stores location information for all media used in a project. Media can be stored in the Media Pool regardless of whether the media is found on the timeline or not. Any event or piece of media placed on the timeline, however, is automatically added to the Media Pool.

 Tip

In Vegas 6, "Media Pool" is now known as "Project Manager".

4.3   Creating and naming the media bins.

Vegas has media management features in the Media Pool. The use of media bins allows users to preset where media will be pointed to and how media is located. A master project bin resides in the Media Pool where all media is pointed to by default. This master bin is labeled "All Media Folder." Beneath it is a folder labeled "Media Bins." Right-clicking the Media Bins folder opens a menu/dialog that allows for new bins to be creaed nd named.

Be aware that Vegas does not copy media and place it in bins. There is no point nor value in having two copies of the same piece of media on the hard drive simply for the point of filling bins as some NLEs demand. On the contrary, Vegas points to a file from within the bin. While the media is always accessed from the bin, it truly resides wherever it was stored in the acquisition of the media. Bins are simply a means of collecting the storage points of all media and putting those indexes in one place.

Bins can be dragged from project to project in Vegas or stored as project bins so that they'll always be found within the preferences of Vegas. Audio, video, graphics, and anything else for which you would like to specify bins can be created, with sub-bins for every bin format. This way, you'll always know where media is stored.

Bins can be dragged from one open instance of Vegas to another open instance of Vegas.

Media can also be imported from other projects by selecting FILE I OPEN, choosing the VEG file from which media is to be imported, and checking the "Merge media from Vegas project files into current project" check box, as shown in Figure 4.5. Media is then automatically added to the Media Pool in the same folders from which the imported Media Pool came. If the imported project has no bins specified in its Media Pool, Vegas will add media to the All Media Folder, where it can be dragged to specific bins within Media Pool for consistent file management.

Use bins to sort media by the name of the tape that media is captured from, a bin for bed music, a bin for various takes, or a bin for JPEGs, BMPs, or PNGs. Good project management starts with locating and knowing where all media is stored at all times. This process also assists in clearing out a project when it is finished.

4.4 Bins separating various media types for efficient file location.

The Media Pool has several additional options for file import. Audio from CDs can be extracted directly from the Media Pool toolbar.

These options include the following:

• Sweep Media Pool—removes all media from Media Pool that is not in use on the timeline of current project.

• Import Media—imports media from other VEG files/Vegas projects to the Media Pool.

• Capture Video—opens the Video Capture application to transfer video from a camera to Media Pool.

• Import Photo—opens a scanner or camera attached to computer for importing photos to the Media Pool.

• Extract Audio—extracts, or rips, audio from a CD to the Media Pool.

• Get Media from the Web—provides a direct link to Sony's partners, some of whom provide free media for your use.

4.5 Importing media from other Vegas projects, which are either open or closed.

👍 *Tip*_____

When Copying Media Bins from one project to another, the media itself is NOT copied. Be aware of this so you don't lose any media thinking you have duplicates due to a copy/paste of the media bin.

4.6   Import buttons from the
        Media Pool.

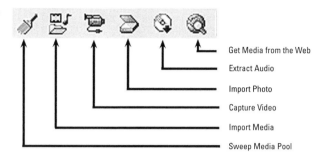

Get Media from the Web

Extract Audio

Import Photo

Capture Video

Import Media

Sweep Media Pool

4.7   Choosing this button auto-extracts audio from a CD inserted in the CD/DVD player.

Imported media is placed in the All Media Files folder in the Media Pool and, once imported, can be dragged and dropped into a specific bin. Vegas supports import to the currently selected bin; bins only contain links or pointers to existing media.

4.8   Search media **bins** to find elusive files that might
        not have been properly named or cataloged.

Bins are also searchable, which makes cataloging files very valuable. Comments inserted in the Batch Capture/Advanced Capture dialog can be searched/located in the bin search operation.

Located media can be dragged and dropped into any bin in the Media Pool.

The Media Pool toolbar contains other useful tools for managing the Media Pool contents, including the following:

• Remove Media—removes media from the Media Pool or bins but does not delete media from the storage drive.

• Media Properties—opens a dialog indicating the type of media, storage location, length, size, and other properties of the media file.

• Media FX—allows FX to be placed on media before it's placed on the timeline. This option is very useful for single, long-length files that need the same format, such as of color correction or special FX, but will be trimmed in the editing process. Select the file to be affected, then press the Media FX button, select the desired FX, and adjust accordingly. This process does not alter the original file.

• Start Preview—plays/previews selected media file in the Preview window.

• Stop Preview—stops playback of selected media in the Preview window.

• Auto-Preview—when pressed, any time a media file is selected, it will be displayed in the Preview window automatically. This process is exceptionally useful when quickly going through media, saving time.

• Views—determines how media is shown in the Media Pool, whether as icons, detailed information, or a list.

• Search Media Bins—uses keywords or attributes to locate media whether captured or imported and does not work over non-mapped network drives.

Vegas and its media management features are helpful, powerful, and useful. Take the time to use them correctly, and projets ill be much easier to manage.

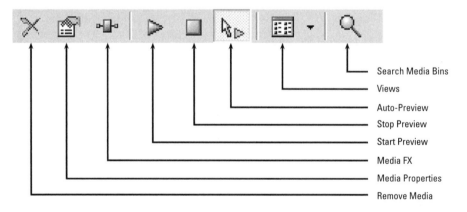

Search Media Bins
Views
Auto-Preview
Stop Preview
Start Preview
Media FX
Media Properties
Remove Media

4.9   File management viewing attributes in the Media Pool.

Editors coming from other NLE applications often ask about having subclips or selections appear in the Media Bins. Vegas does not have this as a destructive function unless subclips are rendered to new files. Subclips may be created in either the Trimmer or on the timeline, yet this does not discard remaining media from the original file. Rendering straight cuts to a new file is faster than real time, because nothing is actually done to the clip. However, some people won't want to render subclips. For those, here is a workaround.

Open a clip in Trimmer. Make regional selections and name the regions. After selecting/naming all regions on a clip in Trimmer, right-click in the open area of the Trimmer and press S or select Save Markers/Regions, which will embed the markers/regions in the file.

In the Explorer window, enable the Regions view as shown here. Notice the regions created in the Trimmer tool are now visible in the Regions view of the Explorer. These regions will not show things such as effects or envelopes, but are a means of quickly locating selected regions especially if the regions have been named with a recognizbl name and then sorted by name.

4.10 Enabling the Region view.

Subclips in Vegas

Vegas the ability to use subclips. What is a subclip? Well, in Vegas they might be better known as "sub-events" as they are reference files to a certain area in a larger event, often called "clips" in other DAW and NLE applications. Subclips may be created in a couple of different ways.

First, a file can be opened in the Vegas Trimmer, a selection made, and the subclip button pushed. A dialog opens, asking you to name the subclip. This does not affect the original event or clip in any way. In this dialog, you can also decide if you want the subclip to play in reverse from the original clip or not.

Second, an event loaded on the timeline might be edited on the timeline for length, selecting different in and out points. Right-click the file on the timeline and choose Create Subclip from the menu that appears. This will deposit the subclip in the Media Pool. The subclip may be renamed in the Media Pool.

Subclips in Vegas are different than subclips may behave in other applications. Creating a subclip is not destructive to the original file. If you used Regions in older versions of Vegas, subclips are effectively the same thing with greater access to the media. Subclips show up in the Media Pool as well, whereas Regions only show in Regions view.

If you are capturing analog tape and planning on editing it, the subclip feature is very useful. This will allow you to load your entire .avi into the Trimmer tool, select the sections you want to keep, and create subclips with them. If they are named sequentially (default) in the dialog boxes, they can be used almost like a storyboard and dragged to the timeline as one group by selecting all subclips in the Media Pool. Performing

4.11   Subclips are useful to identify sections to be reused or to discard unused media. Subclips may be copied from project to project using media bins found in the Media Pool.

a "Save As" and choosing to copy all Media Pool will then save the subclips, and the origating .avi file may be deleted from the hard drive, leaving only the parts you wish to use in the overall project.

> To copy subclips from one project to another, you will not be able to copy or paste them. You must create a new bin in the Media Pool, load the subclip into the new bin, and move the bin from one project to the new project

If for some reason you need to locate other scenes in the media that the subclip originated from, or you need to change the in or out points of the subclip, right-click the subclip in the Media Pool and choose Open in Trimmer. While in Trimmer, press the Select Parent Media button in the upper-right corner of the Trimmer, and the parent media will open with the subclip area indicated by the selection tool. In or out points may be shifted, and the subclip may be re-created with a new name or using the original name.

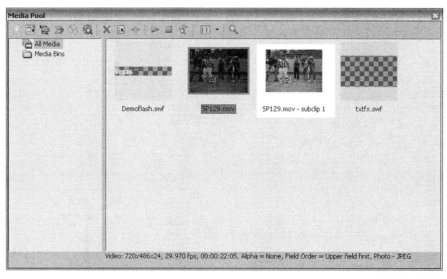

4.12 This is how subclips will appear in the Media Pool.

Subclips are clips of media, and therefore may not be dragged out on the timeline in a standard timeline editing function, as for all intent and purpose, the clip has been "cut" from the original media. If you need to extend the in/ or out point of an event that's been inserted as a subclip, you'll need to open the subclip in the trimmer and change its in/or out points, and then reinsert it to the timeline. Subclips may be added as takes, and therefore can be dropped onto slugs or empty events marking a time space. To open a subclip in the trimmer, simply right -click and select "Open in Trimmer."

Use File>Save As and check the "Copy and trim media" box found in the Save As dialog box, to save subclipped media and delete any media that is not part of the finished project. This is great for saving space on the system hard drive. Be sure to sweep the Media Pool for unused media before saving.

Placing Media on the Timeline

The Media Pool is a great place to start building a project and makes for a much more efficient workflow. Getting media to the timeline from the Media Pool is well organized and easily traceable. The Media Pool is not the only way to work within Vegas, however.

Media can be dragged to the timeline directly from the Explorer within Vegas or from the Windows-Explorer. Notice that the Explorer window also has an Auto Preview button on the Explorer toolbar, just as the Media Pool does. Leaving this checked allows rapid preview of various media formats shown in the Preview window. A search can be done in the Windows-Find feature (START I FIND or START I SEARCH in Microsoft Windows-XP) and dragged directly to the Vegas timeline.

What if you happen to have a long AVI file and only want selected portions of that file?

You can open the file in the Trimmer in one of two ways. First, you can right-click the file and select Open in Trimmer. Second, you can set the general preferences to automatically open a file in the Trimmer by double-clicking the file.

> Consider using the Windows Explorer rather than the Vegas Explorer to locate and identify files. Media may be dragged directly to the Vegas timeline from any window containing files, including the Windows Search application. Moreover, the Windows Explorer provides thumbnail images for video and still image files, making it more efficient to locate and place media on the timeline. The Windows Explorer may be kept open and on top of the Vegas workspace.

Notice that the file takes a moment to build an audio preview. This graphic represents the audio. This process can be sped up by checking the "Build 8-bit peak files" in te OPTIONS | PREFERENCES | GENERAL dialog.

👉 *Tip*_____

The graphic drawing reference files are stored in Vegas (and all other Sony products) as SFK files. These files may be deleted at any time. If a file is loaded that does not have a linked SFK file, Vegas will redraw the file and save as a new SFK file.

After the file is drawn in the Trimmer, select the portions of the media that are to be used. Place the cursor at the point that the video clip should begin and press I for In Point. Place the cursor at the point that the video clip should end and press O for Out Point. This process automatically creates a time selection in the Trimmer. Media can either be scrubbed over or the Play (SPACEBAR) button can be clicked in the Trimmer.

An alternative to pressing the I and O keys to select the in/out points is to draw the selection directly in the Trimmer. Place the cursor where the in point should be and draw by holding down the cursor and dragging the cursor to the out point. You can also work in reverse by placing the cursor where the out point is desired and dragging the cursor to where the in point should be. Notice that as the cursor is dragged the video plays in the Preview window.

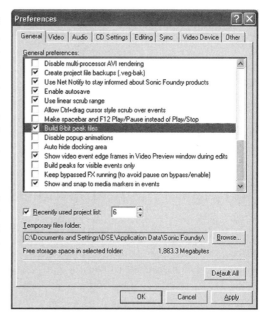

4.13   Reducing the size of screen peak draws will speed up screen draws in Vegas.

Dragging the cursor with the left-click button held down behaves like a scrubbing tool in the Trimmer window.

After a time selection is defined in the Trimmer, a few choices can be made as to how the media can be handled. Media can be placed directly on the timeline by pressing A for Add, it can be dragged directly from the Trimmer to the timeline, or a region can be created. If using the Add feature, place the cursor on the timeline where the added media should be placed. After adding the media tothetimeline, the media becomes an event.

4.14   Time selection created in the Trimmer by pressing I and O for in/out points.

If no time selection is defined as a drawn area, as an in/out point or as a region, media can be selected from the start point to where the cursor is parked. By pressing A, media in the Trimmer is added from the start to the moment that the cursor is set. Alternatively, pressing SHIFT+A adds media up to the cursor to the end of the file.

When placing events on the timeline, keep a fast, visual reference to them by using the scribble strip on the Track Control pane. This feature also helps others quickly know what you are intending with the track. For example, a master track might be named as such, while a picture-in-picture track might be named "PIP track." Good track management is critical, especially in the digital realm where file name on a hard drive can be extremely varied.

Regions are great, as a defined region will stay with the media even after Vegas is closed. To define a region, press R, and Vegas will open a field where the region name can be defined. Multiple regions can be defined, and region in/out points may overlap. When new media is loaded into the Trimmer and replaces the media containing regions, the defined regions will stay with the media file and will be shown any time a file is loaded into the Trimmer. (By default, this option is turned on in the OPTIONS | PREFERENCES | GENERAL dialog. It can be unchecked if for some reason this feature is not desired.)

Markers can also be used in the trimmer to serve as reminders for in or out points. Pressing M will drop a marker. Markers can be named if a name is desired. Should an unnamed marker need to be named later, right-click the marker and choose Rename from the menu. Double-click between two markers to create a time selection from which a region can be named. A region may contain many markers.

Markers and regions are exceptionally important for many editors, especially those that are creating

4.16   Buttons found in the Trimmer tool act as **short-cuts** for the **A** or **SHIFT+A** commands.

keyframes by the frame or in very tight visual spaces. Vegas has the ability to see markers or regions inserted in the Trimmer on the timeline for greater consistency in editing. If a region is created in the Trimmer and several markers are placed at desired points inside that region, these markers (and regions) are visible in events on the timeline. Markers and regions cannot be edited on the timeline if added in the Trimmer. Events can be reopened in the trimmer however, and edited there if necessary.

4.17   Regions may overlap and may also be named. No limit exists on the number of regions that can be created in the Trimmer.

4.18 Markers/Regions inserted in Trimmer appear in events on the timeline.

4.19 To clear markers/ regions on events, open the event in the Trimmer, right-click the Marker bar, select Markers/Regions, and select Delete All or Delete All In Selection.

Placing Still Images or Graphics on the Timeline

Photos play a large role in creating video, regardless of the format. Vegas is capable of reading nearly every photo or image format that the Windows-environment will allow. Some formats, however, are more optimal than others. Whether scanning via the Vegas Get Photo option that uses your scanner utilities or scanning outside of Vegas, the process is essentially the same.

Scan photos at a resolution of not higher than 300 dots per inch (dpi). Because video has a resolution of 72 dpi, extremely high resolutions are not only extra effort, they can also cause

 Tip

Double click a gap in the Timeline. In the Trimmer, mark an In point, but don't worry about an Out point. Now select the "A" key on your keyboard. This will Add the clip to the gap, filling the gap exactly. Should you need to move the In point of the event, simply slip edit that point (Alt-Drag left or right).

your image to look poor if the resolution is set too high. If no pan or crop will be done with the photo, a resolution of 72 dpi is sufficient. Generally, a resolution of 150 dpi is recommended. This resolution is a comfortable size for Vegas to manage quickly and yet provides the ability to pan or crop the image without fear of pixilation. If the Pan/Crop tool will be used to zoom in very tightly on the image, a higher resolution of 300 dpi may be called for.

Earlier in the book, we looked at pixels in the computer world as being square and pixels in the DV world as being rectangular. This issue affects stills and graphics that will be inserted into the Vegas timeline, as Vegas treats graphics and stills as DV when they are square-pixel images from the digital still camera, image editing application, or other source.

With most DV editors, still images and graphics must be created with the correct aspect ratio in mind when planning on dropping the stills or graphics into the DV timeline. Vegas isn't quite as rigid when it comes to this issue as the Pan/Crop tool allows the correct aspect to be maintained. When working with stills in an image editor, however, the correct size (NTSC) for a still image is 655 × 480. This size compensates for the square pixel being stretched in the non-square pixel world of DV. The math to derive this pixel aspect ratio (par) is as follows:

720 × .909 (par of DV) = 654.48

For those who like to round down, 654 works equally well. The correct aspect for PAL images is 704 × 576.

One experiment that demonstrates square versus non-square pixels is creating an image in your favorite image editor, such as Adobe Photoshop or Paint Shop Pro that is nothing but a circle at a project size of 720 × 480. Then drop the image straight into Vegas and don't use the Pan/Crop tool. Create the same image at 655 × 480, place that image in Vegas, and notice the difference. Users of other NLE systems might be familiar with saving files at sizes of 720 × 534/NTSC. For example,

534 × .909 = 485.4

This format works equally well, and either format is usable.

✍ Tip_____

For best results, save still images, graphics, or titles created outside of Vegas at 655 × 480/150 dpi (NTSC) or 704 × 576/150 dpi (PAL). If you plan on zooming deeply into a photograph, consider doubling the resolution, or creating images at 1310 × 960.

Files should be saved as portable network graphics (PNG) files for optimum use in Vegas. Vegas reads JPEG, BMP, GIF, TGA, and most other formats, including the Adobe PSD file format, as well as the TIFF format. The Adobe Photoshop files, however, will not be broken down into individual layers; they will be shown as one layer. If an alpha channel is present, Vegas will recognize the alpha channel, and those areas will be transparent. TIFF files can be used in Vegas only if Quick-Time is installed on the host system (www.quicktime.com). Because Vegas uses QuickTime to read the TIFF file format, TIFF files will slow down the rendering process somewhat. TIFF files also show problematic symptoms in automatically displaying alpha channels. PNG files are a lossless format, so the image is not compressed when saved in the image editing application.

Files may be scanned in at their normal aspect or size and then cropped within Vegas at any time to match aspect ratio, regardless of the original aspect ratio of the photo. This feature is a major timesaver. Sony has created a script (see Chapter 11 for more information on scripts) that will match aspect ratio on all images on the timeline.

In Chapter 7, the pan/cropping section demonstrates how to match aspect ratio of images when they are not of the correct aspect in order to fill the screen.

Editing Events on the Timeline

Each piece of media placed on the timeline becomes an event. Events are then edited to form the final production. Events may be on single or multiple tracks.

Events containing video may be edited in any number of methods. One issue that exists with some NLE systems, however, is that a frame might be split. Vegas gets around this issue for videographers by offering a Quantize to Frames option, ensuring that frames are not split and forcing edits to occur on frame boundaries. When working with video, Quantize to Frames should nearly always be enabled by selecting OPTIONS | QUANTIZE TO FRAMES or pressing ALT+F8. When working with audio only, this feature may, and generally should be, disabled.

The first editing behavior is to edit on the timeline by extending/reducing the length of an event on the timeline. This type of editing is called *trim-editing*.

4.20   When the cursor is placed at the head or tail of an event, the cursor changes to a trim-editing cursor. This allows the event to be dragged out or dragged in, thereby lengthening or reducing the event.

When a trim-edit occurs with the Ripple tool enabled, media subsequent to the edited event will slide to the left to fill the hole left by the shortened event or slide to the right to make room for the lengthened event. Trim-edits can be done with only a numeric keypad. Selecting keys on the keypad moves the cursor to the beginning or end of an event, and the keypad can be used to edit an event by frames or pixels.

Table 4.1   Keyboard Shortcuts Used in Trim-Editing

Shortcut	Description
Press 7 or 9	Moves the cursor to the next event edge, either moving backward or forward.
Press 1	Trims the event edge to the left by one frame.
Press 3	Trims the event edge to the right by one frame.
Press 4	Trims the event by one pixel to the left.
Press 6	Trims the event by one pixel to the right.
Press 5	Exits the numeric keypad trimming mode.
Press 0	Creates a region/loop around the cursor. The length of the region is specified in OPTIONS	PREFERENCES	EDITING.

Pressing and holding CTRL+ALT while the cursor is placed between two events will lengthen one event while the other event is shortened, depending on whether the cursor is dragged to the right or left. This feature allows both events to continue to occupy their current total length, while editing the point at which one event ends and the other event begins.

Slip-editing is another basic editing format that allows an event to remain a static length while changing the in/out points of the event. You can slip-edit by holding the ALT key down while moving the mouse inside an event. During slip-edits, the Preview screen shows the first frame and the last frame of an event based on the slip-edit point.

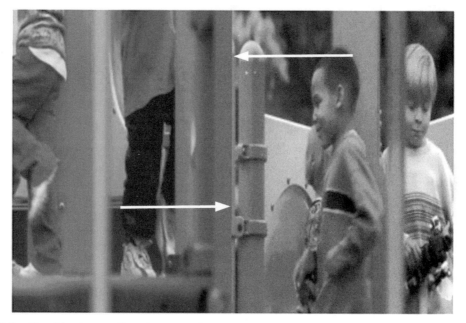

4.21   Slip-editing shows a split preview screen, displaying the in/out points of a slip-edited event.

The second edit function is to perform a transition. The most basic transition is the crossfade, otherwise known as a *dissolve* in the rest of the video world. A crossfade occurs when two events overlap, and one blends into the other as one event fades out and the subsequent event fades in. By default, Vegas crossfades events together any time they are overlapped. Automatic crossfades can be turned off at any time uingth Automatic Crossfades button found on the timeline or by pressing X.

Place two events butted against each other on the timeline. Now drag the front of the second event partially over the end of the first event. An "X" appears in the space in which the two events overlap.

Frame 4 Frame 11

Frame 7

Frame 1 Frame 14

4.22 An example of a crossfade.

4.23 Crossfade is indicated by an "X" between the two events.

Now play the timeline by pressing the SPACEBAR or clicking the Play button found on the control bar of the timeline. The two events will fade from one to the other in equal time. If a faster crossfade is desired, drag the second event farther away from the first event, or trim either the end of the first event or the beginning of the second event directly on the timeline. This process is accomplished by

placing the cursor in the middle edge of either of the events on the timeline and by clicking and dragging in either direction. This process shortens either the outgoing or incoming event and causes the crossfade to be shorter in duration.

The shape of the crossfade can also be controlled. Right-clicking a crossfade brings up a Crossfade menu, which has several choices regarding the way the crossfade should occur.

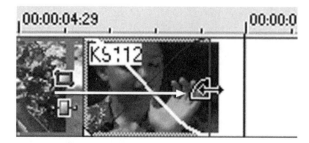

4.25 Grabbing and dragging the end of the first event is shown by a small box-like icon indicating that the end of the outgoing event is being dragged.

4.26 Grabbing and dragging the beginning of the incoming event is demonstrated by a small quarter-circle-shaped icon. This feature helps eliminate confusion as to which event is being edited.

 Tip

Create a time selection over a crossfade, beginning slightly before the crossfade and ending slightly after the crossfade. Then press Q, which instructs Vegas to play continuously and loop over the crossfaded area. While playing over the area, all edits and adjustments are seen in real time in the Preview window as Vegas plays.

After right-clicking the crossfade, choose the Fade Type menu. A series of crossfade attributes opens. Choosing one causes this menu to close. Surprisingly, the attributes of a crossfade have a great impact on how some visual events mix.

Crossfade behaviors can also be applied to the head or tail of an event. Positioning the cursor at the top of the beginning or end of an event will change the cursor to the quarter circle form. The head or tail of the event cn hen be dragged inward to create a fade. This process creates a fade in or out from black.

4.27 Fading in from black is a common editing necessity.

4.28 Vegas offers many crossfade styles.

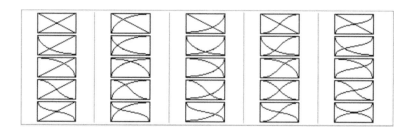

The default fade-in color can be changed by selecting OPTIONS | PREFERENCES | VIDEO and clicking the default colors.

4.29 Track fade colors can be customized to create a specific background color.

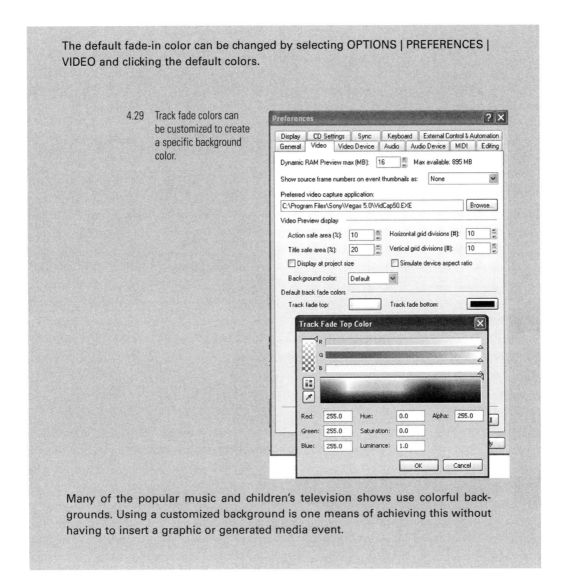

Many of the popular music and children's television shows use colorful backgrounds. Using a customized background is one means of achieving this without having to insert a graphic or generated media event.

A crossfade is a form of a transition. Vegas has hundreds of built-in transition possibilities, and several thousand more transitions can be installed from third-party vendors, such as Pixelan, Boris, and DebugMode.

To change the transition from the default crossfade to another transition, select the Transitions tab in the lower-left corner of the dockable windows area to open the Transitions window. If you can't see a tab, press ALT+7, and the Transitions window is displayed. This window is dockable and may be placed anywhere on the screen that is convenient. To change a transition from any style back to a crossfade, right-click the transition and select TRANSITION | CHANGE TO CROSSFADE or press the / key on the numeric keypad Other transition choices are also available if you right-click the Transition menu.

4.30   Slide Transition replacing crossfade and looped for real-time preview.

4.31   All transitions have dialog boxes to edit transition attributes. The Transition dialog box can be called at any time by right-clicking a transition and choosing the Transition Properties menu.

To preview transitions, click the different transition styles and pass the cursor over the choices. Each transition preset becomes active as the cursor moves over it. When you find a desired transition effect, click and drag the transition over the top of the "X" that defines the crossfade point. The transition dialog window will open, allowing for you to fine-tune the transition, adjusting colors, edges, softness, speed, and other parameters that vary with the different transitions.

Transition properties can be placed on fades as well. This feature is great for bringing in or sending out video for the beginning or end of a presentation.

By creating a fade in or out on a video event and then dragging a transitional element to the fade, the fade creates a transition from transparent black.

When the Transition properties dialog opens, at the bottom of every dialog is a keyframe timeline. This timeline allows for unique and defined behaviors of a transition in time by adjusting keyframes and the sliders around them. (See the "Using Keyframes in Vegas" section for more information on how to use keyframes.) Feathering edges, rates of transition, and color of borders all can be controlled with the available attributes of the specific transitions.

Right-clicking a crossfade or transition opens a dialog that allows for more transition choices. Vegas will also keep the last five types of transitions in meory sotha when you right-click, the last five transitions used are found for rapid access.

4.32   Transitional element applied to the fade in of an event. Notice how the transition flies out of black, which is the default track fade color.

First transition change

Second transition change

Third transition change

4.33 Selecting other transition types with shortcut keys or by selecting in the menu.

Edited sequences can be quickly put together in Vegas using Cuts Only, in which events are butted against each other. Position the dursor at the point at which two events are butted up and press one of the following shortcut keys related to an automatic transition.

Press / to crossfade events

Press * to create a dissolve

Press - to create a linear wipe.

The two events are pulled together to create a crossfade, dissolve or linear wipe.

One unique feature in Vegas is that when an event is slid out of the area in which a transition occurs, Vegas will remember where the transitional element took place and recall all features of the transition. Whether the original event is placed back in the area in which the transition occurred or a new event is placed there, Vegas will still hold the transition location and information. This issue results from transitions living within events.

Users of older versions of Vegas will find new transitions in the Transition Selection menu, including Portals, Page Rolls, Page Loops, and more, as shown in Figure 4.34.

For experienced NLE users, Vegas' method of displaying crossfades and transitions is definitely unorthodox. Vegas can display the traditional A/B roll as well, should this be the desired look in the workspace. Click the Expan Trck Lyers button found on each Video track to show the standard A/B roll.

4.36   Expand Track Layers button.

4.37   Vegas displays A/B roll views, although A/B roll views take up twice the amount of screen space as a single-track view.

4.38   Transition types may be selected by right-clicking any transition, and the last used transitions will be displayed and may be chosen in this submenu.

The concept behind hiding the A/B roll view and showing transitions as crossfades stems from Vegas' origin as an audio editing tool, in which crossfades for audio are always viewed as single tracks. Further, it makes more sense in a real-estate–challenged environment, such as a computer screen, to bring as many elements together as possible.

And the Envelope Please...? Transitional Envelopes

Of course, we've seen how Vegas can easily drop in a transition and preview it on the fly to an external monitor, but there are other features and functions hidden in the transition process.

Crossfade or overlap two events to create a transition as described above. Drop a transition on the overlap. Any transition except the Dissolve will work for this. Now right-click the transition area, and select Insert/Remove Envelope>Transition Envelope from the submenu. This will insert an envelope in the transition area that is similar to a velocity envelope. By double-clicking on the envelope, envelope points or handles may be inserted.

These points will allow the control of the transitional behavior over time. For instance, maybe the transition needs to reverse itself or perhaps only pause in mid-transition. Illustration 4.33b shows a transition reversing and pausing itself.

Transitional envelopes are great for building creative and unique transitions, but the feature may also be used for powerful compositing techniques. By using lengthy transitions coupled with transitional envelopes, entire composites and virtual transitions may be created with only three or four video events. To do this, you'll need to reduce the opacity of the tracks containing the transitional envelopes and layer them over another video event on a lower track. This technique can yield beautiful results when combined with complementary media.

4.39   Right-click the transition for this submenu to appear.

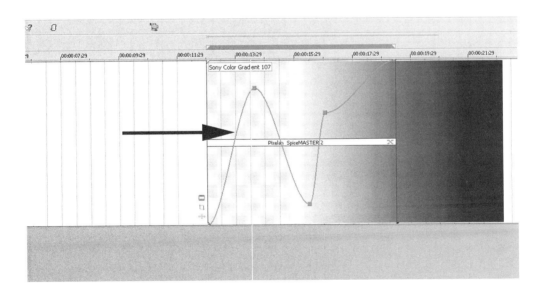

4.40   Where the envelope is pulled down, the transition will reverse. The flattened line indicates that the transition is paused and will hold in that position.

Using Keyframes in Vegas

Vegas has always had a unique method of keyframing. Keyframes are often misunderstood and are sometimes difficult for newcomers to the world of video editing.

Keyframes are nothing more than indicators in time, defined by how an event should behave at a specific moment and an instruction sent to a process at a specific moment during that time. They animate sequences of images or control effect parameters over time.

We live our lives by keyframes. All of us have specific moments in time when we do certain things, such as going to bed, eating a meal, traveling to work, or making a phone call. Appointment books are nothing more than analog keyframes.

In the video editing world, animation world, and audio editing world, keyframes are used to instruct an event to color-correct, change speed, delay, move onscreen, pan, change volume, and much more at specific points in time. The tool that defines these instructions are keyframes. Keyfamewinowsare nothing more than standard clocks, but instead of being round, they are linear.

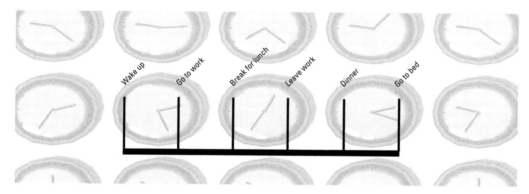

4.41   An average daily keyframe.

4.42   Keyframes instruck an event regarding how to behave over time.

Vegas departs from most applications in regard to keyframes in that Vegas is event-, track-, or project-based, and separate events can have their own sets of processing and keyframing within those processes, independent of the timeline. What this means is that an event can be moved on the timeline, and the keyframes will stay with it!

Imagine doing a 52-minute project for television, and, after the entire editing process is complete, a three-frame error is found in the first two minutes of the program. In most applications, if an event is moved even three frames, the entire project will be affected. With Vegas, this is simply not so. In fact, the entire series of events that exists in the hypothetical three seconds can be moved to the end of the timeline, with keyframes and processing intact.

4.43 The selected event length is displayed in the lower-right side of the timeline.

Notice that the length of the event illustrated is ten seconds and six frames in length. Double-click the event, and, in the lower-right corner of the editing timeline, Vegas displays the length of the event selection. You can also right-click the event and look at its properties, where the media length is displayed.

Insert the DVD found in this book and browse to the `\veg\` folder. Locate and open the VEG file titled `Keyframes`. The timeline will open with the video file shown in the example.

Now, click the Event FX icon found on the event. (If you don't see the icon, go to the OPTIONS I PREFERENCES I GENERAL dialog and check the Show Video Event Buttons.)

4.44 Event properties are seen when the event is right-clicked and Properties is selected.

This process opens the Video FX plug-in folder. In this example and DVD project, the Wave plug-in has been selected.

Note the first keyframe in the keyframe timeline, which is indicated by a small diamond.

Now click the five-second indicator on the timeline in the keyframe timeline window and select the Horizontal Only preset in the Preset dialog box. Notice that a new keyframe or diamond appears on the keyframe timeline. This diamond indicates that over time the slider will begin to move, causing the event image to gradually change over time, getting more and more wavy until at the five-second point, it reaches the full effect as dictated by the slider position.

4.45　The Event FX button is found on every event by default. This feature can be turned off in the OPTIONS | PREFERENCES | GENERAL dialog.

4.46　The first keyframe may be moved anywhere on the keyframe timeline. Attributes of the first keyframe are shown regardless of the position of the first keyframe, as it is the first indicator of time-based event/track/project behavior.

What if you don't want the event to become more wavy over time but instead want the effect to come in only at a determined time? Click and hold the first keyframe and slide it to the right. Now right-click the keyframe and select one of the keyframe behaviors. Attributes that can be assigned to keyframes include Hold, Linear, Fast, Slow, and Smooth.

Hold instructs the keyframe to freeze the settings for the FX in place until a new keyframe is shown, at which point the process jumps to the new settings. Linear creates a gradual change with no curve in the manner in which the sliders move. Fast causes the instructed behavior to slope in quickly and then gradually slow to meet the setting dictated by the slider. Slow does just the opposite; it slowly slopes toward the settings for the second keyframe and speeds up as it reaches its indicated position. Smooth provides temporal and spatial behavior, appearing to start slowly, speed up, and slow down again in tmeas the controls reach their keyframed positions. All of these attributes are demonstrated on the DVD.

4.47 Keyframe velocities/ attributes can be changed by right-clicking a keyframe.

Vegas is efficient in how it syncs the locations of keyframes to a cursor position. This feature can save hours of time trying to place keyframes correctly.

Move to Region 6 on the editing timeline of the Keyframes project. Place the cursor anywhere on the editing timeline inside the event contained in Region 6. Notice that inside the keyframe timeline, the cursor will move in sync to wherever the cursor is located on the editing timeline. Now move the horizontal amplitude slider. Notice that Vegas automatically inserts a keyframe at that moment in time.

Now double-click the time indicator inside the plug-in.

> Be aware that with the automation features in Vegas, keyframes may be automatically created when looping video and adjusting filter attributes. This is a great feature, if you intend for this to happen. However, if multiple keyframes start appearing and they're not desired, be certain to disarm automation in the video track. You'll have to relaunch the plug-in. You can also disable the sync to cursor in the plug-in dialog.

Enter a new time of 00:00:06:10, which will move the cursor inside the keyframe timeline and will move the cursor to the same position on the editing timeline. Now slide the vertical amplitude slider all the way to the right. Notice how the preview of the event image changes to match the setting, while at the same time Vegas inserts a new keyframe at the position of 00:00:06:10. Either move the cursor tool with arrow keys or mouse or double-click the time indicator inside the keyframe tool or the main editing window time indicator to place the cursor with frame accuracy for keyframing effects or other processing.

Nearly everything in Vegas is keyframeable. Pan/Crop settings can be keyframed, as can Track Motion behaviors. Track Motion will show up on the timeline of the main editing window. Region 7 of the Keyframes project contains track motion keyframes. Notice that they are displayed on the edit timeline. Track motion can dramatically affect how events are shown, and, to prevent confusion about oddly sized events on a track, these are displayed prominently.

Keyframes are unlimited as to their application. They can be applied to as many FX as necessary to make an event meet the desired appearance. Some effects seen on television today contain hundreds of keyframes in one-to-two seconds of video.

4.48 Double-click the time indicator inside the plug-in to place the cursor at the exact time.

4.49 Track motion keyframes can be viewed directly on the timeline by double-clikcking a track keyframe and expanding the Track Motion Keyframes view.

Keyframes can be copied and pasted inside the keyframe timeline. Move the cursor to the Region 9 eenton the editing timeline. Click the Edit Generated Media button in the upper-right corner of the event.

4.50   This event keyframes page contains 28 keyframes in less than three seconds of video. Multiple keyframes allow for powerful uses of FX.

The Edit Generated Media dialog will open, and five keyframes will show on the keyframe timeline. While holding the left mouse button down, draw around the five keyframes. When all keyframes are selected, they'll have a white diamond in the middle of each keyframe and will become white in color. Copy the keyframes by either right-clicking and selecting Copy or pressing CTRL+C. Move the cursor inside the keyframe timeline to 00:00:01:15 by either clicking the cursor to position or by double-clicking the keyframe time display. Now paste the keyframes by right-clicking and selecting Paste or by pressing CTRL+V. Repeat the action again at 00:00:03:00. All five keyframes are now repeated three times. Play the media. Notice how it loops the key-frame attributes. These keyframes can also be copied and pasted into another keyframe timeline of a similar nature.

To complete the explanation of Vegas' keyframing attributes and their incredible power, go to the editing timeline of the Keyframes project. Click and hold Region 1, Linear Keyframe setting. Slide it to the end of the project, past Region 8 Multiple keyframes-FX. Place the cursor at the front of Region 1 and play. Notice that the keyframes stayed with the event. Therefore, events can be copied and pasted, slid on the timeline, or moved to completely different tracks. If a keyframed event is copied in one instance of Vegas, it can be pasted into another instance of Vegas with keyframes intact. This feature is unique in the NLE world. Keyframes placed on Events stay with the events. Keyframes placed on a track will stay with the track.

4.51   Keyframes can be copied and pasted within their own keyframe time-line or pasted as event attributes to another event.

Tracks, however, may not be moved horizontally in time; they may only be moved vertically in priority. Keyframes may also be applied at the project setting. Any video plug-in that shows up in Vegas is keyframeable. Audio plug-ins are automatable, which is similar to keyframing, yet are managed and viewed differently. (Vegas uses keyframes to control the surround sound movement, which is discussed in Chapter 6.)

Learning to understand and manage keyframes is perhaps the most important and valuable lesson to be learned and understood in the video editing world, whether working with Vegas or other NLE systems. Various NLEs have unique keyframing attributes, but regardless of the system, all NLEs use keyframes in one form or another.

4.52   Click the Event Video FX button found on each event by default. It is seen on every visual event, regardless of whether it's a still photo, graphic, or video event.

Filters in Vegas

Vegas is jam-packed with filters to enhance, correct, and design graphic and video events, either bringing substandard images to an acceptable level or allowing editors the expression of artistic freedom.

4.53   Dragging FX or clicking an FX button on the **Track** Control pane has the same effect.

Filters, also known as plug-ins, are found in the plug-ins folder and are accessible from many points in Vegas. Opening the VIEW | PLUGINS menu will show the effects found in Vegas. Vegas comes with more than 40 plug-ins, ranging from color correction tools to swirls, waves, and pixilate filters.

While all filters/plug-ins have presets, learning the settings and behaviors of the plug-ins makes for very creative and powerful image processing in Vegas.

As with nearly all other aspects of Vegas, plug-ins can be inserted at the event-, track-, or project-level. Plug-ins can be dragged and dropped or selected from menus selected at the event-, track-, or project-levels.

Plug-ins dropped on

- An event affect only that specific event on the timeline

- A track affect all events on the track that are affected by the plug-in's attributes

- Project/video output level affect every track, event, and final output in the project

- Media in the Media Pool will affect all Events relative to that media in the Media Pool.

To add plug-ins to an event, click the FX button on the event. These buttons are visible by default, but if for some reason they are not shown, the OPTIONS I PREFERENCES I GENERAL dialog has a check box for Show Video Event Buttons that should be checked. If having the buttons visible is not desired, uncheck this box. Events can also be right-clicked and Video Event Effects chosen from the menu.

FX can also be dragged directly onto events from the FX menus. To view all FX at one time, press ALT+8 or select VIEW I VIDEO FX to open the FX selection box.

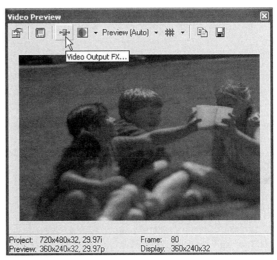

To have a thumbnail preview of some FX properties, keep the FX window open and in the dockable windows section or drag it onto a second monitor. It also makes for a great space from which to drag and drop FX.

Dragging FX to a Track Control pane places FX on an entire track. Each track also has an FX button on it.

Any FX dragged to the Track Control pane will result in all events having FX applied to them. The only way to control FX on individual events is to use keyframes.

FX can be applied at the project-level by dragging FX to the Preview window or by clicking the Video Output FX button on the toolbar in the Preview window. All video, graphics, and still events on every track will be processed at the project- or output-level.

4.54   Inserting FX at the project-level.

The primary use for FX at the project- or output-level is for plug-ins along the lines of the

- Timecode plug-in

- NTSC/broadcast clamp

- Black restore

Any FX, however, can be placed on the project.

As many FX as necessary can be applied to events, tracks, or the project. FX are arranged in the order in which they are applied; this order is easily changed by either dragging one plug-in to its plac onthe plug-in bar or by clicking the "Shift plug-in

4.55   The timecode plug-in places a timecode burn on the project window.

4.56   Arranging the order of plug-ins can be done via button press or by dragging plug-ins to the desired priority.

left/shift plug-in right" button found on the FX Chooser plug-in bar.

You can save chains of FX in Vegas. Many times, a project requires repetitive use of the same series of FX. Creating presets and inserting FX in sequence can be time-consuming. For example, a project might have poorly shot video and requires color correction, brightness adjustment, and broadcast color clamp. Rather than inserting these FX time after time, the series of FX, complete with presets, can be recalled after it is saved as a chain. This process saves tremendous time, especially in an editing house where a set flow of work exists. Each editor can create their own chains to suit their own workflow.

4.57   Find preset chains in the FX packages folder, which are shown each time FX are to be applied to events, tracks, or projects.

To save the chain of plug-ins as a preset:

1.   Select the plug-ins and arrange their priority.
2.   Click the Save-As button. The Chain dialog is displayed.
4.   Name the chain/preset.
4.   Press ENTER to accept the changes you've made to save the preset.

The chain preset is now displayed in the plug-in chooser and is available from the Filter Packages view. (The same process applies to audio presets.)

Vegas has a tremendously powerful feature that allows video output to be viewed at both pre- and post-process settings. Often times, editors find themselves wanting to see original video next to the processed video. This option has not been possible in the past without complex hardware. Now it is possible with Vegas's split-screen preview.

The Split Screen View Selection Tool button is shown on the Preview Window toolbar.

Selecting this button in the Preview window makes Vegas automatically split the preview screen, which shows affected media on one half and original video on the other half. However, Vegas allows users to define the areas where preview or original video is viewed by drawing a square or rectangle over the screen. Drawing the shape on the preview screen creates a hole where original video is seen.

4.58   Split Screen View
         Selection Tool button.

4.59, 4.60   The area to view
            the original (a) versus processed
            video (b) is user-defined.

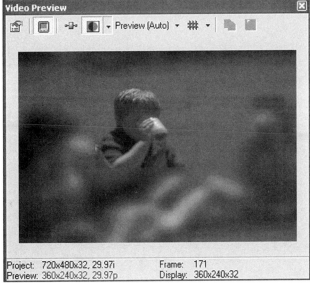

The split preview of processed and original video is also viewable on an external monitor, which makes color correction in Vegas advanced compared to even exceptionally high-end NLE systems. The capability to compare processed video to original video on an external monitor without rendering a file provides editors with a newfound speed, workflow, and freedom from concerns about accuracy in the editing workflow. This feature coupled with RAM renders allow editors to immediately see full motion/full frame-rate accurate views of edited media, limited only by RAM and processor speed.

The Split-Screen Preview window can be used to show contents of the clipboard during the preview of a timeline section. Position the cursor on the timeline and click the Copy Snapshot button in the Video Preview window to copy a frame as a still image to the clipboard. Move the cursor to another point on the timeline.

On the Split Screen View Selection Tool button, click the drop-down menu arrow and select the Clipboard. The contents of the clipboard are displayed in the Preview window or external monitor. The area in which the clipboard contents are displayed is defined by the area drawn with the cursor inside the Preview window area. If the entire clipboard clip is to be shown, redraw the cursor over the entire Preview window area. The underlying clip indicating the location of the cursor is no longer shown. Turn off the split-screen preview or redraw the viewing area to view underlying events. Double-clicking the Preview window returns the Preview window to its default state.

How Filters/Plug-ins Function

While far too many plug-ins are available in Vegas to describe the attributes of each, some common plug-ins are of great benefit to understand. Each plug-in has a series of presets but experimenting with the settings increases the power of the plug-in tremendously. A number of thir-party filters are available, some of which are described in the following list:

- Add Noise—adds grain or noise at various levels.

- Chromakey—removes colors from an image and replaces with other information, similar to the weaterperson on the television news.

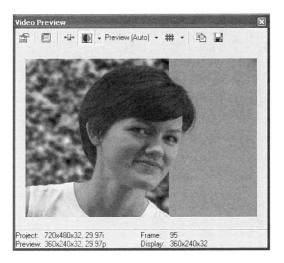

- Convolution Kernel—embosses, finds lines, or creates a motion photograhic image from video.

- Lens Flares—hide anomalies, make still images look more like video, and give flair to wide-video shots.

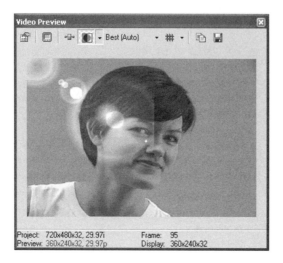

- Mirror—creates mirrored images of any portion of the screen. When used correctly with generated media, the plug-in can emulate a kaleidoscope.

- Pixelan's ChromaWarp—provides infinite artistic choices for the beginning and experienced editor.

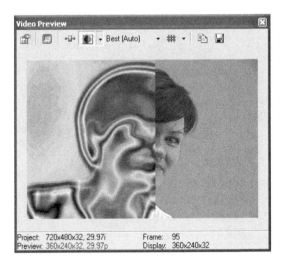

- DebugMode's 3D Pak—adds some wonderful 3-D elements to the Vegas editing toolbox.

4.68   Color correction can be viewed in real time on an external or internal monitor.

These plug-ins are free and are included on the disk in this book.

Vegas has a feature that is often overlooked yet should not be. Vegas has the ability to build a RAM preview of the final appearance of an event so that it can be seen full-motion/full frame rate. The RAM preview is important to be able to see, particularly in situations where keyframes are inserted in tight time spaces. Slower processors or FX-heavy, multiple events can tax the processor so much that some keyframes simply can't be drawn due to lack of processor power. Using a RAM render causes these sections to be drawn without creating a temporary file on a hard drive.

To initiate a RAM render, make a selection on the timeline. Pressing SHIFT+B instructs Vegas to begin rendering the time selection to RAM. The amount of RAM installed in the computer determines the length of time that RAM can render. This is why as much RAM as possible is best in most editing systems. By default, Vegas allocates 16MB of RAM to the RAM preview. Opening the OPTIONS | PREFERENCES | VIDEO dialog gives users the ability to adjust the amount of RAM to be used for RAM preview renders. Vegas subtracts 128MB of RAM from all available RAM for preview purposes. Even if only 128MB are available, Vegas makes allowances for up to 16MB of RAM. However, any available RAM in excess of 128MB can be used for RAM renders. (100 percent of RAM may not be used, as the operating system and Vegas require 128MB of RAM space to operate properly.)

While RAM renders benefit external previews, previews on external monitors are not full frame rate except in the faster machines. If full resolution/full frame rate are required for an external preview, a standard pre-render is required on edited/recompressed media. Pressing SHIFT+M opens the pre-render dialog.

One of the more in-demand, necessary, and powerful plug-ins added is the Color Corrector tool. This palette-based tool offers extremely fast color correction, and, when combined with the Split-Pane Preview window, it's simple to view changes in color on either an external monitor or on a gamma-corrected computer monitor.

The Color Corrector plug-in can be dragged and dropped on an event, track, or entire project. It can be used to simulate color effects as well, such as those seen in the movies *Payback* or *Traffic*.

Double-clicking the dot in the color

4.69 The Secondary Color Corrector makes replacing colors easy and intuitive.

correction palettes resets the palette to zero. Most controls in Vegas act in this manner; double-clicking resets a control to default or null.

Colors can be sampled using the Eyedropper tool found in the low/mid/highlight palettes to assist in selecting the color curve.

The Secondary Color Corrector in Vegas, adding an Invert Mask option. This allows the "Pleasantville" look to be created quickly and easily. See Chapter 5 for more information on how to use this small but powerful update. Secondary Color Correction. It allows for a color or series of colors to be replaced or used as masks through which other media can show. Start by selecting a color to be replaced. Shut off external monitor preview while selecting colors. A single color or gradient of color can be selected. Best results are obtained by working with a single color and using more than one instance of the Secondary Color Corrector.

 Tip_____

Any time video has a final destination where it might be viewed on a television monitor of any kind, it is strongly advised that a good quality television or broadcast monitor be used to preview video; otherwise it is far too easy to have incorrect colors, borders, or margins. If video will only be seen on a computer monitor as streaming media or intranet media, an external monitor is unnecessary.

One of the most sought-after looks in DV production is the ability to have video appear more film-like. While shooting and production are a huge part of this process, there are some steps that can be taken to make video more film-like.

Making video look more like film has been a goal of videographers since desktop video was a concept. Video simply cannot look exactly like film, due in part to the perfection of video and the conversion process, the compression process, and the interpretation of imagery. Film, shot on celluloid, is an analog format that has its own warts but warts that have defined how our eyes see images. Someone once said, "video is what the eye sees, film is what the imagination sees." Kodak's Tom Wallis commented, "Film feels organic to audiences, and that's why they associate a film look with fantasy and video with reality." There is a great amount of truth to this, hence the desire to make video look more like film.

Many companies offer "cure-all" plug-ins to make video more film-like, but in the opinion of all but the most amateur, these plugs merely make video look like video treated to look like film. Compared to the real deal, it's pretty clear what is what. Some of the more expensive tools, such as Magic Bullet from Red Giant, can do an excellent job with video shot like film, but Vegas can approximate most of that same look without the plug-in tools.

First off, to make video more film-like in appearance, the video must be shot like film would be shot. Great lighting, shadows, and depth of field are critical. DV cameras allow for too much depth of field in most cases, so videographers who are aware of this also are aware of the many work arounds to get a good shot with tight foreground focus and weak background focus. For instance, using a Neutral Density filter and opening the iris to full helps. Blurred backgrounds quickly indicate a sense of "unreality" and go a long way to getting video to look more film-like. Shooting through pantyhose behind the lens or shooting through a Tiffen Black Mist filter can help soften the look too. Opening the iris and reducing the amount of light that can pass the filter will call for more and better lighting, too. With cams like Sony's PD150/170, you can easily underexpose and then correct in post if you know what you are doing. Be cautious of this workflow with cameras that are noisy in low light. Take careful notes, either as voice notes on the tape or have an assistant write down the settings. Starting each roll with a gradient or shot color bars will help define colors under conditions when it comes time to correct in post.

Next on the list is cadence. NTSC video is shot at 29.97 fps, and PAL video is shot at 25.00 fps. Film cameras shoot at 24.00 frames per second. The 24 frame "stutter" gets DV closer to film pretty quickly. Many great film makers that find themselves having to work with digital video shoot PAL cameras, as it's not a big thing at all to match 25 frames to 24 frames per second. In fact, if you plan on making a feature that looks like it was shot on film, acquiring a PAL camera should be a consideration. Panasonic offers the DVX100, a DV cam that shoots at 24 fps. Some folks don't care for the video quality while they love the cadence of 24 fps. Some folks just aren't interested in learning another camera or another format. Another difference is the interlaced format of NTSC video and film being progressive scan. But what if you don't have a PAL or 24 fps camera?

This is where Vegas and its format-agnostic, resolution-independent featureset comes in. Vegas is indeed optimized for capture, editing, and output of DV files, yet it does offer other alternatives, too, thereby removing the limitations so many applications impose on the editing process.

Vegas is capable of working with 24p natively, performing what's known as 3:2 pulldown during playback. This is referred to as "inverse telecine." Telecine is the process of converting 24 fps to 29.97 fps. Therefore, pulling the frames back out is known as inverse telecine or IVTC. For a simple explanation about pulldown, go here:

Vegas will easily convert 29.97 fps footage (commonly referred to as 60i) to 24p, which is actually 24.976 fps. This creates the cadence of film, where during the process essentially 6 frames or 12 half-frames per second are removed from the stream. Another way of expressing the difference between 24p and 60i or 50i is: NTSC is 59.94 fields (60i) per second, PAL is 50 (50i) fields per second. Film is 24 full frames per second. NTSC and PAL have the look of reality because of the smooth motion rendition. Part of the film look is the much slower 24 fps acquisition rate. To simulate this with video, you must throw away or blend fields to create 24, 29.97, or 25 frames per second instead of twice as many fields per second. The interpolation of the removed frames is pretty critical to making this all look right. Also important to consider is working with 24p titles, transitions, generated media to keep the image accurate. To my knowledge, Vegas is currently the only application working with native 24p transitions, titles, FX, and generated media. Nevertheless,

4.70 Letterboxing goes a long way to helping video look more film-like. These images are before and after film-like processing as described here.

Editing and Converting

First, edit your media on the timeline as individual events and cuts-only. Do not do any transitions, titles, FX at this time. You might want to leave heads and tails on the rendered events for future transitions or edit requirements. Render these individual clips out by double clicking the event to select the event as its own region. These events will be rendered out to a compressed or uncompressed 24p format. Save the .veg file. Some users might have issues with the render to DV instead of uncompressed, but the Vegas codec holds up just great, and most users will have no issue with the quality of image going from DV to DV. Once all the events have been edited, render them individually by creating a template containing the following settings:

1. Set the Project Properties/Deinterlace mode to Blend Fields (default).
2. Choose File>Render As.
4. Name the file, choose .avi as the file format, and select NTSC or PAL DV (inserting 2:3 Pulldown).
4. If you wish to render Uncompressed, Select the Custom button, In General tab, select rendering quality of Best. Select Video tab, in the Video Format dropdown box, and select "Uncompressed."
5. Render this event to a folder where it can be located later. Render all events as 24p (NTSC-DV or Uncompressed) .

After all events have been edited, open the saved .veg if you've closed it down, and set the Project Properties to 24p (NTSC or PAL). If you've rendered to uncompressed, replace the events in the Media Pool with the 24p uncompressed files you created earlier. Do the same if you've rendered to 24pDV. As soon as all the events in the Media Pool have been replaced, notice that any uncompressed events are letterboxed. (DV compressed files won't have this issue.) This is due to uncompressed media being square pixel aspect ratio and DV media being non-square pixels. To correct this, right -click the first event on the timeline and select Properties. In the Properties dialog, select the Media tab.

Aspect Ratio

If you've rendered uncompressed media, select the Pixel Aspect Ratio dropdown in the Media tab and choose .909 as the aspect ratio. The first event's image will no longer be letterboxed in the Preview window.

Uncompressed or DV, right-click the first event again and choose Switches>Disable Resample. This will prevent the project from trying to reinsert the missing frames for playback.

Copy the first event, then right-click the second event and choose "Select Events to End." Right-click again and select Paste Event Attributes. This will cause all events to have the resample disabled and correct pixel aspect ratio. Now you can begin editing.

One of the first things viewers associate with the film look is letter boxing or 16:9 screen. So, using Pan/Crop on the first event, choose the 16:9 crop preset from the Pan/Crop dropdown menu. If you choose this option, you'll need to apply this to all events on the timeline, so once

 Tip_____

If you're working with HDV, the pixel aspect ratio of the graphic in Photoshop or other graphic editor should be 1.333, not .909 that DV requires.

again copy the first event, select events to end, and choose Paste Attributes. This will apply the letterbox to all events on the timeline. Depending on the framing of the shots, you might need to adjust individual events for composition.

Apply transitions as necessary. Apply titles and any other overlays. These will be generated at 24 fps, progressive scanned as determined by the project properties.

Color correction can be applied at the track level to create a similar look for all events. However, if individual events were shot under different lighting circumstances, it might be advisable to put all similar events on single tracks or save color correction presets per shot location so that color correction may be quickly applied to groups of shots.

Gamma

Another difference in film from video is Gamma, or an adjustment between input and output, and how the eye perceives the difference between film and video. While Vegas doesn't have a specific plug-in for Gamma compensation, it does have Color Curves which essentially accomplish the same goals. Drop the Color Curves filter on the Preview window to apply it to the entire project.

Experiment!

After applying these basics, the next steps are entirely subjective and experimental and subject to personal preferences and will vary depending on the desired final output appearance. However, adding an HSL filter to saturate the colors, adding a touch of Glow will go a long way to getting a great film-like look. For the demo file, I used the Zenoté Glow set to 1/4 Tiffen, plus the Zenoté Film Grain set to 35mm plug-ins. Sony has a good glow filter as well, I find I like the Zenoté a little

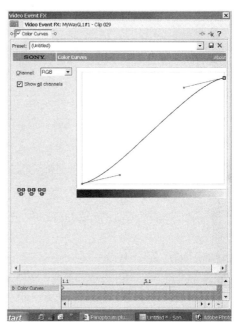

4.71 Notice this curve and how it compensates for differences in gamma. View this on an external monitor and be very surprised at how powerful this underestimated tool is.

better as it's slightly smoother, and the Film Grain are a little more quick to use, but the Sony Film Grain can be tweaked to look similar to the presets of the Zenoté plug. Adding Motion Blur to pans or transitory elements can also make a difference in a shot. Consider using SuperSampling on Motion Blur shots. Don't forget that Pixelan has some excellent film look plugins for Vegas as well. Their Spicefilters are some of the coolest plugs available for Vegas.

From this point it's entirely related to your desire, experimentation, and quality of original video that will determine the final output. The demo video was shot entirely with existing light, backlit, and generally poorly composed, but the quality of color shift and film-like imagery is clear to see regardless of its original quality. Had it been lit correctly and shot with an eye for film-like composition, it would be even more effortless to create a film-like appearance. It can't be stressed enough that the lighting, shooting technique, and composition make all the difference in the world. Don't expect to shoot with a palmcorder and no tripod with a digital zoom and expect to have imagery that looks like it was shot with an Arriflex. It's not only a pipe dream, it's impossible. Even the most expensive, top-end plug-ins can't work these sorts of miracles, but Vegas surely comes close to being a miracle worker with bad footage, and can make really good footage look fantastic.

4.72   The Zenoté plug-ins go a long way to creating a film-like appearance.

Shooting Modes

When shooting with most any DV camera, shoot in interlaced mode rather than in frame or "film mode" as some of the cameras call it. Otherwise you are throwing away pixels that otherwise add to the quality of the original image. Some cameras actually cut the frame rate to 15 fps when shooting in a Progressive mode. Other cams simply shift pixels to create a film look.

It's generally better to do de-interlacing at the NLE rather than throw away data that can otherwise improve the picture. Spend some time studying lighting, contrast, and camera angles. Experiment with ND filters and lighting, and you'll find your image not only improves substantially, but you'll become a better shooter and editor for it. Hollywood rarely uses a zooming lens, but rather uses a prime lens (a fixed focal length) and a dolly or jib to move into or out of a shot. Try shooting without using a zoom. You'll find a better look, and a more disciplined shooting style will help you plan shots better.

Output

In case it's not immediately obvious, to print this to tape requires a camera or deck capable of receiving a 24p stream. If you already have a camera, most of this tutorial is of no value, so we'll

 Tip

Be sure to check out the ReelPak products by David Jimerson, as they mimic many popular film looks, and are very fast to render.

set that aside. This technique is most valuable for printing to DVD, and competing with some of the bigger fish in the market when it comes to film look. I showed a video that was created with these techniques at a small film festival in Milwaukee, WI September of 2004. A reasonably well-known director asked me what kind of film I'd shot it on. He was shocked when I told him it was shot on a pair of DV cameras. The video won first place in the children's category. It was shown from DVD. Render the project out using the Vegas 24p NTSC or PAL template. You can render it as a DVD Architect NTSC/PAL video stream if you intend on rendering an AC3 file for the audio or render as a 24p NTSC/PAL file where the audio will be packaged with the video stream.

These small tips should help you to create a look that approaches film fairly easily. It is indeed a process in terms of the steps required; at the same time it provides a great alternative means to a 24p camera and more importantly as the 24p formats and technologies develop, it allows owners of typical DV cams to have the 24p look without buying a new cam. The greatest advantage of this workflow is that up to 25 percent more media can be stored off on to a DVD when the media is 24p. In order to preview this media on an external monitor, you'll need to insert the pulldown, but Vegas can also do that on the fly. (See chapter 10 for more information) Playback might be a little slower due to the inserted frames in real time, but it's still capable of being viewed on an external monitor for color correction and other filter tweaking. (The output framerate must be at 29.97/NTSC or 25.00/PAL fps to be viewed on an external monitor.)

Opacity Envelopes

Each video track in Vegas has an opacity control, although no shortcut key is available. Opacity is the level at which an event is visible. At zero percent opacity, an event is completely transparent, and at 100 percent opacity, the event is completely visible with zero transparency, which is the opposite of how Photoshop and Ulead control opacity.

The opacity of a track can be altered in one of two methods. The first method is in the Track Control window, where level/opacity for the entire tack can be set. This is not controllable over time but rather sets the level or opacity for every event on the track.

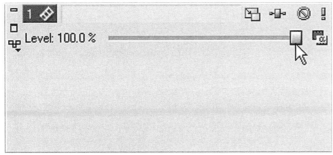

4.73   Track Control pane-level adjustment.

 *Tip*_____

Be sure your opacity levels are always at 100%. If you have a track that seems to be rendering too slow, this is sometimes an indicator that the opacity slider has been moved.

4.74 Adjusting opacity over time. No limit exists as to how many handles/nodes can be placed on the track timeline.

The second method is to set an Opacity Envelope in the track, which is done by right-clicking the Track Control pane and selecting Insert/Remove Envelope and then selecting Composite Level from the submenu that will open. This process will insert a blue line (default color) at the top of the video track. Double-clicking this blue line inserts handles or nodes. These handles/nodes allow the compositing envelope to be pulled down and adjusted for opacity level at any point on the video track. To delete a node, right-click it and select Delete.

The following are the envelope modes you have to choose from:

- Linear—Straight line fades with no velocity or curve to the actions

- Smooth—Smooth fade ramps slightly into the event before ramping back down.

- Fast—Fast fade quickly raises or quickly lowers settings.

- Slow—Slow fade gradually moves in or out.

- Sharp—Sharp fade moves quickly to the peak movement.

- Hold—Hold position has no subtle movement at all and is fairly harsh and obvious.

Using the opacity envelope or envelopes, events can be faded to another event on a different track or to a transparent black.

 Open the project called `Compositing Envelope.veg`, which is on the tutorial DVD. Two video tracks are on the timeline. Track 1 already has a compositing envelope on it. On the control pane for track 2, right-click and select Insert/Remove Envelope, and then select Composite Level. A blue line, similar to the line found on track 1, will appear. Double-click at the first marker on this line to insert handles/nodes. Pull the handle down to 50 and notice how the gradient found on track 3 becomes visible.

By using compositing envelopes, you can create beautiful fades over multiple layers of video. Compositing envelopes also allow for rapid transition from one event to another with overlay or multiple images. With compositing envelopes in place, as many tracks as the imagination might create can be visible.

If multiple cameras are used on the same shoot, the opacity envelope is an indispensable tool. Place video from multiple cameras on different tracks on the timeline, lining up their sync with the audio on each track, so that all video tracks are lined up with sync. Delete the audio tracks that are unused, keeping only the audio master track.

For this example, we'll assume three tracks of video and one track of audio are being used. On video tracks 1 and 2, insert compositing envelopes. Leave video track 3 without any adjustment at this time. Play the video until you'd like a fade or cut to occur and drop a marker at that point, pressing M. Stop playback and double-click the compositing envelope at the top of video track 1 to insert a handle. Double-click again slightly after the first handle. Now pull the opacity envelope all the way down to the bottom of video track 1. Now the events in video track 2 are visible. Play the timeline again, until another fade or cut is desired. Drop another marker and repeat the actions performed above at the new edit point. Now video track 3 is visible. Again play the video until a new fade or cut should occur. Now events from track 2 or track 1 can be brought in by double-clicking the bottom of either video track on the compositing envelope, inserting two points, and pulling the compositing envelope up. In this manner, an entire show can be roughed out quickly.

After all fades and cuts have been made using the opacity envelope, each time a track has been removed from view with the opacity envelope, you can place the cursor on the event, making sure the event is selected. Press S to split the event. Repeat the split at the point in the event just before it fades in again. Now the middle portions of the event can be deleted.

 Open the `compositingenvelope#s2.veg` project from the DVD. (This project also includes the use of the Pan/Crop tools, discussed earlier in this chapter.) This project demonstrates the use of the same video track, panned and cropped, to create the false image of a three-camera shoot from one camera.

The compositing envelope is used to create the original edit points. In this project, you'll need to split out the unused video. Removing the unused portions of the event is not necessary, merely helpful in viewing the overall project.

Compositing envelopes may be automated, including Mutes, just as Volume, Pan, and other envelopes may be automated. If you own a Mackie Universal Control, you'll be able to use the faders as compositing controls for video, thus giving you an automated video switching system as well as an audio mixer.

Velocity Filters

Velocity filtering allows for media to speed up, slow down, reverse, or freeze-frame, all without cutting clips of media into individual pieces as previously required in most applications. Velocity filtering, or envelopes, as they are known in Vegas, can be applied to any number of clips. The speed at which the envelope interactswith the media can be controlled as well via keyframes. Every effect, envelope, or filter can be keyframe-controlled in Vegas, with a variety of shapes for the envelope properties.

Open the `velocitytraining.veg` file found on the DVD.

Notice that on the timeline a green (default color) line is in the midde o the event. This line demonstrates how the velocity envelope is adjusted. The second event on the timeline is for you to adjust your own velocity envelope.

4.80   Velocity envelope inserted, with regions expressing each change in velocity. Handles have various envelope settings on them.

Start by previewing the first clip. Notice how it slows down during the first moments of the event, slowly climbs back to regular speed, and then freezes frame at the end? (You might need to perform a RAM render [SHIFT+B] if the processor cannot draw the video at normal speed.)

In the second half of the event, the video actually reverses to give an instant replay type of feel. Again, the event freezes frame at the end, allowing time for a blur, added title, special effect, or just a simple dissolve to the subject shot. This option is especially effective with video of high motion, such as sports, chases, or fight scenes. Notice how during the freeze frame, the Pan/Crop tool is used to create an artificial camera zoom. Another great space to use the velocity envelope is when you have a series of camera zooms that maybe weren't as smooth as they could have been. The envelope can slow down the jerkiness of a poor zoom or speed up a zoom that was too slow. A velocity envelope applied to speed up a fast zoom makes it faster, more frantic, and draws immediate attention to the subject on the screen.

To insert a velocity envelope into a media clip, right-click the clip and select Insert/Remove Velocity Envelope. A green line will appear. (This line is green by default in v4 and blue by default in v4.) The line will be set by default to normal speed, or 100 percent. Double-click the timeline, and a node or handle will appear. Move down the timeline a few seconds and double-click again, inserting a second handle. These handles are similar to keyframes, allowing the setting of velocity or speed on the individual event. To delete a node, right-click it and select Delete.

Now, move the handle up or down to set the desired speed. If the desired percentage of speed change can't be precisely achieved by moving the handle up and down, right-click the handle.

The dialog box shows the fade choices and speed settings. Select Set T and type in the desired setting. Slow the envelope down just as the zoom reaches its end and make sure the handle on the keyframe is set to Smooth if the media is being sped up or slowed down over a short number of frames. By setting the envelope handle to Smooth, the media won't appear to jerk or jump from slow to fast or from fast to slow.

As the event is sped up or slowed down, artifacts can occur, particularly in Vegas 2.0. Avoid this problem by right-clicking the clip, selecting Properties, and checking the Resample box. This process causes the render to slow down somewhat, yet carefully resamples the video to assure smooth picture and motion in almost every instance.

In Vegas, a feature for resampling has been created, which allows for smart, forced, or disabled resampling, as shown in Figure 4.81. If Smart Resample is enabled, which is the default option, Vegas determines whether the event requires resampling or not. Force Resample is similar to the resampling found in older versions of Vegas, in which Vegas is instructed to resample the event whether it requires it or not. Disable Resample turns resampling off.

4.81 Resampling features found in Vegas provide for smooth **slow motion** and velocity events.

Velocity envelopes have been used in nearly every form of special effect there is and can be used for titles, movement control, color keying, and other forms of effects. One favorite is to use an envelope during a title shot, slowing or freezing the subject matter, panning/cropping the media as though the camera zoomed in on the subject, and dropping the opacity of the media so that he title can punch through. This method is exceptionally effective when coupled with a mask and moving media behind the text. Velocity envelopes can be applied to all moving media, including GIF files.

⮞ Tip

Here's a tip for using velocity envelopes on long files: use the Split tool (S key) to split the clip before the actual change/handle of the velocity envelope. Otherwise, the envelope affect te entire file and slows down the render process if the rate is accidentally set to any level but 100 percent, when only a small portion of the event needs to be affected and perhaps resampled.

4.82 Right-clicking oan event calls up the Switches dialog.

Open in Tri<u>m</u>mer	
Video Event Pan/C<u>r</u>op...	
Video <u>E</u>vent FX...	
✂ Cu<u>t</u>	Ctrl+X
▣ <u>C</u>opy	Ctrl+C
Paste Event A<u>t</u>tributes	
✕ <u>D</u>elete	Delete
Select Events to E<u>n</u>d	
Insert/Remove <u>V</u>elocity Envelope	
Swit<u>c</u>hes	
T<u>a</u>ke	
<u>G</u>roup	
P<u>r</u>operties...	

Submenu:
<u>M</u>ute
<u>L</u>ock
Pushpin
✓ L<u>o</u>op
✓ Maintain <u>A</u>spect Ratio
Reduce Interlace <u>F</u>licker
● Smart <u>R</u>esample
Force Re<u>s</u>ample
Di<u>s</u>able Resample

Event Switches in Vegas

Right-clicking any event in Vegas calls up a Switches dialog. These switches dictate how selected events are treated. Events can be muted, locked, looped, video events maintained to aspect ratio, interlace flicker reduced, and audio events normalized. As mentioned previously, Smart Resample, Force Resample, and Disable Resample are also options in the Switches dialog.

Muting a selected audio event or video event prevents the event from being heard or seen on the timeline. Muted events are dark on the timeline, demonstrating the muted status.

Locking an event prevents it from being moved or edited. Locking events is good practice when a section is complete in a long-form video. Locking events causes those events to be grayed out, indicating that they are locked.

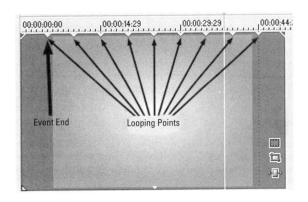

4.83 Looping events is helpful for extending titles and generated media.

Looping events causes events to repeat if they are dragged past their actual end. This option allows events to be extended on the timeline.

If FX have been applied to an event that is being looped, the FX holds at the last keyframe. This option can be a valuable artistic editing tool with titles, generated media, and backgrounds. If a loop is applied to a generated media event, keyframes loops with the generated media length.

Normalizing an audio event is typically for bringing audio to its maximum volume, based on the highest peak found in the audio. When normalizing is used, Vegas looks for the loudest point of the audio and adjusts the entire file to the loudest possible level without clipping. The maximum level for normalization can also be set manually, if necessary.

Aspect ratio lock can be applied to an event as well. This option prevents Vegas from stretching the aspect of the events' contents should it not match the project settings.

Sometimes graphics or stills that are converted to video do not display well on an interlaced monitor, depending on the colors and resolution. Reducing interlace flicker generally repairs this condition. Without applying the reduce interlace flicker, graphics and stills often show fringing on video edges or show crawling lines on the screen.

When editing long-form video and some short-form videos, it's helpful to be able to lock various events together in a group. By doing this, cut, copy/paste, and delete can be executed simultaneously, and multiple

4.84   Setting the level at which normalization peaks.

events can be moved simultaneously. It's also an efficient means of tracking sectionalized video.

To create a group:
1.   Select all events to be included in a group.
2.   Press G or right-click any event.
4.   Select GROUP | CREATE NEW in the submenu that opens.

No limit exists as to how many groups may be created; however, no two groups may share the same event.

Groups may be shifted, copied and pasted, or deleted together. After a group is created, right-click any event in the group to select all events in the group. Select GROUP | SELECT ALL from the submenu.

Audio and video files are grouped by default when placed on the timeline. To remove audio or video from a group or to separate them, select the event to be removed from the group and press U to ungroup that event. The event will be removed from the group.

To remove all events from a group, right-click any event in the group and select Clear.

Grouping can be temporarily ignored by clicking the Ignore Event Grouping button on the toolbar.

This option instructs Vegas to ignore the groups temporarily, while allowing events to be moved. After this button is released/selected again, however, the group is restored with all event members.

Groups or individual events can be locked on the timeline to prevent them from being moved.

The Shuffle feature, which is part of the new Ripple Editing toolset, is also a powerful and efficient means of creating a storyboard and rough cut on a single Vegas timeline.

At Sundance Media Group, we commonly use one instance to rough cut, one instance to edit/finish, and a third instance rendering in the background.

In a facility that uses multiple editing stations, one editor creates the rough cuts and saves them as a rough-cut VEG file. A second editor grabs the VEG file without ever copying media and does the color correction and finish work on the project. With a network, this workflow is exceptionally fast, particularly in a small company setting.

4.85   Six events are grouped. Notice the dark color at the top and bottom of the events. The seventh event is not grouped. Notice the white at the top and bottom, which indicates that this event is not part of the group.

4.86   Two open windows of Vegas. The first instance, or copy-to instance, doesn't need the Explorer, Trimmer, or other tools open. The second instance, or copy-from timeline, is where media location, sequencing, markers, and other finishing aids are created.

Some NLE systems use a layout concept called storyboarding, which uses thumbnails that can be dragged into a specific order and placed on the timeline for fine editing. Vegas does not have this feature. The following two methods, however, can be used for those desiring to edit with a storyboard workflow.

AVI clips in the Windows-Explorer (not the Vegas Explorer) show thumbnails if the thumbnail view is enabled. Clips can be shuffled from position to position in the Explorer, creating a sort of storyboard that works for most general purposes.

A more powerful and useful method of storyboarding is to have two instances of Vegas open at one time. The first instance is the active editing workspace, and the second instance is used for creating a storyboard/rough cut that is then copied and pasted into the first instance. What makes this option the more powerful storyboarding tool is that comments, markers, regions, and trims, in addition to storyboarding capabilities, are retained in the second instance. With either a single or dual monitor setup, this is a fast and powerful way to storyboard and edit.

Create a rough cut in the second instance, copy the timeline by selecting a region (press CTRL+A) or the entire timeline (press CTRL+C) and then paste into the first instance (press CTRL+V). Be certain to ave"Automatically save markers and regions" enabled in the OPTIONS | PREFERENCES | GENERAL dialog. Othewis, markers and regions created in the copy-from instance will not be carried over into the copy-to instance.

4.87 Notice that clips are not in numeric order, rather they have been shuffled to create a storyboard.

Filters and Add-ons

Working with Plug-ins in Vegas

Several third-party manufacturers have stepped up to Vegas and have written plug-ins for the product. The tools that come with Vegas provide a wide variety of additional expressions and emotions for editors in Vegas; however, these plug-ins give editors far more arrows for their bows, as well as a feel that the Vegas plug-ins don't come with. Pixelan Software, BorisFX, Red Giant, RM Tools, Panopticum, and DebugMode have released powerful new tools for Vegas, and demos of some of these products are found on the DVD in the back of this book.

Pixelan SpiceMASTER 2

Pixelan, long famous for their plug-ins for Avid, Adobe, Pinnacle, Media 100, Ulead, and other fine editing products, created the SpiceMASTER plug-in several years ago. Often mistakenly thought to be just a transition tool, this plug-in provides tremendous power to users. This tool has 500 BMPs alone that can be used as backgrounds, foregrounds, masks, and more. Combine this feature with other tools, and all of a sudden, there are millions of possibilities.

5.1 Spice explosion with Bump Map applied over Generated Media makes a very realistic solar flare.

Installing SpiceMASTER takes only a few minutes. Five hundred Spices provide the backbone of how images are manipulated, and the Spices are automatically installed to a folder that you can find quickly and easily. When working with Vegas and DV, load only the DV/720 × 480 Spices (for NTSC) and 720 × 576 (for PAL), as the other sizes will be of little use in Vegas. (If other applications are used, loading other Spice sizes might be of benefit.)

After installing the SpiceMASTER application, open Vegas and insert a video track, placing two events on a track with a crossfade.

In the Transitions tab, select the Pixelan SpiceMASTER 2 plug-in. Drag it to the transition between the two events, or right-click the crossfade and choose Pixelan SpiceMASTER 2, and a dialog box opens. This dialog can be confusing to first-time users. The dialog box instructs users to disable the Sync Cursor button in the Vegas keyframe timeline.

5.2   Locate SpiceMASTER 2 in the Transitions tab.

5.3   Disable the Sync Cursor button in the Vegas keyframe timeline.

The Sync Cursor button must be disabled in order to use some of the more powerful features of SpiceMASTER. SpiceMASTER 2 has its own keyframe timeline that allows for a level of control that the Vegas keyframe timeline cannot allow on its own.

The first window that opens shows the keyframing area, Preview window, the Choose Spice File button, and controls for how the Spices behave and appear.

5.4   Main SpiceMASTER 2 window with the keyframing area to the lower left, the Preview window in the upper left, and the control panel to the right.

The Keyframe window is where the velocity or attack/release of the Spices are controlled. The keyframer controls every aspect of how a Spice behaves, based on user input. SpiceMASTER has added a Bezier curve control that allows the user to smooth or ramp keyframes. The keyframer allows images to be brought in and out with a Spice, to be frozen, and even to be reversed. The line in the keyframer is a linear indicator of how the Spice will flow from start to finish. In the case of a transition, the keyframe controls the outgoing event, with Spice behavior on the left and the incoming event controlled on the right. Where the Spice falls in the center and how it behaves is entirely up to the user, who can slide the curve to satisfaction. A line from 0 on the left to 100 percent on the right and without a curve represents a traditional, straight transition. A line shaped like the line shown in Figure 5.5 creates a slow outgoing transition with a slight hold in the middle of the transition and a rapid curve to the new event at the end. With the two events on the timeline and a SpiceMASTER 2 transition inserted, click the Choose Spice File button, which opens the menu of Spices from which you can choose. Spices are animated in the Library, demonstrating how the motion of the effect will appear in the transition. Select a Spice. The effect is shown in outline in the SpiceMASTER's Preview widow

5.5   Notice the keyframes holding a curve, controlling how the Spice flows between two events.

5.6   Spices are animated and will display their action in the Chooser window.

Just below the preview image is a Transport bar. This bar has a Play button that can be used to play the built-in preview or to show how the keyframe points are controlling the effect. This option saves time by allowing users to see how a Spice transition will flow in real time. At the same time as adjustments are being made to the keyframes in the keyframing tool, the Vegas Preview window can also be active, showing in real time what adjustments are being made to the transition and Spice behavior.

5.7 A selected Spice displayed in the Preview window.

5.8 Click the Dual Pane button to see all controls in the SpiceMASTER 2 interface.

The keyframer takes a bit of adjustment for Vegas users familiar only with Vegas' keyframing techniques. The concept of keyframing in SpiceMASTER, however, is exactly the same as Vegas, minus the sync cursor capability. Users will find the keyframer in SpiceMASTER more capable and very fast to use. The cursor bar in the keyframer allows scrubbing in the keyframe window in order to see exact points in the behavior of the Spice il.

5.9 Above the keyframe tool is a cursor that can be scrubbed across the keyframer, allowing for frame-by-frame adjustment of keyframes.

Using the mouse or cursor, grab the top of the cursor bar in the keyframer and scrub across the timeline. Notice how in both the Vegas Preview window and in the SpiceMASTER Preview window, changes are seen as the cursor bar rolls over time. This ability allows keyframe points to be set to exact moments in time. Stop the cursor in the keyframer where a desired change should be made. Adjust for softness, adjust for color or transparency, or just adjust the curve. A new keyframe is inserted. When the new keyframe is inserted, observe the small Bezier curve indicator that appears to the right and left of the keyframe. This small line is what controls the Bezier curve properties of the keyframe. Raising the line upward causes the keyframe to adjust the image rapidly, while lowering the curve slows down the keyframe's adjustments to the image, depending on whether the event is the incoming or outgoing event.

5.10 Changing the Bezier points in a file, coupled with the use of a Climactic Spice, gives a sense of foreboding in this image overlay. Using a standard overlay without a Spice would be too sharp or clear and would not have the "mysterious" nature of this image.

5.11 Bezier curves control the velocity and depth of the incoming event's transparency, coupled with the moving position of the transition. Transition appears slowly in the upper-right corner, moving to the center, with a rapid slide to fully opaque in the last frames of the transition. These Bezier curves function in a similar manner to the Bezier masking tools found in Vegas's Pan/Crop function.

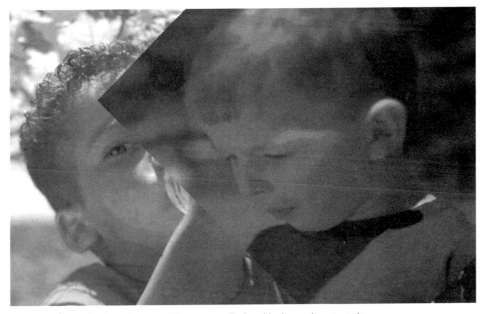

5.12 Image appearing from the upper-right corner as displayed in the previous example..

Nearly every aspect of the SpiceMASTER interface has a built-in preset that can be mixed with other presets to give deep functionality and a unique transition between events. Using a softness preset coupled with a texture preset presents more than 1,000 possibilities alone, and all five of the control panes contain dozens of presets in addition to any random manual adjustments you might wish to make. To reach the presets, select the Light Bulb icon found on each control pane.

5.13 Each control pane contains a series of presets for users starting out. Personal presets can also be saved.

The true magic behind how Spices function is the ability to make Spices more organic and rich in motion and depth, in addition to allowing editors more creative inspiration. SpiceMASTER and accompanying Spices are not simply transitions. The Spices can be used as filters or as associates to filters in Vegas that create extremely deep and creative images and effects over text, still photos, video, or generated media. Combined with bump or height mapping, the compositing tools found in Vegas take on even greater power and opportunity for creative flow.

Inserting a Spice as an effect or filter is as simple as dragging the SpiceMASTER effect from the Video FX tab and dropping it on an upper event. (You'll need two tracks; otherwise, the Spice will be flowing over the default solid color background.) This process is useful as a means of showing an event via a created mask, for creating a virtual transition, or for moving a Spice over an event as if it were an event on a separate track. The angle, opacity, softness, and so much more can be controlled in the SpiceMASTER tool, but possibilities are virtually without limit. Colors can be applied to borders with one color on the outside border and a second color on the inside border, with varying opacities for each border setting. Keyframes can be applied to change the opacity or color of the borders, or simple presets can be applied.

5.14 Same transition as in Figure 5.12, with a texture and softness preset applied.

Spices can be added to an unlimited number of tracks. One creative opportunity is to place three or more tracks of video on the timeline, with different Spices flowing over each track. Shift different Spices around to find what best displays all tracks as a deep composite. Spices make incredible masks that can be inverted, softened, position-whifted, and more.

5.15 Combining a Spice with a Cookie Cutter Mask and a Spherize filter creates the appearance of a super fish-eye lens coming out of a fog-like mist.

Spices can also be used directly on masks, creating beautiful flowing titles or other masked information. Using multiple Spices on multiple masks and events allows for even greater creativity. In the next example, the image flows from one Spice to another without one Spice interfering with the flow of another. One Spice is applied to the mask/letters, while a second Spice is applied to the generated events, acting as a child to the parent. The background event also contains a Spice masking a still of camera lenses in a very subtle background motion.

Extremely soft, subtle transitions or filter flows can be created; in fact, far too many to list in this book. The tips and tricks presented here were intended to whet your appetite.

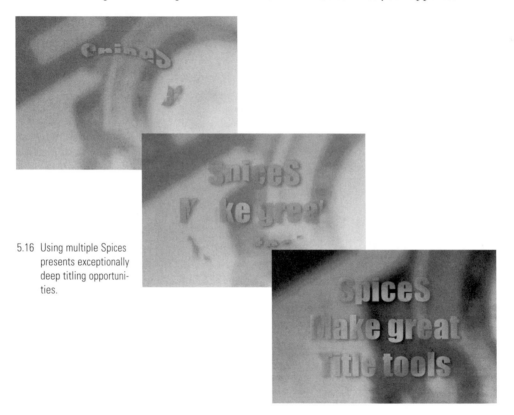

5.16 Using multiple Spices presents exceptionally deep titling opportunities.

Tip

The SpiceMASTER 2 projects seen in the previous examples can be found on the disc in the back of this book, in spices.veg.

SpiceFILTERS

SpiceFILTERS, also from Pixelan, open many, many doors in Vegas. Five primary filter tools are available: ChromaWarp, FlowTexture, NewNoise, StepMotion, and StepTime. If there was one set of plug-ins that I think all Vegas users should own, this is the set.

The ChromaWarp plug-in is a color-shifting plug-in that displaces pixels over time or over color space. Psychedelics, inversions of colors, additive or subtractive tints, or even complex color correction can be performed with the ChromaWrap plug-in.

5.17 ChromaWarp can be used to create a psychedelic among many other user-adjustable settings. This plug-in can be used to quickly simulate an infrared heat signature, a negative film image, or other color-based effects.

The FlowTexture plug-in uses Spices from SpiceMASTER or other graphic files to create textures with displacement mapping. Extremely complex textures, bump maps, displacement maps, and rippling effects can be created with this effect. Coupled with other effects, the possibilities are essentially endless. This plug-in is great for flowing over titles, creating motion backgrounds, or for creating unique visual images. The next example provides the appearance of a Monet-style painting over video using the Moderate Displacement preset and some minor adjustment using the Seep1 Spice.

The NewNoise plug-in is used for creating film noise, color streaks, random color patterns, and grain effects among other effects that are noise or granular based. The streaking on the screen in Figure 5.19 is just one of the many presets in the NewNoise plugin.

5.18 A stipling-style painting is simple to achieve with the FlowTexture plug-in.

5.19 Streaks preview in real time with the NewNoise plug-in. Reduced opacity and a slight blur create the illusion
      of high-speed motion while an event is playing at normal speed.

5.20 Properties of the Spice-FILTERS are adjustable and have tremendous options. All filters have several presets in addition to adjustable parameters.

The StepMotion plug-in is similar to an audio time delay or reverb, creating visual echoes of the event. Dark or light pixels can be selected for delay, either via preset or manually adjusted parameters. No wedding videographer should be without this filter; when applied to a bride with a flowing wedding dress, the filter creates a beautiful effect of dream-like motion. Applied to motion graphics, such as the echo rings found on the DVD in this book, applied to the sweep hand of a clock, or to another motion over the top of reasonably still backgrounds, the filter creates a stunning effect. Try using this filter on bullets or other fast-moving images on a screen to give a new look to an old image. Images can be frozen in time, ghosted, and echoed.

The StepTime plug-in can also provide ghosting, but more importantly, low-frame rates can be simulated, in addition to strobing, stop action, and more. Using keyframes, various strobe and stop motion effects can be blended or keyed to other clips, music beats, or other effects. By using the key parameter and a strobe, events underlying the event with a strobe on it can be revealed, creating a timed alpha revealing any underlying events without needing to composite them together. This feature is powerful for titles or for creating a dream sequence in which two different images are required to set up the feeling of alternating perspectives. One powerful effect is to take the same image on two tracks, reverse the lower track, and apply a strobe with a key. At the mid-point, the two images come together and then fly apart again. This same technique can be used to create a stunning effect by copying a track and desaturating the lower track so it is black and white, while the strobe on the event above is in color. This process creates a strobe between the black and white event and the color event.

SpiceFILTERS open many doors to creativity, color enhancement/correction, and special effects. Have fun with the demo version on the DVD!

5.21 The StepMotion plug-in acts like a video version of an audio delay. Added to high motion, it provides amazing effects.

5.22 Using a key and a strobe, events can be composited without using a parent/child, with opacity creating a unique good against evil effect. To add some softness to one or the other, add a StepMotion filter to one or the other event in the adjust, or overlay, mode.

5.23 Blend the strobe with a black-and-white image beneath to create color strobing over a monochrome image. The SpiceFILTERS are powerful, effective, and inexpensive.

5.24 Boris RED Vegas.

BorisFX

BorisFX makes a series of compositing, titling, and special effects tools for a wide variety of NLEs, in addition to providing a stand-alone product. Boris FX has released Boris Red and Boris Graffiti for Vegas. Graffiti LE is bundled with Vegas, giving users an upgrade path to the full version of Graffiti or Red. Figure 5.24 shows the Boris RED interface working within Vegas. Boris RED is both a Vegas transition and filter, with a surface generator (or what Boris terms a *synthetic importer*) in the works. BorisFX is very aware of the workflow that Vegas offers users and molds their development around this. Within Vegas, users can both apply a Boris effect to the timeline and preview it in the same manner they are accustomed to with other Vegas filters. After the effect is applied, users can launch the Boris user interface from the native Vegas FX Property page, create their effect, and upon closing, automatically import the Boris effect into the Vegas timeline.

From this point, whenever the Vegas cursor is scrubbed across the Boris effect in the Vegas Timeline, users can view the Boris frames natively in the Vegas Preview window. *Instant Boris FX* by Chris Vadnais is an outstanding resource for those wanting to learn the Boris Interface inside Sony Vegas.

5.25 Drawing morph and warp characteristics can be done with built-in shapes or freehand drawings in the WinMorph workspace.

Wax/Debugmode Software

The DebugMode products that work under Vegas are the result of the work of Satish Kumar, a software programmer who also enjoys Vegas. These plug-ins bring new capabilities to Vegas not otherwise possible with X-Y-Z plane adjustment to create multidimensional imagery.

The WinMorph plug-in allows images similar to those seen in the smash hit movie *The Matrix,* wherein the subject freezes and the background spins around the subject, or similar to the Michael Jackson music video *Black and White,* wherein one face morphs into another with different parts of the image changing at different times. Warps of specific sections in the event, whether a still image or video image, can be created with shifting space based on shapes drawn in the WinMorph main workspace. WinMorph is included on the DVD in this book, complete with tutorials on how to use it to create some of these effects.

The Plug-inPac filters offer similar attributes to WinMorph in that shapes can be rapidly shifted in three dimensions and moved on various X-Y-Z planes and aspect ratios. Three Plug-inPac filters are available: PixelStretch, Shatter3D, and 3D LE.

PixelStretch allows pixels at a defined space to be shifted, stretched, and pulled into unbelievable shapes. Laser beams can be created from letters, faces distorted, and, when combined with other plug-ins, amazing images can be quickly created. Like the Pixelan plug-in tools, the Plug-inPac tools can unleash incredible creativity.

As its name implies, the Shatter3D plug-in creates the image of shattered glass or other fragile material. The number and size of the shards or shattered pieces are controlled by the parametes of the plug-in.

5.26 PixelStretch stretches a defined area of pixels, keyframable over time.

5.27 Shattered images can be very complex with the shatter 3D plug-in.

5.28 The Shatter 3D plug-in controls. Although Vegas has terrific 3D tools, some users might find the Debug Mode tools more controllable and intuitive..

Tip_____

The images from the PluginPac examples can be found in the `debugfiles.veg` files on the disc in the back of this book.

The parameters of the Shatter3D plug-in allow The The parameters of the Shatter 3D plug-in allow images to be simple or deep, with keyframe ability over time. Shattering images can be reversed in the middle of an event, allowing an image to be shattered and restored during an event. The plug-in has controls to simulate the amount of force with which the image is struck, the angles of the shards as they fly across the screen, the angle at which the shards are viewed, the rotation of the shards, and the perspective/depth of focus.

The 3D LE plug-in is fantastic for creating 3D images that fold together and move apart with varying angles and depths and for creating trapezoids and multiplane angles. These can be combined with shadow and glow from the Track Motion tool and used as transitions or event flybys. This tool is also great for creating the ubiquitous *Star Wars* titling effect.

 Tip_____

More tutorials and information on the Pixelan and DebugMode plug-ins are available at `www.pixelan.com` and `www.DebugMode.com`. The tutorials for WinMorph on the disc in this book are courtesy ofSatish.

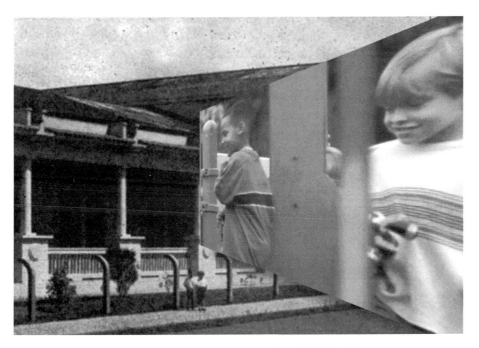

5.29 A 3D transition flies in to lock to one side of the screen before closing like a door.

5.30 Trapezoidal screens created with the 3D LE PluginPac are fast and simple to do.

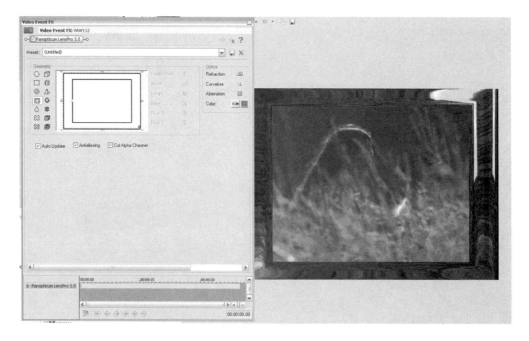

5.31 The Panopticum LensPro plug-in offers wonderful effects. It's a slow rendering plug-in; be sure to check the auto-update box. Frames and lens effects are beautiful, and well worth the wait. No other plug-in currently offers these effects. "Visit http://www.panopticum.com for more information on the Engraver and the LensPro plugins for Vegas.

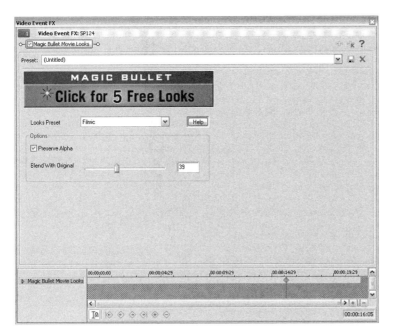

5.32   The Magic Bullet plug-in installs with Vegas and is a great tool, albeit a slow renderer. Similar looks may be achieved with Zenoté plug-ins. Magic Bullet's Film Looks plug for Vegas does not allow any control over the parameters of the plug-in.

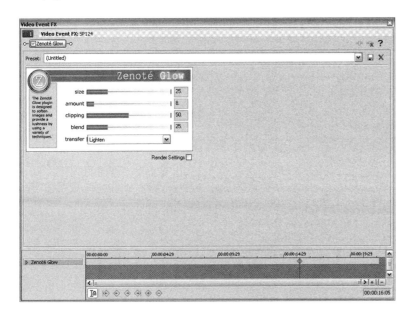

5.33   The Zenoté plug-in suite is fantastic for getting a good film look, cleaning up noisy DV files, adding blur, or jitter to an image. The Zenoté plug-ins are not heavy on the processor and allow for very fast real-time previews, and render very fast. Visit http://www.zenote.com for more information on these fine plugin tools for Vegas.

Audio Tools in Vegas

Recording Audio in Vegas

Vegas was one of the early multitrack editors available for the PC before the advent of Vegas Video 2.0. Having set the standard for audio on the PC with Sound Forge several years previously, a multitrack tool was a logical step, and like Forge, it became a standard for the Windows-environment.

Vegas can be used for a basic voice-over-only setup or as the heart of a full-blown multitrack studio setup for recording live bands, film scoring, television production work, or other professional audio requisite.

For those doing audio for video, it's often thought that video is more difficult to edit than audio. Perhaps so, but audio is the greater importance in the two media forms. Those who would argue the point might want to take any movie, turn the sound off, and see how enjoyable the film is. Even in the days of silent film, a musical score accompanied the film, and most theaters had a piano or organ player who performed the score along with the silent film. In current times, audio and video artists and engineers are crossing formerly strongly drawn lines in the authoring of various forms of media.

Vegas manages media at three levels:

- Event
- Track
- Project

Events contain graphic, video, text, or audio information. Events can be individually edited, and have effects added, processed, and controlled. Events live on tracks.

Tracks contain multiple events. Tracks can control, process, and add effects to all events on the individual track.

Projects contain a single track or multiple tracks. All events contained in all tracks can be controlled, processed, and finished. (Effects may be added in the Project Media as well, however, this is not a Timeline management of media/filters)

Basic Setup

To record audio from a microphone plugged into the computer, a microphone and sound card are needed. Plug the microphone into the soundcard's microphone input and open Vegas. The timeline/workspace will open with no audio or video control panes. An audio control track will need to be inserted, which is done by pressing Ctrl+Q or by selecting INSERT | AUDIO TRACK. Click the Record button on the control pane of the new track. Vegas displays a dialog box asking for the location to which audio files are to be recorded.

6.1   Clicking the Record button will call up a dialog asking for the destination of audio.

 Tip _____

Recording to a second hard drive is highly recommended for purposes of keeping audio files off the system drive. This process allows input/output (I/O) to run more efficiently and helps ensure flawless recording.

Audio is now ready to be recorded. Click the Record button on the transport control to begin recording. Click the Stop button on the transport control to stop recording. You won't believe how many people will not think of that! This is all there is to recording basic audio in Vegas. From here, much, much more can be done.

When the Record button is armed (clicked), an icon that looks like two speakers is located in the Track Control pane next to the Record button. If a multichannel card is installed on the system, a number will appear instead of the dual speaker icon.

Clicking the speaker or number icon allows audio input to be converted from stereo to mono or a unique input channel to be selected on the multichannel device. If voice or a single instrument is all that needs to be recorded, it's good practice to use a mono input, as it saves disk space.

The Input Monitor option also appears in the same menu as the stereo/mono inputs. Vegas allows inputs to be monitored with effects/processing as it's recording. For musicians, this upgrade is fantastic, as a reverb can now be monitored with compression added during the performance. The reverb/compression/other processing is not recorded to the track—it is only there to assist the vocalist in getting the best performance possible, without using additional external hardware. This upgrade gives Vegas the ability to be a multitrack recording system with no additional hardware whatsoever. The ability to monitor inputs with processing is entirely dependent on processing speed and system ability. FX Automation envelopes are bypassed during monitored recording.

6.2   Click the Record button on the transport control to begin recording.

6.3   Audio may be recorded in stereo or mono and may be live-monitored in Vegas.

6.4   6.5

Checking the Input Monitor box enables processing to be heard through the output specified in the output/bus assignment dialog. To assign outputs other than the default sound card outputs, select OPTIONS | PREFERENCES | AUDIO and specify input/output settings. If only a two-channel sound card/Blaster-type card is present, nothing more can be set, as there is nothing for audio to be assigned to.

If a multichannel sound card is available, such as an Echo Audio Layla, M-Audio Delta, or other similar card, up to 26 input/outputs can be specified. Multichannel cards are required for mixing 4.1, 5.1, or 7.1 surround sound.

6.6   Echo Audio Layla.

To use multichannel audio cards, select OPTIONS | PREFERENCES | AUDIO and choose Windows-Classic Wave Driver or ASIO Driver in the Audio Device Type list box; otherwise, multichannel cards will not be properly accese.

6.7   Setting preferences
       for a multichannel
       sound card.

If latency is encountered with Mark of the Unicorn 2408 interface, perform the following steps:

1. Select START | FIND | FILES OR FOLDERS.

2. Search for a file named `motu324.cfg`.

3. Open it in WordPad or Notepad.

4. Underneath the `DDHELP.EXE=17` line, insert the following line:

`VEGAS.EXE=392`

In general, multichannel sound cards do not have microphone preamplifiers (pre's) in them; however, a few models do come with them. In the event that your multichannel card does not have a pre-amp built in, you will need one in order to properly drive channel inputs. If you don't have one, audio will be very noisy and not very loud. Separate pre-amps are typically better; however, many of the built-in pre-amps, such as the M-Audio Quattro and PreSonus FIREstation, are excellent and for the investment, a terrific value.

Additionally, Vegas is capable of working with multiple sound cards. Consult your sound card manual for information on configuring more than one soundcard.

6.8   M-Audio Quattro.

6.9   PreSonus FIREstation.

The volume control found in the Track Control pane is for playback volume only. Adjusting this during the recording process does not affect the recording process at all. Output from the sound card, sound card mixer, pre-amp, or other external input device determines the level of incoming audio.

To adjust the volume of incoming audio when not using a sound card mixer, select START | PROGRAMS | ACCESSORIES | MULTIMEDIA | VOLUME CONTROL. Select OPTIONS | PROPERTIES and click the button to adjust the volume for recording. In the Record Control window that is displayed, recording input volume can be increased/reduced.

Recording audio in the digital realm can be tricky, particularly if one is familiar with analog techniques and practices. In the analog realm, it's acceptable to hit 0dB and sometimes go slightly past 0dB. Tape has a saturation level that digital does not enjoy. Record audio in the digital realm with peaks hitting at around -.03dBFS and averages at around -15dBFS. Because of the low-noise/no-noise digital signal-to-noise ratio, it is also easier to expand audio levels later in the editing/recording process. Bear in mind that digital 0 and analog 0 are -20dB apart based on the Advanced Television Standards Committee (ATSC) standards (www.atsc.org). When using analog meters to view digital information, be sure that tones are used to match up analog meters to digital output. When working with audio for video broadcast, the analog broadcast standard is +4dB into a source impedance of 600 ohms. Traditionally house reference meters are set to 0VU based on the +4dB level. -.03dB is a good maximum level to target for maximum levels at input.

6.10   Levels peaking at approximately -6dB. The instrument is an acoustic guitar with no compression and is prone to unexpected peaks. Therefore, levels are marginally lower than they might otherwise be.

6.11   Level set correctly for the loudest point in recording.

Recording Multiple Tracks

Multitracking is what Vegas is all about. The ability to monitor tracks while recording is critical. Vegas provides this ability with most low-end sound cards and with nearly any multichannel card.

Recording and monitoring tracks is fairly fast and self-evident. Start by inserting a second audio track (Shift+Q) and assigning its inputs as you did for the original mono track. If the second audio track is to be mono, set it up this way now. Track 1 will play back through whatever sound card is assigned. Track 2 will play back through the default assigned sound card as well. Depending on the sound card, this process can demonstrate latency during the recording process. This process is also where a professional sound card is invaluable. Professional sound cards use ASIO drivers, which dramatically reduce latency in the hardware/software relationship.

In a computer audio system, latency means any delay or wait time that increases real or perceived response time beyond the response time desired. More specifically, latency is the time between when sound is input to Vegas, processed, and returned to headphones or speakers. A contributor to computer latency includes mismatches in data speed between the CPU and I/O devices and slow buffers. Drivers and buffers can be set in Vegas to reduce latency. Small buffers reduce latency but increase the risk of dropouts. Larger buffers lessen the likelihood of dropouts but increase latency.

Vegas has the ability to access ASIO drivers used by most professional sound cards. Latency can be reduced to as little as five milliseconds (ms), which is virtually indiscernible to the human ear. This idea means that although the CPU is processing the incoming, outgoing, and effected audio information, the ear will hear audio playback in correct time.

Clicking the Record button (Ctrl+R) on the Transport bar starts the recording process, while at the same time audio is playing back through the sound card.

Advanced Recording Techniques and Tools

Vegas has many advanced tools for recording audio. Vegas has a metronome for monitoring a click track during recording sessions. (This feature requires that Vegas' properties be set for beats and tempos.) While this feature doesn't affect playback or record speed from the timeline, it does affect the tempo at which the metronome is heard. Metronomes are useful for video editors as well, as they can help set a cadence for video to be edited at.

 Tip

Ask the scorist for the video for a tempo map, and Vegas can be mapped out accordingly, so that when the score is complete, the audio is dropped into place if tempo-based editing is the goal. The metronome will speed up and slow down according to the tempo map created in the production stages.

Tempos cannot be adjusted over time, as they are fixed in the setting specified in the AUDIO | OPTIONS dialog. While Vegas can't change tempos without an ACID loop acting as the driving click track, true tempo maps may be created in Vegas by using an ACID loop as a click track, shifting tempo over time.

6.12 Setting a tempo grid in Vegas.

6.13 Completed tempo grid.

Recording with Takes

Rarely is a performance perfect every time; consequently, Vegas allows for takes to be recorded, just like in the movies when you hear "take 1, take 2." In Vegas, takes can be recorded in a number of different ways, as the number of takes is limited only by hard drive space.

Setting up a loop over the area where multiple performances are wanted instructs Vegas to continually loop over the area. If the area that requires multiple takes is a single event, double-click the event, which will set up the loop. Press Q or click the Loop button on the Transport bar.

Click the Record button on the Transport bar, and Vegas begins recording. To stop recording, press the Spacebar or click the Record button again. A new take will appear on the timeline, living over the old audio. The old audio is still there. Pressing T or right-clicking and selecting the appropriate menu item toggles back and forth between the various takes. Takes can also be directly monitored, by stopping playback, right-clicking, and selecting Choose Active, and then clicking Play in the dialog box.

6.14   Using Takes is an efficient method of recording a section over and over, keeping only the best performance.

Takes can be renamed to help identify them. Takes can also be opened in the specified audio editor for further editing and then saved as a new take or saved as the name of the take opened in the audio editor. Takes can be deleted from an event as well, leaving only the desired audio in the event.

Takes can also be added to the timeline in yet another fashion, albeit not necessarily in time. Right-click and select multiple audio clips in the Explorer or Project Media, drop them on the timeline, and when the menu is displayed, select Add as Takes to put all files into one take. Takes can then be selected using either the right-click method or scrolling through takes by pressing T or Shift+T. This method is handy for just about anything, as it allows for toggling back and forth.

> Takes are very handy for cutting together the best performance and for having the performer record the same piece several times and then cutting the unwanted parts of a take. Press S to split takes and then choose the best of each line. This process is known in the industry as comping. With Digital Audio Workstation/Non-Linear Editor (DAW/NLE) software, comping is easy and fast. In the past, engineers had to take several tracks, and using mute buttons and fader moves, comp parts of several similar performances together to a new track. With Vegas, it's all done on one track, with no difficulty like there is in the analog world where it either needs loads of hands on the mixer or good automation.

Pre- and post-roll settings are available in Vegas. Pre- and post-roll also act as punch in/punch out settings and can be combined with takes. To create a pre- or post-roll in a single event, split the event where the record in/out points are desired. Then create a loop or selection that begins before the split point and ends after the split point. Use the Loop tool if multiple takes are desired, and use a time selection only if a single punch in/out is desired.

Then click the Record button (Ctrl+R), and Vegas begins playing at the beginning of the time selection, begins recording at the split point in the event, ends recording at the split point at the end of the event, and stops or loops at the end of the time selection or loop point.

Recording actually occurs through the entire selection. This process allows you to expand the event out in either direction if you nede to get a pickup note.

6.15   Defining pre- and post-roll on a single event.

How About a Flyin' Smooth Punch?

Punch-ins have long been challenging for Digital Audio Workstations (DAW) like Vegas because of the look-ahead required to make punches smooth and clean. However, Vegas has conquered the punch-in problem and given it a total K.O.

A punch-in takes place when audio that has been previously recorded is monitored during playback, and Vegas is put into record mode during the playback process, allowing a new section to be re-recorded. For example, perhaps a voice-over (VO) has been recorded and only one word is problematic. The VO is monitored during playback, and when it comes time to replace the bad word, a punch-in takes place that allows only the bad word to be replaced. Once Vegas has gone past the punch-in region, Vegas disengages record mode and continues in playback mode.

6.16 The record button can be punched in manually in Vegas 6 with glitch-free punch-in.

While earlier versions of Vegas had punch-in capability, it was significantly improved in Vegas 5. To accomplish a punch-in:

1. Record a track. Assuming the track has errors, position the cursor prior to an error in the existing recorded track.

2. Locate the flawed section and using the S key, split the recorded file section prior to the error, and split again at the end of the flawed area. Create a time selection with a few seconds prior to the split, extending slightly past the split. Looping may or may not be enabled.

3. Arm the existing audio track for recording by pressing the record enable button found on the track header.

4. Start playback of the project or file. The original audio will be heard until the Record button is pressed.

5. Press the Record button on the transport bar or hardware device connected to the computer. Vegas will begin recording at that point. If Input Monitoring is enabled, the new audio will be heard.

6. To stop the recording process, press the Record button again. Vegas will continue rolling (post-roll) for a few moments and then stop.

Vegas will also allow you to record multiple takes if looping is enabled. Press the Looping button or the Q shortcut key, and Vegas will create a new take each time the loop repeats. This provides multiple choices of various performances, allowing the best one to be chosen. Vegas will actually create regions with each take. These regions will not be part of the project, but will be displayed in the trimmer.

6.17 Illustration of trimmed section with pre/post roll

If you have multiple punch-in sections, each may be selected by holding Ctrl and clicking on each split-out section. Vegas will automatically punch in and out at these sections, allowing multiple re-takes to be created over the length of the entire file.

Prior to the recording process, a file location should have been specified in the Project Properties dialog. If one has not been selected, Vegas will prompt for the file to be named and saved. If the track was named prior to the recording process, Vegas will automatically select the track name as the file name. The file may be renamed in the post-record dialog box.

6.18 Post-record dialog box

Assigning Buses

Buses can be used to route audio to anywhere it must go. A bus can feed another bus, creating virtually limitless routing if necessary. Vegas is capable of handling up to 26 simultaneous buses, which is the same as the alphabet.

This fact means that up to 26 channels of audio can be streaming out of the computer at once, if enough hardware devices are owned. It takes four to eight channel converters to meet this output, and to leave six output channels empty. The norm is to have 24 channels of output.

This feature does not mean Vegas is limited to 24 channels of audio. Not at all. Vegas is limited to up to 26 channels of audio busing, but the number of audio tracks is limited only by the processing power of the computer.

If several tracks are on the timeline, insert buses into the mixer by clicking the Insert Bus button.

6.19 Adding a bus to the mixer.

On the Track Control pane, click the small square that appeared when the first bus was inserted. Choices for busing are listed here.

6.20   Select bus routing by clicking the square on the Track Control pane.

Select Bus A. Audio on that track is now sent to the Bus A mixer section. For example, Bus A could be sent to the normal right/left outputs of a mix, or it could feed a rear channel of a surround system. Alternatively, it could feed a signal processor, such as a flanger, reverb, or delay; perhaps it's a submix that eventually routes back to the master output.

Assign the bus outputs in the Mixer window in the same manner. Click the small square that is found on the bus control. On track 2, assign the track to the same Bus A output. This step routes Tracks 1 and 2 through the Bus A outputs.

6.21   Assigned and unassigned buses.

Buses can be used for submixing, such as all drums going through one submix, all keyboards through another submix, and all rhythm instruments through yet another submix. This feature is of value as then all drums can be pulled down or up in volume without affecting the mix levels of each instrument/track or all keyboards can be raised or lowered. Signal processing is less taxing on the CPU if processing is done at the bus level as well. Putting six compressors on a drum kit is much more processor-intensive than putting one compressor on a drum submix. Generally, kick and snare drums are left out of submixes, as are lead vocals. These primary instruments/tracks are typically controlled individually.

Using Buses for Routing Effects

Buses can be used to route effects as well. Effects can be placed on individual tracks, but as the number of tracks grows, the load on the processor increases. It's a good idea, therefore, to place effects on buses to affect several tracks at once. This process can be done using direct track assignment or the multipurpose fader, or through assignable FX envelopes. Envelopes can be used to automate effect levels, sends, and returns.

In the Mixer window, click the Insert FX button, choose a delay effect, and set the effect to the parameters you'd like to hear. Now right-click in the Track Control pane and choose the bus to which you assigned the delay. An envelope is displayed in the track timeline. This is the send to for the specified bus. Raising the line will increase the amount of audio sent to the delay and lowering it will decrease the amount of it. Double-clicking the envelope places a handle/node on the envelope, allowing for automatic send changes. If a delay is needed only on a specific phrase or moment in an event contained in the track, the envelope can be pulled all the way down until that moment when the envelope will be raised to the desired level. Handles or nodes can be right-clicked, and the Set-to percentage or volume can be specified that way as well.

6.22 Inputting specific values from the right-click.

FX can be set as pre- or post-fader in Vegas. This option is found on nearly all mixing consoles and is important, particularly for sound designers. This option allows audio to be sent to the processor before the fader, so regardless of where the track fader is set, even if it's off, FX receives an audio signal. Post-fader is how most processing is done, in which reducing the output volume of a track also reduces the send to the FX. As an envelope fades on the track, the send to the FX fades as well. Bus sends are post fader by default. To change them to pre-fader, right click the Bus send to change it to post from the submenu that appears. You can also right click a us utput fader in the mixer section.

6.23 Right-click the FX send on a track to select pre- or post-fader send to the FX.

6.24 Vegas bus assignment.

Buses can be viewed as tracks for automation. Bus outputs/returns can be automated for much greater mixing power. For example, if there were several tracks with background vocals, all vocals needed to be raised in volume at once, and all required a reverb to rise with the volume. The vocals could be sent to one bus, with the reverb sent to another bus. The reverb is controlled by an inserted bus send, and the vocal levels are controlled by an envelope assigned to another bus, just like a bus routing on a typical mixing board.

With busing and automation, mixes are capable of being very deep and exacting.

6.25 Analog mixer bus as-
signment.

Could I Get a Transfer Please?

Buses are used to route audio from place to place, being used for submixes or effects send and returns. However, Vegas 6 provides the option of routing buses to buses. This allows for much easier patching of submixes. One use of this is to patch separate mixes to two different locations such as perhaps sending one mix to a hardware device or external mixer while sending the other to a master bus. Buses may be used in a recording studio to set up master mixes while also having a headphone mix for the talent to listen to. Artists usually like to hear their performance with a little more reverb than the producer might like to hear, or perhaps they need a little more of this or that in their mix that is different than what is being heard in the control room monitors. Buses can provide all of that.

The bus panel indictes where audio is being routed. If the ⬚ is seen, then the audio is beng routed to a hardware device. If the ⬚ is seen, then audio is being routed to the Master, and if the Ⓐ is seen, audio is being routed to another bus. Up to 27 buses are available.

Vegas also has a wonderful failsafe capability that prevents a bus from being routed back to itself. If you have two buses in your project and the first bus is routed to the second bus, the second bus may only be routed to the master output or a hardware device.

FX Packaging

Creating FX chains is an important aspect in Vegas. Often, presets in FX are simply not enough to recall. If multiple FX chained together with specific presets are needed, Vegas can save a chain of FX with presets. For instance, an EQ, a compressor, and a chorus can be used for vocal processing with each of the individual FX having their own presets. Rather than having to insert and choose presets for each effect manually, all three can be saved as a chain/package complete with presets.

To create a package, perform the following steps:

1. Click the Insert FX button in the Bus, Mixer, or Track Control windows, which opens the Plug-In Chooser.

2. Choose the plug-ins you wish to use.

3. Arrange them in any manner by either dragging a plug-in before another or by using the Shift Plug-In Left/Right buttons found in the upper-right corner.

4. Click the Save As button and name the chain, which will now be stored as a package in the Plug-In Packages folder.

5. Click OK. Your preset is now stored and can be recalled at any time.

FX To Go, Please?

Moving FX settings from one computer to another has long been a challenge for users of most any non-linear editing system. Vegas has a new feature that allows FX folders to be moved from system to system, permitting users to share folders. These may be copied, but may only exist in one folder. Find these files in the C:\Program Files\Sony\Vegas 6\Presets\FX Packages. Subfolders can be created from the plug-in explorer's context menu or toolbar under the "packages" folders in order to organize your packaged chains. Each package only occurs once under the appropriate package folder; that is, you can only move packages, not copy them.

Works the same as all the other plug-in explorer folders, but now for Audio FX packages, Video FX packages, Transition packages, and Media Generator packages. Newly created packages go in the appropriate top-level package folder. (You'll need to close and re-open the plug-in explorer to see the new order of FX packages.)

To move packages from one computer system to another, copy the .veg file and paste to the new computer system via a network, USB drive, hard drive, or other means. Once the .veg is opened in the new computer system, the FX Package will reside on the new system.

6.26   A single track feeding four buses and two auxes with automation.

Inserting Effects Without Using a Bus

Effects can be directly routed and controlled in Vegas without inserting a bus. This process is similar to an aux send that doesn't return to a bus on an analog mixer.

Click the Insert FX button in the Mixer window, which calls the Plug-In Chooser dialog. Plug-ins can be viewed by All, Chains, Automatable, Sony, Third-party, or Optimized. All shows every Direct X plug-in installed in the system.

Choose the FX desired. If multiple FX are desired, press and hold down Shift while selecting FX. They will all be placed in the mixer as a series. FX selected this way cannot be individually controlled, as they all share the same send and are chained together.

FX can also be inserted individually. Every FX plug-in that is inserted in the Mixer window is also available to every track or bus. Keep in mind that this can be very processor-intensive during preview, although it will not affect the final render.

Use FX assigned to buses, as opposed to individual tracks when several tracks need the same effect. For example, a group of tom-toms, cymbals, and percussion might be able to share a reverb or delay. Rather than insert a reverb and delay on every track, send all relative tracks to a bus and insert the FX, controlled by the bus.

To do this, perform the following steps:

1. Insert FX.

2. Insert a bus.

3. Assign all desired tracks to the bus.

4. Select VIEW | SHOW BUS TRACKS.

5. Right-click the bus track and insert an FX envelope.

6. Set envelope as desired.

Now all tracks have the necessary FX, with automation to those FX controlled from the bus. Choruses, verses, fills, bridges, other sections of a song, or sound design for a movie can be unique in the way that FX are heard and managed as a result of this method, and yet processor and RAM resources have been spared the heavy load of having many plug-ins active.

Using Track FX

Every audio track in Vegas has a chain of FX installed on it already. A Noise Gate, EQ, and Compressor are found by clicking the FX button on each audio track. They can be heard during recording by using input monitoring, they can be removed from the track, or they can be appended to or replaced all together. These FX are optimized to keep processor resources at their peak but still place a load on the processor.

Set the default track properties by setting up the track the way you'd like it to default to. Set up an FX chain for the track FX, right-click the Track Control pane, and select Set Default Track Properties. Checking the boxes in the dialog that opens will cause the current track settings to become the default settings for future tracks inserted into the current project. Now every time Vegas opens, these track settings become the default, saving time and preventing the user from having o rmember how the last mix was set up before beginning.

6.27 Set the track defaults before recording so that all audio tracks have the same settings when inserted.

Tip

Set up a blank project with all track settings in place, so that when a project is started, a template of several tracks is already built. Starting with 8 to 16 tracks, complete with commonly used compressor, EQ, and reverb settings, not only saves time but also impresses clients when they hear how quickly a tight sound can be dialed in. On the DVD enclosed with this book, you will find a recording interface with tracks in place that can be used as a starting place for your preferences.

Recording Multiple Tracks

When working with a band or ensemble, several tracks might need to be recorded at one time. A multichannel sound card is best used in this situation. If a two-channel sound card is used, only stereo information will be recorded, and an analog mixer will be required to manage all of the microphones. With multichannel cards, an unlimited number of microphones can be input directly to Vegas, depending on the number of cards used. (Many manufacturers of hardware cards have limits as to how many cards can be stacked.) These can be individually controlled without using an external mixing device. To select multiple inputs with an individual microphone routed to each input, assign the input of each track as Mono and select either the right or left input of the sound card.

Remember, if your sound card does not have pre-amps built in, a preamplifier is needed for every input channel.

Select a channel input for each microphone, and with every channel that has an input assigned, be sure the channel is armed. Click the Record button (Ctrl+R), and all tracks that are armed will record in sync. Enable input monitoring where necessary—the more tracks that are set for input monitoring, the heavier the processor load. Without using ASIO drivers, latency can be unreasonably high. Use ASIO drivers for input monitoring for best results.

6.28 The Echo Layla has eight analog inputs and eight digital inputs

6.29 Typical session armed for recording. Double-click the right side of the track header bar to show or hide track headers.

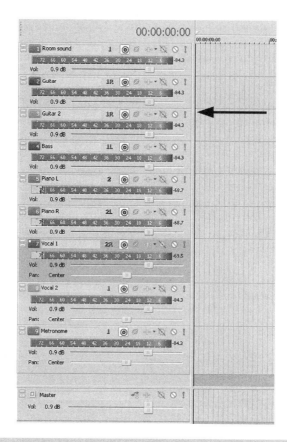

Vegas has the ability to support ASIO drivers, found in most professional sound cards. ASIO drivers are low-latecy driver sets specified by Steinberg Media Technologies AG.

Tip

Pressing Ctrl+A selects all tracks at one time, and clicking the Record button on one track simultaneously arms all tracks. Clicking the Record button again after the recording is finished disarms all tracks. Use this same technique to insert volume, pan, bus, or FX envelopes on every track.

Synchronizing Vegas to External Devices

Some studio setups can call for a multitrack tape machine, sequencer, or other external device to control Vegas, or conversely, Vegas can be the master device controlling external equipment if the proper hardware is in place. To do this, a device that can convert SMPTE to MIDI timecode (MTC) is required.

Most MIDI distribution devices are capable of converting incoming MIDI timecode to SMPTE or outgoing SMPTE timecode to MIDI timecode. Most tape machines will accept either MTC or SMPTE. Some accept both.

If Vegas is to be the master device, Vegas needs to generate timecode. Set this up in the OPTIONS | PREFERENCES | SYNC dialog.

6.30   Setup of a timecode de-
vicce to connect Vegas
and external recording
devices.

 Tip_____

If you click Play in Vegas and it starts/stops an external device, Vegas is known as the master. If starting and stopping the hardware starts and stops Vegas, Vegas is the slave.

To generate a timecode that an external device can read, have the owners' manual of the external device handy so you can learn the incoming timecode specs that it requires. Most devices default to 30 frames per second, while other devices call for 29.97 non-drop. The standard for most professional audio equipment is 30 fps. DV has a different standard, based on American television standards.

Vegas generates timecode that is sent to the conversion device, where it is distributed to whatever external devices that Vegas needs to control. Timecode connection is necessary if Vegas will be used to edit external media that will be returned to the external recording device after edits are completed.

In the OPTIONS | PREFERENCES | SYNC | ADVANCED dialog, Vegas has an option to use either an internal clock from the CPU clock or the clock generated by the sound card. Most instances will call for the clock to come from the sound card. Vegas also has the ability to send full-frame messaging to external devices. Full-frame information can speed up location in some external tape machines. Not all devices can respond to full frames, and some devices can become confused. Check the documentation that came with the device that Vegas is controlling.

If Vegas is to be a slave to timecode generated by an external device, Vegas must be set to trigger from timecode. In the OPTIONS | PREFERENCES | SYNC dialog, set the trigger from the device sending timecode into the computer. Be certain that Vegas' frame rate setting matches the frame rate being sent from the external master device. Otherwise, audio will drift ahead or behind the master when Vegas is played in time with the external master. For Vegas to operate consistently with a word clock connection, trigger must be used. Trigger refers to Vegas seeing a point in timecode, at which point it will begin to play. It is not locked to the timecode specifically. Chasing timecode means that Vegas remains synchronized with incoming timecode and follows the timecode as best as possible. Vegas has a Freewheel mode that allows Vegas to continue to play for a period of time even if timecode input is occasionally lost, playing until it sees timecode again that it should be synchronized to. If timecode is consistently lost, check the hardware or signal flow from the master device.

Sync is set up in the Preferences dialog but must be enabled in the Options menu (Ctrl+F7).

 *Tip*_____

Use Vegas to edit audio from a tape machine and apply EQ, noise reduction, and processing. This process saves buses on an external machine, frees up reverbs and other processing hardware during a mix, and generally affords an opportunity to make a smaller studio have the capabilities and power of a much larger recording facility.

To view incoming or outgoing timecode, right-click the time display, which defaults to the upper-left corner of the timeline. Choose which timecode you wish to display: time at cursor, incoming, or outgoing timecode.

The timecode window is docked by default but can be moved to a convenient space on the timeline or wherever it is most visible. It cannot be completely removed from the workspace.

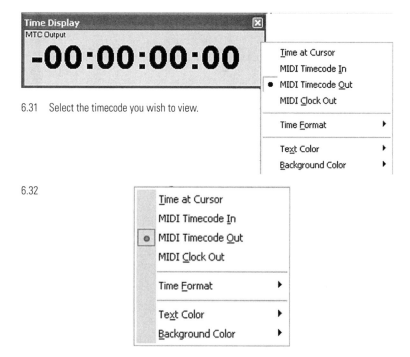

6.31   Select the timecode you wish to view.

6.32

Editing Audio in Vegas

The audio editing tools found in Vegas are among the best in the world. Moreover, the audio tools in Vegas are superior to any audio tools found in any NLE system available today. Playback and recording tracks are limited only by the amount of available CPU, hard disk space, and RAM.

Placing Audio on the Timeline

Audio recorded is immediately found on the timeline and is also found in the Media Pool. However, it's often necessary to place audio on the timeline that might be a take, from a stock music collection, an ACID loop, sound FX, or other stored audio file.

To do this, open the Explorer in Vegas and find an audio file to place on the timeline. Double-clicking the file inserts the file directly on the timeline. Right-clicking a file opens several options, such as opening the file directly in Trimmer, which allows audio sections to be trimmed beoreputin media on the timeline. After audio is placed on the timeline, it becomes an event.

6.33   The Explorer in Vegas looks similar to Windows Explorer.

6.34   Audio opened in the Trimmer, with selections chosen to be added to the timeline. Regions for insertion may be specified and saved in the Trimmer just as video regions may be saved

Right-clicking also offers the option of placing the audio in the Media Pool or opening the file for editing in a third-party audio editor or in Sound Forge, depending on settings in the OPTIONS | PREFERENCES | AUDIO dialog. Opening the file in the Trimmer is a simple workflow that allows phrases or sections to be marked and added to the timeline.

After making a selection in the Trimmer, press the R key. This creates a namable region in the Trimmer that stays with the audio and will be seen anytime the audio is opened in the Trimmer. After creating the region, place the cursor on the timeline where the audio is desired and press A. This step adds the media to the timeline, where it now is an event on a track. Selected audio can also be dragged to the timeline from the Trimmer. Do whichever is comfortable for you.

Audio in the Trimmer can also be inserted in Ripple mode (see "Using Ripple Editing" later in this chapter for more details) by copying the audio in the Trimmer and enabling Ripple or by copying and pressing Shift+Ctrl+V. The audio is pasted as an event at the cursor, and subsequent events ripple down the timeline for the length of time equal to the size of the pasted event.

Extracting Audio from CDs

Vegas has tools to allow audio to be extracted from CDs. While a single track will play back from a CD, multiple tracks or clips from a sample library that are scattered all over a CD might not play back so well, due to the limited speed of a CD or CD-R. There are two menu areas where Vegas can be instructed to extract audio.

The first is the Media Pool. Clicking the Extract Audio from CD button opens a dialog where users are asked to choose which tracks are to be extracted. Audio can be extracted three ways:

- By track (individual indexes can be selected)

- By time selection (a range of time for extractin an be specified)

- By the entire CD (the entire CD is extracted to the hard drive as one large file)

6.35 Clicking the Extract Audio from CD button calls up a dialog requesting information as to where files should be extracted.

When placing any media on the timeline, it's easy to lose focus on what the media is or where it came from. Selecting OPTIONS | PREFERENCES | GENERAL and checking "Show active take names in events places the name of the take on each event whether graphic, video, or audio in nature.

6.36 The Preferences menu has many choices to make editing in Vegas easier and more personal.

6.37 Active take names help identify events.

With audio on the timeline as events, it is ready to be edited. Basic edits would include cutting, copying, pasting, fading audio in and out, cross fading, splitting, and moving a file.

Cutting, copying, and pasting are handled in Vegas as in most applications. To cut an event, select the event and press Ctrl+X or select EDIT | CUT after selecting the event. Events that are cut are available from the clipboard. To copy an event, select the event and press Ctrl+C or select EDIT | COPY after selecting the event. To paste an event, first cut or copy the event and then place the cursor where the event is desired to go. Pressing Ctrl+V pastes the event(s) to the timeline wherever the cursor is located. Cut, Copy, and Paste commands are also accessible by right-clicking any file and choosing one of the commands from the context menu.

Vegas also has a Paste Repeat command that allows events to be pasted multiple times. Events can be pasted end-to-end the number of times specified in the dialog or can be spaced at intervals defined in the menu.

Selecting events to the end of the timeline is an option when all events need to be moved up or down the timeline as a group. Rather than Shift+Clicking each file, right-click only the first file in the series, and from the menu choose Select Events to End. This process will go all the way to the end of the timeline and select every event on that track after the cursor/selected event.

To fade an audio event in or out, it's as easy as clicking and grabbing the upper corner on either end of the event. A small quarter-circle will appear. This circle indicates that the tool is prepared to fade audio in or out.

6.38   Pasting multiple instances of an audio event.

Splitting an event or series of events that are on different tracks is accomplished by placing the cursor where the split should occur. If no single event is selected, all vertical events on the timeline will be split on the point where the cursor is. PessS to split the audio files.

If an individual event is selected, only that event will be split.

6.39   Creating a fade in.

Fades can be customized by right-clicking the fade and choosing from the menu of five different types of fades. If on of the five fade types still doesn't provide the desired sound, use the Audio Envelope tool to create the desired fade type.

6.40   Different fade types available in Vegas.

Creating a crossfade, in which two audio events overlap each other and one fades out as the other fades in, is achieved by sliding the two events over the top of each other for the desired length of fade. Automatic Crossades must be enabled on the toolbar. Although defaulted to Enabled, check to be certain that the following button is pressed:

Double-clicking inside the crossfade selects the lengh of the fade. The exact timing of the fade can be read in the Time Display window at the lower-right corner of the timeline.

6.43 Double-click a crossfade to make a selection. The length of the crossfade is displayed in the Time Display window.

6.44 Vegas has many cross-fade choices available. Right-click the crossfade to call up the Fade Type menu. Properties of a crossfade can be adjusted by inserting a volume envelope (V) over a crossfade..

Vegas has the ability to create auto-crossfades of a preset length. In the OPTIONS | PREFERENCES | EDITING dialog, crossfade times can be preset. Set the desired length for crossfades by time or by frames and select multiple files in the Explorer by pressing and holding ctrl and selecting media by clicking them. Drag tem o te imeline, and the media will drop in as automatically crossfaded events. This same behavior applies to video files.

6.45 Several files can be dragged to the timeline and automatically crossfaded by selecting several files in the Explorer.

6.46 A mono event faded into a stereo event.

When interviewing with a DV cam and using one mic to the interviewee and one to the interviewer or another interviewee, the two channels are captured as one audio file with right and left information. With most NLE systems, separating channels requires editing in a separate sound editor. In Vegas, place the two-channel audio on a timeline. Duplicate the track by right-clicking the Track Control pane and selecting Duplicate Track. Click the upper of the two identical tracks. Right-click the audio in the upper track and select Channels | Left Only. Right-click the lower track and select Channels | Right Only. There are now two tracks of mono audio on the timeline, capable of being edited and processed separately. This method is a fast means of accomplishing two tracks with separate control.

All tracks added to the timeline are stereo. Only events are either mono or stereo. A mono signal, however, will remain mono when dragged to the timeline. Mono and stereo signals can occupy the same track, and a mono event can be crossfaded over a stereo event on the timeline.

Audio that is stereo, but should be mono, is quickly converted by right-clicking a stereo file and choosing Combine from the pop-up menu. Files that have been combined can be restored by selecting Both. Audio can also be selected as Right Only or Left Only, and channels can be switched by selecting Swap.

Audio that is not at nominal level can be normalized non-destructively by right-clicking an audio event and selecting Properties. Check the Normalize box, which will bring audio to a level normalized as specified in the OPTIONS | PREFERENCES | AUDIO EVENT dialog. On the disc in this book, a JavaScript is found that can be run as a script in Vegas, normalizing all audio on the tielie as a script rather than normalizing all audio manually. The file is located in the \scripts\ folder as normalizeall.js.

6.47   Audio event before normalizing.

 *Tip*_____

Normalize in Sony Sound Forge as opposed to Vegas, so you can normalize on the RMS value, as opposed to the peak value.

6.48   Audio event after normalizing, a 4.1dB increase in gain. Normalizing an entire project may also be accomplished with scripting tools available for free, at vasst.com.

Audio events have an individual gain reduction on each event as well. Place the cursor at the top of the audio event and watch for the cursor to turn into a handico. Then click and hold, dragging the hand icon downward. Vegas indicates the gain level reduction as the gain line is pulled downward.

6.49   Reducing the gain of an audio event on the timeline..

Right-clicking an audio event calls up several menu options. One of them is the ability to loop an event, which is different from setting up a playback loop for previews.

Right-click an event, choose Switches, and check the Loop box. This step allows the audio event to be dragged out infinitely, and the audio will constantly loop. Vegas inserts an indicator that looks like a small divot or carrot in the event at the point of the end/beginning of a loop. Looingis terrific for repeating sounds that might fade together or for using an ACID loop that should repeat. Looping is set to On by default.

6.50   Setting an event for looped playback. Looping may also be enabled by pressing the Q key.

Looping is helpful in most situations; however, it can also work against a mix in some instances. If a reverb or delay is desired to continue reflection for a long time after an audio event ends, looping must be disabled, and the file dragged out for the length of time that the reverb/delay is desired. Otherwise, the plug-in sees the end of the audio event and thinks it needs to shut off if the end of the project is eaced. Dragging out an empty portion of the event with looping turned off allows the reverb or delay to continue to be audible.

6.51   Event dragged out with looping off. Because looping is disabled and the audio has ended, Vegas treats the stretched event like empoty media.

Get ACIDized!

Speaking of loops, ACID has long been recognized as one of the most valuable creative tools for composing royalty-free music for video and recorded productions. ACID uses pre-recorded loops, recorded by some of the finest musicians in the world. Imagine having Mick Fleetwood play drums for you, Rudy Sarzo on bass, Ken Jordan from Crystal Method on keys and sound design, and some of the world's best-known R&B vocalists all performing on your video soundtrack! With ACID loops and Vegas's ability to take advantage of ACID metadata, you can have these great performers and more.

Visit http://www.acidplanet.com and download some of the free eight-packs of loops. Unzip them, and start creating music in Vegas.

ACID files are .wav files containing metadata that informs Vegas of the tempo, key, and length of the audio file. Vegas will take recordings of disparate tempos and lock them up to whatever tempo is set in the Project Properties. Using the Pitch Shift functions, loop pitches may be shifted up or down to be made to be harmonically acceptable.

One of the caveats about using ACID loops in Vegas is that Vegas, unlike Sony's ACID application, cannot shift tempo on the fly by using tempo markers. This doesn't mean that soundtracks or underscores can't change in tempo, however. This merely means you need to work around the limitations.

In Vegas, whatever the project tempo may be, it determines the tempo of the loop. Therefore, if the project tempo is left to the default value of 120 beats per minute (BPM), then any loops dropped on the timeline will conform to the 120 BPM tempo. However, the project tempo may be changed downstream/later in the project, and any loops dropped on the timeline prior to the tempo change will retain their tempo of 120 BPM, while any loop dropped on the timeline after the project tempo is changed will retain the new tempo value. Put another way, if you drop loops on the Vegas timeline with the tempo at 120, any loop you drop at any point will always be at the 120 tempo. If you shift tempo later, and attempt to place loops on the timeline in sync with the earlier inserted loops, the loops will not synchronize correctly. So be sure to get your compositions correctly assembled prior to changing any project tempo in Vegas. It's also handy to save various versions of your project if you expect to be changing tempos or creating mapped tempos later on.

Vegas does not indicate the current tempo, so it's a good practice to create markers on the timeline to indicate where tempo changes are occuring.

Another workaround is to create your project the way you want it to sound in Vegas, create a tempo change, and then reload the loops after the tempo change has occurred, loading them from the Project Media. The loops originally dropped on the timeline will retain their original tempo information, and the loops inserted from the Project Media will exist at the new tempo.

Key changes are not possible as a global function in Vegas. Individual loops may be pitch-shifted to create key changes, but this is only done on an event by event basis. Vegas will not recognize the actual key of a loop, but loops may be tuned by using the pitch-shift capability found in Vegas. If Show Active Take Name is selected in the Options>Preferences dialog Vegas will display the original pitch or key of the loop. (Drum loops rarely contain pitch data, and so will be blank.)

A workaround to the lack of global pitch shift is to select all loops to be shifted by holding the Ctrl key and using the minus or plus keys to shift them up or down according to desired amount.

> Shifting loops in amounts of two semitones, five semitones, and seven semitones will follow the average pop song format. There are 12 semitones in an octave. Music today is often written in what is called I, IV, V format or 1,4,5 format. This means that the chord or pitch changes will reflect a shift up by a fourth or a shift up by a fifth. An interval of a fourth is equal to five semitones, and an interval of a fifth is equal to seven semitones. To shift a pitch down to the fifth the downward value would be -5 from the original pitch and to shift down to the fourth, the value would be seven semitones down. It's rarely a good idea to shift a loop more than 12 semitones up or down unless a specific sound or effect is being sought. Loops in higher octaves will display less of a negative effect than a lower octave loop, because of the distance between frequency amplitude. Don't expect to shift a bass guitar loop by more than a couple of semitones without damaging the integrity of the loop.

If you have two loops of disparate or dissonant pitch, select the loop that is different from other loops, or lower in pitch overall from the opposing loop. Using the hyphen or equals key, pitch the loop up or down until it is harmonically acceptable, or in the same pitch as the other loops on the timeline.

6.52   Notice that the pitches do not match. This generally will mean that audio will be discordant and not sound correct.

Using ACID loops in Vegas is a powerful addition. This allows video editors to create rudimentary beds or sound design tools. If greater or more powerful music creation tools are required, I recommend that readers check out ACID, another of Sony's desktop media applications.

And there goes the pitch! (Vegas still hits a home run)

Vegas has always had amazing audio manipulation tools since the inception of Version One1. Vegas 5 brought some new audio tools to the game, and one of them involves pitch-shifting on the fly. This feature is simply amazing. A weak voice-over, a music bed that conflicts with dialog, an unintelligible word or two can all be improved or even repaired just by using this new feature.

To shift pitch in Vegas, make a selection of an audio event. If only a single word or section needs to be shifted, use the S key to split the audio event, singling out the area to be shifted. Create a time selection above the selected event, and press the Q key to enable looping. Start playback. During playback use the plus and minus keys to shift the pitch up or down. Pitch may be shifted up or down as much as two full octaves, or as much as 24 semi-tones in either direction. By holding the Ctrl key while shifting pitch, changes will be made by cents rather than semitones, giving very tight control to critical pitch shifts. Use this feature to correct an out of tune vocal, or to thicken a doubled/duplicated track.

Any shift greater than approximately five semitones in either direction may have adverse effects on the quality of the audio, depending on content. Entire music beds may be shifted up or down as much as a fifth or plus or minus seven semitones to compliment dialog or make way for other audio events, while stingers or other special effects events might be shifted very low or high for maximum impact.

Try inserting a cymbal or other hard attack and long sustain sound and pitch it down to -24. You might find it very powerful as an introductory sound or perfect accompaniment to a fly-in transition or graphic object. Coupling this with the new real-time reverse found in Vegas makes for a wonderful effect in some circumstances. Experiment with different sounds to learn how this effect might best suit your workflow and creative opportunity.

 Open the "dropped pitch.veg" file on the DVD in the back of this book and experiment with how the new audio-processing tools function.

Shifting stock music or other music found in the project down or up by a pitch or two will have a tremendous impact on the feel and texture of a scene and usually will clear the frequency range for a better dialog track. Experiment with this new feature, and it may well become your favorite tool in Vegas. It's definitely in the top two or three favorite features in Vegas for me.

Get the Mark Up

Vegas has improved managing of markers in a substantial fashion. No longer bridled with only 10 markers with names, Vegas now allows numbering of up to 99 markers that are auto-numbered when inserted to the timeline. Of course, all markers may be renamed and renumbered to user preference, but just having the ability to insert more than 10 markers and have the numbers stay sequential is a great thing. Earlier versions would allow for lots of markers, but only one through nine were named.

Further enhancements include being able to click the Marker indicator in the upper-right corner of the workspace causing the Marker bar or timeline to take focus from the rest of the application. This allows the arrow keys to be used to jump from marker to marker. The left - arrow key moves cursor and playhead to the previous marker, and the right-arrow key moves cursor and playhead to next marker. Markers also move with media when a multiple selection is created and moved. Markers may be individually or group deleted in addition to now being able to selectively delete the markers. When focus is shifted away from the Marker timeline, the Marker tools are disabled.

To work with the new features in the Marker timeline, click the Marker tool button in the upper-right corner of the window.

Now click on any marker. (Insert a few markers if you don't have any. To insert a marker, press the M key.) Notice that when the marker is clicked, it becomes selected with its number highlighted in the marker box. Click Delete to remove the marker, left-arrow to move to previous marker, or right-arrow to move to next marker. You may select multiple markers by holding Ctrl as each marker is selected. Markers may be moved in tandem when multiple selections occur, or multiple markers may be deleted at one time by selecting each marker while holding the Ctrl button. If you have a number of markers to be deleted, click on the first marker, hold Shift, and click on the last marker. All markers in between the first and last markers will be selected and may be deleted with the Delete key.

6.53 The Marker button is new, allowing Vegas to focus on the Marker timeline, providing users with several options.

Inserting Markers

Markers are often needed to indicate a specific point on the timeline that requires an edit, to serve as a cue, to insert metadata, and for many other helpful uses. Vegas allows for three different types of markers:

- Markers—reference points to be returned to later, which identify timing or act as a reminder for later edits. Markers can be inserted on the timeline or in the Trimmer. Markers can be named at any time.

- Regions—defined sections on the timeline. Regions can behave as permanent indicators of a selection either in the Trimmer or on the timeline. Regions can act as reminders of specific sections to be returned to later or can act as edit length indicators in the Trimmer. Regions can be named at any point in time. All training materials on the DVD contained in this book are built with regions.

- Command markers—used to insert metadata in streaming media files. Text data, such as lyrics, promotional information, URL locations, and closed captions, can be embedded with command markers. (See Chapter 11 for more information.)

Markers and regions can remain with the audio file when inserted in the Trimmer tool. The OPTIONS | PREFERENCES | GENERAL dialog has a check box to automatically save markers and regions in the Trimmer tool.

To insert a marker, place the cursor where the marker location is desired. Press M, right-click the Marker bar, or select INSERT | MARKER. This step places a marker on the timeline. Markers can be deleted by right-clicking the individual marker or by right-clicking in the Marker bar and choosing Delete All Markers. A group of markers can be deleted by making a selection on the timeline that contains the markers to be deleted, right-clicking in the Marker bar, and selecting the menu option Delete All in Selection. Markers can be named when inserted or later by right-clicking a marker and selecting Rename. Pressing Enter or clicking out of the box on te tieline sets the marker's name.

Markers can be navigated by pressing Ctrl+Left Arrow/Right Arrow. This step will jump the cursor from marker to marker.

6.54 Be certain that the check box for "Automatically save trimmer markers and regions with media file" is checked to save the indicators in the Trimmer.

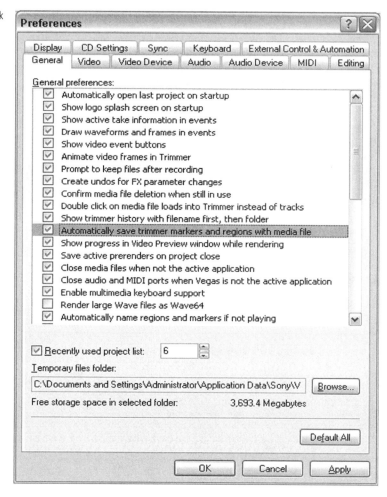

6.55 Inserting, deleting, or editing markers can be done by right-clicking the Marker bar.

Regions are defined by creating a selection on the timeline and pressing R or by selecting INSERT | REGION. Double-clicking an evnt creates an automatic selection for the length of the event. The region can be named in any way that you choose. Regions can be renamed at any point.

6.56 Cursor behaviors inside a region can be selected by right-clicking a region marker.

👍 **Tip**

Use regions to indicate mini-projects or mini-sections, such as a verse, chorus, or bridge. This option makes it easier to find full sections or loop full sections during the recording session. It also makes it easy to fly in a repeat chorus or bridge later on, if necessary.

Regions can be navigated or toggled. Regions can be navigated by selecting a corresponding number on the keyboard (not the numeric keypad) or by pressing Ctrl+Left Arrow/Right Arrow. This step allows rapid navigation within Vegas of various regions on the timeline.

Command markers are created when the cursor is placed at the desired point for a metadata event to occur, and C is pressed or INSERT | COMMAND is selected. This step calls the Command Properties dialog, in which the desired type of metadata is selected.

Metadata allows for media to become rich media or media that is more than just audio. (See Chapter 9 for more information.)

The command marker can have a different name than the properties associated with the marker. Right-clicking the

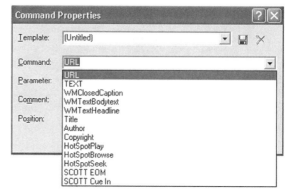

6.57   Different types of metadata that can be inserted.

command marker provides a menu for renaming the file. Command markers can be deleted individually by right-clicking the marker and selecting Delete. Right-clicking in the Marker bar and selecting Delete All does not affect command markers.

Rubber Audio

Vegas has a feature known as Rubber Audio. Audio can be stretched by grabbing the right side of an audio event, pressing and holding down Ctrl, and dragging the event to the right. This option is useful to correct a slightly off-sync voice or to expand or compress an audio event to make it fit within a specified period. Audio that is expanded/stretched much more than 10 percent, however, will sound very strange indeed. Perhaps long stretches are valuable for a specific effect; however, the audio is quickly recognized as affected after it has gone pat the 10–15 percent stretch point. Use the Rubber/Time Stretch feature only as a means of achieving sync on an out of sync and time format event or as a special effect.

 Tip

Rubber Audio.veg is a project on the DVD that allows you to hear what rubber audio/stretched audio sounds like at various speeds and pitches.

Time stretch can also be accomplished by right-clicking the audio event, selecting Properties, and adjusting the length of the file.

Audio pitch/tuning can also be adjusted in this same dialog box.

Use Semitones to move pitch in musical half steps and use the Cents dialog to change by hundredths of semi-tones. For example, a pitch shift of -7 semitones is equal to a fifth interval down from the tonic, or original pitch. Shifting a pitch by +4 is a minor third up from the tonic or original pitch.

 Tip

Sound designers will find the Pitch Shift/Time Stretch tool invaluable. Using household sounds, such as blenders, flushing commodes, gelatin being slowly sucked out of a can, and other creative sounds, coupled with the Pitch Shift/Time Stretch feature yields usable sounds for any kind of video or audio production. Adding reverbs, delays, flanges, and panning information to these sounds further enhances value and realism.

Variable Speed Audio in Vegas

Currently, Vegas does not have the ability to gradually speed up, reverse, or slow down sound on the timeline. If audio speed must be gradually reversed or slowed down, the file must be opened in either Sound Forge or another audio editing application. If a multichannel sound card is available on the system, however, there is another option.

Create a new bus and route the audio to be sped, altered, or reversed to this bus. Create a new track and select the output of the new bus to feed the new track. Click Record and play away with the Playback Rate control in Vegas. This process is a lot more accurate and fun than using the J, K, or L keys or a Contour ShuttlePro/SpaceStation AV. The altered playback shows up on the new track where it can now be filtered, EQd, or otherwise processed.

This process can also be accomplished with the Windows-Media Recorder by selecting the inputs from the Windows-Media Mixer.

To reverse audio with no gradiation in speed, right-click the audio event and choose Reverse from the submenu options. This is a real-time process, so you'll see the audio event reverse itself and re-draw its waveform.

6.58 Changing pitch of an audio event can bring a slightly off-key singer into tune or create that "news television" sound for a slightly thin voiceover.

Reverse Decisions

Ever wanted to reverse an audio or video clip? In the past, video could be reversed by using the Velocity envelope set to a value of –100 percent and video would be easily reversed. In Version 5, Vegas made this even more simple by offering a right-click and selecting the Reverse option from the submenu that pops up. The beauty is, this reverses audio too, if audio is selected. Any audio may be reversed whether tied to a video event or not.

Any time audio is reversed, a subclip is created that will be found in the Project Media. This subclip may be placed on the timeline as a separate event. An incredible use of the reverse tool is to apply it to a cymbal that has a strong attack and a light decay. Reversing this provides a great opportunity to create a stinger or audio event that can lead up to and impact a particular scene or action in a video. The Beatles were the first to take great advantage of reversed audio, but one of the best examples is where Roy Thomas Baker used reversed tape on a piano for the "We Will Rock You" and "Bohemian Rhapsody" songs recorded by Queen. Try this on a variety of instruments, combined with the pitch shifting tools now found in Vegas. You'll be surprised at the creative inspiration you'll find in doing this. For even greater effect in dialog, try placing a duplicate of a dialog track, and reversing one of the two tracks. It creates a mess, but where the two tracks converge, it's a very interesting effect. You may want to split out one section of the dialog and do this. Alfred Hitchcock used this technique in Psycho to create a sense of babbling and underlying confusion, and it certainly worked well. It might just make your production take on a whole new meaning.

Snapping Audio Events

Vegas can snap audio events to a marker, region, grid indicator, or to an abutting event. Two events on the same track always snap together if snapping is enabled.

Two events can also be snapped together on different tracks, however. To do this, follow these steps:

1. Double-click the event to which you want the next event to snap. This step creates a time selection.

2. On the track that holds the event to which the selected event should be snapped, move the event toward the front or back of the region or selected event. Vegas auto-snaps the moved event to the first event that is selected, regardless of tracks. Several events can be snapped at once.

Events can also be snapped to a grid line. Pressing F8 enables snapping, and pressing it again disabls napping. If snapping is not enabled, timing grids are not visible. To snap an event to the grid, press Ctrl+F8. To snap an event to a marker, press Shift+F8.

6.59 Snapping several
events to a selected
track event.

Trimming Events on the Timeline

Events can be trimmed in the Trimmer window before being placed on the timeline. They can also be edited for length directly on the timeline as well. Position the cursor over the start or end of an event, and the cursor changes to the trim cursor.

Grab either the start or end of an event by clicking and holding, and drag the end of the event to the left or the start of an event to the right. The event shortens as it is dragged or trimmed.

If auto-ripple (Ctrl+L) is enabled, any trimming on the timeline will result in events following the trim filling the space/hole left behind because of the trim.

6.60   Before trimming on the timeline.

6.61   After trimming on the timeline.

6.62   Trimmed on the timeline, media following trim filled in time vacated as a result of trimming on the timeline.

6.63   Rippled on the timeline, media following trim filled in time vacated because of trimming on the timeline.

Another option to trimming on the timeline is to slip or shift the contents of an event. By pressing and holding down Alt and dragging right or left inside an event, audio can be slipped forward or backward in time without moving the actual event. This feature is great for moving audio within a specified time space without having to be concerned about losing space in time. The event remains a placeholder while audio can be fine-tuned. This feature is also useful for fitting audio in a stipulated time space, where time is specified but the contents can be determined later.

Deleting Events from the Timeline

Selecting events by clicking them and then pressing Delete removes them from the timeline. Multiple events can be selected by pressing and holding down Shift and clicking events to be deleted. Deleting events removes them from the timeline but does not eliminate the empty space that remains unless auto-ripple is enabled (Ctrl+L). If an entire space in time across multiple tracks is to be deleted, make a selection on the timeline. Select Delete (Ctrl+X). (Selecting Delete does not place deleted media on the clipboard.) If Ripple is enabld, all events remaining on the timeline shift to fill the empty space; otherwise, the time selection remains behind and is left empty.

Events or time can also be deleted by selecting EDIT | DELETE.

 Tip
If in the process of deleting events where ripple is needed but not enabled, use a post-edit ripple to close deleted areas. Post-edit ripple behaviors are selected in the Edit menu or by pressing F, Ctrl+F, or Ctrl+Shift+F.

Using Ripple Editing

Vegas has Ripple features that make rippling intuitive and easy. Entire tracks, multiple tracks, and individual events can all be rippled collectively or individually. Enable rippling by selecting the Auto-Ripple button.

Select Affected Tracks from the three options displayed in the drop-down menu. Drag several events to the timeline, butting them together. Trim the outpoint of the first event. All events subsequent to the first event slide to the left, remaining butted up against the first event. At random, place markers on the timeline. Now drag the out point of the first event back to where it was when originally placed on the timeline.

The events subsequent to the lengthened event slide forward in time for the exact length as the event being dragged moves. However, the inserted markers stay where they are.

6.65　Vegas draws an arrow indicating the direction of the ripple that also demonstrates the length of the ripple.

Return to the Auto-Ripple drop-down menu shown above and select Affected Tracks + Project Markers, Keyframes, and Envelopes. Drag the out point of the first (or any other event) to the left, and this time when all events slide to the left, regions, markers, envelopes, and all other attributes of all tracks slide to the left as well, keeping the project timeline intact. This process is called a *ripple edit*.

 Tip
Notice that the Ripple tool in Vegas will give a display of the amount of time the media is being moved backward or forward in time.

Inserting from the Trimmer is easy and fast as well. Select or regionalize audio in the Trimmer and either press A with rippling enabled or, if rippling is not enabled, press Shift+Ctrl+V. The audio inserts as an event with all subsequent audio sliding down to make room for the new event. Ripple editing is useful in quickly cutting together on-air commercials, or in a musical setting, it's excellent for cutting out entire sections or bars of music.

Grouping

At times, it's helpful for entire sections or types of events to be grouped or locked together so that when one is moved, all of them move. Grouping events is quick and easy in Vegas. Select a number of events and press G. This step ties all of the events together so that when one is moved, all the others move with it. For instance, perhaps all events related to a chorus, bridge, or verse might be grouped so that when one section is moved, all related events to that group are moved with it.

To remove an event from a group, select it and press U to ungroup. Grouping can be temporarily ignored by clicking the Ignore Event Grouping button on the toolbar.

Groups are great for applying edits to multiple events at one time. To apply an edit to all members of a group, perform the following steps:

1. Press Shift+G or right-click one member of the group.

2. Select GROUP | SELECT ALL. You can cut, copy, or paste edits to the entire group. Grouped, but unselected events, are not edited together.

Events can only belong to one group at a time. Adding an event to a group essentially dissolves the existing group and creates a new one. As many groups as needed can be created, yet no two groups can contain the same event.

6.66   Grouping can be temporarily ignored.

Working with Audio Plug-ins

Vegas has a tremendous assortment of plug-ins that come with the application and that provide massive mixing and editing power. Particularly necessary in the digital audio world, there are multiple types of compressors and equalizers, plus reverbs, delays, flangers, noise gates, resonators, and more. As a result of the open Direct X platform, plug-ins from companies such as WAVES, Ozone, Sonitus, Cakewalk, and dozens of other manufacturers, can be used in Vegas.

Sony was the first adopter of what was once called Active Movie, which later became Active X, which then once again changed names to Direct X. Sony supported Active Movie in their 4.0a version of Sound Forge. Because of Sony's pioneering work in the plug-in interface market, most every video editing application, as well as audio application, supports the Direct X audio platform.

Plug-ins, such as compressors, reverbs, delays, and noise reduction, all take the place of hardware counterparts in the analog world. In fact, many software plug-ins look just like their hardware counterparts, and, in some cases such as WAVES, the software tools were so popular that the company followed up the software tools with hardware tools for the non-digital environment!

Sony offers nearly 30 plug-ins with Vegas. Rather than examine each of them, we'll look at what each family of plug-ins does.

Dynamic range plug-ins offer the ability to ensure that audio doesn't exceed the dynamic range capabilities of digital audio. This includes compressors, limiters, and combinations thereof, such as WaveHammer, Sony's final-step plug-in.

While digital audio has an extreme dynamic range, it is also less forgiving than its analog counterpart, in that the zero point in the digital world is cold, harsh, and unforgiving. In the analog world, the dynamic range is fairly limited by any comparison, ranging in the upper 60dB area depending on the quality of equipment used. Twenty-four bit digital recordings have a dynamic range of 138dB, or more than double the dynamic of analog. Dynamic range plug-ins help reduce dynamic range, while maintaining most of the nuances of a fairly dynamic performance. They could be considered automatic volume controls. By limiting, or subtly compressing the exceptionally loud portions of a performance, the performance still maintains its soft to loud moments but

Sony Dynamic plug-ins include:

- Express FX Dynamics
- Track Compressor
- Graphic Dynamics
- Vinyl Restoration
- Multi-band Dynamics
- Wave Hammer

Frequency-based plug-ins/FX function by varying the amount of volume of a given frequency or group of frequencies to change the way a recording sounds. Equalizers, wah-wahs, phasers, and similar tools work on either moving a frequency's amplitude up or down to change the audio's sound or timbre. Wah-wah and phaser sounds sweep/shift the amplitude and frequency over time, giving the sound of motion, similar to the concept of a Doppler effect. In fact, some plug-ins are written to simulate the Doppler effect.

Frequency-based plugs include:

- Wah-wah
- Graphic EQ
- Paragraphic EQ
- Smooth/Enhance
- Track EQ

The Doppler effect, discovered in about 1845 by Christian Doppler, an Austrian mathematician, demonstrates that shifts in frequency occur as the article generating the sound moves. This effect is how our ears perceive sounds coming toward us and moving away from us. Listen to a train as it approaches. The frequencies contained in the sound that the train makes shifts as it moves toward you or away. The shifting frequencies result in shifting pitch as the object moves in either direction.

at the same time doesn't exceed the preset point. More on dynamic range control is found in the "Mixing Techniques" section of this chapter.

Time-based plug-ins/FX are based on just that: time. Delays, reverb, chorus, and flangers are all based on delaying, recombining, and/or reflecting a moment in time. When a sound originates, roughly 40 percent of its sound that we perceive is based on reflection of sound in a given space. In other words, singing in the shower is so much more fun than singing in a closet because the reflections of the voice in the shower hit the ear much more quickly than the reflections in a closet do. Some types of music are predominantly based on reverbs and delays, used to create emotional expression and to fill holes in a song. Without long delays and reverbs, many of the ballads and arena anthem rock songs would sound empty and powerless because the lead vocal and chorus vocals would lose their presence and power through the absence of filled time and massive reflection. Time-based effects are used more than any other effect to create emotional responses. Dripping water combined with huge reverb settings is part and parcel of nearly every horror movie made, and the simulated sounds of space (space has no air and therefore sound cannot pass) also include reverbs and delays.

Time-based plug-ins include:

- Flange/Wah
- Multi-tap Delay
- Reverb
- Simple Delay
- Acoustic Mirror*
- ExpressFX Chorus*
- ExpressFX Delay*
- ExpressFX Flange*
- ExpressFX Reverb*

* Optional FX from Sony

On the DVD enclosed with this book, you will find demonstration plug-ins from PSP Audio, WAVES, Ozone, and Sonitus. A wide variety of plugs are available for you to experiment with and enjoy.

Upgrading from Vegas 3 or 4 to Vegas 5 or 6, and your plug-ins disappeared?

Use the Plug-in Migration Wizard in your Vegas toolkit. Go to Start>All Programs>Sony> Utilities>Migration Wizard. Run the register DirectX plug-ins utility. This should restore all of your plug-ins to Vegas 6. This generally only happens once you delete Vegas 4. I recommend you leave Vegas 4 loaded for a period of time, until you are entirely familiar with Vegas 5 or 6, if only for the compositing tools found in the video toolset.

Automating FX in Vegas

One of the most exciting tools in Vegas is the ability to automate FX. Many of the Direct X plug-in tools have the ability to be automated. EQ settings, delay times, reverb decays, and much more can now be controlled by Vegas' automation envelopes. Many of the high-tech sounds demanded by production music today require either several hands at the mix console or automated FX control.

For instance, if a vocal line reaches a break just before a chorus and a long delay is needed, automated FX can change the length of the delay time as opposed to using another FX send just for the vocal breaks. Perhaps an EQ sweep just as a car passes from right to left, creating the illusion of a Doppler effect, would make the sound more believable. Frequency sweeps added to drum mixes or to a main instrument sound become part of the instrument itself, creating an unmatchable identity. Remember "Axel F," the theme song from BeverlyHills Cop? The sweeps heard on the bass lines in that song were created by synthesis, but the sound itself was a huge part of the song. Techno music is nearly always automation-dependent because the repetitive nature of the music.

To hear an example of automation, open the FX Automation project on the DVD.

On track 1, you can observe an inserted automation envelope by right-clicking the Control pane and choosing FX Automation Envelopes. Notice in the Track EQ settingstht Bnd3Gain and Band3 Bandwidth boxes are checked. Click OK.

6.67 Select the boxes related to the automation parameters you wish to control.

A pair of dark-colored envelopes are on the track in the timeline. These are the bandwidth and gain controls for the EQ that you have set for automation.

6.68 Automation envelopes appear when Automation parameters are selected.

6.69 The FX Automation button opens up a dialog where tool automation features can be viewed and selected.

Every two seconds, insert a handle on the Band3 Gain envelope or the envelope that appears in the middle of the track. (The project grid is laid out in seconds.) In between the handles on the Band3 Gain envelope, handles are already inserted on the Band3 Bandwidth envelope. Now drag every other handle of the Band3 gain handles down to the bottom of the track, or -15dB worth of adjustment. Experiment with the type of fade by right-clicking the handle and selecting different fade types. You'll be astounded at the degree of control this offers the sound.

Not all Direct X plug-ins have the ability to be controlled by automation envelopes. iZotope, Sonic Timeworks, WAVES, Wave Arts, and the plug-ins found in the Automated plug-ins folder are all examples of automatable plug-ins. If a plug-in is capable of automation, a selection button will appear in the upper-right corner of the plug-in. When the button is clicked, the parameters available for automation will appear.

Some plug-ins have to be added to a chain at least once before they are recognized as automatable. Don't be alarmed if you don't see them in the automatable folder right away.

Working with Other Types of Plug-ins

Noise Reduction

In 1995, Sony released a product called Noise Reduction 1.0. This new tool revolutionized the music industry. As in the past, only very expensive hardware tools or the Digidesign Intelligent Noise Reduction (DINR) tools found in ProTools or No Noise from Sonic Solutions were available. One was too expensive and only occasionally effective, the other not satisfactory in extremely noisy circumstances. Sony's Noise Reduction tool gave working musicians the ability to clean up poor sounding rooms or environments.

Noise Reduction uses an algorithm known as Fast Fourier Transform (FFT) as part of the power behind how it functions. This algorithm is large, requiring millions of calculations based on information selected in the noisy portion of the file. A basic explanation is that when noise is present in a sound file, the noise can be isolated in sections between words, instrument attacks, or in heads or tails of a file. The noise is then sampled, and the algorithm applied to the rest of the audio file, removing the sampled sounds but leaving behind the original sound. Sometimes, if the sample is too large or contains too much information (sounds other than noise) or if the noise sample is frequency unstable (sound is moving), the process can remove some of the original, pre-noisy sound, resulting in artifacts. These artifacts often resemble the sound of rushing water or a waterfall. Other times, it has a metallic, robotic sound. In fact, some films have used this extreme noise reduction technique to create alien sounds. In this section, however, we're interested in removing noise to make a file sound cleaner. In short, Noise Reduction is similar

6.70 Select the preferred audio editor in the PREFERENCES | AUDIO menu.

to a frequency-depended noise gate that is divided into several hundred bands. The noiseprint determines the threshold or open level of each gate, and any time the volume of a frequency is below that threshold, it is suppressed/silenced.

Noise reduction i particularly effective when trying to remove a constant noise source, such as an air conditioner, refrigerator, or AC hum. It is least effective on moving sources, such as constantly passing traffic, running water, or varying wind noise.

A demonstration version of Noise Reduction is located on the DVD in the back of this book. Install it now, if it has not already been installed.

To apply Noise Reduction to a file, first open the file in a Direct X–capable audio editor by right-clicking in Vegas and choosing "Open copy in (audio editing application)." This option should already be configured if you followed the steps in Chapter 1. If you have not done so, select OPTIONS | PREFERENCES | AUDIO and use the Browse button to locate the executable for your favorite audio editor. It is located in the `C:\Program Files` directory in most instances.

On the audio file, select a very small slice of audio that contains only the noise that needs to be removed. When selecting a noise sample, less is more. Fewer frequencies in the sample make for a more accurate reduction in those frequencies.

Now open Noise Reduction from the DirectX plug-in host, and the screen shown in Figure 6.75 will be displayed.

Check the Capture Noiseprint box and click the Preview button. This step allows you to hear what section has been selected. At the same time, a noiseprint has been captured. Click the Noiseprint tab if you wish to see what the noiseprint looks like. Thousands of handles are on the noiseprint, so that custom or excetinaly ccurate control of the noiseprint can be had. It is

6.71 When the file opens up in the sound editor, it looks something like this. Notice the noise between words spoken.

generally best to allow the plug-in to function automatically, however. Playing with these handles does offer the opportunity to create some fairly inventive and radical sounds.

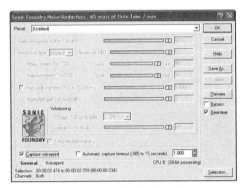

6.72 This is the main window for Noise Reduction, where all control of noise removal takes place.

6.73 A view of how Noise Reduction interprets the noise information.

After the noiseprint has been captured, the area that the filter should be run on must be selected. Noise Reduction allows for selectable time spans, entire files, regions, or specific areas to be processed. Generally, files will be the entire area, but you can specify an area if so desired. Generally, choose All Sample Data because if noise is present in one area, it's typically present in the entire file. (Other host applications can operate differently.)

6.74 File after noise reduction applied.

Trying to use large noise samples is counter productive, damaging wanted information while possibly ignoring unwanted information. Use sal samples multiple times rather than trying to use a larger sample one time. Noise Reduction can be run as many times as necessary to remove noise from the file, and using small selections usually has little impact on the desired sounds.

6.75 Select the smallest space possible for noise sample.

Narrow noise selection

Click OK when you have determined what time selection of the file should be affected. Now you'll be able to move the Reduce Noise By slider, listening in real time as Noise Reduction processes the noise out. Typically, it's rare to get more than -50dB of noise out of a file, but occasionally more aggressive settings will work.

A useful feature in Noise Reduction is the Keep Residual Output box. Checking this box inverts the signal, so that the information being reduced/eliminated is heard and the audio that will be kept is masked. This process allows you to hear if too much of the original signal is being affected or not.

After the desired level of noise is reduced/eliminated, click OK. The Noise Reduction plug-in will process the file. Closing the file in Sound Forge will prompt you to save the file. Save the file, and it will be deposited on the timeline in Vegas in the exact place that it came from, but it is now named the original filename with take(numer) in the filename. It can be toggled back and forth from the original audio file for comparison.

Some files require multiple passes of Noise Reduction in order to obtain the best results without affecting the original audio/desired audio.

The DVD in the back of this book includes a project called Noise Reduction Project. Open this file. You will see two video files; the first has had no noise reduction on it, the second has been noise reduced. If you monitor the project through a good set of speakers or through any headphones, the hum in the background is very clear. The noise source is a refrigerator, three rooms from where the interview was being conducted. In the case of the second file, -70dB of noise was taken out, without creating artifacts in the desired audio file. Even if you don't have speakers that can accurately reproduce the noise, pay particular attention to the master meters.

Practice on the first file. If you don't capture a small enough segment for your noise file, you'll most likely create artifacts in the speech. FFT processing doesn't require a large slice; use a 100ms slice of noise at most for your sample.

> Noise Reduction can be used for other purposes, such as creating unique sounds over a drum loop, voice, or sound effect. Experiment with it and find what works creatively for you. Drastically removing the high end by sampling the decay of a high hat or snare can give unique personality to the sound of any drum loop. Try using Noise Reduction on a heavily compressed speech file and make any human sound become more robotic.

As a side effect of Noise Reduction's capability, it is not intended to be used as a real-time effect. It is exceptionally processor-intensive, and all but the fastest computers with loads of RAM will stutter and pop. This plug-in is best used as a destructive edit, as a take over original audio, or used in an audio editor as a destructive or take-based event. It's common that noise reduction will require multiple passes to reduce noise to a satisfactory level. To accomplish this in Vegas will require several instances of the Noise Reduction plugin on the offending track, whereas by using Sound Forge, it's very fast to process, and provides immediate result with no hit on the processor.

Fingertip Mixing; Using the Mackie Control (and Other Control Devices in Vegas)

A significant barrier to using Vegas in the all-digital recording studio was that until version 5, Vegas was incapable of working with any hardware device except the Contour Shuttle Pro, which offered no mixing capabilities whatsoever. Vegas 5 changed all that, providing direct access to external surface control with the Mackie Control device, and with generic controllers that can be programmed to work with Vegas. For instance, for fading and panning, no mouse is needed, simply use the Mackie Control in the same manner as you'd mix with any mixer. Accessing all parameters of FX such as compressors and EQs is very simple and intuitive with the control. Any generic device such as the M-Audio Oxygen keyboard or a Tascam 424 can be set up to function with Vegas as well. Once you've mixed with a mixer, mixing with a mouse becomes extremely irritating and almost painful.

6.76 The Mackie Expanders and Control together make a very powerful control for Vegas as well as many other audio applications. The console housing for the Mackie Control was built by Omnirax and contains many racks for external audio gear.

To set up a Mackie Control within Vegas, you'll need:

- Mackie Control

- MIDI interface device (many sound cards can manage this)

- A Mackie Extender. This is a nice addition, but not necessary. The Extender expands the capabilities of the Control so that the Control for instance, manages channels 1 through 8, and the Extender manages channels 9 through 16. However, the Mackie Control can manage up to 128 channels of audio at a time. Switching from one channel set to another is a minor inconvenience; the video editor might not find it cumbersome nor inefficient in the same manner that an audio engineer or mix engineer might.

Connect the MIDI input of the Mackie Control to the Output MIDI connector of your sound card or MIDI I/O device. Connect the MIDI output of the Mackie Control to the MIDI Input of your soundcard or MIDI I/O device.

6.77   Connect the Mackie Control to the MIDI interface device.

Select Options>Preferences>External Control and Automation. This opens the dialog of the external control parameters. This is where Vegas will be instructed to access the Mackie Control hardware interface.

6.78   This dialog, found in the track header, is used to tell Vegas how to read or write any automation or level settings from the Mackie Control.

In this dialog, select the Available Devices dropdown menu and choose the Mackie Control from the dialog. Then click Add to add the Control to the Active Control Devices dialog. This should cause the Mackie faders to move to indicate that the device is communicating with Vegas. (If it doesn't respond, don't be concerned. The next step will determine communication.) When the device shows up in the dialog, double-click the box containing the Mackie Control.

This opens up the Configuration dialog, which allows Vegas and the Mackie to be set up to not only be compatible, but to also be as efficient and powerful as you'd like it to be.

Click Scan in the Configuration dialog. This will instruct Vegas to scan the MIDI connections to see what is connected to the ports. If you have Mackie Extender devices attached to the MIDI interface, they'll show up here as well.

Each device must be configured separately, but the engineers at Sony and Vegas have done most of the work for you. However, you'll need to instruct the Configuration dialog to set up the channels on the various devices. For instance, if the system is set up for one Expander and one Control, the Control can be set up to be channels 1-8, or 9-16, and the Expander can be set to control whatever channels the Control is not controlling. Since I'm right-handed and find my need to access the Control more imperative than reaching the Expanders, I set my system up as follows:

- Expander 1: Channels 1 through 8

- Expander 2: Channels 9 through 16

- Expander 3: Channels 17-24

- Mackie Control: Channels 25-32

Notice in illustration 6.73 that the Control is set up to the far right of all the Expanders. (Expander control should soon be available for Vegas.)

After clicking Scan and setting up each device for its controlled channels, click OK. Now click the Apply button in the External Control and automation dialog. All is set for Vegas to know what to do, except one last detail.

Close the Preferences dialog and go to Options>External Control, and click on External Control. This will place a small check mark next to the External Control words. This tells Vegas that you'd like to control the application externally. Of course you'll still be able to operate Vegas via the keyboard and mouse, but this tells Vegas to accept information from the Mackie Control.

6.79   Set Vegas and the Mackie Control up to behave exactly as you'd like to have it behave in the Configuration dialog.

6.80   Enable External Control from the Options>External Control dialog.

Vegas will automatically be mapped to all the knobs on the Mackie Control, so nothing more is needed. The Mackie Console should have come with a Lexan overlay that you can stick to the surface of the control. The Lexan overlay is specific to Vegas, indicating how each push button relates to Vegas, and what it controls. As mentioned earlier, you may customize the keymapping to set any button to perform a specific task in Vegas.

A single Mackie Control may be set up to operate as many as 128 channels at a time on a single device, but this does require a lot of paging through various views to look at each channel past the eight that are automatically displayed. Since most of my audio mixes require me to have immediate access to all channels, I find it more efficient to use a series of Extenders and Controls. One powerful side benefit of the Mackie Universal Control (and any other controlling device) is that the device may be used as a video switcher as well, providing access to color correction plugins, and other plugins found in the Vegas filterset.

Other Controlling Devices

Any MIDI control device may be set up to control Vegas. For example, the M-Audio Oxygen keyboard has eight generic control knobs that may be accessed within Vegas, and may be used like a mixer via generic surface control.

Some MIDI devices won't use a MIDI connection, such as the Oxygen. Control data is passed back and forth via the USB connection.

To use generic surface controls, the set up is very similar to using the Mackie Control setup. First install the device drivers and connect the device to be used as a generic surface control. Open the Options>Preferences>MIDI dialog. The generic device should appear in the dialog box. Tick the boxes related to the connected device, telling Vegas which devices you'd like to control Vegas with.

6.81   The eight knobs on the Oxygen may be assigned as controlling devices for Vegas.

Click the External Control and Automation and select Generic Control from the dropdown in the Available Devices dialog box. The dialog below will display the generic devices. Right-click or double-click the Generic Control and open the Configuration dialog. In the Configuration dialog, you'll need to map the keys and controllers to specific functions within Vegas. Some devices may be ready to roll with Default Mapping. Devices such as as the Tascam 424 and the eVolution U Controller should link up fairly quickly, although no mapping has been created for the device. You can locate the files for surface controllers in the C:\Program Files\Sony\Vegas 6\External Control Drivers\Generic Control Maps folder.

Locate the Quikmap.xml file on the VASST.com/login.htm website, which will set up all automation needs for the M-Audio Oxygen. You will also find other controller parameters on the VASST site.

Audiomation?

Even if you don't have HUI devices connected to Vegas, you can still take advantage of the automation found in Versions 5 and 6.

Each audio track header's automation button contains several options. Right-click the automation button to view the options.

The automated Mute feature allows audio to be muted during the recording of automation during playback of a file.

To insert an automatic mute in your project, place an audio file on the timeline. Click the automation button and select the Show Automation Controls from the submenu. This will insert the Automated mute button into the track header. Click the automation button again and choose Write/Latch or Write/Touch from the submenu.

Begin playback, and while the playhead is moving down the timeline, press the Automated Mute button. Vegas will insert an automated Mute point in the timeline, and each time the playhead crosses this point the audio will be muted. Press the automated Mute button again and the audio will be un-muted.

Audio may also be mixed on the fly with Vegas using a mouse, clicking on the track and inserting envelope points during playback. Choose a track header, press V to insert a Volume Envelope or P to insert a Pan Envelope. During playback, click the volume or panning envelope. This will insert an envelope point or handle in the timeline. Moving this envelope point or handle will modify the volume or pan position of the track. All movements of the volume or panning envelope will be remembered and recalled automatically for future mixing. Setting up a time selection and loop will allow mix points to be tweaked on the fly.

Training Vegas

Vegas can be trained to work with most standard controller devices. To train Vegas to accept input from your MIDI Controller device, open the Options>Preferences>External Control and Automation tab. Double-click the Generic Controller, or right-click and select Configure from the submenu. The Configuration dialog will open.

In the Configure dialog, click on the parameter you wish to control.

Touch any controlling device button, slider, or knob. This will cause the Learn Button in the dialog to light up. Tick the Learn box, and turn, slide, or press the parameter knob, fader, or button to instruct Vegas to link it to the specific parameter. Repeat this step for each parameter you wish to control. Be certain you save the map so that it's available for your next session. (Maps are saved as XML files.)

6.82 Select the parameter that you'd like to control by clicking on it and then moving, sliding, or pressing the controlling device, knob, slider, or button. You'll need to tick the Learn box.

Every Breath You Take, Every Move You Make!

Automation is the act of the host application remembering every move made on the external control device. In past versions of Vegas, automation was entirely controlled by a mouse. While intuitive and functional, it is certainly nearly impossible to generate an inspired mix with a mouse. Music is supposed to be inspired by the whim of the moment, and sometimes generating mixes by hand at moments of random will spark the most amazing muse and mixes. Moreover, being able to recall random mixes at will and create multiple mixes to play back for a director or producer is a wonderful thing.

Nearly all parameters of Vegas' functions may be automated and recalled. With a higher-end controller such as the Mackie Control, you can access parameters of all effects, bus sends, auxiliary sends and returns, reverbs, and compressors.

Automation in Vegas is a wonderful thing to experience because of its simplicity with underlying complexity.

To automate, even a small Griffen knob can be used. It's a little challenging to set up, but once the controller is set up, here are the steps to automate a mix:

1. On the track to be automated, click the Automation settings button.

2. Choose Automation Write in one of the two modes offered, Touch and Latch.

3. Click Play or press the spacebar, and start to twist knobs, slide slidrs, or push buttons.

4. Stop playback. If you are pleased with the mix, it may be put into Automation Read mode, where no movement will be taught to the application, it merely will read the moves previously input with the controlling device.

 Tip_____

If you are an experienced audio engineer, you can mix all tracks live just as you would with an analog mixer. Select all tracks in Vegas before putting a track in automation mode, so that when one track is placed in automation record mode, all tracks are put into automation record mode. You can always go back and over write all fader moves quickly on individual tracks if necessary. If you have a hardware device such as the Mackie Universal Control, it's fast and easy to write a full mix, and then go back and tweak later. If you have more audio tracks than you have fader control over, only enable automation for the tracks you have faders for, then switch the faders to the remaining tracks, writing automation, and tweaking as you go. Remember, you can always reorder tracks in Vegas by dragging tracks to where they are most convenient in layout and priority.

Touch Me, Latch Me! Automation Modes

There are two forms of writing automation. One is Latch mode, and the other is Touch mode. Each has their benefits, and each is fairly common to automated studios. Generally the workflow between the two processes are managed in a specific order. For most recording scenarios, you'll be working with Vegas by starting in one mode and finishing in another.

For a fresh mix with no automation moves inserted, start in Latch mode. Play the mix by pressing the spacebar or clicking Play, or pressing the play button on your controlling device. Move knobs or faders during the playback on however many tracks you have in automation mode. This creates a 'rough mix,' as it's called in the industry. Now Vegas will remember all movements you made regardless of whether they are volumes, pans, or FX automation movements. This is usually done with all tracks in record mode, but just because it's usually done this way doesn't mean you have to do it this way.

Latch mode will continue writing settings regardless of whether you are making fader movements or not, and will overwrite any existing movements that you may have created earlier, making Latch mode excellent for writing over an entire mix or an entire track if you are dissatisfied with the mix or want to create an alternative mix.

Following the mix set up or rough mix, the mix can be fine -tuned either by individual track, or tweaked with all tracks still in automation mode. However, switching tracks over to Touch mode is best. In Touch mode, keyframes and control points are only created when you are touching or adjusting the parameters of the track. As soon as you stop moving sliders or knobs, Vegas quits writing movements, and the already existing movements you inserted in Latch mode or the first write of automation take over again. This is why Touch mode is best for tweaking a mix.

On each track header, there is an automation icon. You can see it next to the Mute and Track FX button. Click it and a submenu appears.

Automation is found on all track headers and may be setup for all tracks at once or set for individual tracks.

In the submenu, you can select Show Automation Controls, and this will cause the Automation icon to display the mode that the specific track is in. This is handy if you find yourself wondering why a specific track is behaving in a particular way.

Mutes may now be automated too. A device like the Mackie Control or the eVolution 33 have Mute buttons on them. Mutes may also be inserted by clicking on the Mute button found on the track header or by pressing the Mute button found on the controlling device. Automated muting is very handy for music or dialog composites, where various sections and takes are on multiple tracks and you want to comp together all the acceptable parts of different tracks to create one final track.

6.83   The four icons that indicate track status are Off, Read, Touch and Latch. Notice Read and Touch are very similar. The Read icon is green and the Write icon is red.

Automation disabled

Read Automation

Latch Mode Automation

Touch Mode Automation

Feeling Fat? Get Thin!

Automation will literally write thousands of nodes, also known as handles or keyframes, during a write. This can be exceptionally tasking on the CPU if left to its own. However, Vegas has a feature known as thinning where the number of nodes and keyframes can be thinned out, controlled by the user. In the Options>Preferences>External Control and Automation dialog, there is a check box for thinning. Thinning will be necessary on slower machines that are used for large mixes. Otherwise, the thousands of envelope points generated by fader motion will be more than the processor can handle.

6.84   Use this menu to reduce or increase the amount of Thinning of keyframes and handles found in a mix.

Video editors may or may not find the nuances of thinning necessary to control. Musicians will demand to have as much control as possible and so will want to set this to preference. If you still feel that thinning is missing or hitting an area that doesn't feel just right, you can always manually adjust handles by using a mouse and clicking and moving the node or envelope point until it is sitting just right in the mix. One suggested workflow is that the mix be created in Latch mode with Thinning enabled. Turn thinning off, and tweak or fine-tune the mix using Touch mode. Only use Touch mode on the areas that need fine-tuning or you may end up rendering the earlier-thinned sections moot.

Though it may seem odd, various controllers may send differing amounts of information and some may insert far more values or less values than necessary. Experiment with your controller device to determine whether thinning is necessary or not for your mix.

Faders Flying Everywhere

Fader movement can be viewed on or off, the question becomes one of whether fader movement is distracting to the mix or too much information for a lesser video card to draw move-

The small marks nserted either manually or with a controlling device may be called nodes, handles, keyframes, grips, envelope points, and or rubber band markers by various applications. All of these names mean the same thing. Sony calls them envelope points.

👉 *Tip*

> If you need extreme control over complex mix sections, do a rough mix and get things as close to finished as possible, then turn off Thinning in the Options>Preferences> External Control and Automation dialog.

ment for. With a complex mix of more than 16 channels, viewing fader movements might be too big a load on a 4MB or 8 MB video card. Any 16 MB or larger VRAM video card should easily draw fader movements. If by chance your video card can't write the movements, visit the Options>Preferences> External Control and Automation dialog. In this dialog, uncheck the Animate Screen Faders during Playback. If you have a flying fader device such as the Mackie, faders will move on the device regardless of whether the screen is drawing the movement or not. This is a very sexy and impressive event for those not familiar with fader movement. Watching faders move, meters bouncing, and all functions doing what they do while the user is hands-off is quite exciting.

Another great reason to use a device like the Mackie for an external control surface is that metering can be viewed on the LCD screen of the Mackie Control. Sony has made this work in such a manner that you don't have to constantly look at the computer monitor while setting a mix up on the Mackie, as the meters are very accurate and laid out above each channel strip, making it easy to see, and familiar to audio engineers used to viewing metering on the console. The meters will show up as long as the Mackie is in I/O mode, found on the console view section.

Mixing Audio in Vegas

Mixing audio is a practice based entirely on personal preference, but some standards and techniques are used by most engineers and producers to achieve mixes that meet with industry expectations. Each person's ears are different; this is what makes one producer more popular for various kinds of music than another. Mutt Lange, a very well-known producer of heavy metal music and pop-rock, is one of the few to jump from one musical style to another. (Marrying country legend Shania Twain didn't hurt.) Peter Gabriel is renowned for his production of world-pop music, just as William Aura is known for his adult contemporary work. Alan Parsons, Tom Lord-Alge, Ross Collum, and Danial Langios are all unique and well-known producers/mix engineers. All of them credit their years working with the equipment and producers in the studios they cut their teeth in as third engineers, janitors, or receptionists. All of these producers got to where they are not only because of their inspired sense of what people want to hear and how to bring an artist's talents to the fore but also because they knew the basic principles and practices of mixing audio. Knowledge and a practiced ear are the two most important things to creating a great mix. Knowledge is easily found. Having a practiced ear can take years. The basic principles of understanding a mix are fairly simple; from there, it simply becomes a matter of expanding on experience.

Mixing Techniques

Setting up a mix is entirely dependent on the contents of the track, whether it's instrumentation, bed music with a voice over, Foley, sound design, or full-blown orchestra. Bass frequencies tend to be more centered in a mix than are high frequencies, where a right-to-left spread is more evidently heard. Bass frequencies below 250 Hz aren't really even directional but rather omni-directional. Higher frequencies are very directional, which is why bass drums and bass guitar/synthesizers are generally mixed to the center of a mix and higher frequency sounds are spaced throughout the right-to-left areas of a mix. An easier way to think of it is to look at a photo of a beautiful mountain vista. The mountains form the base of the image, and the eye is drawn to the bugling elk in the forefront, slightly off center. You notice the green trees and the stream or brook flowing through the picture. The primary subject of the picture is the elk in the foreground, but without the surrounding beauty, the elk looks rather stark. Creating a good mix is just like that: lots of individual elements that draw the ear to a primary element. Try to picture a mix visually with the score or performance in your mind's eye, which will help achieve the end goal.

> Fine-tune mixes by holding down the left mouse button and use the 2 or 8 key on the numeric keypad to fine-tune any envelope up or down. The 4 or 6 key moves a node forward or backward on the timeline. The amount of control is determined by the depth of track focus. With maximum zoom, superfine envelope increments are possible. The Quantize to Frames (F8) option might need to be disabled to have accurate access at maximum zoom.
>
> The same keyboard trim features affecting the video timeline are also found in the audio toolset. Use the 7 or 9 key on the numeric keypad to select an event edge; use the 1 or 3 key to edit longer or shorter by samples. The depth of track focus determines how fine the keyboard edits are made. Zooming in deep on a track causes up to sample-by-sample edits; zooming out on the track edits larger sections of audio. (See Chapter 3 for more information on keyboard editing.)

Some mixes are built from the bottom-end elements first, finishing with the primary element, and other mixes are built starting with the primary element and the other sounds are built around it.

For working with a dialog-based mix for film or video, this is a good way to start, getting the voice to a level that is comfortable. It should be loud, but never crossing the -3dB mark so that room exists for other elements to maintain their dynamic expression. Adding a compressor to the primary element is fairly standard practice. If the primary is a voice, start with light compression settings of 1.5:1, or 2:1, working with the threshold to suit the mix. Be cautious of squashing the sound too much, as this element is the most out front one of the mix.

Next, begin to place the foundation elements, such as static walla, traffic, or background noise. In a musical context, these elements would be the kick drum, bass guitar, or other bottom-end elements. If the bottom sound is muddy or tubby, remove some of the frequencies in the 300 Hz region. In a musical mix, add a little 1.5 KHz for some snap in the kick drum and bass guitar. In a mix for video with dialog, leave some of the upper frequencies out, perhaps even dampen them a bit, so as not to fight with the frequencies in the primary element/front voice. Use a compressor, starting with a basic setting of 3:1 or 4:1, and work with the settings from there to keep the mix

The term walla stems from the early days of radio, when extras were brought in for a radio or film show, and actors would say "walla-walla-walla" over and over, with just a few people saying the words out of sync with each other to create the sound of a murmuring crowd. No individual words were spoken at all. To this day, background dialog is called walla, but actors no longer use the fixed word format.

from becoming too dynamic in the low frequencies. Send all the bottom/foundation elements to one submix/bus, with an additional compressor if necessary on the bus.

Sound design comes into the mix next, with motion and depth filling the speakers with moving elements that can be musical or not. Either way, the sound should be a filling sound that underlies the other pieces of the mix. In a music-oriented mix, this is the rhythmic element. Try to avoid panning this sound hard right or left if possible. More of a 9 o'clock and 3 o'clock is the ticket, washed wide rather than being too loud, so as to take away focus from the aural subject. Guitars, synths, and background vocals all fit into this space too. Be cautious of wanting too much sparkle or bottom end in these elements and leave room for the primary sounds and foundation sounds. Use reverbs or delays to wash these sounds across the sonic canvas, rather than increasing the volume of an individual instrument. These sounds contribute a sense of color or timbre of the musical element. If everything were taken away except this element and the lead element, there would still be something worth listening to. If inconsistent sounds are in this element, try to bring them in and out gently rather than with surprise. Otherwise, they'll detract from the front elements.

Next placed are the special FX or signature sounds of a piece. In the musical context, this is the moving sounds of a synth that has a signature to mark the song, rather than a synth that is emulating a traditional keyboard. In a video context, these sounds are the cannon fire, bullets flying, spaceships, aircraft swoops, or other action sounds. These should be placed to move right to left or front to back in a surround mix. These are the exciting elements of a stereo or surround mix.

Remember, these tips are mere rudiments. From here, the mix can be tweaked according to the individual ear.

Compression

One might say that it is simply impossible to do a good digital mix without compression, yet compression is one of the most misunderstood parts of the mix and audio process. First, it's important to understand the difference between a compressor and a limiter.

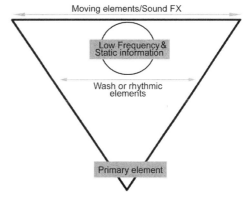

6.85   An overhead view of mix elements.

6.86   Audio before being limited.

6.87   Audio after being hard limited.

A limiter prevents audio from passing at a predetermined volume. Any audio that attempts to pass the preset level is squashed to fit the preset level. Limiters are generally not good for music or audio for video mixes but are more suited for situations in which not all elements of the media can be controlled.

There are hard limiters and soft limiters. The difference is how much of a dynamic the limiter might be set at before the hard limit point. In other words, a limiter might be preset to ensure that nothing greater than -3dB is allowed to pass, but the majority of the audio information is at -5dB with lots of dynamic that wants to go much louder than the -3dB allowable maximum. Using a setting that instructs the limiter to start reducing levels at -9dB allows some dynamic feel to remain in the audio track. Limiters often squeeze the high end and life out of a mix, making it dull and boring. Television commercials are often hard limited and compressed to give maximum volume (one of the annoying things about the overall volume of a television commercial).

The term soft limiter is really just drawing a comparison to a hard compressor. Most compressors also have limiting ability built in.

Compressors operate a little differently from a compressor limiter, being more elastic or malleable only in the way they control dynamics on release. A limiter is a compressor with a ratio of 10:1 or greater but usually with fewer adjustable attributes than a compressor. Compressors can make audio louder, while at the same time making sure that the dynamic range is reduced. Generally, a compressor is used to keep dynamics as accurate as possible, while at the same time preventing audio from crossing a chosen threshold. This feature makes it easier to get an event/signal louder in a mix, while still maintaining control over the apparent signal.

For example, compression might be required for a singer or voice-over artist in the studio who moves toward and back from the microphone. Recorded levels are not consistent. Perhaps the same vocal artist has very quiet to very loud passages in their speech. A compressor evens out the differences between the two sections.

A compressor is used by guitar players and bass players to maitai th sutai ofa plucked or strummed note/chord. A compressor smoothes down the attack on the strings and then opens up/releases gradually by allowing the note/chordto ppear as though it is going longer than it would have otherwise been heard.

6.88   Threshold set at -30dB, with variable compression ratios: 2:1, 5:1, 10:1. Notice the compression curve at the different settings.

6.89 Mastering level compression at 2:1, with threshold at -8dB allows the signal to be louder overall because of the reduced dynamic range.

6.90 Compression applied at 2:1, with threshold at -24dB. Beginning the attack earlier in the signal with a lower threshold makes a huge difference in the behavior of the compressor.

Here's how a compressor works. Comprehending the ratio, threshold, attack, and release are the most important pieces to understanding compression.

6.91 Attack, threshold, and release.

Vocals generally won't sound right with compression of greater than 6:1. All dynamics of the voice will be squashed to the point of having no performance or nuance left in the audio.

On the DVD included in this book are five demonstrations of audio and audio for video. Listen to the differences in how the audio cuts through on the repaired sections.

Sony provides a multiband dynamics processor in their plug-in arsenal. This multiband tool is a combination of four compressors with frequency-dependent settings. Rather than compressing an overall instrument or mix, individual facets of the audio can be affected while leaving other portions alone. For example, a snare drum might be exactly the sound you want but is too loud at one particular frequency or range of frequencies. The multiband dynamics plug-in, or EQ-based compressor, gives the ability to compress only the offending frequency or range of frequencies without affecting the rest of the audio information.

De-Essing

A component of both spoken and sung word is sibilance. Sibilance is the hissing sound made when speaking or singing s or sh. Difficult to repair, this issue, known as essing, creates distortion or apparent distortion on cheap speakers and high-end systems alike, regardless of how much compression or EQ are applied. In fact, EQ is the last resort to repair essing, and compressors are only one step ahead of EQ when it comes to de-essing sound. A de-esser is just a band-specific compressor.

When sibilance from s's get in the way of the mix, open up the Sony Multiband Dynamic plug-in and start with the De-Ess preset. Reset the attack time to .5 milliseconds. Reset the decay time to 40 or 50 m. or a male voice, set the frequency center to 5 KHz, and for female vocals, set the frequency center to 6.5. True sibilance is usually centered between 8 and 10 KHz. Both of these settings are starting points. It might be that further adjustment is required.

6.92 Saving the De-Ess preset setting preserves it for another session, or other de-essing in the same project.

The compression ratio should be set at 30:1 to start with, and the threshold set at -30dB. Now start a loop over a section where sibilance is present and adjust the multiband settings as the loop is heard. Be cautious of applying too much of a ratio; a singer or voice-over can quickly gain a lisp if it's set too high. Sometimes as little as 6:1 is enough. Experiment with raising the threshold and reducing the ratio until the desired fix is found. Save this setting as a preset by typing a preset name in the preset box and pressing the icon that looks like a floppy disk. This preset is now part of your toolbox.

Using Equalization

Equalizers, also known as EQ, are one of the most oft turned-to tools in the plug-in arsenal. EQs are used to cut frequencies of fat sounds that occupy space in the audio spectrum that other sounds can also occupy, creating confusion about what the ear is hearing. EQ is also used to correct problems with a tracking room, poor frequency balance in a microphone, or sometimes simply to enhance a performance or characteristic of an audio event. While invented initially to flatten sound over the telephone, today's EQs are predominantly used to unflatten sound, and so in jest, some engineers call these tools un-equalizers.

The use of an EQ must be judicious. Too much boost of any frequency can cause overload of the outputs, can cause a compressor to work harder than it needs to because of excess volume boost, or can even create distortion in the harmonics related to a sound.

EQs typically come in two formats: graphic and parametric.

6.93 Graphic equalizers set at octaves.

6.94 The Timeworks Parametric EQ resembles a Graphic EQ. However, frequencies can be selected, and the bandwidth or Q of the frequencies can be defined.

With graphic EQs, frequencies are preset, and only the gain of specific frequencies can be increased or reduced. It is found in octave, half octave, and one-third octave in most instances. An octave is determined by a frequency multiplied by two. The octave of 125 Hz is 250 Hz, the ex ocav being 500 Hz, and so forth. The half-octave of 125 Hz is 187.5 Hz, and the one-third octave of 125 Hz is approximately 160 Hz. Frequency centers are International Standards Organization (ISO).

Vegas has four different graphic EQs available as plug-ins.

6.95 The Q is fairly wide, affecting frequencies on either side of its center.

6.96 The Q is very narrow, affecting only the immediate frequency selected.

With parametric EQs, users can select a specific frequency center, select the amount of bandwidth that the frequency has control over, and control the gain or reduction of that same frequency band. Usually parametric EQs allow several frequencies to be specified and controlled.

A derivative of both graphic and parametric EQs, paragraphic EQs are mixed mode equalizers that generally have fixed frequencies for the bottom and top frequency spectrums, and midrange frequencies that can be shifted. This type is rarely seen in software-only forms.

Tight Q is useful for cutting out a pecific frequency that can be a hum, distortion, or simply a problem frequency. Tight Q is also valuable for enhancing specific frequencies, such as boosting presence in a vocal to give an airy quality in order to obtain the pop vocal sound that is popular today.

 Tip

On the DVD, open the Equalization Demonstration project. The file contains the same event in duplicate. The first version is the broadcast version; the second has presence and compression added to it using a parametric EQ with a boost at 4.1 KHz. Notice the difference between the two. Either of these two mixes is acceptable for final output, but a difference exists in how the two are perceived.

Using Reverb

Reverb can be used for any kind of audio mix, whether for video or audio, spoken word or music. It is also one of the most overused effects in the palette of tools available. Reverb is used to artificially reproduce various room environments. In the past, music had to be recorded in large chambers or in rooms with large reflective areas. The reverb created in such large rooms helped blend sounds together, creating a cohesive yet individual expression of instruments or vocal authority. Ever notice how the voice of God in film or recording always is accompanied by a large reverb? As technology and creativity grew in the music industry, reverberation was emulated in tubes, springs, complex room systems, eventually electronics, and now in software. Reverb can express a vastness and spatial distance or be part of an intimate communication, made unique by how certain consonants, syllables, or instrumental inflections sound within a reverberant sound. Every environment common to the world has a sound. What makes up this sound is the reflections within that environment. Singing in the shower makes even a poor voice sound rich, while that same voice, singing in a closet sounds dull and lifeless. The shower is full of hard surfaces, while the closet is full of soft surfaces. The hard surfaces effectively create a doubled voice sound that the ear hears immediately, where the soft surfaces absorb nearly all sounds, preventing almost all reflections and making the sound harder to hear. Large rooms with reflective surfaces, such as cathedrals, auditoriums, and long hallways, not only reflect the sound, but reflect it repeatedly, expanding and elongating sound, while all the while softening the sound, giving an illusion of infinity.

Somewhere between the sound of a closet andcathedral, there are reverb settings useful to nearly every situation. Vegas has lots of great reverbs built in, and incredible software reverbs are available from several third-party manufacturers, such as PSP Audio software, WAVES, iZotope, Anwida, and more.

 Tip
Several reverbs are included on the DVD with this book, including freeware from PSP Audio software.

Overusing or overly loud reverb can wash over too much of the audio spectrum, making audio sound muddy and without clarity. Use carefully.

Consider using reverb in very short, quiet settings for interviews that might be too dry from being in a very tight, quiet room or that might have some ambient noise that can't be washed with other sounds or beds. Reverb is also useful for making a mono audio signal appear to be stereo by creating artificial reflections that reach the ear at different times. Feed a mono voice or instrument into a bus or FX send that is only the reverb and then route back to the master output. Make sure the reverb is fairly short and has very little pre-delay. Panning the reverb/ sending the reverb to the same location as the dry sound also is a great technique for keeping the sound large, but located. Pan the original signal to where it sounds right in the mix before adding reverb. Use an FX send to route the dry sound to the reverb. Pan the reverb to the same space. This technique works well with vocals mixed with a music bed, as well as with single instrument sounds, such as guitars, snare drums, keyboards, and other single-point source instruments.

Be cautious about reverb sounds that are too bright. While they usually warm up a voice, bright reverbs also tend to elaborate sibilance and can easily create distortion in the high end. Use a de-esser or EQ before the reverb if this problem occurs.

When mixing audio, sometimes a need arises to lower the audio volume quickly, whether for a phone call or visitor or because it's too loud for a conversation. Vegas provides a Dim button that dims audio by 20dB. This option ensures immediate volume reduction without changing the audio output level sliders and without affecting render output. The Dim button is found just above the Master Volume slider or can be enabled by pressing Ctrl+Shift+F12. Of course, with Vegas's keymapping feature, you can map the Dim button to be any key setting you'd prefer.

Mixing for 5.1 Surround Sound

Surround sound mixing brings an entirely different perspective in prepping and setting up a mix. Rather than being concerned with just two speakers in a stereo field, there are now six speakers, all individually controlled. The term 5.1 is derived from there being a right/left speaker for the front and rear, a center channel, and a subwoofer (the .1 of 5.1). Each speaker has its own input, and setting the mix for each speaker can quickly become a challenge, as the stereo field all of a sudden becomes small. Moreover, having extra sound points excites most any engineer who hasn't had experience in the surround realm, and it's very easy to create an over-the-top mix, which while sounding exciting in the control room, loses its excitement in the listening environment. Sometimes mixes don't even make sense to the ear when taken in the context of a non-visual setting. In short, it's easy to over-emphasize the rear channel speakers simply out of the novelty of having them.

Vegas has the ability to do 5.1 channel surround mixing. This type is the standard for most DVDs, and many music recordings are moving into the realm of 5.1 surround. The Eagle's Hell Freezes Over CD was one of the first immersed-experience CDs on the market and is an excellent example of a 5.1 surround sound audio recording.

The room must be set up correctly for mixing in 5.1 surround. Having a 5.1 sound system from the local office supply and a 5.1 surround card is barely going to suffice and will not suffice at all if the room is not set up correctly.

6.97 Wiring the surround system properly is important. Use high-quality cables to connect speakers to a sound card.

Multi-channel sound card

Rear left

Left

Center

Right

Sub woofer/LFE

Rear Right

6.98 Select the surround setting to create buses for the surround mix.

On the DVD contained in this book is a test clip, which allows audio to be tested on the output of all speakers in the room. It's critical that they all be equal in volume to achieve a balanced mix. Use these tones to test the output.

Do this process by placing the tone as an event on the timeline of Vegas and then open the FILE | PROPERTIES dialog. Select the Audio tab, and, in the Master Bus Mode dropdown list, select 5.1 surround.

This process automatically inserts buses in the Mixer docking window to allow for mixing levels to front, rear, and center speakers, plus a low frequency enclosure (LFE) control. It also adds a surround panner to each audio track on the timeline.

Set levels on the soundcard's mixer at 0dB to ensure that Vegas is the only mixing device being used to control levels. Otherwise, it's possible that rendered files will not be accurate to what is being heard. Having unequal sound card mixer settings guarantees an unbalanced mix.

6.99 Some soundcard mixer control levels outside of Vegas. Check this carefully for accuracy in the mix.

This panner control is how Vegas maneuvers audio around the audio space. Notice that five speakers are in the panner. Clicking the LFE button in the upper-right corner of the Panner control sends the channel only to the LFE output.

Audio is panned from front to rear and right to left using keyframes. Vegas uses keyframes in the audio tool slightly differently from how it uses keyframes in the video tools. Automatic mixing makes this very effective and powerful; rather than using hardware to set up the mix, audio positioning can be exactly keyframed and edited at any point in the mix, with Vegas graphically showing the placement of audio at any point.

After opening the surround panner, right-click the Track Control pane associated iththe open surround panner. Select Insert/Remove Envelope (Shift+P) from the menu and then Surround Pan Keyframes from the submenu. This process allows for keyframes to be placed on the timeline, instructing audio to pan to wherever you wish it to be, at any point on the timeline.

6.100 Double-clicking the surround panner on the Track Control pane splits it off as a movable window, making panning easier to define.

Normal Surround Control   Film Mode Surround   Low Frequency channel

6.101 These are the three surround pan modes in Vegas. Right clicking the first/default pan mode allows selection of Film Style or LFE control, shown to the right. Selecting the LFE button sends audio only to the LFE channel output.

With the surround panner open, follow these steps to move audio in the listening space:

1. Place the cursor where movement should occur or should finish, if the location is different from the default front-center position.

2. Move the orange dot found in the Surround Panning box to where the audio should be at that moment. Audio will slowly pan to this point from where it originated at the first keyframe. Notice that the reference position is followed by small dots, indicating how the audio will move.

3. Place the cursor on the next time point to which audio should be moved.

4. Move the reference position in the surround panner to the desired point.

5. Repeat until all panning is complete for the project on that track. Keyframes/audio position can be edited later.

When panning stereo signals, moving right to left can create problems when audio becomes louder on one side than on the other side when audio is off balance during a pan. Add Channels, the default setting, can easily create distortion. The Constant Power setting moves audio around the audio spectrum at equal volume with no change in volume at any point. Notice that Vegas displays the relative volume for each channel in the Surround Panner tool. Experiment with various settings during panning operation if audio seems to jump in volume during a pan.

Vegas has separate control of the center channel per track, rather than assigning it to a bus as some 5.1 systems do.

Right-clicking keyframes in the Surround Pan timeline opens a menu, which shows choices for the velocity attributes of how the keyframe will move sound. Hold freezes audio until the next keyframe. Smooth gently speeds up as it leaves the keyframe and slows down as it approaches the next keyframe. Fast ramps the audio quickly to its next keyframe. Slow ramps the audio to the next keyframe fairly slowly. Linear provides a straight movement. This is the default keyframe setting in Vegas. While not always easy to see, the various keyframe settings draw the audio path differently in the Surround Panner window.

6.102 Right-clicking the surround panner offers choices regarding the audio power at a specific point in the pan.

6.103, 6.104 Center channel is at OdB by default. Notice how the sound field draws to the rear as volume from the center speaker increases.

The center channel is at zero volume by default. As the volume is increased in the Surround Panner window, however, notice that the sound grid draws backward, as the power/volume increases in the center channel.

Vegas has surround modes that may be accessed by right-clicking the surround panner and choosing Film from the submenu that appears. The film panner mode more closely simulates the theatre environment for more accurate mixing of surround. Notice that the Center channel is now defaulting to 0dB rather than the _inf position that it defaulted to in Vegas 4. This will have an impact on currently existing projects, so monitor carefully, as your monitoring environment may not have changed, but you may not have had an accurate mix.

6.105 Film Panning more closely resembles a theater sound system, and you may find it easier to mix in this mode.

When using motion in the center channel, experiment with the Smoothness setting. If dialog or center audio is fairly transient in nature, such as intense dialog, fast-attack guitar playing, or other sharp sounds, and the smoothness is set too high, the audio will sound very slow moving from center channel to the left or right. If set too low, audio will appear to jerk into other speaker fields. This issue varies with the listening environment, which again demonstrates the necessity of having a good monitoring system.

The room should be set up with equal distances between audio speakers (audio monitors), and it should also be damped and have reflective surfaces minimized. Monitors should be equidistant to the listening space, measured from where you'll be sitting.

Try to set the room up similarly to a home listening environment, as this environment is how most recordings will be heard.

It is possible to mix through a typical home stereo system, if the receiver allows for separate audio channel inputs. Vegas does not send a decoded AC3 stream, so you'll need to have connections that allow for line input. Many receivers/amplifiers today do. Run cable from each output on the sound card to the inputs on the receiver back. Using high-quality cable is critical if radio frequencies (RFs) and other noise in the room is to be avoided. Mix in the room, perhaps referencing a favorite or similar DVD.

Additionally, many professional sound cards have TOSLINK outputs/optical outputs that can feed consumer receiver/amplifiers for monitoring over home theater systems. This process is not advised, as home theater systems are anything but flat, and it is very difficult to create a quality mix on anything but reasonably flat speakers.

The primary elements of a surround mix are:

- Dialog
- Music
- Sound design
- Effects

6.106 Monitors should be equidistant to the listening space, measured from the listening position.

Dialog is obviously the most important consideration in most situations. Typically, it is in the center channel and should receive attention first. When setting up the mix, find the peak point of the dialog and then lower the dialog by -6dB relative to the peak. This process allows for headroom/increase in the dialog channel, as it usually is needed after the final mix is prepared. If the peak is lower than -3dB, consider normalizing that event or perhaps raising the level at the track.

Conversational dialog or direct dialog belongs in the center channel in most instances. Working with the center channel presents some challenges, particularly in music mixes. If sound isn't properly handled in the center channel, listeners on a stereo system or a four-channel system missing the center speaker will hear strange artifacts in sounds mixed for the center channel. Adding a slight reverb to the center channel is always good practice, even if it's merely a small room bounce with no pre-delay. Walla or background conversation goes in the left/right or rear left/right, so it won't be brought into the mix at this point.

The next element is music in most instances. Music typically is placed in the front right/left monitors, with some elements moving to the rear speakers, depending on the point of view or movement of the camera, the sound design, or moving dialog.

This point is where the actual mixing starts. Bring the music up to the level that it should be, monitor at a comfortable level. Listening too quietly makes the mix out of balance in both levels and equalization. Listening too loudly means your ears fatigue fairly quickly. Low-quality speakers also tire the ear, so use the best monitors that you can afford.

Active monitors are typically cleaner, flatter, and easier to work with in a surround environment.

Begin bringing in any sound design underneath the music, leaving the dialog channels alone for the time being. Mix the music and the sound design, working the sound design to the rear channels. Be cautious of too much movement in the rear channels as it quickly becomes distracting to the ear.

As an example of a mix, we'll take a city-scape shot with a dialog in the foreground and examine some of the aural potential, as shown:

- Center speaker—contains dialog between two people. Low frequencies rolled off/high passed from 120 Hz and above.

- Left/right front speakers—contain traffic, walla, moving audio, bed music, and sound design. Low frequencies rolled off/low passed from 120 Hz and above.

- Left/right rear speakers—20/30 percent sound design, 10/20 percent bed music, traffic noise panning from front at camera movement or when dialog permits. Motion front to back related to transitions in video. Music moves to rear speakers during dialog, as scene elements require.

- Subwoofer/LFE—contains dialog elements, bed music elements, and sound design. High passed at 120 Hz by default in Vegas' surround setup and as ISO. Although this is a standard, experience suggests that a high-pass filter, rolled off at 24dB per octave, starting at 80 Hz, be inserted in the LFE channel.

Be cautious of moving audio into rear speakers during dialog.

In this scenario, when dialog is the focus but music is required along with traffic and walla, move the music to the rear before moving traffic and walla to the rear. Cut midrange in walla and traffic to make room for dialog. With dialog taking place, the cut frequencies are not noticeable unless the mid-cuts are too drastic.

Use smooth keyframes for sound design and music that is moving to the rear. Don't be afraid to use hard keyframing/abrupt shifts in audio placement, based on hard cut editing. Smooth visual transitions call for smooth aural transitioning. Hard visual transitions can use either hard aural transitions or smooth transitions, based on what is happening on-screen.

Overall, do not tread on the dialog mix. As keyframes start to fly bed/design/FX audio right to left or front to rear, it's easy for the dialog to get lost. This point is when the extra 6dB of headroom left in the early stages of the mix are invaluable. If you find that 6dB isn't enough, something is not correct in the other audio mixes.

View buses as tracks in Vegas. Doing so provides automated mixing of the buses, offers easier surround control, and is visually more comprehensive to follow. Assign dialog, bed music, FX, and sound design to separate buses. If a single track doesn't provide enough control of a sound/series of events, duplicate a track and keep the volume out of the track until it's called for in two aural locations. At that point, raise the duplicate track volume assigned to the correct bus.

When planning a project that will include a surround mix, camera shots can be a consideration as well. Panning the lens toward and away from a scene makes an easy transition both visually and aurally. Dollying into a scene makes a wonderful rear-to-front transition. Panning from the bottom of a scene with upward motion or panning down from above a scene into the subject makes wonderful visual transitions that sound readily enhances.

Do not remove all low end from the right/left/center/rear mixes. If there is no bass in these mixes, listeners in a collapsed environment (stereo only) will hear no low end. Most everything in the mix goes into the LFE mix anyway, but if there are exceptionally important low frequency elements, such as gunfire, cannons, and extremely low end in sound design, it's advisable to duplicate those tracks, roll th lo end out of one copy of the tracks, and roll the high end off of the other copy. Send the copy that has high end removed to the LFE channel to supplement the bottom, while not distorting the other surround speakers and ensuring that audio collapses properly in a stereo listening situation.

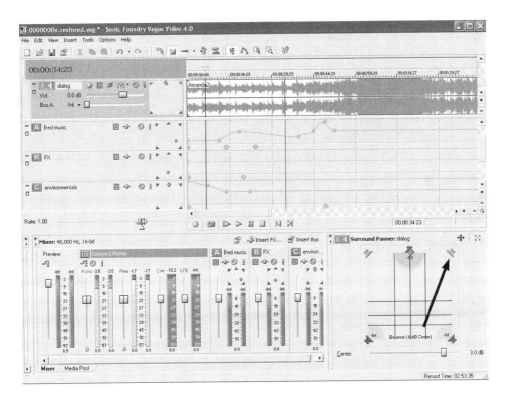

6.106 Viewing buses as tracks offers tremendous control. Notice each bus in the mixer and that the left/right speakers are disabled in the dialog bus.

Surrounded by FX: Surround Plugins

Yet another feature of Vegas is to bring specific plug-ins to the surround-sound toolset. Vegas 4 provided surround-sound tools to the desktop editor, but effects can only be placed on the individual tracks and buses that make up the surround project, thus making a controlled mix a challenge. Vegas 5 not only provided the ability to place FX on the master output but also provides customized plug-ins specifically for a 5.1 mix.

Digital audio requires very tight control of outputs. Sony now offers the Wave Hammer tool first made popular in Sound Forge, in a 5.1 surround-sound formatted tool. This 5.1 plug-in allows users to control the output levels on all buses in the surround environment, preventing distortion on any output, and making it easier for editors to create a robust yet clean, surround audio signal. The Wave Hammer plug-in may be enabled or disabled per channel of audio by checking or unchecking the check box found in the Routing tab of the 5.1 Wave Hammer.

There are three components to the Wave Hammer 5.1 plug-in tool.

First is a compressor. The compressor can be used to smooth out dynamics and add power to the overall mix. Used improperly, it can also create a somewhat warm distortion in the signal, but this is rarely desired in a surround mix. Wave Hammer's presets are set up quite well for most video-mix situations, but you may want to experiment with the settings to find what works best for you. Refer to Chapter 3 and Chapter 8 to learn more about using dynamics processing in Vegas and video applications. Particularly in a surround mix, be sure to keep the threshold set fairly high and the overall compression levels set low. Using a fair amount of compression starting at low trigger levels will nearly always create distortion. Particu-

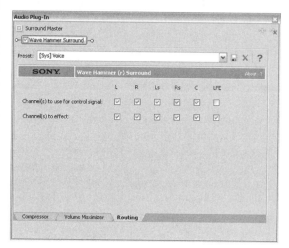

6.107 Enable/disable the Wave Hammer on individual surround channels by checking or unchecking these boxes.

larly for video-output mixes, leave the Auto Compensate for Output levels check box unchecked. This will nearly always result in distorted signals that will be obvious with dialog.

Wave Hammer now allows for either peaks or RMS levels to be scanned for processing. Either scanning method works fine, but be aware that setting this to RMS may allow fast transients such as gunshots or other fast and hard sounds to escape processing, creating distortion that you may not be able to easily hear but that clip beyond the output level of zero dBfs.

If very light compression is used, it's a good idea to turn on "Longer Look Ahead" for best results. This allows the plug-in to scan audio farther ahead in the file for information, usually creating a smoother attack when slow attack times are used. However, if a large transient is encountered it can sometimes create a fadeout or breathing or pumping effect just before the transient, so monitor transients carefully if the longer look-ahead is used.

Next is the Volume Maximizer, found in the second tab of the Wave Hammer plugin. This could easily be one of the most important plug-in tools for any broadcast-destined audio for video mix. The Volume Maximizer works exactly as its name implies. It maximizes volume of an audio track or bus without creating clipping on output. When using the Volume Maximizer, any levels that go beyond the threshold are limited to whatever level the threshold is set to. Audio not crossing the threshold is managed and increased in overall level. Since digital audio does not have the flexibility for going beyond zero in the same manner analog does, this is a terrific means of maintaining maximum output while assuring that at no point will audio exceed the output level. More importantly, using the Wave Hammer tool provides the ability to have a house-standard level of output as part of a final render process. If files are destined for AC3 output, this also assures that the AC3 encoder receives maximum information for the best possible encode. I recommend using the Wave Hammer set to the "Master for 16 bit" preset on virtually all audio for video mixes. In the absence of my favorite WAVES Ultramaximizer plugin, this is the next best thing, and is the only plug-in available for a 5.1 surround output.

The Routing tab is next in line on the Wave Hammer plugin. While this seems to be a simple row of check boxes, it's much more than it appears to be. For example, a setting that instructs the Wave Hammer to begin compression on the surround speakers when the center/dialog channel reaches a specific point might save an otherwise muddy or loud mix. Any one of the 5.1 output channels may be used to determine the point that other channels will be ducked or compressed.

Also available as a 5.1 surround plug-in are the Track EQ and Dither tools. EQ is important as it allows editors to fine-tune the EQ of individual surround buses as opposed to inserting EQs on the individual tracks or mix buses. This not only saves processor power but also prevents EQ settings that may conflict with each other. Track EQ does not provide a specific EQ for each bus, but rather provides a master EQ that affects all buses. You may enable or disable the track EQ from affecting a specific bus or buses.

Use the Track EQ settings to create a tighter mix signal in your surround, repair muddy or weak areas, or to balance the overall signal. Automation may be applied to Track EQ found on the surround bus, including the enabling and disabling of the EQ on specific buses. Therefore, if you have an EQ setting in place that should only affect a specific portion of a mix on a specific bus, you may enable the EQ on that bus only via automation. The 5.1 EQ is the only automated 5.1 effect that Vegas has available.

6.108 Track EQ's can be automated while in 5.1 format in Vegas. By selecting or deselecting these check boxes, individual buses may or may not be affected by EQ settings.

Generally you'll want to have the EQ precede the Wave Hammer in a final output or mix. Otherwise, the Wave Hammer will not have the equalized signal information and won't be able to react appropriately. This could easily lead to distortion as well, if the Volume Maximizer is used prior to the EQ and the EQ is being used to boost any frequencies in the audio signal.

Dithering is the process of adding noise to an audio signal to mask or hide quantization noise. With surround, this is particularly useful on mixes that contain a lot of high-frequency information to keep the information clean in fadeouts. See the Dithering guide on the DVD found in this book for more information. In most instances, however, you'll be using a Rectangular or Triangular dithering shape.

Mixing Surround or DVD Audio

Musical DVD is an entirely new soundstage with surround sound, offering musicians, producers, and engineers entirely new methods of presenting their art. The quality of digital versatile disc-audio (DVDA) finally goes past the consumer-hype words of "CD quality." CDs are 16 bit/44.1 KHz, while DVDA is 24 bit/48 KHz.

Mixing audio-only for surround presents new opportunities, while also presenting new challenges. Caution must be taken with placement, EQ, and sonic spacing in order to keep the mix cohesive and credible. One major advantage of surround is that it requires far less compression as currently called for in a stereo-only environment.

In a recording of a vocal-based group, the lead vocal takes center space. It's very important, however, that the lead vocal not be assigned exclusively to the center channel, or collapsed listening environments (stereo-only) will hear artifacts and ghosting of the vocal. Using a slight reverb on the vocal helps dilute this phenomenon, if the reverb is added to the right/left mixes.

Percussion, acoustic guitars, and ethnic instruments all share the listening space of left/center/right/center quite well, which opens up more frequency space for vocals or lead instruments.

Picturing the soundstage as it would appear to a concert-goer helps build the mix. Drawing the mix in advance can't hurt and often provides a great visual reference for an engineer.

Consider pairing left/center, and right center, rather than thinking of left/right as separate elements. Treat the rear speakers predominantly as assignments of the reverbs, delays, and audience responses. Audience members don't often sit in the middle of a stage, so placing much musical information in the rear speakers is not often a good practice. Placing the audience, however, where a lead vocalist might stand is a wonderful place to be. Save the rear surrounds for effects and aural surprises.

Mix the bass guitar/bass synth to all speakers, without regard for the LFE enclosure. If more low-end punch is needed, bus the bass and any other low-frequency information to a separate output, feeding the LFE. While the bass channel in a surround system has 12dB more headroom than the remainder of a surround system, few consumer-grade subwoofers are able to handle the extreme volumes of low end, so be mindful of your listening audience. Save the LFE for exceptional low end, such as the five-string bass or synthesizer that really needs the punch. Kick drums should be sent to the LFE with caution.

Feed reverb returns to the rear speakers, along with any vocal or instrumental effects. Sending the vocal to two reverbs or delays with similar settings allows for separate control to front and rear speakers, giving listeners a more intimate seat in the listening experience.

Use the rear channels for any audience information, such as applause and walla. Don't forget to feed a little to the front speakers as well, or stereo-only listeners will hear odd anomalies at the end of songs in a live environment. Panning reverbs and delays to the rear as part of an effect makes the rear speakers become part of the art of the mix. Keeping the rear speakers at full volume, full of a surround element can quickly dilute the value of a surround mix. Use the rear speakers as a paintbrush, not as a canvas.

Always check a surround mix in a stereo-only environment as well to ensure that it is collapsing correctly. Headphones are great for checking this out. (Remember never to mix in headphones.)

Blue Man Group's self-titled CD, the sound track to the movie *A.I. Artificial Intelligence*, the Eagle's *Hell Freezes Over* Tour, or Jon Anderson's *Deseo* CD are all excellent examples of surround sound in non-visual settings.

Surround sound is part of the future, and eventually nearly every facet of video and audio production will call for it. Artists like surround productions because they are harder to pirate. Consumers enjoy 5.1 because it's a sweeter entertainment experience. Radio stations are starting to broadcast in surround, and surround systems are becoming fairly common in the car as well. All in all, the industry has many motives for moving in this direction. Engineers with surround chops will find their talents more and more in demand.

I'm All Mixed . . . Down! Downmixing in Vegas

Mixes on DVDs are often 5.1 these days, yet many viewers of DVDs don't own speaker systems or receivers capable of playing 5.1 surround sound. Furthermore, some viewers only have mono televisions. Most systems have a feature in them that allows for audio to be downmixed so that the viewer is capable of watching the show even though it's not being heard in the original mixed format of 5.1 or stereo. However, whether the mix is downmixed correctly is the responsibility of the editor and engineer. No playback system can repair a bad mix when the six channels are collapsed to be heard over stereo speakers or even a mono speaker. Even the small DVD players that are used for flying or automobile viewing can't accurately play back 5.1 mixes that are not correctly assembled.

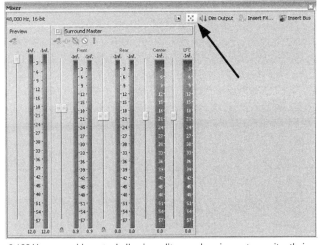

6.109 Vegas provides a tool allowing editors and engineers to monitor their mixes for all playback situations: mono, stereo, or 5.1.

Downmixing is not an arbitrary process; it is controlled by information embedded in a metadata stream contained in the AC-3 file. This metadata is present in all AC-3 bitstreams. For example, the dialog channel sets the normal information for the stream. This is what tells the program how loudly it should be played by way of the information being received by the Dolby Decoder in the system. In a downmix to stereo or mono, this information is combined and modulated to allow it to be heard on a standard stereo or mono system.

Needless to say, if the mix isn't correct, or if there are parameters out of whack in the 5.1 mix, the downmix at the viewer's end will also be strange and could mask dialog, lose bottom end entirely, or create an overburden of bottom end. Other information may be either lost or overbearing, depending on the way the mix was managed in the authoring stages.

In order to allow Vegas users to combat this issue or at the least address it, Vegas provides a DownMix button that allows users to hear what their mixes sound like in stereo or mono and compensate for those scenarios during their 5.1 mix session. Users of earlier versions of Vegas will need to convert their mixes to mono or stereo by changing the project properties, but this won't provide the same sort of information.

To use the DownMix feature, click the DownMix button, found on the Master bus in Vegas.

6.110 Select the AC-3 format in the FILE | RENDER AS dialog, which has a stereo or 5.1 option.

Encoding Audio to AC-3

Encoding audio to AC-3 is included in Vegas+DVD. AC-3 is a compressed audio format that allows audio for DVD or DVDA. DVDA typically doesn't use AC-3; it uses meridian lossless packing (MLP). The whole point of the separate format is to allow ultra-high quality audio to be compressed to fit six channels of information onto a DVD for video or audio. This process allows for greater bit rates of video on a DVD and allows for higher sampling rates for audio on a DVDA. AC-3 stands for Audio Coding—Third Generation. AC-3 is licensed from Dolby and follows their specifications. Sony became one of the first licensees in the PC environment with their Soft Encode product in 1996.

After a mix is finished in Vegas, it's a simple matter to select the AC-3 encoding option in the FILE | RENDER AS dialog. Audio is output that is then imported to a DVD authoring application. If you are working with DVD Architect (available only in the Vegas Professional package), AC-3 becomes a selection in the final creation of the DVD or an be imported as a separate stream. Vegas does not allow the monitoring of AC-3 files, so be certain that the mix is correct before encoding.

Creating and distributing an AC-3 file technically requires any packaging to contain the Dolby Digital trademark. For more information, visit www.dolby.com.

6.111 Dolby and the double-D symbol are registered trademarks of Dolby Laboratories.

*Tip*_____

When rendering audio to AC3, consider trying setting the dialog normalization level at -31, and setting the Pre-pro-cessing Line and RF modes to None. This will often more closely approximate what's being heard from the Vegas 6 timeline. Sometimes encoding audio from uncompressed files to AC3 doesnÅft have quite the robust sound once encoded, so experiment with audio files to see what most closely approximates what is coming off the timeline.

How Come the Audio Cats Get All the Cool Stuff?

Actually, they don't. With mapping, all audio features can also be made to apply to video. Muting tracks, fadeouts, compositing envelopes, and transition modes may be automated using a controlling device. Control of playback and rewinding can be controlled with a Mackie or other controlling device. I suspect with this kind of control, it won't be long til we start seeing A/B roll devices for video editors to have external control with. Fade to Color and Compositing Envelopes come to mind as two of the most common uses for automation in video editing. This is an exciting new paradigm and possibility for video, even to the point of copying audio movements and tracks and applying those envelopes to a video track. In Vegas, the following parameters may be automated and controlled with an external surface controller:

- Video envelopes and compositing envelopes
- Video bus track envelopes
- Track FX parameters
- Parent overlay modes
- Track level mask generators
- Track motion keyframes

Thinning will apply to video envelopes as well. They may be thinned after the automation input, with as much or little control as necessary. Automation is accomplished on video tracks the same way as audio tracks are managed. Click on the Automation icon found on the video track header to determine how you want the automation to work. This will set up the automation to work the way you'd like it to function. For those audio folks that have a Mackie Universal Control or other MIDI controller connected to Vegas, try doing automated camera/composite fades just as you would do with a live switcher. This is a fabulous way to automate shots between camera scenes on the Vegas timeline.

6.112 Pressing the automation icon will give video editors an entirely new toolset for working with video. You might sur-prise yourself how much you may be inspired by using these tools to create composites. Experiment with a controller and see what it does for your creativity.

Compositing in Vegas

What Is Compositing?

Compositing is the combination or interaction of two or more graphic or video images to create a single finished image. Compositing can be as simple as laying a title onto a visual image or as complex as combining hundreds of photographs, video, and animated elements to create complex images.

Compositing in its most complex forms is absolutely an art; there are compositing artists all over Hollywood, Austin, New York, Sydney, and other major cities who do nothing but create complex imagery for major networks, film, and corporate media departments. The fantastic imagery seen on ESPN, CNN, and in most major motion pictures is the result of these artists' work. It is most likely that not one major motion picture has been released in the past few years that didn't contain significant compositing, whether it's titling, green/bluescreen work, or overlaid imagery. *The Matrix* is an amazing example of how greenscreen work is brought to the big screen through the creative use of composited images, as is the *Lord of the Rings* and even the heralded Titanic. Many of the full ship images in Titanic were composited together, including animations of people walking, driving, and loading the ship. Most of the scenes including fish are composited and animated. So in short, compositing is very much about eye candy and illusion.

Basic Compositing

Compositing in its most basic form is titles laid over images. Vegas has a fairly powerful titling toolset, capable of creating all but the most complex of titles.

To insert a title over an image, first place a visual event on the timeline. Right-click the Track Control pane and select Insert Video Track or select INSERT | VIDEO TRACK.

In the new video track, right-click the timeline and choose Insert Text Media from the menu.

The Title tool opens with the Edit tab displayed, showing the words Sample Text inside. This area is where the words found in the title are inserted. Text size, font, and attributes, such as bold, italic, and justification are also selected here. These attributes and the Edit window work just like a word processor.

7.1 Right-click brings up this menu, then choose Insert Text Media to insert a title.

7.2   The Title tool with the Edit tab displayed.

Get your title to exact length the first time. Create a time selection in the project that is the desired length of the title. In the track where you'd like the title to live, right click and choose "Insert Text Media." A title dialog will open up, set to the length of the selected area. This will override the default title lengths in the Options|Preferences|Editing dialog.

The frame size can be selected at the top of the titling tool. In Vegas, generated media always defaults to 720 × 480, (non-square pixels) but appears correct as to frame size. (If you are creating titles outside of Vegas for NTSC DV, the frame size should always be 655 × 480, and for PAL the frame size should always be 704 × 577.) This factor compensates for the non-square pixel aspect ratio of DV.

The media length is set by default to whatever the length of stills is set at in the OPTIONS | PREFERENCES | EDITING dialog; however, the length of the media can also be selected in the top of the Title tool, overriding this value.

Often, the setting in the Options menu is for stills, yet titles need to run longer. It's speedy to extend a title by specifying a longer title in this dialog. Titles, of course, can be looped to any length. Presets are available in the titling menu. These presets are there to assist you in creating great titles out of the box, but for truly powerful and professional-looking titles, you need to learn the features of the rest of the titling tool.

Titles can be positioned anywhere on the Text Placement dialog, which is under the Placement tab.

To manually place a title, click the text in the window of the Edit tab and then drag the title to the desired location. By default, a safe area is defined at 10 percent. This safe area indicates the area in which a title should live if it's being shown on television. Televisions have an area that is partially covered by a bezel in addition to being unscanned. This area hides approximately 10 percent of the video signal. Some televisions cover more and others less. The safe zone can be defined from a zero size area to a 30 percent safe area, by clicking in the Safe Zone text box and entering the desired safe area size. Ten percent is a typical safe area for NTSC and PAL video. Streamed media requires no safe area.

Title placement can be keyframed if the title should move onscreen.

Title Properties

Under the Properties tab, the color, tracking, scaling, and leading of the title can be controlled. Selecting the color is done by placing the cursor in the color palette and clicking. The cursor changes to a small target icon that can be dragged inside the color selector.

If a specific color is desired, the RGB values of the specific color can be entered into the color value boxes. Vegas also offers a color picker, which allows you to use the Eyedropper tool to select a color or range of averaged color.

The Eyedropper tool can be applied to any image on the screen. If a commercial color set is available, exacting color selection is possible.

Color can also be selected based on hue, saturation, and luminance (HSL) by selecting the HSL button just above the Eyedropper tool.

A background color can be specified if necessary. If the title is overlaid on a video image, a background color probably shouldn't be specified and should be left transparent instead. This feature can be used as an effect over video, and if the opacity of the background color is reduced, the visual image will show through the color, causing the background color to act as a color filter. All color aspects are keyframe-controllable.

7.4   The Editing tab found in the OPTIONS | PREFERENCES dialog allows users to preset title and still default lengths.

7.5   Titles can be manually placed anywhere, or presets can be used to place a title.

The Text Properties area of the Properties tab in the Title tool allows for adjustment of the kerning, leading, and spacing of text. By default, auto-kerning is disabled. Check the button to enable it.

7.6 Using the Eyedropper to match the color title to the flower on the shirt.

7.7 Selecting a background color's transparency/opacity.

Tracking controls the distance between letters in the text/title field. Leading controls the space between two lines. Leading fine-tunes a single line of text up and down. Scaling controls the sizing of the letters. All three text controls are keyframable. Scaling tends to be jerky in the scaling of text, so use with caution.

A check box is available for automatic kerning of letters above a preset, user-controlled size. Kerning is the specific spacing between a pair of characters. Some letters take up more space than others, and without kerning, sometimes letters appear to be too far apart in a word. Kerning generally alleviates this problem, although some fonts use more space than others.

Adding Effects to Text

The Effects tab offers a number of options to edit and enhance text. Effects often are used to make text stand out on otherwise busy visual screens or to create a specific mood.

Adding a glow to text can make letters show up when the underlying media is of a similar color. Glow is also often used to give text an image of depth, such as coming out of a vacuum.

Clicking the Draw Outline check box adds a glow to the text. This effect is great for outlining light-colored text with a slightly darker color, creating a slight illusion of 3D.

7.8　　The tracking control.

7.9　　The leading control.

7.10　　The scaling controls.

7.11　　Using Outline to create a glow around text causes the text to stand out.

7.12   Adding a shadow adds depth and dimension to text.

The outline can be feathered, which smoothes out the transition between the text and underlying media and softens the edge of the glow. Use this effect to add a bit of flair to text that might otherwise be dull.

Drop shadow, or shadowing, is one of the most useful tools in the Effects tab. Click the Draw Shadow check box, and a shadow will appear beneath text. This shadow can be colored in any color found in the palette by clicking the Color button and then selecting either a preset color or choosing a custom color by using the color picker/eyedropper to select a color.

Shadows can be keyframed to add depth to a title, moving in a direction opposite the original text, which creates an image popular in Hollywood titles today. Colors and opacity can be keyframed and combined with glow to create very rich and deep title attributes. Feathering smoothes and softens the edges of shadows and adds perspective to the depth of the text.

The Deform tool can shear, bend, squish, or compress text. Text can be wrapped around images by curving, or text can be used to give the impression of urgency by keyframing a fast bend as the text comes on or off the screen.

7.13   Bending text around an image can create an illusion of text and image being one image.

You can keyframe text with any one of the many effects in the tab and create flowing text that appears to be very deep, particularly when combined with other text effects.

Each of the three effect sections has slider controls for different text features. Double-clicking a slider returns the slider to its default "null" position. Clicking on the slider activates the effect, and the control can be controlled either with the mouse, or if active, can be moved with the Right Arrow and Left Arrow keys for more precise control.

Learning to manipulate titles is an introduction to compositing, and titles are one of the most creative and yet difficult aspects of film and video production. In the past, complex applications were required to do in-depth titling, while today Vegas contains many of the same tools as the more complex tools offered in the past. With some creativity and inspiration, Vegas can be use to create Hollywood-level titles. In fact, many Hollywood-level films and television productions contain title work created in Vegas.

7.14   Inserting a mix of effects can create complex titles.

Using the Pan/Crop Tool

Vegas has a Pan/Crop tool that can be used on any video event. This powerful tool can be used to correct camera depth, create motion on a still image, match aspect ratio, or crop out unwanted material from an image. While simple in use, this tool is exremely powerful.

Open the Pan-Crop.veg project so you can follow along visually with this section.

After capturing video and placing it on the timeline, each clip will contain a small Crop symbol. Notice that in Figure 7.14 the image in the monitor screen does not entirely fill the video preview area. Clicking the Crop tool opens a dialog that allows the user to entirely fill the Preview screen and match the image view to the aspect ratio of the Preview screen.

This feature is particularly useful when creating videos of scanned-in still photos or cropping unwanted content from a video image. See Chapter 4 for details on photo sizes and scanning.

With the Crop dialog open, right-click the image inside the Crop window and select atc Output Aspect.

7.15   The photo does not fill the entire Preview window.

This action causes the image to be cropped to a size that will completely fill the preview area. Now, the Preview window is completely filled with no black background showing. The aspect ratio of the photo, however, appears to be correct even if the photo itself really isn't. This aspect ensures that all imagery mixed with DV and other graphics can be made to fill the viewing screen completely at all times, matching the aspect ratio of the project. This accomplishment, however, isn't without its specific issues. For example, we no longer can see the entire

7.16 Selecting the project aspect ratio crops too much of the image out in some instances.

image that comprises the photograph shown in Figure 7.15. Notice that the gramophone has lost the overall view in Figure 7.16. The viewer can now see only the part of the gramophone that the editor allows them to see—useful in some situations, but not in others.

Wouldn't it be great if the still image could move, almost as though a camera had been used to capture the image rather than a scanner?

We can create that movement by the use of keyframes. Right-click again and select the Pan/Crop tool or click the Crop tool icon found on every clip or image on the timeline. Now, move the

Selection/Crop window to a new position. The Keyframe tool automatically inserts a keyframe, telling the timeline that at a specified time, the photograph should be cropped differently. Zoom in on the photo and zoom out of the photo, placing keyframes at each point of movement. Notice the added keyframes in Figure 7.17.

Producers of PBS specials, BBC documentaries, wedding videos, and broadcasts apply this same technique to create the illusion of movement. Even if the image is exactly the correct aspect ratio, no one really likes looking at a static photo on a computer or television screen. Even the smallest bits of movement are far more interesting to watch than a static photo.

In the past, tracking cameras, or remote control-operated cameras that mount on a rail, shooting motion images over a still photo, have been used to create this effect. Ric Burns, celebrated filmmaker/documentary genius of *The Civil War*, *The Way West, New York*, and others, has employed still images coupled with motion to change the entire face of documentaries. This effect can now be easily accomplished with a scanner and the Pan/Crop tool. This tool is tremendously powerful and useful for putting together slide shows, wedding montages, or other photo-heavy presentations.

Another application uses the Pan/Crop tool to correct bad camera movement. It can also be used to generate camera movement where the camera is static or not moving at all. If the clip of a soccer game, for example, is tripod-shot and static the camera movement could be generated to tell the viewer where they should be looking. A word of caution: don't zoom in too far, or the pixels will become too large and the detail of the event will wash out. This tool should be used in a subtle way for video. It's a terrific precursor to a transition.

Still images can usually handle deeper zooms if the resolution is set high enough on the original photo. Typical sizes of photos generally are considered best at 72 dpi for video; in most cases, saving photos at double the standard resolution provides a clean image for zooming and panning. However, preview stills in your scanning software to ensure the best resolution for your needs.

In addition to the Match Output Aspect menu in the right-click dialog, additional choices include the following:

- Restore—restores pan/crop boundaries to the edges of the image. No pan/crop takes place.

- Center—centers pan/crop boundaries around the centering dot found in the middle of the crop boundaries.

- Flip Horizontal—flips images horizontally, making the right side become the left side. (This feature is great for changing a view. Open multicamera.veg for more information.)

- Flip Vertical—flips images vertically, causing most images to be upside down.

- Match Output Aspect—matches the image aspect ratio to the settings in the FILE | PROPERTIES dialog, which is usually 720 × 480 for DV editing.

- Match Source Aspect—matches the image aspect to the original aspect ratio. Use this setting when applying full photos over other montages and when it is acceptable for the photo's borders to be seen. This feature will still allow an image to be resized smaller; however, the aspect ratio is that of the original image, not of the project.

7.17 Notice the keyframes created to build the illusion of a camera-shot still photo.

 Tip

Having photos at too high a resolution creates artifacts on the video image, containing too much information for a video image.

Standard-size graphic images, such as titles, backgrounds, and generated graphics, should be created at no higher than 300 dpi, or double the maximum zoom, and should be sized at 655 × 480 for insertion into a DV project. This configuration compensates for the non-square pixel issues found in DV. Always reduce interlace flicker for photos and consider using the Broadcast colors filter on stills if they are beyond legal colors. The Broadcast filter can be dropped directly on a still image event, or if the timeline contains a large number of stills, the filter can be dropped on the Project window instead. Instead of a Broadcast filter, you might want to try a Levels filter, set to convert Computer RGB to Studio RGB. Set this by reversing the Studio RGB to Computer RGB settings, which will ensure that the entire dynamic range is passed. (See Chapter 8 for more information on legal colors.)

The Pan/Crop tool can also be used to create 3D–like imagery. By spinning an image, whether video, photo, or graphic, the illusion of 3D can be created by adding a glow or shadow to the image. Of course, with the 3D Track Motion tols, this merely becomes an added bonus.

In the second section of the `Pan-crop.veg` project, a flip or rotation is found on the project. Glow, shadow, and keyframed motion of the pan/crop is applied to the image.

Use the Pan/Crop tool to flip images horizontally, vertically, or to squeeze an image onto the screen. Partnered with the Spherize plug-in found in Vegas, this process is one means of creating unique titles or animations of transitioning video.

Masking with the Pan/Crop Tool

Like the Track Motion tool, the Panning and Cropping tools have undergone a significant face lift. Users of earlier versions of Vegas will find the new tools to have a slight learning curve, but once understood, the power of this new toolset in the Pan/Crop tool is fabulous.

> If the Pan/Crop icon isn't visible on each video event, go to Options>Preferences>Show Video Event Buttons, and tick the check box there. This will cause the Pan/Crop and FX buttons to be visible on each media event. If you are working with single-frame events, you may want to turn this feature off. You can always access Pan/Crop and FX by right-clicking any video event.

Place a video event on the timeline. This can be a generated media event or a video event. Insert the Pan/Crop tool by selecting the Pan/Crop icon found on the event or right-clicking the event and choosing Pan/Crop

7.18   The Pan/Crop tool in Vegas 5 and 6 is different compared to earlier versions of Vegas.

For users of previous versions of Vegas, notice that the familiar interface has changed significantly. Rather than a series of dialogs with dropdown menus, the new tool is slider-based. A parameter is chosen, and the slider used to set the parameter. For example, notice the Zoom option. Click the word Zoom, and the slider next to the parameter lights up. This allows you to zoom more deeply on the image in the Pan/Crop window, and work at fine detail levels without the Pan/Crop preview window requiring a shift in size as it did in previous versions of Vegas. I find that setting this to a level of 50 is a good starting point for most Pan/Crop motion work. As with all of the Sony tools, double-clicking the parameter slider or button resets this to the default. The default setting for the Pan/Crop tool is 100, which may prove to be too large for some work spaces.

The Pan/Crop tool still may be manually moved in the workspace as in previous versions of Vegas, and values may be inserted with the keyboard as previously possible. But the slider tool found in this latest revision may prove to be more creative or intuitive for some users. I find that I grew used to it very quickly and find it a great way of getting my images to position or size very quickly.

Open the Pan/Crop tool the way you usually do, and you'll see a new control in the Pan/Crop keyframing tool labeled "Mask." The Mask allows bezier curves to be drawn in the Pan/Crop tool as masks, opening up an entirely new creative realm.

Click the Masks indicator so that Masks is selected in the keyframe tool. Now hold down the Ctrl button, and this will cause the cursor to turn to a pen tool in the Pan/Crop preview window. Left-clicking the pen tool in the Pan/Crop Preview window will insert a point in the

window. Now move the cursor to a new location, hold Ctrl, and left-click again. This will create yet another point in the Pan/Crop preview window. Create at least three points, joining one to another. As the pen tool is rolled over the first point in the mask, a small circle will appear, and all mask points will turn yellow, indicating that the mask is a completed path. A selection is now made. Pressing the Alt key and clicking on any of the yellow anchor points will select all anchor points. Clicking on any single anchor point allows it to be selected and the Bezier curve to be adjusted to work with the angle or curve you'd like to create. These curves and selected areas are completely keyframe controlled, so this sort of selection may move with any object or subject that you might have in the video image. Multiple selections may be made in the Pan/Crop window, allowing for multiple objects and selections to be cut out and defined.

7.19 Closeup view of the Pan/Crop tool with all tools expanded.

But How Is This a Mask?

On the left side of the Pan/Crop tool, you'll find a new interface and control set. In this control set is a setting labeled "Path." Click on the Path Mode dialog or on the + symbol next to the word "Path," and a drop down menu appears with the choices "Positive" and "Negative." When Positive is chosen, the area inside the curve is visible and the remaining space is transparent. When the Negative option is chosen, the area inside the curve is transparent, and the area outside the anchor points and path is visible. This is a great tool for removing a subject from a background, placing them in a new background, or removing a background from a current scene and replacing it. One way to consider this tool is that it's like a Chromakey tool that will work regardless of the number of colors found in the background. At many levels, this feature brings some of the tools found in rotoscoping tools to Vegas.

The opacity of the mask may also be controlled via the new Pan/Crop Bezier tool. Opacity, like all other aspects of the Bezier tool, is keyframe-controlled. One benefit is that masks may be faded in or out over time by using the keyframe tool to create the type of image needed to complete the composite or overlay.

Open the Path dialog by clicking the + symbol next to the word "Path." Note the Opacity parameter in the Path dialog.

Opacity may be controlled by entering a value via the keyboard, sliding the Opacity slider, or using the spinner controls next to the slider tool. Use the Page Up and Page Down arrows for coarse control, moving the value in increments of + or –10, and use the Up and Down arrows for fine control moving in fractional values. For example, setting the first keyframe in the masking timeline to a value of zero causes the mask to be transparent, or invisible. Setting the next keyframe to a value of 100 will cause the mask to be completely opaque. This may be used to fade the mask in or out of the image composition.

> Values in the Pan/Crop and Track Motion dialogs may be controlled by the keyboard or programmed HUI device. Use the Page Up and Page Down keys for coarse control of parameters in these two dialogs. This shifts the value in increments of + or –10. Using the Up or Down arrows shifts values by single-digit increments. You can also use the Tab key to scroll downward through the attributes of the dialogs and use Shift+Tab to scroll upwards.

Next in the list of power tools found in the new Pan/Crop tool is the Feathering tool. This allows you to blend the masking lines created in the Bezier mask with the background. When working with moving media, this is exceptionally helpful as it can assist in blending moving images against a moving backdrop.

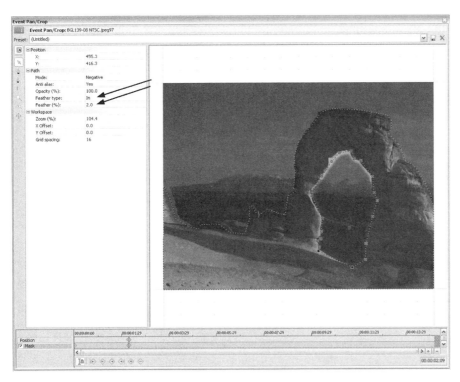

7.20   Use Feathering in the Pan/Crop tool's masking toolset to blend the mask with the background if the lines seem too visible. Feathering may be either inside, outside, or in both directions from the mask line.

Feathering can take place either inside the mask, outside the mask, or in both directions.

No Feathering   Feathered Out   Feathered In

7.21   Three examples of feathering with the Bezier masking tool.

To take advantage of the Feathering tool, first create a mask as described above. Open the Path dialog by clicking the +symbol next to the word "Path." Note the feathering dialog beneath Opacity.

Choose how you'd like the path feathered. Experiment with all three feathering modes to determine what works best for the mask.

Masks created in the Pan/Crop tool may be copied and pasted to other events. The most common method to copy or paste a mask is to copy an event containing a mask contained in the Pan/Crop tool, right click on the destination event or video clip, and select Paste Attributes from the submenu that appears. However, if the destination image is of a different size or aspect ratio from the original, this will not apply the mask correctly in the destination image, as Vegas will interpolate the position based on the value of the source image. For example, if a mask has been created by drawing points around a .jpg image and the mask is copied or pasted to an .avi file of a different size, the mask will not paste in the same location or aspect as created in the source .jpg. The correct method of copying and pasting a mask attribute from differing file types is to copy the keyframes from the source image and paste them into the keyframe timeline of the destination image. This will ensure correct aspect and location.

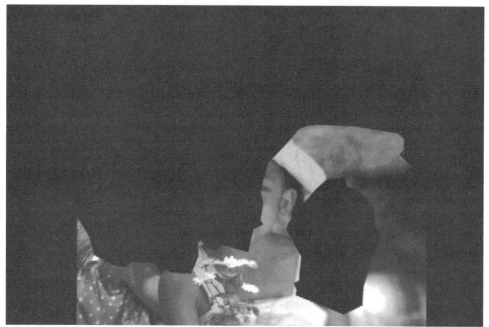

7.22   To copy mask attributes from a source image that is different in size or aspect from the destination image, copy the keyframes from the source image rather than using the more common copy and paste attributes. This will ensure that regardless of the aspect ratio of the image being pasted to, the aspect of the mask will remain correct rather than scaling to fit the aspect of the new image.

Using Track Motion in Vegas

On each video track, Vegas assigns a Track Motion tool. This tool is exceptionally powerful and goes far beyond its initial impressions.

The Track Motion tool in its most basic form can be used to create a picture-in-picture presentation, allowing one motion video event to be placed over another motion video event while reducing the size of either event and alowig bth images to be visible simultaneously.

7.23 The Track Motion button is found on every video track in Vegas.

7.24 The Track Motion dialog has many choices with which to manipulate an image.

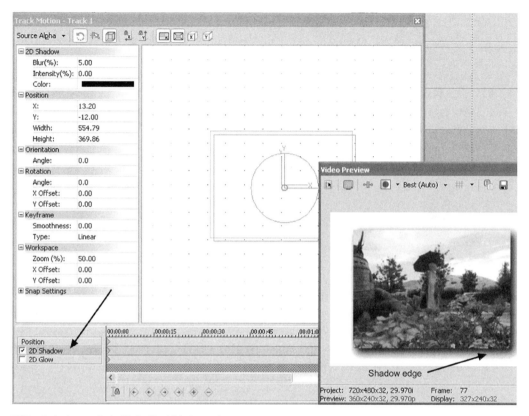

7.25   A shadow applied with the Track Motion tool.

Clicking the Track Motion button opens a dialog that is similar to the Pan/Crop dialog. In fact, these two tools share many of the same attributes but accomplish completely different tasks.

As an example, a shadow can be applied with the Track Motion tool, as shown in Figure 7.25. Shadow can be applied to any image with the Track Motion tool, even if the resize or motion features of the tool are not used. This fact will be useful when using text as masks as shown later in this section. It's also a simple task to apply shadow to a still image or graphics with a transparency by using this tool.

Starting with the top-left corner, a number of tools are found within the Track Motion dialog. The Show Properties button hides and shows the position, angle, zoom, and other views found on the left side of the Track Motion tool. The Normal Edit button, just below the Show Properties button, is the tool predominantly used to size, rotate, and manipulate the images in the track motion frame window.

The Zoom tool, which looks like a magnifying glass, allows for tight zooming on the frame window area and is very helpful when trying to align images in the frame to a small grid space or when creating exacting keyframes.

Enabling Snapping causes the frame in the Track Motion tool to be snapped to the nearest grid and is also useful for accurately locating the frame during editing.

The Lock Aspect Ratio in the Track Motion tool functions in the same way as the Pan/Crop tool. Unlike the Pan/Crop tool, however, the Track Motion tool causes the frame in the Preview-windo to rmai in he correct aspect ratio, but size-reduced.

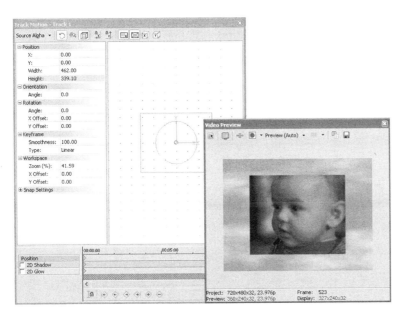

7.26, 7.27   Similar settings in the Pan/Crop tool (a) and Track Motion tool (b) frame windows, but very different results in the Preview window. Try inserting a Border filter with the Soft Edge preset on this sort of composited shot.

The Lock Aspect Ratio function should be used in most operations of Vegas so that the vertical and horizontal aspects of the image remain equal. The aspect ratio, however, can often be used as part of a creative edit. Turning off aspect ratio and adjusting generated media, for instance, is great for creating lines or other shapes. (Generated media is discussed later in this chapter.) By default, these buttons should be enabled.

The Size At Center button found on the top side of the Track Motion tool to the right of the Lock Aspect Ratio causes the frame and subsequent view in the Preview window to center around the dot found in the middle of the track motion frame. When you move the dot to another location, right-click, and then choose Center while this button is enabled, the dot will return to the center of the track motion frame. In addition, the frame image will move with it while keeping the dot where it was moved in relation to the original center of the frame. The center dot is actually designed to move a frame off center during movement, providing a pivot point for rotation of the frame.

Sizing a frame down to one-fourth screen and snapping at the centerline causes the frame to be part of a quad image on a screen. Figure 7.28 shows three images reduced in size and snapped to centerlines of grid. The gradient is generated media with a title overlaid.

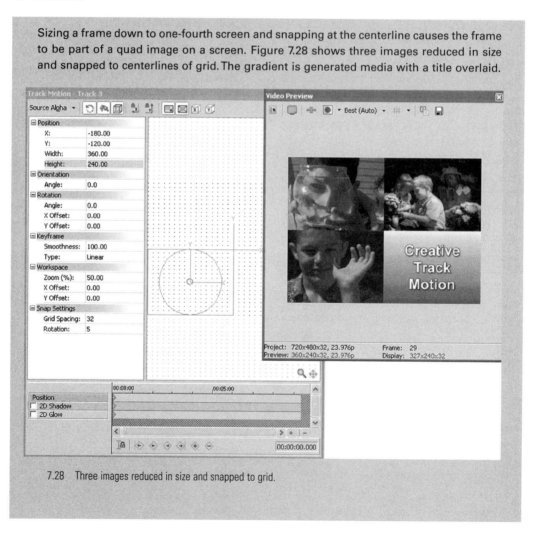

7.28   Three images reduced in size and snapped to grid.

7.29   Note that in Vegas 6, the Track Motion presets that had been removed in
         Vegas 5 have returned. Users can now specify presets for Track Motion.

Track motion is where most users become acquainted with the concept of deeper compositing, as opposed to just creating titles overlaid on images. Another common use of track motion is to create a picture-in-picture image. Creating a picture-in-picture is fairly simple and is a good exercise for getting started with manipulating images.

To create a picture-in-picture image, create two tracks of video, with events on both tracks. Place the cursor in the middle of the two events.

Track 1 is the overlaid event that will become the picture-in-the-picture. Select the Track Motion button on track 1.

Make sure Lock Aspect Ratio is enabled, grab the lower-right edge of the frame in the track motion frame view, and reduce in size, watching the Preview window as the frame and preview image are reduced. Reduce the track 1 event to the size of x + 317.0, y = 210.0. (Size is displayed near the cursor during resize or can be directly input in the Track Motion Properties dialog.)

In the Properties Center dialog, input a value of 180 for the left box and a value of 120 for the right box. These settings will place the video slightly to the right of extreme left and slightly below the top of the screen.

Preview the image by pressing W (rewind) and the Spacebar (play).

The track 1 event will be previewed in the upper-left corner, while playing over the top of track 2's event. If both tracks are video tracks, full motion will be seen in both events.

7.30 Picture-in-picture images are very fast to create with Track Motion.

Be sure that the Sync Cursor button is disabled when working with this exercise unless the desired effect is to shrink the track 1 event to the proscribed size. Otherwise, the first keyframe, which in most cases will be a full frame view of track 1, will gradually shrink the track 1 event until it reaches the second/new keyframe generated by shrinking. It is easy to accidentally create unwanted keyframes during the track motion or pan/crop actions. In the event of a second keyframe being created in the Track Motion dialog, right-click the first keyframe found in the keyframe dialog and select Delete from the menu. This step will then cause the second keyframe to be the initial size of the event. You will quickly create a workflow based around your personal preference for managing these two tools.

The picture-in-picture image might seem flat or without dimension, as the two images are at exactly the same depth of field. To create a depth of field, insert a shadow.

Shadows can be inserted in any color, opacity, and size within Vegas. Open the Track Motion dialog again by clicking the Track Motion button on track 1. A check box for a shadow is located at the bottom of the dialog on the left side of the keyframe timeline. Checking this box adds a shadow to the frame in the Preview window. One of the more creative uses of the Shadow tool is to turn off the aspect ratio of the Track Motion tool when applying shadowing and to create shadows that stretch, move, shrink, or rotate while the image that the shadow falls from remains in aspect ratio. To disable aspect ratio on the shadow, which is enabled by default, press Ctrl while moving the shadow about the screen. To disable it for the duration of the editing process, click the Lock Aspect Ratio button, turning this tool off. If the image on the timeline has an alpha channel, the shadow will work with the opaque image. This method is one way to create layered shadows under PNG, TGA, GIF, AVI, or other alpha-capable image formats. Shadows are keyframable for opacity, color, size, and position.

7.31 Shadow applied to PNG file containing alpha channel.

7.32 Glow can be subtle.

7.33 Glow can be exaggerated.

Glow may also be applied to images in the frame. Glow on its own, or combined with shadowing, allows for very complex image manipulation. Glow is adjustable in opacity, color, and size. Glow can also be feathered to blend into background or other composited images.

Using glow in a subtle manner around letters whose color properties closely match a background color can help offset the letters from the image underneath. Glow is keyframable for opacity, color, size, and position and can be used in a similar way to a shadow in that it can have a separate path from the image to which it is assigned. Using a combination of glow and shadow allows for two separate moving images beneath a single event.

The project seen in Figure 7.34 is on the DVD in this book, labeled `composite1.veg`. This project can be used as a template.

The Track Motion tool can be applied to just about any project in some form or fashion, splitting screens, creating multiple screens such as seen in the opening f the Brady Bunch television series, used to fly titles in or out and any number of other creative uses.

 The project displayed in Figure 7.36 can be found on the DVD in this book and is labeled `composite2.veg`.

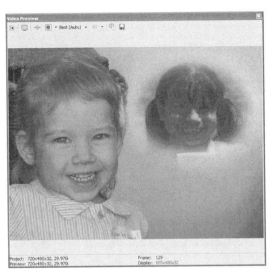

7.34 Glow combined with a mask and shadow makes for a seamless transition between the foreground and background events.

7.35 Mask soloed to demonstrate the cookie cutter, blur, glow, and shadow combined.

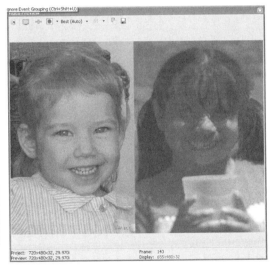

7.36 The split screen is achieved quickly with the Track Motion tool.

The Next Dimension: 3D Track Motion Tools

Vegas 5 and 6 take a great leap into the next level of creative power by offering a few 3D creative tools. If you've worked with the Plugn'Pak from Debugmode for Vegas 3 or 4, then you are more or less familiar with how this tool is going to work for you, however the new feature is embedded in the Track Motion tool. Access to all planes of movement may be keyframed from within the Track Motion tool.

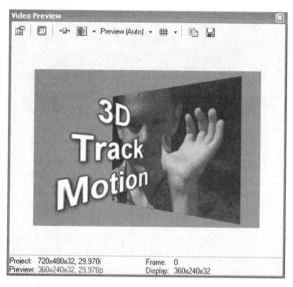

7.37   The new 3D feature is great to use with text to create alternate planes and angles for text.

The new Track Motion tool featureset will be unfamiliar to previous users of Vegas, as it marks a departure from the interface that users are familiar with. However, in order to accomplish some of the features now found in Vegas, these changes were clearly necessary.

To get started with the new Track Motion tool, create a new video track and drop a video event on the new track.

Select the Track Motion button on the track header.

A new dialog opens up, showing the new Track Motion appearance. (If you are new to Vegas 5 and 6, this will not be new to you.)

Notice that in the upper left of the dialog there is an option for Source Alpha modes. This is where you'll access the 3D behaviors for Vegas.

Click the dropdown menu from the Source Alpha Modes button and choose 3D Source Alpha from the menu choices. A new dialog opens up within the Track Motion tool.

In the left -hand side you'll find several controls for the 3D parameters. The primary controls are for X, Y, and Z axis. Manipulating the X axis moves the media along a right or left horizontal plane, manipulating the Y axis moves the media placement along a vertical plane, and manipulating the Z axis moves media forward or backward in a vertical plane.

7.38 The three planes are accessible in the Track Motion workspace. Zoom in for greatest control if you are moving planes with the mouse rather than using the spinner, slider, or dialog box.

Notice that there are controls for Position, Orientation, Rotation, Keyframe, Workspace, and Snap settings. Each of these control groupings may be minimized or maximized by pressing the plus or minus sign next to the parameter control heading.

In the Position group, select the X parameter. (You may need to maximize the group by pressing the + symbol if the group is not fully visible.)

When the parameter is selected, a small dialog containing numeric value, a spinner control, and slider control open up. Position value information may be input manually by typing a value into the numeric dialog, or values may be determined by moving the spinner or slider values up or down, allowing preview of the media position.

For the purposes of this exercise, set the value to 1.0. This will move the media to the right, nearly half way.

Select the Y parameter and set the value to 00.00.

Now select the Z parameter. It will adjust in exactly the same manner as the X and Y parameters. Set the Z parameter at a value of –100. This will cause the media to zoom forward.

To adjust the 3D placement, enlarge the Orientation dialog if it's not already open. (You may wish to minimize the Position dialog by pressing the "–" button next to the Position indicator.) Select the X plane.

Adjust the values of X to 148, the value of Y to 50, and the value of Z to 130.

This adjusts how the image floats in 3D, but these positions are also keyframeable. Place the cursor at the out point of the video on the timeline. Enable the Sync to Cursor button in the Track Motion dialog.

Notice how the cursor moved in the Track Motion keyframe timeline, to a new location that matches the location of the cursor on the workspace timeline.

Here's where you can learn another method of manipulating how the parameters are controlled in the Track Motion dialog.

7.39 The window view may be varied by selecting the window description in the upper-left corner of the dialog. Notice the sync to cursor button in the lower-left corner of the keyframe dialog. This will sync the cursor in the Track Motion keyframe dialog to match the location of the cursor on the timeline.

In the lower portion of the Track Motion dialog, the Perspective Window is found. When the cursor is rolled over the center, or location of media, a box will highlight. This box indicates the X, Y, and Z axis of the media.

Roll the cursor over the edge of this box, and a small circle will appear in the corner of the spatial indicator box. Click and drag on this circle, enlarging the image. Notice how the numeric values in the Width, Height, and Depth dialogs change in the Positioning window)

Drag the corner of the spatial indicator box until the Z value reaches 3732 in size. If you try to input the numeric value, the aspect ratio of the media will change unless you have Lock Aspect Ratio enabled.

Beneath the Orientation group, you'll find the Rotation group. In this group, the media may be rotated on any of its three axes. For this exercise, click on the keyframe that was newly created in the previous step, where the size of the media was dragged larger.

Now select the Z plane in the Rotation dialog, and input a value of –60 by either manually entering the value, using the spinner, or using the slider to set the value.

> Like all other tools within Vegas, double-clicking the slider will reset the slider to default value. This is very useful when finding yourself a little lost in the early stages of learning the 3D tools.

Double-click the file and press the spacebar to begin playback of the file. Notice how it flies across the Preview window and rotates.

To see an example of how this functions, open the 3D#2.veg file found on the DVD in the back of the book. It may also be located on the VASST.com website.

Nesting Composites

Another great and very powerful feature found in Vegas are the nested compositing features. In earlier versions of Vegas, the compositing tools were powerful but were limited in creating in-depth composites. Vegas 5 and 6 can have multiple tracks entirely controlled by one parent track. Individual tracks may have their own motion in space using 3D or 2D tools, with a master composite track controlling all tracks beneath it that are assigned to it. This is great for building monster composites and having one final track control it. In the audio world, this is similar to a mixdown, with a master volume, pan, and effects. The tracks of video are all controlled by the master. In the case of nested tracks, even the master track may have its own 3D properties as well, that affect all tracks nested, or acting as children to the parent or master.

7.40 For those familiar with Vegas 4, parent/child switching is slightly different, due to the nested compositing modes.

Follow these steps to understand the basics of Parent/child tracks:

1.   Create four new video tracks (Ctrl+Shift+Q)

2.   In tracks 2-4, place either video or generated media.

3.   On each track, open the Track Motion dialog, turn on 3D Alpha mode, and create 3D motion in each track so that all three tracks reveal themselves at some point in the project.

4.   In each track header, there is a Parent/Child switch. Press the switch to cause all tracks to act as child tracks beneath the parent.

5.   In track one, open the Parent Track Motion dialog, and enable the 3D Alpha mode on the parent track.

6. Create movements on that track, using X, Y, Z planes, orientation, and rotation. All three tracks beneath the parent will respond to the parent track motion regardless of their own motion.

7. In the Parent track, insert text or other form of media.

8. In the track header of the Parent track, click the Track Motion button. Enable 3D Alpha Channel mode in this dialog. Assign 3D motion in this dialog as well, creating keyframes to animate the track. This track animation is independent of the other three tracks that are children to the parent track, yet the parent track controls this track's motion as well. Therefore in this composite, there are five track motion elements occuring at one time. Each of the four beneath the parent will respond to the parent track motion regardless of their own motion.

9. In the parent track, insert text or other form of media.

10. In the track header of the parent track, select the Track Motion button. Enable 3D Alpha Channel mode in this dialog. Assign 3D motion in this dialog as well, creating keyframes to animate the track. This track animation is independent of the other three tracks that are children to the Parent track, yet the parent track controls this track's motion as well. Therefore in this composite, there are actually five track motion elements occuring at one time. Each of the four tracks has its own track motion element, with the parent track controlling each of these tracks in a separate motion path. You also may need to move the parent position by a few pixels in order to see the shadow or glow beneath the child tracks.

> As you are working on individual tracks, notice that the track header number contains a small blinking indicator signifying which track is being affected by whatever process is being applied. This is particularly helpful when working on parent/child comps, as this makes it clear as to which track is currently selected. Even when multiple tracks are selected, only the track whose properties are going to be affected will blink.

Effects may be set up to be pre or post-process in the keyframing tool for that particular effect. Pressing the Pre/Post Toggle button in the effect will instruct Vegas when to process the media with that specific filter. Tracks in 3D mode may not be pre- or post-toggled.

Select the Pre/Post Toggle button in the keyframing tool for each effect. Vegas will automatically reroute or reorder filter position for you.

7.41 If the triangle points left, it's pre-compositing, and if it points right, it's post-compositing in behavior.

Parental Guidance/Shadows and Glow

Another benefit of a master parent track is that all child tracks may be assigned a master shadow or glow. This allows for a more cohesive composite as opposed to creating separate shadows and glows individually.

In the composition created earlier, open the Parent Track Motion, and disable the 3D Alpha Channel mode.

To the left of the keyframing timeline in the track motion dialog is a checkbox for Shadow and for Glow. Enable the Shadow, and you'll see the child tracks have shadow showing where the background allows it to be seen. You may need to create a non-child track at the bottom of the timeline that contains a white generated media slug in order to see the shadow, depending on the color of your shadow and media content.

You can also insert a white slug on the parent track, and insert a compositing envelope on the parent track. This will allow the parent track to control opacity of all nested media. Open the Rings-opacity.veg file found on the disk in the back of this book. Notice how the parent tracks control opacity of tracks nested as child tracks. Move the handles on the composite envelopes on the tracks to get a feel for how this works.

To insert a composite envelope to control nested tracks:

1. Create the composite as you'd like it to appear.

2. Insert a new video track above the composition.

3. Parent the new video track to the tracks beneath.

4. In the new parent track, choose the compositing mode tool in the header, and select Multiply/Mask mode.

7. Choose the Parent Track Motion button in the parent track. In this track, you'll assign 3D motion (or any other motion to the child tracks). Assign any motion you would like, if any. Otherwise, right-click the track header and insert a compositing envelope. Double click the compositing envelope to assign handles to the envelope, allowing the opacity or transparency of the track to be adjusted.

Growth Curves from Vegas 4 Users

The new Track Motion tool and Pan/Crop tool are definitely and deeply different from what previous versions of Vegas offered. However, these new tools, in spite of a slightly more difficult learning curve, offers a tremendous new power in Vegas. Opening composites from Vegas 4 and opening them in Vegas 6 will help learn how the new tools function. Essentially, the masking tools are the same, with the exception of the addition of 3D. There are some minor irritations for those familiar with the former track motion and Pan/Crop tools, for instance, the lack of ability to move the target inside the Track Motion dialog via up and down arrows is something I find challenging. According to the engineers at Sony, this was a challenge to keep implemented along with the addition of 3D tools. I also find the lack of a background to be difficult in these tools, as I was used to the black or gray gridded backgrounds found in earlier versions of Vegas. In spite of these differences, it's fairly simple to learn to work with the changes and discover all the new tools which allow and encourage you to be more creative.

Generated Media

Vegas has the ability to create or generate media using nothing but plug-ins (no physical file is required) that can generate titles, solid colors, noise, gradients, checkerboards, and other graphic elements. You can quickly and easily generate colors for inserted media, masks, filling backgrounds under titles that don't have associated video or graphic events, and many other uses.

To learn how to create generated media, insert a new video track on a new project by right-clicking the Track Control pane and choosing Insert New Video Track or by pressing Ctrl+Shift+Q.

Right-click in the timeline area of the new track and choose Insert Generated Media from the menu. The Generated Media dialog opens.

Select Sony Solid Color. The Solid Color dialog box opens, and you can select the color of choice. For this exercise, choose Black.

After setting the color, set the length of time that the event should last and close the dialog by clicking the × in the upper-right corner of the dialog. A black event now appears on the screen.

Click the Event FX button found on the event, or right-click and choose Event FX.

From the FX dialog, select two plug-ins: Add Noise and Black Restore. Both can be selected at the same time by pressing and holding Ctrl down while selecting the second FX plug-in. On the top/header of the plug-ins dialog, you should see both FX names displayed.

Click the Add Noise box. In the Add Noise plug-in dialog box, uncheck the Animate check box, and slide the Noise Level slider to 1.0. In the Black Restore dialog, set the threshold for 0.600.

You have just created a star field from nothing more than computer-generated media.

To add more media to the star field to make it more realistic or interesting, insert a new video track above the existing track. Right-click in the timeline area and choose Insert Generated Media just as you did before.

Now follow these steps:

1.   Choose Sony Color Gradient.

2.   Select Sunburst from the menu. Notice that by moving the target marker around in the Gradient Preview screen, the curve of the gradient can be adjusted.

7.42   The Solid Color dialog box is used to define solid colors on the timeline.

3.   Define the length of time that the event should occur. This length of time should be the same length of time as the previous event created. Now close the dialog.

The new gradient now covers the entire Preview screen. To show only the portions that are to be actually seen, select the Video FX tab on the bottom left of the screen or click the Event FX button found on the new gradient. Choose the Cookie Cutter FX plug-in.

In the Cookie Cutter dialog, select the Arrowhead in the Shapes menu. The screen can still be covered with the Sunburst image. Using the Size slider, size the arrowhead so it is not filling the entire Preview window. A size of around 0.050 is a good choice. Close the Cookie Cutter dialog.

Now open the Track Motion dialog on the track with the arrowhead. Place the cursor on the upper-left corner handle of the frame. The cursor will change into a circular shape, indicating that the Track Motion tool is prepared to rotate the frame.

Rotate the frame so that the arrowhead in the Preview window is pointing at the lower-right corner of the Preview window.

Click and hold in the middle of the track motion frame and slide the frame to the upper-left corner of the frame window. The arrowhead in the Preview window will move to the same location and should still remain pointed at the lower-right corner.

Enable the sync cursor in the Track Motion Keyframe section. In the timeline, place the cursor on the right edge of the generated media event. In the Track Motion tool, move the fameto the lower-right corner. A new keyframe will be inserted in the timeline as a result of the sync cursor being enabled.

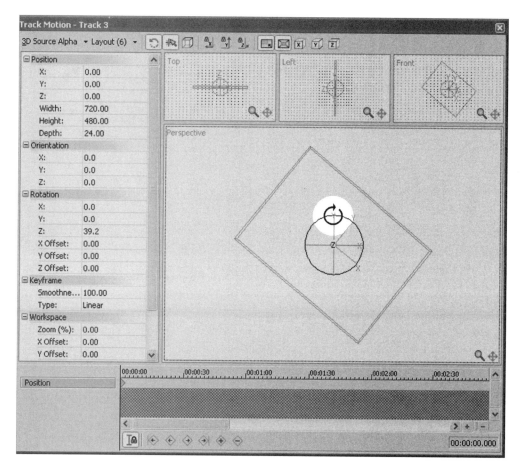

7.43 The cursor changed to a rotating cursor, used for rotating the frame inside the Track Motion tool.

Now press the Spacebar or click Play on the Transport control. You should see the arrowhead flying across the star field, and if the loop is enabled (press Q), the arrowhead/starship will fly across the screen from the upper left to the lower right.

Adding an orange glow and sizing it to cover only the back of the arrowhead will create a flame coming out of the back of the arrowhead/starship. By animating the feather, opacity, and intensity of the glow, the lames can come to life, moving at different depths and opacity, giving a realistic sense of video to an otherwise static image.

 This project can be found on the DVD included in this book and is labeled com-positerocket.veg. The keyframes animating the flame are also found on the VEG file.

7.44 Flames created with glow give a realistic edge to the starship.

Credit Rolls

Inserting a credit roll is one of the generated media options in Vegas. Credit rolls are used for more than only titling at the end of a video project; they are great for showing specific product information, creating introductions to a video, or creating fast-moving numbers or letters for a specific effect, particularly when used at reduced opacities.

Insert a credit roll by right-clicking a track and selecting Insert Generated Media from the submenu. In the Generated Media chooser, select Credit Roll from the listing of available generated media types.

7.45 The Credit Roll plug-in is found in the Generated Media chooser.

The Credit Roll plug-in offers many choices to manage text in the credit roll. Three text settings are allowed in the roll: a Title Text (headline), Subitem Text (main topic), and Item Left/Item Right (sub-topics). Each of the three settings can have its own font size, color, style, and position.

The type of line can be adjusted by clicking next to the field in which the text will be entered. For example, a single line of text can be either a Title Text field, or it can be a Subitem Text field.

👉 **Tip**_____

You can also use the standard title tool and the Pan/Crop tool to create credit rolls. Simply type text into the Text Generator for its full length. then use the Pan/Crop tool to pan up/down the generated text, creating a very controllable credit roll. This method offers more options tha the standard credit roll function.

The type of text is selected by clicking the small box next to the input field. Clicking in the field allows text to be input to the field.

In the Style dialog, kerning, spacing, and connecting styles, such as dashes or dots, can all be specified. All aspects of the credit roll can be keyframed. Because of the nature of the credit roll and generated media, there is no sync cursor ability.

The length of the event determines the speed of the credit roll, and the number of lines determines how fast the roll moves through the length of time. Longer event lengths with fewer lines create a very slow crawl, while short event lengths with several lines scroll more quickly.

From the Properties dialog, a timed sequence can be created. In a timed sequence, titles can be zoomed in and out, faded in and out, and slid from the bottom, top, and side depending on selection in the menu. The number of lines and length of credit roll event determines the length of time of each title image on screen.

By default, credit rolls are of transparent background. Background colors, transparency, and letter colors, however, can all be adjusted. Shadows and glows are not options in the credit roll.

Using the 3D Track Motion tools, DebugMode 3D plug-in, a ump map, or height map (discussed later in this chapter) can add a number of options and creative ability to the credit roll.

 *Tip*_____

To add a shadow or glow to a credit roll, open track motion. Leave the track position at default but check the shadow or glow (or both) check boxes. These settings add a shadow or glow to the characters on the credit ol. Tes ca bekeyframed on or off or for position if the shadow or glow is desired to flow differently from the direction of the credit roll.

7.46 Selecting the Styles tab allows parameters of each of the three styles to be adjusted. Clicking the Style button on the left side of the Credit Roll plug-in chooses which text style the line will present.

7.47 Connect the left and right credits on the scroll with dashes, dots, or lines.

7.48 Using Track Motion in 3D mode (or using the DebugMode 3D LE plug-in), text can be angled on the screen, resembling a wall or doorway. Height mapping can be used to wrap the text on a tex-tured surface.

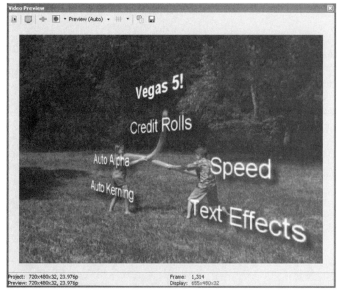

👉 *Tip*

If credit rolls have jagged edges or aliasing, try resizing the generated media to double size, or 1440 x 960, and reduc-ing opacity of the credit roll to 98% rather than 100%. Don't use fonts with serifs or fine linens. Adding .001/.002 of Gaussian Blur can sometimes help clean up soft edges on credit rolls, as can the Unsharp Mask filter.

Creating/Using Masks in Vegas

Masks are exceptionally powerful tools for creating composited media. The generated media project created earlier contained a mask, inserted with the Cookie Cutter plug-in.

Masks can be made from just about any photo editing tool, font, or shape that exists. Vegas auto-senses an alpha channel from most images that contain them and has options to force recognition of an alpha channel if it is not automatically sensed.

To force Vegas to recognize an alpha channel if it is not seeing the channel automatically, right-click the event containing the alpha channel. Select Properties from the submenu that appears. Select the Media tab in the Properties window and at the bottom is a menu labeled Alpha Channel. Next to this, locate a drop-down list that offers several choices. Select Premultiplied from the menu.

An alpha channel defines the areas you want to be transparent. Each image on the video screen is comprised of four channels: red, green, blue, and alpha. The alpha channel acts as a mask, instructing the other channels on how the pixels should blend or merge. Alpha channels can have gradations, allowing blending of multiple images on top of each other at various levels of transparency. Another way to understand how an alpha channel functions is to imagine a stencil laid over an object and a can of spray paint. The alpha channel reveals the events beneath much as a stencil reveals the object beneath. Alpha channels usually display transparent areas as white space, while hidden areas are displayed in black.

Masks can either hide or reveal information/images in a video project, allowing image areas to be defined within an event. Another name for a mask is a matte or a key. All terms mean the same thing: hiding or revealing an area so another image can show through, or hiding an area so that another image can be composed over the top of it. In any definition, a mask, matte, or key defines the transparent pixels of an image for superimposing or revealing another image.

Just as titles are one of the simplest forms of compositing, they are also one of the most viable uses of masking. Titling is an excellent method of learning exactly how a mask works.

Open a new project in Vegas. Insert three new video tracks. Choose a video or still file to serve as a background. To create the mask, place the video or still image on track 3.

Place a title on track 1. Do not use fonts that contain serifs or small lines. A font such as Impact or Arial Black will serve best as you learn this technique.

7.49 Right-clicking and selecting PROPER-TIES | MEDIA allows alpha channel recognition to be forced if alpha channel is present.

On track 2, place a video file that has high motion with bright colors for the best effect in the learning stage.

The text is a mask but is not seen as such just yet. On the extreme left side of the Track Control pane, there is a small arrow pointing upward, which is the Make Compositing Child (Parent/

7.50   The Parent/Child button is found on the left side of every video track.

Child) button. Clicking this button will cause all areas of tack 2 to become transparent. The only portions of track 2 that are seen are seen inside the letters of track 1. Click this button.

The event on track 2 disappears and becomes visible only inside the title letters. The letters are a mask; the letters become the parent, and the event beneath becomes the child. This process causes the parent to instruct the child how to be shown. Multiple tracks can be the child, but only one track can be the parent. As many parent and child relationships as necessary can exist across multiple tracks; however, but no child track can have more than one parent. If multiple parents are required of a child track, the child track must be duplicated.

To gain a better understanding of the masking process, change the color of the text on track 1 to black. It will cause the letters to become invisible. Reset the color of the title to white in order to continue this section.

This process is masking in its most basic form. Any image that contains transparent/ alpha information can be used in place of a title. To continue the concept of manipulating the title appearance, however, keep this project on the timeline.

In track 1, right-click the title to edit it or click the Edit Generated Media button found on the title event. The Title tool opens. Navigate to the Effects tab and select a shadow on the text. The shadow can't be seen. Changing the color of the shadow will result in the shadow being seen.

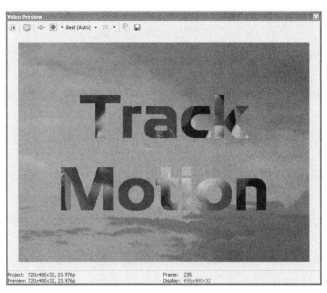

7.51   The video of track 2 (the child) shows through the letters of track 1
(parent track).

To place a shadow on the mask, or placing letters in this instance, select the Track Motion tool on track 1. In the Track Motion tool, check the Shadow check box. A shadow will appear beneath the mask/letters on the Preview screen. This shadow can be keyframed in exactly the same way that a shadow in a normal track motion instance would be keyed. Color, size, feathering, transparency, and position can all be user-defined using keyframes.

Open your favorite photo editing application. In the application, create a new project/photo image that is 655 × 480 pixels for NTSC or 704 × 576 for PAL. Flood the entire work area with black.

Paint a design or shape in the work area, using white as the color. Save the design as a PNG file for best results. A GIF, JPEG, TIF, or Targa will also work.

Open a new project in Vegas. Create three new video tracks. Place the new image on the timeline on track 1. The explorer might need to be refreshed in order to see it in its newly saved location. Refresh the explorer by clicking the Refresh button on the Explorer toolbar.

Insert the media that should be showing through the mask on track 2. The length of the event doesn't matter, as the length of the parent event determines how long the underlying event is visible. (Of course, if the child event is shorter than the parent event, the child will not be seen for the full length either.)

On track 3, insert an event that contains video or a still image that functions as the background image.

7.52   You can have fun while learning
to make masks.

7.53 Adding a shadow to the mask with the Track Motion Shadow tool. Glow can also be added to a mask.

7.54 Any shape can be used to create a mask, so long as it contains a mask and an alpha image.

In a gradient mask, white areas are revealed, while black areas are hidden. When using other colors as the mask, the closer a color is to white, the more revealed it becomes, while just te oposite is true for gradient colors approaching black in value. However, when using other colors in a mask, those colors reduce the opacity of the underlying image.

7.55   Black to white gradient changed to solid blue gradient, reducing the opacity of the image shown through. (See Figure 7.34 for the original mask appearance.

Now click the Parent/Child button on track 2, and the image you created becomes transparent, except the visible mask areas, which now show the event on track 2.

Filters can be applied to the events on the child track, which will affect how the events on track 2 are shown. Applying blurs will blend the mask into the underlying events.

Another means of creating a mask in Vegas is to use generated media to define what will be masked out. One useful way to do this process is to create a mask that splits the screen in two or three parts, using blur and mask to create a completely smooth transition from one side to the other.

To create a split screen with a seamless transition:

1.   Insert three video tracks. Track 1 is for the mask, track 2 for one half of the screen, and track 3 for the remaining half of the screen.

2.   Insert the desired events on tracks 2 and 3.

3.   On track 1, insert generated media by right-clicking in the track 1 area of the timeline and selecting Insert Generated Media. In the Media Generator plug-in dialog, select Sony Solid Color and choose white as the color.

4.   Select the Pan/Crop tool on the generated media by right-clicking or by clicking the Pan/Crop button found on the media. In the Pan/Crop Preview window, slide the frame to the right until it divides the frame in half. (The Center should be at 720 and 240.) Close the Pan/Crop dialog box.

5. On track 2, click the Parent/Child button on the right side of track header. This step will cause the screen to split in half, showing track 2 on the left side of the screen, as it is being masked by track 1 and the pan/cropped image. If the images on tracks two and three are not centered, the Pan/Crop tool should be applied to the images to center them.

6. With the screen split, apply a Gaussian blur to the event on track 1 either by dragging the blur to the event from the Video FX docking window or by clicking the Event FX button on the solid color event on track 1. Apply the blur to the desired setting.

7. This process can also be applied in a series of two ofttrasitonsas well, by adding two more tracks to the project. This step will display three split sections Pan/Crop will need to be applied in opposite directions and in thirds of the screen.

7.56   Splitting the screen with the Parent/Child feature.

7.57   Splitting the screen into three parts is fast and simple with masks made from Generated Media.

👍 *Tip*

The project shown in Figure 7.57 can be found on the DVD in this book. The filename is 3screen. veg.

7.58   Access the Mask Generator by clicking the Mask FX button found on any Parent/Child combination.

Vegas also has a Mask Generator for every video track parented to another.

Five different mask modes are available in the Mask Generator dialog. Each mode blends or masks media differently, based on color or luminance found within the parent image, and are described here:

- Luminance—uses luminance in the image to determine transparency.

- Alpha—uses an alpha channel to determine transparency.

- Red Channel—uses the color red to determine transparency.

- Blue Channel—uses the color blue to determine transparency.

- Green Channel—uses the color green to determine transparency.

7.59 Specific color channel controls determine the transparency of that color's channel..

Open the `colorchannel.veg` file on the DVD in this book.

Use the Low in/High in sliders to limit or delimit the information in the Child events in the Parent/Child relationship. These attributes are keyframable and can be used to limit/delimit transparency of a channel over time. Use this tool as one alternative to animate lines on a map, create handwriting on an image, or mask out a color channel over time.

There are many creative ways to use masks in Vegas. Using masks, a reflection of text can be quickly composited.

Open a new project. Insert six video tracks. Do the following steps in this order:

1. On track 6, insert a background image. For purposes of this exercise, use generated media, preferably a color gradient.

2. On track 5, double-click the media on track six to create a selection. On track 5, right-click to insert text media. For this exercise, keep the text to one single line. Use a creative font for best results.

3. On track 4, with the selection still active from double-clicking track 6, right-click and select INSERT GENERATED MEDIA | SONY COLOR GRADIENT. (If the selection is not active, double-click track 6 again.) In the Gradient dialog, select the Linear White to Black from the menu. In the Aspect Ratio Angle dialog box, enter a value of 37. In the keyframe timeline of the Color Gradient dialog, click the Last Keyframe Button to move the cursor in the dialog to the end of the selection/event. Rotate the Aspect Ratio Angle to –180.0, which will cause the gradient to rotate in the project. Now select the Parent/Child button on the right of track 7.

4. Right-click the text on track 5 and select Copy. Right-click in track 3 and select Paste. Vegas will ask if you wish to create a reference to existing media or if you wish to create a new copy. Select New Copy.

5. On track 5, select the Track Motion button. In the Track Motion dialog box, right-click in the Track Motion Preview window and select Flip Vertical. The "F" in the Preview window will now be upside down in the Preview window. Now resize the track preview to 947.1 × 568.3. Center the image at 360.0 × 360.0.

6. Still working on the event on track 5, insert the following event FX: Add Noise, Gaussian Blur, Deform, and Light Rays. These plug-ins create the illusion of a reflected surface. Set the Add Noise plug-in to 0.168, with MonoChromatic and Gaussian Noise boxes checked. In the Gaussian Blur dialog, set the Horizontal value at 0.023 and Vertical at 0. In the Deform dialog, set the Amount to 1.00. Check the Center Image box. Leaving the Left and Right sliders set at 0, set the Top slider value to –0.209, and the Bottom slider value to 0.510. Finally, set the Light Rays to the values shown in Figure 7.58.

7. Place the cursor in the center of the Light Rays keyframe timeline. Set the Strength value to .550 and move the Light Source indicto toth center of the preview box. Move the cursor to the end of the keyframe timeline in the Light Rays keyframe timeline. Set the Strength value to .250 and move the Light Source indicator to the far right of the preview box.

7.60   Light ray values.

7.61   Settting values

8.   Right-click the mask on track 4 and select Copy. Paste this copy on track 2. Once again, Vegas will ask whether a new copy should be created or a reference to the original file should be made. Create a new copy. Click the Edit Generated Media button found on the generated media on track 2. In the Aspect Ratio Angle dialog, on the first keyframe, enter a value of 0.0. Now click the last Keyframe button in the keyframe timeline and enter a value of –180.0. On track 3, click the Parent/Child button to cause track 2 to be a parent to the text event found on track 3.

9.   Create a selection again by double-clicking any event on the timeline. On track 1, place a Sony color gradi-

7.62   Creating a reflective surface is very fast, and requires no additional plug-ins.

ent. In the Gradient dialog box, set the values to the settings shown in Figure 7.61.

Use the RAM Preview Render setting by creating a selection of all the media and pressing Shift+B. Vegas will take a moment to render the project to RAM. Be sure that RAM preview is set to the maximum available amount in the OPTIONS | PREFERENCES | VIDEO dialog. The default setting is 16MB of RAM. To render this project, you'll need at least 300MB of RAM available.

Compositing Modes in Vegas

Vegas has 14 different compositing modes. Source Alpha is the default mode, while additional modes can be used for a number of image manipulation and creative settings.

7.63 Compositing Mode button on each video track.

7.64 Various compositing modes in Vegas

7.65 Original foreground and background events.

Compositing modes define the manner in which a higher track combines with a lower track. As higher-level tracks dominate, for purposes of reference, the higher-level tracks are referred to as foreground, and lower-level tracks are referred to as background.

Compositing Mode tools allow for rapid access to creating multilayered images quickly. Compositing mode parameters are not adjustable. Using compositing envelopes allow you to adjust compositing level, or color management plug-ins can be used to provide opacity, chroma (color), and transparency control over all events. For instance, in the Add mode, using the Color Correction Secondary plug-in, combined with blur, creates a moving sonic wave. Using the Screen mode creates a more organic property in the sonic wave, almost as if it were a moving cloud.

Vegas 5 introduced a new compositing mode feature. When tracks become parented to one or more lower tracks, a new icon will appear in the Track Control pane of the uppermost track of the parent/child set. This is the Parent Track Overlay Mode button.

The Parent Track Overlay Mode button provides options to manage masked events above other events.

Out-of-focus video is sometimes an issue with even the most experienced of videographers. Using the Hard Light composite mode and a plug-in or two, marginally out-of-focus video can be brought to a faked focus or at the least, a more sharpened image.

Place the problem footage on a track and duplicate the track. On the upper track, apply the Convolution filter and the Sharpen preset in the Convolution filter. Reduce the opacity of the upper track to approximately 50 percent. Various settings will apply to individual events. On the lower track, apply a Hard Light compositing mode.

Some events with good color balance can also benefit by applying a Hard Light overlay mode in the compositing modes selection.

7.66 Before and after applying Hard Light and Convolution Kernel filter.

7.67 Parent Track Overlay Mode button.

7.68 Parent Track Overlay mode.

When you select this button, there are two menu choices. The first is the default Multiply mode, and the second is Custom. Selecting Custom opens a dialog offering three compositing overlay modes: Displacement Map, Bump Map, and Height Map.

Displacement Map

This mode uses the parent image as a controller to offset the pixels in the composited child tracks along the X and Y axes. his process uses a two-channel displacement. In other words, pixels are displaced to the left, right, up, or down depending on their relationship to colors in the mask. The displacement map is also useful for following contours of shapes.

7.69

This plug-in can be challenging to control. Working with solid colors or gradients as masks will yield the best results, particularly when learning how to use this tool.

7.70 Using a red mask causes the image to shift in a clean four-way split.

7.71 Using a blue-to-green mask causes the image to shift all pixels to the right, creating an extremely wide-angle appearance around the center of the screen without the associated rounding of the image, or vignetting.

7.72 Ordinary clouds shift to streaks of movement using the height map to shift pixels farther from their original position.

Original image from generated media

7.73 Three tracks are required to create the project illustrated in Figure 7.72.

To learn more about the displacement map, create two video tracks and place the stone.png image on track 2. Create a title using a bold font on track 1.

Duplicate track 2 and slide the new track so that it is track 1, the text is on track 2, and the original image is on track 3.

Now make track 1 parent to track 2, which will cause the text to be masked.

Check the Composite Mode button and choose the CUSTOM | SONY DISPLACEMENT MAP from the menu that opens.

In the dialog box, change both channels to Red. In the Horizontal axis, set the value to-0.018 and the Vertical axis to 0.027. The appearance of the text in the Preview window will vary depending on the font used. Experiment with the slider values to find the appropriate setting. Notice how the lettering conforms to the rocks in the photo. Using a text color slightly lighter in hue over the rocks completes the effect.

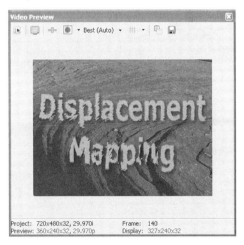

7.74 Three tracks were used to create this effect.

Height Map

This mode uses the parent image as a controller to cause pixels in the composited child tracks to appear closer to or farther away from the viewer. Adding a height map is a great tool for creating the appearance of moving water or viewing an image through glass or water, creating shimmers, fire, or smoke over another image. This mode can be added to gradients, masks, or other images above lower images.

To learn more about the height map, create a new project. Insert two video tracks.

Place the image rings.png from the DVD in this book onto track 1 and place a video or generated media event on track 2. Now make track 1 parent to track 2 by selecting the Parent/Child button on the left side of the Track Control pane.

On track 1, click the Compositing Mode button on track 1. From the menu, select CUSTOM | SONY HEIGHT MAP.

Enter the following settings in the dialog box:
• Amplitude—0.023
• Elevation—0.319
• Height Scale—0.320
• Smoothness—11
• Source Channel—Intensity (menu selection)
• Edge Pixel Handling—Wrap pixels around (menu selection)

Add a pan/crop to the event on track 1, zooming in by 40 percent. Experiment with the Amplitude and Elevation settings in the Height Displacement dialog box in order to better understand how this plug-in functions.

Any track-level keyframes can be viewed, moved, and edited directly from the timeline. By expanding the keyframes in the track view, keyframes can be slid forward or backward in time and double-clicked to open the track motion or compositing keyframes Tis feature provides a visual reference at all times when there is track motion or compositing information on a track, which allows for cursor placement on musical beats, specific musical or dialog points, or simply provides a reference to what is being seen in the Preview screen.

7.75 The Expand Track Keyframes button opens a keyframe pane directly on the timeline.

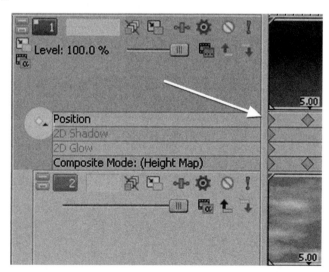

In nearly all of the previous projects, a gradient mask is used. Gradients and other generated media forms are very useful as masks. As an example, try this method of creating a mask:

1. Insert a gradient mask.

2. For mask shape, select rectangular.

3. In the Gradient Preview window, slide the color placement control points so that they are lying over top of each other with very little overlap.

This process takes some attention, because if the control points are not placed correctly, the mask will reverse itself and change from an outer mask to an inner mask. This element can also be used as a valuable tool. A color with reduced opacity can also be added to the mask's outer area, acting as an overlay, if desired. This type of mask is similar to the way the Cookie Cutter filter functions; however this method has greater flexibility in some instances.

7.76   Masks can be any shape at all.

Practice using the black-to-white gradient as a mask in projects, as it is one of the most powerful masking tools Vegas offers.

 Open the file called `jellyfishswim.veg` from the DVD in this book. It is a fairly complex project and contains many attributes found in Vegas.

Let's look at each track individually.

- Track 1—contains generated media and height map and is at 20 percent. The generated media acts as a guide to shift pixels generated on track 2.

- Track 2—contains generated media from the new Noise Texture generator. The Noise Generator is shifting in bias, causing it to create ripples on the "water."

- Track 3—is a gradient mask over track 4. It's composited in an Add mode, which brightens the image and adds contrast to allow the jellyfish to stand out over the other elements.

- Track 4—is another Noise Generated event, with color shift and pan/crop to create motion in the water.

- Track 5—is a simple blue generated media overlay at 50 percent opacity.

- Track 6—is another gradient, in Subtract compositing mode, acting as a mask for track 7. This feature helps bring out the colors in the jellyfish by masking brighter color values. With some work, a similar effect can be had with a secondary color corrector.

- Track 7—is a Noise Generated event, shifting across the Frequency, Noise, Offset, and Amplitude settings. Masked by the gradient on track 6, this color sets the shimmer over the jellyfish.

- Track 8—is the still image of the jellyfish, using pan/crop to move the fish, while two instances of the Spherize plug-in create the motion in the jellyfish. There is also a minor adjustment to the color of the still, reducing the exposure of the flash in the original shot. It also contains a height map to give the jellyfish texture and shine and is mapped to the event on track 9.

- Track 9—is a Noise Generated event, creating a texture of movement under the water, beneath the jellyfish.

Underneath all these layers is a motion blur added only to the jellyfish and Noise Generated layer found on track 9. Motion blur is applied at a value of 15 percent.

With this project open, change the compositing modes, opacities, and generated media gradients or colors. See how these changes affect the jellyfish appearance. This demonstration provides a visual overview of the function of each aspect of the tools.

Bump Map

This mode uses the texture of the parent image to create a map of light and dark information. This tool is very handy for creating 3D titles, creating textures over an event, and mapping a texture to an underlying event.

Lighting angles are definable with the Lighting Type menu. Use the Intensity slider toinceas ordeceae the presence of a light. The X, Y, and Z parameters can be controlled by inputting values to the input field or by moving the target dot in the Bump Placement window. Reset the X-Y parameter by double-clicking the yellow dot or by right-clicking in the Bump Placement window and selecting Reset.

7.77   In this image, the stone creates a texture, mapped to the outlines of the cowboy, creating a handdrawn effect.

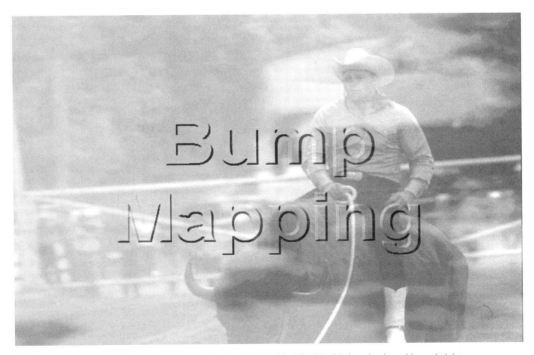

7.78   In this image, a simple text event takes on 3D attributes with definable lighting, depth, and bump height.

7.79 Controls found in the Bump Map dialog box control light, focus, depth of mapping, and light displacement.

The Z slider (vertical) controls the height of the light on the mapped image. When Spotlight is selected from the menu, the distances of X and Y are controllable, and the focus slider is enabled as well. Focus controls the tightness or breadth of the light image. Omni-directional and Directional menu options automatically disable the focus and X-Y distance controls. The Destination of X-Y can be adjusted by moving the X in the Bump Placement window.

The Shininess slider controls the reflective surface of the map, and the Ambience slider controls the amount of light seen in the mapped image.

The White is high check box causes the bump map to view white areas as the highest areas of the bump texture. Leaving this box unchecked causes the black areas to define the high areas of the texture.

Finally, flipping the input surface reverses the two images, causing the upper and lower tracks to flip images.

Open the `bumpmap.veg` file found on the DVD in this book for examples of the bump mapping shown in the images earlier.

Learning to work with these tools helps build titles, scene atmospheres, and magical shots quickly and powerfully. Compositing itself is an art form and requires a great deal of time and experimenting. Vegas has some of the most powerful compositing tools in its class of editing systems and, over all, has more compositing tools than any NLE system that doubles as a finishing editor. On the DVD in this book, several compositing projects are available, although not described in this chapter.

Using Chromakey Tools in Vegas

Chromakey, also referred to as greenscreening or bluescreening, is an art form that must first be practiced at the camera and shooting stage of a production. Even fairly weak footage, however, can be usable in Vegas when filtered with the color correction tools and chromakey tools.

Chroma (color) and key (mask) come together to create a mask from selected color(s). A quality mask or key can also be made from nearly any color or reasonable gradient of color. Selectable colors/chroma can be keyed or masked out, so that other events can show through those sections. Although industry tradition uses a screen of blue or green, any color can be keyed. Due to the luminance and chroma sensitivity of the bright green used in screens, however, in most situations, green is the best choice for DV.

(For more information on the relationship between chromakey and DV, visit `http://www.sundancemediagroup.com/help/kb/` and read the tutorial on 4:1:1 DV.)

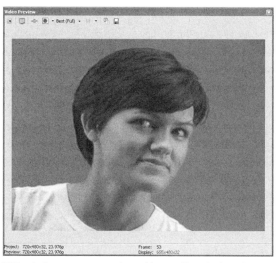

7.80 A clean greenscreen shot, with no spill on the face of subject.

Shooting a clean screen is critical to having a relatively smooth experience with keying. Many tutorials are available on how to shoot a clean screen, and the Sundance Media Group V.A.S.S.T. training course teaches this as well (`www.vasst.com`). Some basics to know are presented here to assist the inexperienced cameraperson/editor in creating a clean shot to be keyed in the editing stage.

Use Rosco green paint or a commercially produced greenscreen. We recommend the Photoflex dual-color screens that have flex hoops in them for easy storage. When shooting on DV, green is the only safe choice. Blue can be used in analog shooting.

Good lighting is critical. To shoot a clean screen requires at least three lights: a key light for the talent and two lights for the screen itself. A reflector for the key light to light the opposite side of the subject is valuable too, as are flags (masks) to keep the key light from spilling onto the screen.

Shoot the subject at a minimum of six feet from the screen. This practice is necessary to prevent green reflection from spilling onto the subject. This kind of reflective spill is very difficult to remove in editing, regardless of the application used for creating a key or matte.

Vegas has excellent chromakey tools that allow for rapid and clean keying of colors. A successful key, however, is also dependent on practice and experience on the part of the user.

From the DVD, open the `greenscreen.avi` file on the timeline in Vegas. Select the Event FX on the file and open the Sony Chromakeyer tool.

In the Chromakey dialog box, uncheck thechck oxin the upper-left corner. The Chromakey dialog defaults to blue, and unchecking this box allows Vegas to sample an accurate replacement color. Select the Eyedropper tool, found in the left center of the Chromakey dialog. With the Eyedropper enabled, click the color to be removed from the event in the Preview window.

7.81 Chromakey tool at default setting. Uncheck the Chromakeyer
box in the upper-left corner.

7.82 Draw or click in the Preview window to select color for removal.

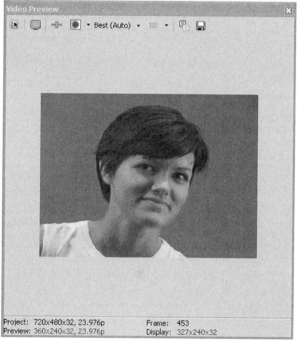

Enable the Chromakey tool by placing a checkmark in the check box in the upper-left of the
Chromakey dialog. A portion of the selected color will immediately change in the Preview window. Now the Chromakey tool must be adjusted to create a clean key.

Start by placing the event to be seen beneath the keyed event. This process helps adjust the key for best matting. Generated media is great for this, esecially generated media that is a similar color to the replacement event. Of course, the replacement event can also be used. If it's a fairly busy event with lots of detail, however, it is sometimes difficult to create clean lines, as the detail in the background event hides lines during the key process.

 Tip

> Viewing the key process on an external monitor is helpful to ensure a clean key process. During the color selection, however, the preview must be on the computer screen. After key color is selected, video can be sent to an external NTSC or PAL monitor.

After an event is placed beneath the event being keyed, slide the Low Threshold slider to the right and slide the High Threshold slider to the left. On the `greenscreen.avi` file, a clean key will be achieved with the Low Threshold slider at 0.400 and the High Threshold at 0.800. The Blur setting is dependent on the background media used. In the instance of the greenscreen. veg file found on the DVD, the Blur setting is at 0.015 to soften the harsh transition between the background color and the edges of the key. Some keyed events require a fair amount of blur while others can require no blur whatsoever.

Creating a Garbage Matte in Vegas

A garbage matte or mask is a simple mask, created from an event or image in Vegas, which removes one element from other elements on the screen. This option assists in the keying process, particularly where more than one color must be keyed out. The earlier project does not require a garbage matte; however, many instances exist in which a garbage matte is beneficial.

To create a garbage matte, click the Show Mask Only box in the Chromakey tool. This step displays the areas being masked and quickly shows a clean or unclean key. This matte/mask can

A popular effect is to create an image that is entirely black and white, except one or two colors. This is part of a color pass, which allows a color to pass through an image that is otherwise black and white.

To create this effect quickly, place the events on the timeline to be color passed. Duplicate the track so that two identical tracks exist. On the upper track, insert a Chromakey and Black and White filter in order.

Using the eyedropper in the Chromakey tool, select the color to be passed, or allowed to be shown. Use the View Mask Only check box to see what areas will be knocked out in black and white. Adjust the Black and White filter to the desired level of black and white blend. For maximum effect, the lower track can have a slight blend of black and white with the color. This option reduces the amount of contrast between the color and black and white areas if this is the desired effect.

Although this is one method of color-passing in Vegas, see the section on Color Correction in chapter seven which discusses alternative methods.

7.82   A clean and simple garbage matte/mask.

7.84   An improper mask/matte.

7.85   Track 1 soloed and with Show Mask Only enabled in the Chromakey tool. This
process is done to render a matte/mask to a new track.

be rendered to a new track, which is then parented to the original event, saving processor time and allowing multiple masks to take place on the timeline/project. To render the matte to a new track, solo the track containing the mask. Double-click the event to be rendered to a new track, creating a selection. Select TOOLS | RENDER TO NEW TRACK. In the dialog box, select Custom and select the Audio tab.

After the new track is rendered, it should be parented to the original track. Click the Event FX button on the original track and disable the Chromakey tool by un-checking the check box in the upper left of the Chromakey tool. Parent the mask event to the original event by clicking the Parent/Child button to the left of the original track.

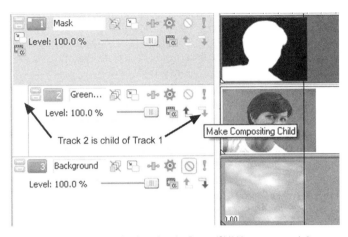

7.86   Parent track 1 to track 2 by using the Parent/Child button on track 2.

7.87   A clean composite

The two events over the third track, which contains the background information, create a clean composite over the background image if all parameters are adjusted correctly, as illustrated in Figure 7.87.

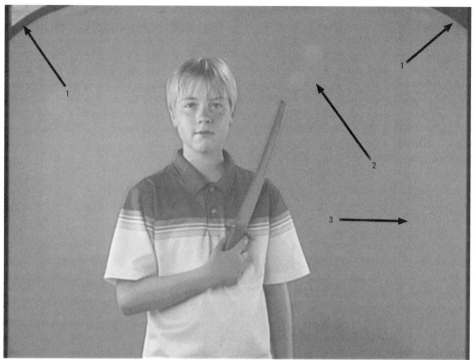

7.88   Identifying problem areas in a screen isn't always easy or obvious.

The original image can be color corrected, blurred, or otherwise filtered for creative presentation if desired.

Figure 7.88 shows three problem areas in the screen.

1. The corners of the screen are visible. These areas will not mask cleanly.

2. Lens flare/reflection shows across screen. This will not mask cleanly.

3. There is spill getting past a flag, allowing backlight spill on the screen and creating two colors of green. This will not mask cleanly.

These problems can be overcome, but the time involved, coupled with the loss of resolution, quickly demonstrate the necessity and time savings of having media shot correctly in the production stage.

 To see how to correct the poorly shot footage, open the `badscreen.veg` file on the DVD in this book.

A clean mask has been rendered to track 1. This garbage matte is required to create a clean composite. Track 2 is parented to the mask/garbage matte, which is similar to the way the first greenscreen project was done. To be able to create a clean mask, however, a secondary color corrector and black restore were used to cause the mask to render cleanly. The event is also panned/cropped to remove the corners from the scene and to create a clean masking area. Still the original event requires color correction to blend into the background with a believable presentation. The original settings for the color correction and chromakey have been left in place on the original event in region one. Click the Event FX to enable these two FX, allowing you to see how the mask was created. Color correction has been added to the event as well. Disable this by unchecking the check box in the upper-left corner of the FX dialog. A very small amount of blur has been added to the mask to smooth over the transition from the masked area to the background area.

These are two examples of how a chromakey can be used to repair a background image or to insert new media. There are other instances where a screen is valuable however.

Open the `tvscreen.veg` file on the DVD in this book.

The `tvscreen.veg` file contains a still image: `tvshot.png`. This image is an old photograph of a child watching television. The television screen has been replaced with green, allowing for a motion picture to be placed in the television screen. This method can also be used to replace screens in television studio-type shots or military establishment-type shots to create a sense of realism. There are more examples of this sort of masking on the tvscreen.veg file. Play with them and notice how the Track Motion tool is used to fill in the masked sections.

Never be afraid to experiment using various FX, track Motion, Pan/Crop, and other tools on composited media. Turn lots of knobs, slide the sliders, and check the check boxes. Various combinations turn up lots of artistic possibilities, and, as mentioned at the front of this chapter, compositing is an art form. Be creative!

Create a Holograph in Vegas!

Remember the beamed holographs seen in Star Wars episodes? At the time the movie came out, this was an exceptionally cool thing, never seen nor conceived before. Star Trek had a simple transporter beam effect that used masks to create the look of being transported, but the holograph was a method of communication and projection never before seen. Playing around in Vegas on a VASST tour, I was working with a piece of footage and realized how simple this would be in Vegas. To accomplish this look you'll need to shoot against a solid backdrop, preferably green if you are shooting with DV. (See my tutorial on why green is better.) Shoot your footage with your actor dressed in imaginative clothing, but color of the clothing won't matter much, as we'll be apply-

ing a blue filter over the original footage to mask most color detail. Just be sure the clothing doesn't contain colors that are the same or fairly similar to the background color. You'll have the most effective look if your actor is shot full-body, but even half or three-quarters works acceptably well. However, to mimic the Star Wars look, you'll want to do a full body shot. Remember, if this is to look like a communication transmission, your actor should look at the camera just as though he can see a video or holographic representation of who they are speaking to.

7.89   The original image is shot against a green background.

First, I used the secondary color corrector to pop my blues, allowing for better extraction from the background which has a few gradients, as we didn't use the cyc's full lighting system. I then added a chromakey tool, and using the Show Mask Only check box, I cleaned up my output. The project .veg file has left these two tools in place, merely turned off, so you can work with the demo media to see how I popped the blue and cleaned up the output. I then used the Pan/Crop tool to create a 16:9 letterbox, and used the Track Motion tool to stretch the body and create a thinner and off-aspect appearance to the shot. After getting the mask set up, I found a background .jpeg that I wanted to insert the original image into. In this case, it's a shot of a living room.

Next, I rendered a new track with the Show Mask Only box still checked. I unchecked Include Audio from the Render>Custom options, as I wanted the new mask track to lie directly above the original track with no audio, and the audio from the original track was used in the project, removing the need to have a second, duplicate audio track. This allowed me to create a garbage mask or matte to be used as a parent to the original image. Don't create the mask or matte til the Pan/Crop and Track Motion attributes have been determined. Be sure ripple is disabled before rendering to new track. On the original track, remove the Secondary Color Corrector and Chromakey from the original. With the matte above the original track, Parent the matte to the original by pressing the Parent/Child button on the original track. This will allow the original track to show through. At this point, you should see a fairly clean image over top of the selected background. Set the opacity of your matte to 75 percent for starters. This will allow the background to be seen through the hologram.

Using selected filters, we'll now create the image of the hologram. Drag the Gaussian Blur filter to the matte. Set the values for both horizontal and vertical blur to approximately .025 for starters. This will likely be tweaked later. (The project veg is set to .027.) The blur helps create a soft edge on the original media. It also washes out the screened edges and blends the image into the background a little more smoothly.

Drop the Secondary Color Corrector onto the original video track. Choose the Desaturate All but Red preset for starters. Slide the Saturation slider to the right, to a value of 3.000. Now slide the Limit Hue value to the full right, to a value of 360. Slide the corrector target dot to the lower left in the color wheel, setting the track to a blue color. Set this to the desired level. This should blow out the edges of the original media. This step is not necessary for creating this particular look. I simply wanted to blow out my edges.

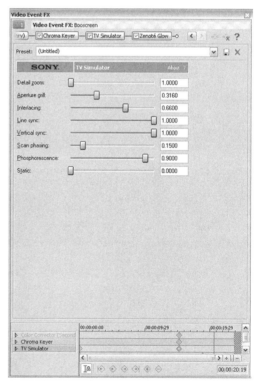

7.90 Match the sliders in this screen shot to create fast pulsing sync lines.

Now drop the TV Simulator on the original media. Select the TV Look preset. Slide Line Sync, Scan Phasing, Phosphorescence all to the right to create a fast scan image. Add a tiny value of Static if you'd like to distort the image a little further. If you want less interlacing (the horizontal lines in the image) reduce the Interlacing value to zero. For a really unique look, keyframe Line Sync and Scan Phasing value movements to make the picture break up every now and then. Notice there are no keyframes in the project. I left these blank so you could experiment with these values on your own.

Now drop the Brightness and Contrast filter on the original image, setting the Brightness value to .22. That's all there is to it. The project ready to be rendered.

Some options you might want to try, depending on source footage if other than the media used in the training file:

- Drop the Glow filter on the footage. (The Zenoté plugin was used for the original render seen in the demo footage. It's an excellent tool for smoothing out the highlights.)

- Drop a Film Grain filter on the original along with the TV simulator to create noise in the file.

- Use the Convolution filter to create unique effects. This won't work for all looks but is a great look for some effects.

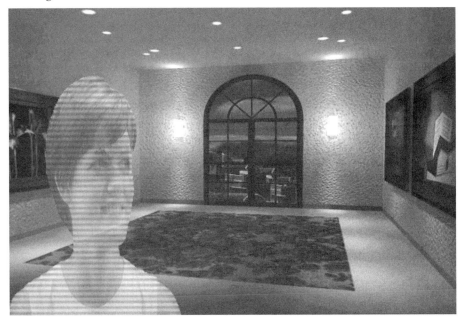

7.91   Here is the look of the final product.

Motion Blur

Vegas has a feature called Motion Blur that allows an envelope to be applied controlling the duration and shape of the blur applied to the motion of video. What makes motion blur unique is that it applies blur at the frame level, creating a blur over time (temporal) as the video shows

7.92   Motion blurred at full value with the Motion Blur tool.

7.93   The original image from Thomas Edison's 1900 fim, The Kiss. Notice black edges to
        be cropped out, bringing the image to correct aspect ratio.

movement. This option makes zooms, pans, and motion in the image blur smoothly. A standard blur applies a blur in 2D space or a spatial blur. A motion blur acts more like a wide-open shutter, allowing for a greater exposure time.

Applying the envelope is performed by selecting VIEW | VIDEO BUS TRACKS (Shift+Ctrl+B) and then right-clicking the video control pane and inserting a Motion Blur envelope. Double-clicking the envelope and adding handles/nodes controls the amount of blur.

Applying this filter to sequences of still images, fast or slow motion video, and animations can add a sense of realism to the media. It can also be inserted with great intensity to generate a dream-like quality.

One really great effect to try with motion blur is to render an event with lots of motion to a new track and to add a motion blur to suit the eye. In that new track/event, right-click and select Undersample. Undersample the event by at least .750, which will create a unique and stuttered look with blur shifting. The most unusual effect comes from using extremely low undersampling/ frame rate in which the frames skip enough to cut the blurred frames to the point that they are almost unrelated in motion.

Another terrific use of this tool is to blur a camera pan when transitioning from one scene to another. A motion blur, coupled with a velocity filter and transition, is a good combination for the popular effect of stuttered motion or stopped-motion blurring during a pan into another scene or shot sequence. Motion blur does add considerable time to a rendered section, so make sure the envelope is completely off when not being used.

Every track will be blurred when this envelope is up, unless the Bypass Motion Blur button is chosen. This option allows you to selectively blur tracks. The button is next to the Scribble Strip

7.94   The same image after cropping and supersampling at a value of 2 frames.

on each video track in the Track Control pane. Leaving it enabled causes the video track to be blurred.

Super Sampling

Super sampling resamples each pixel of video information in Vegas 6 and significantly improves the smoothness of the pixel edges and matches to adjoining pixels. This feature is primarily valuable when used in conjunction with the Motion Blur envelope but is also beneficial when used in upsampling smaller resolutions to DV or higher levels. Super sampling will not be as noticeable with video containing high motion or with video that is not being changed in output size or resolution. Use super sampling in connection with Motion Blur, upsampling small resolution video, or when working with extremely low resolution stills. It works exceptionally well when shifting the aspect ratio from one size to another, such as converting video that is 160 x 160 to 720 x 480.

The way this works is that Vegas creates interpretive frames based on the difference between the project frame rate and the frame rate of the media, or the computer-generated imagery. This process also creates smoother flow and edges for generated behaviors, such as Pan/Crop, Track Motion, Transitions, and other new media created in the timeline during the editing stages.

Insert a Super Sampling envelope in the same manner as inserting a Motion Blur envelope by selecting VIEW | VIDEO BUS TRACKS (Shift+Ctrl+B) and inserting a Super Sampling envelope. Use the envelope to control how many interpolative frames are created. For instance, by using an envelope setting of four, four times as many frames are rendered as existedin he rignal event. This means that render times are significantly slowed, so don't plan on doing a super sample while you are answering a phone call or grabbing a quick bite to eat. Super sampling, however, is a fantastic tool when shifting resolution, frame rate, or both. It often is beneficial to add a small amount of Gaussian blur as well, to spatially shift the image. Supersampling won't benefit media that isn't changing aspect ratio or framerate, if it merely is being employed to go from one format to another format of matching dimension.

Color Correction and Manipulation

Understanding the Color Correction Tools in Vegas

Vegas has many color correction tools capable of repairing even the most difficult footage with greatly improved result. A color correction toolset, a secondary color correction toolset, waveform monitor (WFM), vectorscope, parade scope, histogram view, and optimized hue saturation luminosity (HSL), color curves, broadcast filter, and more make Vegas one of the more powerful color correction–capable NLEs available today. (See Figures 8.1, 8.2, 8.3, 8.4, and Color Plate 8.1.

8.1   Vectorscope

8.2   Waveform monitor.

Tools that can be used for color correction include:

- Black Restore
- Brightness and Contrast
- Broadcast Colors
- HSL plug-in
- Color Curves plug-in
- Color Balance
- Color Corrector
- Color Corrector—Secondary
- Gradient Mapping
- Pixelan Chromawarp (third party)

The new color correction tools found in Vegas provide the ability to set apart colors or a range of colors and to command isolated colors in order to suit emotional, artistic, accurate, or whimsical expressions.

Also, tools are available to maintain color shift from event to event in Vegas, which assists in matching shots from two different cameras or from DV to other video sources. Finally, Vegas provides tools that can limit or force colors to remain legal or become broadcast legal in Vegas.

These scopes and monitors are all tools to help identify color values and luminance values and to assist in color matching. Just having them doesn't correct color; they are for reference. Although we'll briefly discuss how to use them, this chapter is not intended to teach you how to read them and gain an in-depth understanding of how they work.[1]

This chapter, however, provides a basic overview of how these monitoring and display tools function within Vegas and the editing world.

Broken down to the most simplistic form, a waveform monitor is for reading *luminance*, or brightness, and most other tools are for reading *chrominance*, or color. Keep this information in mind while working with the tools. In the majority of color correction use, both the WFM and vectorscope are open at the same time, which is why menu choices for both are in the Video Scpes menu.

 Tip

Before starting any color correction processes, be sure you've got exposure set correctly. My method is to convert the image to greyscale using the B/W filter, and then using Levels to adjust the exposure. Once exposure is corect, then you'll want to remove the B/W filter.

8.3   RGB Parade display.

8.4   Histogram.

Displays and Scopes

The Histogram tool is one of the most valuable tools in Vegas. A histogram gives a good indication of color balances overall, s sown in Figure 8.5.

8.5   The histogram on the left contains illegal colors; however, the histogram on the right is legal, using the Broadcast Colors filter.

A histogram also provides a very fast way to view illegal colors. Illegal colors are usually created by inserting text, adding color-altering filters, or using improper color correction. Use the Broadcast Colors filter to bring colors into legal status.

The parade display in Vegas shows which colors are within individual limits and also demonstrates the level of the total video output, as shown in Color Plate 8.2. This important tool can help you discover color distortion at output. A standard parade display shows level information on RGB, instead of showing the total level of the modulated video output.

Illegal colors are colors that are not compliant with NTSC standards. Illegal colors overmodulate the broadcast signal, causing distortion of video and audio. No one will put you in jail for using illegal colors, but the strain on the eyes and ears in most instances, will drive viewers crazy. If you've ever seen a low-budget car-lot advertisement on television with buzzing audio and distortion on the announcer's sibilants, chances are great that the commercial contains illegal colors, most likely the whites used in titles. (Distortion is actually across the entire audio signal but seems more apparent with an overmodulated color signal.)

Color value in the NTSC world is measured in IRE. Color value in the RGB world is measured in RGB component values. For example, in the IRE world, extreme black is 8.5 IRE. Extreme black in the IRE world, however, is really just a very dark gray, measuring at 16.5 in the RGB world. Extreme white in the IRE world is 100 IRE. Again, this is really just very bright gray, measuring at 234 in the RGB world. RGB extreme black is 0, while extreme white is 255. Any color value in the RGB world that goes below 16 or above 234 is illegal by NTSC broadcast standards. Any color value in the IRE scale that goes below 8.5 IRE or above 100 IRE is also illegal.

Legal colors are related to NTSC broadcasting. Because most video equipment in the NTSC realm is calibrated or manufactured to the same specification, however, practicing legal color on DVDs, video tapes, and hard drives is a good practice. The Internet currently has no color limits.

8.6   Shows the video event with illegal colors.

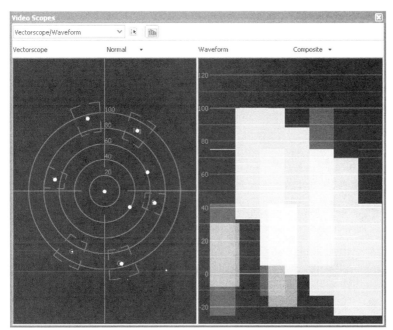

8.7   Standard SMPTE colorbars, inserted as generated media in Vegas 6. The white dots represent positions of the individual colors found in SMPTE colorbars (WFM in Composite mode, with indicators enlarged for illustration).

8.8   Shows colorbars with saturation in the Color Corrector tool at 1.500 (all
other settings reset to null).

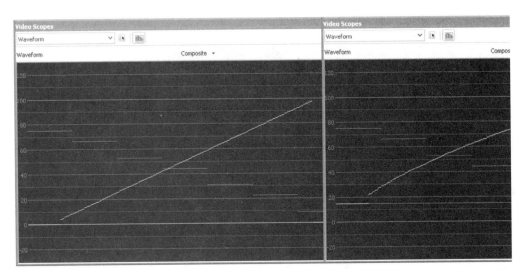

8.9   Shows ramp with gamma at 1.500. Notice that the curve of the waveform display has changed significantly in the right
image (all other settings reset to null). The ramp is used to demonstrate gamma, as colorbars aren't a good choice to
express gamma.

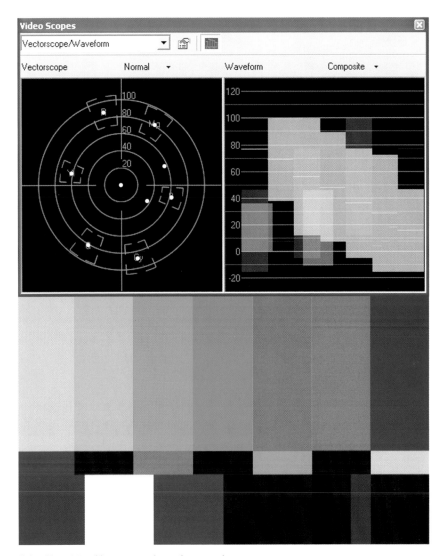

Color Plate 8.1　　Vectorscope/waveform monitor.

Color Plate 8.2   In this screenshot, the blues are clipping in the image, even though the eye doesn't see extreme blues. This result occurs because a blue gradient is being overlaid. The gradient is only five percent opaque, yet that is enough to clip the blue channel.

Color Plate 8.3   Easy-access color correction controls.

Color Plate 8.4   The original shot.

Color Plate 8.5   The image on the left is dull and uninteresting. The image on the right has
depth and more interesting detail.

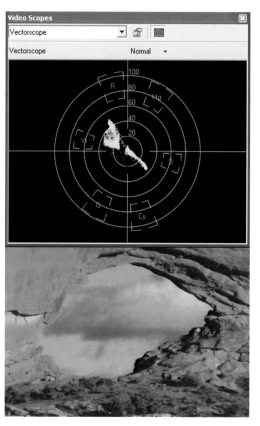

Color Plate 8.6   Video event on scope.

Color Plate 8.7   Still image event on scope before color correction.

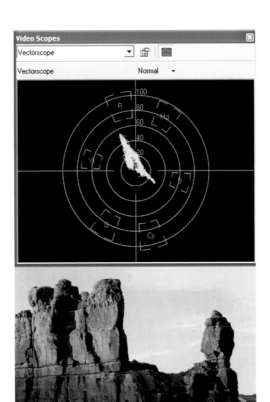

Color Plate 8.8   Still image event on scope after
color correction.

Color Plate 8.9   This image is dull and lifeless and lacks contrast.

Color Plate 8.10   Using a brightness/contrast filter, the image now has contrast and color but appears cold, harsh, and unfriendly.

Color Plate 8.11   The left half of image is improved, or corrected. The right side is the original image. The Split-Screen Preview tool is invaluable for comparing events while editing.

Color Plate 8.12   The original image coloring is on the left, and the corrected image is on the right.

Color Plate 8.13   The original image. White balance was not taken before the shoot, hence the white spotlight on performer's face on a dark stage. Overblown whites have destroyed any hope of detail.

Color Plate 8.14   The image after correction. Rather than trying to restore detail that doesn't exist, bring up the surrounding colors to make the image less objectionable, more realistic, and potentially usable in the absence of more acceptable footage.

Color Plate 8.15 The left side is the original image, and the right side is the gradient-covered image. Notice the male dancer on the right image is clearer, and the colors from the right to left side of the screen are more balanced.

Color Plate 8.16 Gradient applied to the image using the Gradient Map plug-in.

Color Plate 8.17 Which contains more detail—the warmer images on the right or the cooler images on the left? The images are exactly the same. The image on the left has the Sony Gradient plug-in with the Warm preset, and the image on the right has the Sony Gradient plug-in with the Cooler preset.

Color Plate 8.18   The original and color-enhanced image using the Secondary Color
                    Corrector tool.

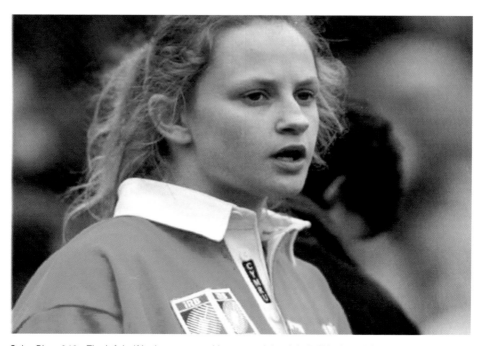

Color Plate 8.19   The left half is the processed image, and the right half is the original image. The Secondary Color Corrector tool removed all color except for the red in the jersey.

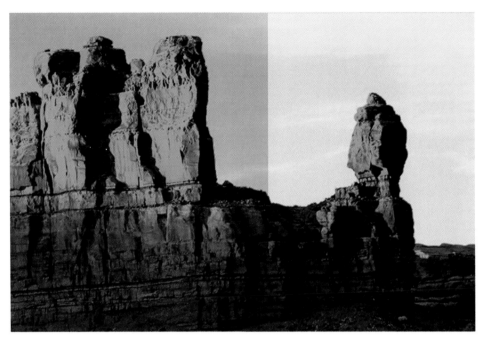

Color Plate 8.20 The processed image is on the left, and the original image is on the right.

Color Plate 8.21 The left side is deinterlaced using duplicate tracks.

Color Plate 8.22 Gamma reduced, saturation increased, dual tracks of interlaced video, top track at 50 percent opacity.

Color Plate 8.23   Settings for the Saturation Adjust filter remove all saturation except for lower mid-levels and leave the clothing
in color while everything else is desaturated.

Color Plate 8.24   By blowing out or overextending the gain and luminance
of an image, a look of infrared or night goggles can be
created.

8.10 Shows colorbars with gain at 1.500. Notice that the WFM breadth and height have expanded significantly (all other settings reset to null).

The parade display can be updated by enabling the "Update scopes while playing" button. Place the cursor over the highest part of a color display in the parade scope to display the RGB value of that color point.

Figure 8.6 demonstrates the waveform view of the same video event, which is showing illegal colors. This instance shows how the waveform monitor can demonstrate illegal or clipping colors.

Figure 8.7 shows the same event with the Broadcast Colors clamp set to Lenient. This tool brings the colors to a legal status, but the blue channel is still clipped.

Working from an SMPTE colorbar pattern, examine how various changes affect the display of the WFM/vectorscope. (The waveform monitor displays IRE in percentages, not IRE levels. Use the Broadcast Colors clamp/plug-n if a 8.5 IRE pedestal is required.)

The images shown in Figures 8.7 through 8.11 are in `colorbars-scopes.veg` on the DVD in this book.

These figures demonstrate how the sliders in the Primary Color Corrector tool affect the display of images and how they appear in the WFM/vectorscope. Knowing how each of these controls works is key to using the tools correctly and to achieving the desired image quality.

Pedestal, also called setup or lift, is a base line for indicating black. Without knowing exactly where black exists in relationship to other colors, it's difficult to process colors accurately. Each video display (histogram, WFM, vectorscope, parade) has a Settings button in the upper center. Select options from Setting to determine a Studio RGB setup (RGB-16forblak,8.5IR for black, or none).

8.11   Shows colorbars with offset at 50.0 Notice the positioning of the colorbars (all other settings reset to null).

8.12   Color Corrector tool found in Vegas

8.13 The updated Secondary Color Corrector tool found in Vegas 5 and 6. Note the Invert Mask feature.

These new tools allow concise and accurate color selection in Vegas to be isolated and managed. Each of the color wheels is controllable with a mouse or a joystick, making it easier to fine-tune each color. The color wheels match the position of colors on the WFM.

The Primary Color Corrector tool works much like an equalizer in an audio system. The three wheels control lows (blacks), mids (largest range of color information), and highs (whites). Thinking in this mode may help some editors work with the colors more comprehensively.

Shadows and contrasts fall into the category of black. Facial colors, clothing, paints, and predominantly everything focused on in a frame, all fall into the midrange color category. Whites are the sparkle and the high end of various hues of color, providing detail in most instances. Dulling the high end, as in audio, generally results in less clarity of a picture image. Sometimes illegal colors, however, function much like distortion and need to be reduced to bring colors to a more reasonable and appreciable level. Depending on how the image was captured/acquired and with what, resolution levels might not allow colors to be intensified without seriously degrading the image.

All plug-ins in Vegas are now dockable with scroll bars. This feature means that the workspace is less cluttered, yet all controls are accessible from within the docking space (see Color Plate 8.3). This process makes color correction more efficient when working on a single screen, such as a laptop, as all correction parameters are accessible without having thesceencoered with the correction tools.

8.14 Color wheel and vectorscope color distribution is the same.

8.15 The Define Effect Range is enabled by using the Eyedropper tool to select the color range to be affected.

It should also be understood that when working with most of the color correction tools, manipulating images in the midrange will usually have some impact on the blacks/lows, the whites/highs, or both.

We'll use the color image in Color Plate 8.4 as a color correction starting point. This image is flat and dull. In reality, however, we know that the rocks of Moab should be red and vibrant, and the sky should be deep blue, with white clouds. A brightness/contrast filter could be applied to the image to bring up the brightness; however, that process would then brighten the shadow and landscape areas as well, causing detail to disappear. The overall image would appear washed out and soft in appearance. Using the Secondary Color Corector, colors can be selectively adjusted.

Open the `rocks.veg` file found on the DVD in this book.

Four views of the same event are provided in the `rocks.veg` file found on the DVD that accompanies this book. Version one has no color correction whatsoever. Version two has red added to create a richer and deeper color. Version three has the red added in version two, and the sky has been brought to a deeper color for greater depth. Finally, version four has green added to the trees to set them more in the foreground of the shot. In Color Plate 8.5, the left half of the screen is the original shot, and the right half is the color corrected shot.

Let's look at how this was done.

Apply a secondary color corrector by selecting the Event FX button on the event, which opens up the Secondary Color Corrector dialog. First, select the color intended to be isolated and to be enhanced or edited. Use the Eyedropper tool found in the Secondary Color Corrector tool to select the rocks and define the effect range.

After the color range is selected, move the color wheel target around in the color wheel. This step causes colors in the Preview window to change with the rotation, demonstrating how the targeted colorspace is affected. Open the scopes view (Ctrl+Alt+2) and look at how the image shows up in the vectorscope.

With the orange of the rocks selected as the target color, move the target dot to an angle of 118.5 and the magnitude of .480. You can either key the numbers in the dialog box or drag the target dot to that quadrant/location. Adjust the Saturation slider to 1.00. The rocks take on a reddish/orange hue. Adjust the saturation to the point that it is satisfying to your eye. These numbers are relative to a computer monitor and not previewed on an external NTSC monitor.

After the color of the rocks is brought to a point where you are satisfied, click the Event FX button on the same event and insert another Secondary Color Corrector tool by clicking the tool and the Add button.

Use the Eyedropper tool again to select the blue in the sky. Now set the angle to 324.5 and the magnitude to 0.382. Adjust saturation to 1.00. Adjust the Limit Saturation/Low setting to 20.0 and the Limit Saturation/Smooth setting to 50.0. Finish the correction on the blue/sky area by adjusting the Offset setting to 6.5. Now the rocks and the sky should be a pleasing color and depth. Again, keep in mind that various monitors display the images differently, so check this image on an external monitor or adjust to your eye and satisfaction.

Notice that after the red and blue have been corrected, the trees in the foreground are darker and inconsistent in color with the rest of the image. Another Secondary Color Corrector tool is needed, so click the Event FX again, select Secondary Color Corrector tool, and click Add to insert it. Using the Eyedropper tool, select the green trees and bushes in the foreground. Set the angle to 211.0 and the magnitude to 0.485. Set the Saturation level to 1.070. In the Limit Luminance, set the High level to 76.0. Notice how the color of the green pops out to match the color levels of the rocks and sky.

8.16   Original color in vectorscope.

8.17   Color display for corrected version. Notice the extended blue, red, and yellow/green display.

On the timeline is a still frame event that must be color-matched as closely as possible to the video event preceding it. This process is difficult to do because of differences in resolution, location, and time of day. A reasonable compromise, however, can be made between the two images, making a transition between the two less objectionable. Secondary Color Corrector tools and Color Curves tools are used to bring the two events closer together in color value. The vectorscope is used to match the colors more closely together in terms of relevance. The rocks and sky are the two common subjects in the two events, so we'll use those to make our corrections and changes (see Color Plate 8.6).

Finding a middle ground for the two images, particularly when the original video image is washed out (see Color Plate 8.7) and has been corrected to bring out more color, means that the still image event must be washed out and colors reduced to match the video event. Using the vectorscope, we can see a footprint of the two images. Because little can be done to realistically bring the video image up any further in resolution quality and color depth, the still image event must be corrected and brought to resemble the footprint displayed by the video event.

The Primary and Secondary Color Corrector tools are exceptionally powerful. However, don't forget the other correction tools. Color Balance, Color Curves, HSL, and Saturation Adjust are all tools that are equally powerful. Color Plate 8.8 has a Secondary Color Corrector tool, Gaussian Blur, Color Curves, and Saturation Adjust on the image to bring it as close as possible to the video event transitioning into it. Select the Event FX button on the still image evet to see how the image is brought to corrected color values.

Open wedding.veg from the DVD found in this book.

In this wedding scene, we can see how the opening shot is lacking contrast, depth, and personality (see Color Plate 8.9). It's also fairly dark, which would make most of us reach for the brightness/contrast tool.

Using the Primary Color Corrector tool, highlights and color can be brought out while maintaining warmth and personality. In this example, the face tones, the green in the trees, and the red in the bunting can be brought out, which will make for a warm and interesting image (see Color Plate 8.10).

When matching two events on a timeline, one technique is to do a screen capture of one of the two events, preferably the correctly colored event. Move the cursor to the second event so you can see it in the Preview window. Select SPLIT SCREEN | CLIPBOARD and draw a rectangle around the area of the second event on the timeline. The screenshot will be shown next to the second event, making it easiertocolor match/correct the second event to the first event.

8.18 Use the Select Adjustment Color eyedropper to select colors to be restored/repaired.

On this same event, several individual Secondary Color Corrector tools can be used to bring out the same features while maintaining the mountain shadow in the background. This particular image has many approaches, depending on whether you are matching other imagery to the shot. In this case, many images needed the same level of color correction, so the Primary Color Corrector was applied to a single video track, affecting all events.

Another way the Primary Color Corrector tool is used is to sample low, mid, and highlight colors. Sometimes, this process is all that is needed to correct a color.

Select the Event FX in the first event on the wedding.veg timeline and insert a Color Corrector tool. Using the Eyedropper tool, choose Complementary Color from the Highlight tool and sample the color of the shirt collar from the man in the Preview window. Notice how this sets the neutral white for the entire shot. Using the Midrange Color Selector, use the Select Complementary Color eyedropper to sample the green in the evergreen bush. Sample a brighter portion of the green for best results. The color will immediately pop and balance the overall image. Because the colors are still not as saturated as they should be, increase saturation to a value of 2.00 and decrease gamma to a value of .900. These settings create a warm and pleasant color space without washing out the resolution of the shot (see Color Plate 8.11).

As you can see, the Primary Color Corrector tool is useful and powerful with the ability to repair or improve errors or difficult shot situations. For example, white balancing a camera is often overlooked, or in many cases, not possible with lower-quality DV cameras. Consequently, images might be too blue or green from fluorescent or mercury vapor ighting, yellow from tungsten lighting, or washed out from too much light.

 Open `colorfix.veg` from the DVD found in this book.

Color Plate 8.12 shows how tools in Vegas can compensate for a forgotten white balance in a classroom containing fluorescent lighting. Skin tones, neutral whites, and color depth are all regained by using this tool.

To understand how this process works, insert a Color Corrector tool on the first event on the `colorfix.veg` file.

Using the Select Complementary Color eyedropper in the high tones, draw a square on one of the ceiling tiles on the upper part of the image in the Preview screen. The angle/magnitude settings should automatically set to approximately 130/0.584. Using the Select Complementary Color eyedropper on the High color wheel, select the ceiling where it's slightly darker. A sample can also be taken from the lightest portion of skin. The angle/magnitude settings should automatically be approximately 130/0.450. The skin tones immediately become warm, the surrounding colors are no longer blue from the lack of white balance, and the image is much deeper and interesting to look at. This same method works equally well with footage shot under tungsten lights that is overly yellow in color. The Primary Color Corrector tool is powerful and may be turned to for quick color repair on almost any image.

Some images simply cannot be brought to a correctable state, however. Sometimes, poor quality shots must be used. In this case, adding noise, saturation, and generally unacceptable color management helps rather than trying to hide poor color balances in the image (see Color Plates 8.13 and 8.14).

Another use of the Color Corrector tool is to apply a color gradient over an image. In buildings with large walls or obstacles, it is sometimes difficult to get a good balance with lighting if it's a live shot or a run-and-gun. Using a gradient over the image creates a balance and offers unlimited possibilities (see Color Plate 8.15). Used like a Neutral Density filter on a camera, gradients can be used to restore or enhance images.

When working with the Color Corrector filter/tool, remember this order of use:

1. Select the brightest point of an image with the High Complementary tool.

2. Select skin tones or mid-range colors with the Mid Complementary tool.

3. Select the darkest point of an image with the Low Complementary tool.

By doing so, color balancing is almost automatic, white balancing a shot that was incorrect is virtually hassle-free, and a great starting point is established for correcting colors.

This element can be built with any kind of image—simply create a gradient, such as the one in the `gradient.veg` file.

In Color Plate 8.16, notice how the warmer look of the original image seems to be flat on the left side, while the bluer image created by the gradient on the right side appears to have more depth.

In addition to using a gradient to correct a color space, gradients can be used to enhance an image overall. Warm images generally seem flatter, shallower than cooler, more contrasted images. Our eyes tend to believe that warmer colors have less detail.

Sony has a Gradient Filter plug-in that provides exceptionally fast and simple changes to the emotion of an image (see Color Plate 8.17).

Using Color Correction as FX

Color correction tools can also be used for artistic expression, creating certain moods and emotions that cannot be obtained with lighting or camera lens filters in a low- to mid-budget project, or in some cases, cannot be obtained in the real world at all.

Inserting or replacing colors that aren't part of the original shot is fast and easy with Vegas. Using the Secondary Color Corrector tool, colors can be selectively replaced, graded, or enhanced.

In Color Plate 8.18, the original black-and-white photo is given a sense of warmth from the Secondary Color Corrector tool. A similar effect is possible with a Sepia filter or by layering a sepia-generated color on a track above and reducing the opacity. When you use the Secondary Color Corrector tool, however, you can insert keyframes, changing the transparency and chroma value of the overlaid color.

Color Plate 8.19 shows how colors may be desaturated using the Secondary Color Corrector tool. This particular image has the "Desaturate all but red" preset selected. We'll see how this same effect can be managed with another tool later in this chapter.

Color Plate 8.20 demonstrates a shot taken with a low-end camera, which did not allow compensation for a bright sky. Using the Secondary Color Corrector tool, the sky was brought to a richer and more vibrant color. Without using a glass filter on the camera lens, this shot would have been difficult for even the most high-end camera.

As an example, the movie Pleasantville, along with various commercials on television, have made the all-black-and-white-except-one-color look very popular. This type of work is nearly impossible to create with only a camera without doing lots of preproduction work. In Vegas, it's a few steps to create this look cleanly and quickly.

You can use a Saturation Adjust filter in Vegas to single out a color quickly, while desaturating all remaining colors. Color Plate 8.23 demonstrates the Saturation Adjust filter, applied in order to remove the color of the rocks and surrounding color. Only the climber's clothing is in color. The Saturation Adjust filter works much like an audio equalizer, allowing colors to be selectively reduced or enhanced in order to create an artistically pleasing image. Of course, the Saturation Adjust filter may be applied to any image to bring down oversaturated colors, pop up undersaturatd colors, or bring an overall balance to images on the screen (see Color Plate 8.24).

Tip

When using the Secondary Color Corrector tool in Vegas, use caution, as overextended colors can quickly become illegal, washed out, or destructive to detail in an image. Color correction is meant to be a corrective tool, not a fix-all for poor camera skills or poorly shot footage.

Inversion Layer

Using the Secondary Color Correction tool, Vegas users have been easily able to create the "Pleasantville" look that is so very popular, particularly with wedding videographers and editors. Vegas 6 and later versions make this even easier by adding an Invert Mask to the Secondary color corrector, making this effect possible without using a copy of the same event as a mask.

Open the Secondary Color Correction tool and apply it to an event, selecting the color you wish to remain, or pass through. Now simply slide the Saturation control completely to the left, or to none, and select the Invert Mask tick box. Notice that the image is now black and white/ and desaturated, but the color you selected is allowed to pass through.

The new Invert Mask option makes for very easy creation of the popular "Pleasantville" look that many videographers use. This is particularly effective in wedding videos, used to pass only red found in bouquets or perhaps the white found in the bride's dress.

The wedding examples are just salvageable but can't really be brought to full life, as the video camera was not white balanced, the backlight was brighter than the foreground, and the entire scene was shot in the shadow of a building. Sometimes footage can only be saved, not enhanced. Plan shooting schedules accordingly and remember that footage shot well saves a tremendous amount of time in the postproduction process.

Making Digital Video Look Film-Like

Notice that this section heading says "film-like" and not "like film." Video cannot look just like film. It's a different medium. It can be made softer, with adjusted gamma, grain, and color saturation, but it still will not look the same as 16mm or 35mm film. I'll preface this section by saying that if you are interested only in shooting media that looks like it was shot on film, shoot on film. If you are interested in exploring how to make DV more palatable to the eye, read on.

Making DV look more film-like requires starting at the lens and shooting aspects of the production. Using nothing but prime lenses, using dolly shots rather than lens zooms, and shooting with lighting intended for film are all part of the process. Shooting through filters, such as the Tiffen Black Mist series filters, helps warm the image as well. Practice shooting in a progressive scan or frame-based mode rather than shooting interlaced images, and, if the camera is capable of multiple frame rates, shoot at 24p, shoot with a PAL 25 frames per second (fps) camera, or learn how to operate the camera properly in progressive scan mode. In progressive scan mode, the camera must be handled differently from when shooting in interlaced modes. Pans can easily become mush and blur in the hands of the inexperienced. Hand-held shots become a wash of colors in those same hands. Managing the camera correctly is half the battle in getting a good film-like appearance from the digital information.

Interlaced or Not?

One of the first exercises in the process of making DV look film-like is to deinterlace. We discussed interlacing in Chapter 3, but to revisit, interlacing is the process in which lines, known as fields, are drawn for every frame of video. NTSC-DV has a frame rate of 30 fps or 29.97 fps. PAL-DV has a frame rate of 25 fps. This information means that NTSC DV has 30 half frames of lower fields/lines and 30 half frames of upper fields/lines. PAL has 25 half frames of upper fields/lines and 25 half frames of lower fields/lines. These lines generally should be removed or blended to gain the smooth look of film. Video shot in progressive scan mode does not have these temporally offset fields. Be certain that when editing progressive scan footage in Vegas the project properties are set for Progressive Scan. If the setting is not correct, Vegas might insert the fields in transitions or other generated media.

Removing interlacing can be done within the project itself, by setting Vegas to the project settings of progressive scan versus interlaced. Several ways to accomplish a properly deinterlaced image are available. The first and fastest way is to set the project properties to Progressive Scan. To do so, open the FILE | PROPERTIES | ADVANCED dialog, and in the Deinterlace menu, select Blend Fields. This method is fast and easy and assures continuity.

Another way, or "look," is to blend fields manually. This process creates a slightly softer image and may be preferable to your eye.

When manually deinterlacing, create a new project. Set the Project Properties to Progressive Scan, and insert a new video track (Ctrl+Shift+Q). Place events on the timeline. To deinterlace for a film-like appearance, duplicate the video track. Select an event on the top track, right-click, and then select PROPERTIES | FIELD ORDER | UPPER FIELD FIRST. Using the Track Opacity/Level slider on track 1, set opacity to 50 percent. On track 2, be certain that events are lower-field first. This process deinterlaces the footage by drawing all parts of the frame, rather than drawing only half the frame (see Color Plate 8.21).

There is no wrong way to achieve deinterlaced footage with Vegas to obtain a film-like appearance.

Another big difference between DV and film is the gamma curve. In Vegas, the gamma can be reduced using a color correction tool (see Color Plate 8.22). Increasing saturation is also good practice for obtaining a more film-like look.

You need to know a few things about shooting for a film-like appearance. First, if the video will ever be transferred to film, do not shoot with filters such as the Black Mist 2 from Tiffen. Shoot clean and with clarity. The same goes for using film-look plug-ins, such as grain. All of the digitally created film look is created in the transfer from DV to film. You need to understand going in that DV-to-film transfers are exceptionally expensive. An average 90-minute project will cost a minimum of $30,000 to transfer from DV to film. http://www.dvfilm.com has lots of information on how to make this happen if this is your end-goal. If video will be shown on a large screen, digitally projected, test the footage before sending out the entire project as an uncompressed file. Projection can create problems, such as pixilation or overblown colors, so the entire project should be checked over before public viewing. Rendering uncompressed footage, which is generally advisable for large-screen projections, can take a long time, particularly when motion blurs and super-sampling are applied. Be sure to have everything checked out before starting this process to avoid long periods wasted because of haste in the postproduction process.

Legal Colors

Video that will be broadcast or displayed on NTSC-display equipment must be brought within legal color guidelines to avoid clipped colors and clipped/distorted audio and to avoid embarrassment as a professional. The best means of handling illegal colors is to have color correction, titles, still images, and filtering monitored so that the video isn't allowed to become illegal in the first place. Fulfilling this requirement, however, sometimes can be a challenge. Vegas provides a Broadcast Colors clamp that ensures that colors are legal. Although Vegas 2.0/3.0 had the Broadcast Colors clamp as well, Vegas brings a number of parameters to this tool that were previously unavailable. The Broadcast Colors plug-in can be considered in a similar light as a limiter in the audio world. The new tools can be considered more of a video compressor as the new tools allow some elasticity as to how Vegas treats illegal colors.

These options give editors many choices in working with color values. With technology changing rapidly in the broadcast industry, these limitations are less stringent, although the standards will most likely persevere for many years to come.

Rather than dropping the Broadcast Colors filter on an entire project, which would absolutely assure that the project is legal, consider inserting the plug-in on events that are demonstrably beyond legal colors. Use the histogram or waveform monitor to display and indicate luminance issues.

Inserting the Broadcast Colors filter on troublesome events rather than on an entire project will speed render times. More importantly, adding the filter to individual events will not clip or affect color values that may border on the edge of legal and then have a potentially negative impact on the overall picture if much of the project is at near-illegal levels.

8.19 The new Broadcast Colors tool has a broad palette of options.

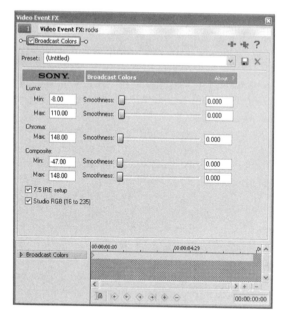

The Broadcast Colors plug-in presets bring colors to within 8.5–100 IRE levels or 16–234 RGB levels. Luma and chroma (light/color), however, are adjustable separately, as is the composite blending smoothness of luma/chroma.

Even though the Internet does not have color limitations, inserting a Broadcast Color, Black Restore, or Levels filters on events can indeed benefit video streams over the web. Encoding is an art form, have no doubt. The fewer color variations in a stream, the better the stream. Redundant frames are the key to good streams. The Levels plug-in can limit colors. This process would not be useful if the HSL and Restore Black filters were used to crush blacks and reduce color saturation. Be aware, however, that the Broadcast Colors plug-in will not ever add anything to colors but only assure that colors are within legal ranges.

Endnote

[1] For more in-depth reading on WFM/vectorscopes, pick up *Color Correction for Digital Video* by Steve Hullfish and Jaime Fowler. Available from CMP Books.

Streaming Media Tools

Creating High-Quality Streaming Media

Just as television was to radio, webstreaming is to television today. Television, in its infancy, delivered exceptionally poor information with fairly poor quality. Streaming media is much like that today; while the information might be high quality, the quality of the view is compromised because of the delivery medium. Until greater bandwidth is available for the public, a need will always exist for editors that have the ability to edit just for the web.

Vegas is one of the most powerful web-delivery authoring and editing tools available today. Preproduction, however, is equally important as the editing and encoding ability when it comes to creating great streaming media. While many resources are available for great streaming media authoring techniques, I've included some tips in this chapter for shooting and producing great media.

Shooting, Editing, and Delivering

Perhaps the most important part of streaming production is knowing more about video than simply knowing how to turn on a camera. Understanding the basics of production is equally important to the flow of the production process and to the quality of the media itself.

People trained for working directly in broadcast are often the worst at generating quality streaming media shoots. Much of what is known about broadcast shooting is diametrically opposed to shooting good web video. Keep in mind that television is a lean-back experience, in which viewers are laid back, perhaps with a bowl of popcorn in hand, relax-

9.1   Rule of thirds applies to broadcast images.

ing in some form. Streaming media, or media on a computer, is generally known as a lean-in experience, in which the viewer is close to the computer monitor, leaning in to view a fairly small image. This issue alone forces a completely different perspective for production of media. Of course, with the convergence of television and streaming media close at hand, this issue might well change in the near future. Both REAL and Windows-Media support high-definition streams with surround sound ability, and the quality of these streams is outstanding. For the moment however, more than 80 percent of the world is still on dial-up, so bandwidth will continue to be an issue in the near future.

Three processes are in the chain of web video production:

- Production

- Editing

- Encoding and delivering

9.2   Streaming media works best using more of the screen space or the Rule of Two Thirds.

Production

Rule number one for shooting good web video is to always shoot with a tripod. Handheld camera work, regardless of the ability of the cameraperson, simply has too much movement to be encoded well. Redundant information in the frame encodes well, whereas moving media, even if it's only slight movement, encodes poorly.

Shoot close in. Normally in broadcast-destined footage, shots are based around the rule of thirds. The rule of thirds is simple—divide the viewfinder into a grid that looks like a tic-tac-toe game. Any two points where lines intersect become the focal point of your subject matter, preventing the subject from being in the exact center. With streaming media, however, the message is more important than is the aesthetic of the picture. Clarity and a less informational background is the goal. Shooting for two-thirds imagery means bisecting three lines rather than only two in the framed image.

Be as tight as practical. Limit any background movement. Never shoot in front of moving trees, roads, or other backgrounds where there is movement. In fact, shooting against a backdrop, greenscreen, or bland fixed set is generally best. Keep background information/imagery to its simplest form. This process makes it easier for the encoder to process information.

Don't forget audio. Audio is even more important in the streaming world than in the broadcast world, and it's pretty important in the broadcast world. Viewers of streaming media will forgive the poorer video quality of a stream. They generally will not forgive bad audio. Always use lavaliere or boom microphones. Never use the microphone built onto the camera. The proximity of the microphone to the subject is too distant, and the sound is muffled and full of reflections, noise, and ambience, which is difficult to remove. Use Sony Noise Reduction if necessary, and it usually is. Unless the production is being delivered over the Internet or if it's absolutely live-or-die necessary, audio should be in mono rather than stereo. Aside from phasing issues, stereo audio is more difficult to encode than is mono audio, and the audience can rarely appreciate stereo audio on most computer systems.

Limit or curtail reverb decay times, and cut off bottom- and top-end frequency information with an audio equalizer. This process leaves less information for the encoder to deal with. Normalize or maximize audio to assure that it's as loud as possible. The encode process works best with

9.3 Well-lit face for streaming. High contrast and a tight shot make for a great stream at any speed. If the background is static, of one or two colors, and contrasted highly against the subject, Windows-Media 9 is capable of delivering even a full-screen stream at 56 Kbps. This image is a 56 Kbps stream projected in a training session. (Photo by R. Grandia.)

9.4 Using a split screen allows camera angles to be less important and still keeps a two-part conversation visible and clean

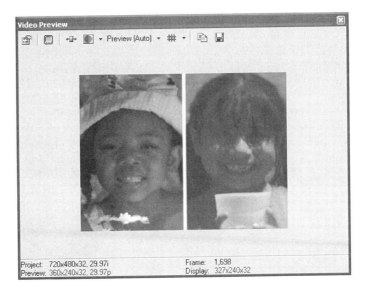

highly compressed, loud media. Large dynamic ranges (quiet to very loud) do not encode well. Try to limit dynamic range to 12dB or less.

Light well. Having great lighting is critical to any web-video production. This issue is true more so than in the broadcast world because encoders have a difficult time distinguishing as many colors as the broadcast equipment does. High contrast and low saturation always work best for web media.

Editing

Edit for clarity, content, and cropping in mind. Beautiful panoramic shots are wonderful for demonstrating high-definition TV (HDTV) or for displaying the great outdoors. Such shots are horrible for the web, however. Detail becomes so small as to be invisible. Is that detail really critical to the message that's being delivered? The message is the most critical consideration, and anything not directly related to the message should not be found in the stream.

In the edit process, if two talking heads are needed, rather than showing the two heads in one frame, consider the CNN-style appearance where each head has its own space, divided by a clean line down the middle. This setup accomplishes two tasks. First, it keeps the background frames redundant. Second, it requires less distance between the heads, so both heads may be cropped in more tightly.

Removing unnecessary information limits what the encoder has to look at. Encoding tools are not capable of separating a few pixels of a reflection on a window from the blowing hair of the subject. To the encoder, it's all just moving pixels, and nothing is prioritized over anything else. Cropping helps alleviate this concern because cropping allows for less information to be on the screen.

Less saturation is best in streaming media. While the RGB color space allows for millions of colors, keeping colors to a minimum is best because it offers fewer color choices to the encoder. Reduce colors whenever possible. The Hue, Saturation, Luminance (HSL) filter in Vegas is excellent for this concern. Insert the Black Restore filter as well to ensure that black is really black. Gradients of black are difficult for the encoder to compress and difficult for the eye to see in the production stage. This filter, used correctly, flattens out black in the stream.

When editing for streaming media, forget about long, beautiful dissolves and fades. These sorts of transitions do not encode well. Use linear wipes, hard cuts, or other straight-line transitions. Don't use titles with serifs, but do use clean-cut title fonts and keep them as large as possible. Sometimes no title is necessary if metadata is used to convey text inforaton.

9.5 The broadcast shot allows for more background to set the stage and location of the shot.

9.6 Cropped for the web, this shot is more interesting when viewed from very close up, such as with a computer monitor.

9.7   Streaming media should not have as much background. This example shows a poorly cropped screen. Too much information is in the background, and the subject takes up too little of the viewing space.

Also, in the edit stage, be aware that extreme contrasts are harder to encode, so keep extreme variants in saturation limited. Remember that placing media on the web is about messaging, not brilliant colors and flashy editing.

To summarize:

- Use clear fonts for titles.
- Limit dissolves; use cuts or hard wipes instead.
- Avoid moving paths when possible. Use picture-in-picture or split screens.
- On headshots, crop to half, rather than thirds.

- When you want to deliver to low-band systems, keep audio in a mono setting. For both low- and high-bandwidth delivery, consider using both stereo and mono audio. Does stereo really add value?

- Don't limit yourself to the standard 4.3 aspect. If your video is about something involving heights for instance, consider scaling the video to be tall and narrow. This process might also use less bandwidth and might allow for better audio or compression. It also might be that the stream quality will suffer, depending on the aspect selected. Either way, do not be afraid to experiment.

- Try a variety of codecs to see what allows for the best look. Perhaps put low bit rate media in one codec and high bit rate media in another codec.

- Try frame rates of 12 fps rather than 15 fps when bandwidth or file size is a concern. For slide and still-type presentations, use even slower rates, such as 5 fps.

- For headshots, try using color key or chroma key tools to create background masks. Then fill in with high-speed, blurred imagery. This process keeps the headshot clean, while causing the eye to focus on the headshot and not the black behind it. It also lends an MTV-type quality to the interview or presentation.

- Impress viewers by embedding metadata into the end or middle of the video files that direct their browser to open at the end, so that they are given other images to view following the video/audio presentation. If you are selling a product, the metadata could potentially send the viewer to a "purchase me" type of page.

Audio for Internet Delivery

Preproduction of audio for web-streaming or Internet distribution is often overlooked in the streaming preparation processes. Oftentimes, videographers intent on placing media on the Internet or an intranet use tools built into the applications that are being used for editing media for the web. If these tools are the only ones available, little can be done to prepare the audio for the web without going through multiple renders and loss of video quality. The processing described in the next paragraphs apply equally to audio only, as well as audio for video.

9.8   The image on the left shows a slow fade and letterboxing. The image on the right incorporates a hard wipe and no letterboxing. This image will encode/compress much better.

If third-party editing tools are available, use them to the best advantage possible. Most non-linear editing packages come bundled with Sony's XP audio editing software. For this book, I've used Sound Forge 7.0, a full version. The tools used in this book, however, are all found in the XP version.

Audio takes a tremendous amount of unnecessary bandwidth in the streaming world. Most computer speakers can't reproduce sounds of any quality above 10,000 Hz (10 KHz) or below 125 Hz. If unnecessary audio is taken away, it leaves room for more efficient use of both video and audio bandwidth.

All video and audio compression tools use both high- and low-pass filters of some sort. The question is what is the quality of the filters, and where are they cutting? Video tools simply aren't designed well for most audio processing chores.

How Is Audio Preprocessed for the Web?

First, start by fully rendering your file. If you are working with most audio editors, you'll want to be sure your file is smaller than 2GB, as current limitations prevent larger WAV files from being opened in audio editing tools on FAT32 drives. Moreover, you probably don't want to create too large a file, as large files are a bane in streaming media. If you want to save a step in the production process, render your file in an AVI format that is the view size for streaming media, such as 320 x 240 at 15 fps (using square pixels).

9.9   Notice the dynamic range of audio in the waveform.

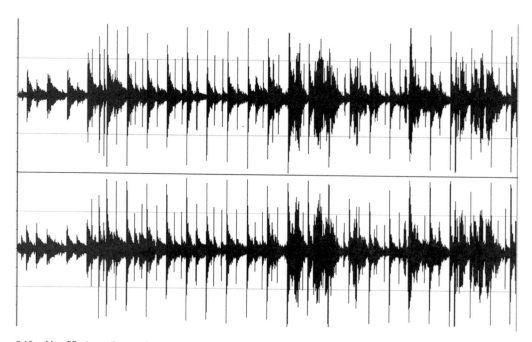

9.10   After EQ, the audio waveform contains less transient information because extreme low/bass frequencies and extreme high frequencies have been cut.

Open the rendered file in your audio editor. Notice how the audio dynamic is fairly consistent across the spectrum. This audio has full dynamic range, containing both frequencies that multimedia speakers can't reproduce and also frequencies that can't be heard. If it's a live recording, sounds, such as microphone stand rumble, use up to 100 times as much power to reproduce as the breath in a singer's voice. Those frequencies use bandwidth/streaming space that can better be used for video or audio enhancement/quality.

Using the graphic, paragraphic, or parametric equalizer in the audio editing tool, locate the high and low roll-off controls. Set the low-pass filter at 10 KHz and the high-pass filter at 100-Hz. These settings will cut off the extreme high-end and low-end audio right from the start. Just this preproduction task alone makes a tremendous difference in how the compression application accepts files for compression.

At this point, it might be advisable to do any final tweaks and enhancements with the audio. If you have any stereo widening, reverb, or ambience adding effects, now is the time to add them. Time delays and long reverbs do not compress well. Care and consideration, therefore, should be used at this point, so that streaming media will sound the best it possibly can on the receiving end. Multimedia speakers have a tendency to have a bump in the 5 KHz region, so if your media is music intensive, it might be advisable to reduce this frequency area by as much as -3dB.

Notice the difference in the audio file's appearance in Figure 9.11 following the compression change. The waveform has less mass, and the transients become less apparent.

Be sure to have a preview listen to the file before moving on, making certain that the audio is the way you would like it to sound when it is received on the listening end of the stream.

9.11 Use light compression to smooth out waveforms. In this illustration, a 2.1 compressor has been inserted, with compression starting at –12dB.

Often in multimedia creation, particularly dealing with files generated directly in the computer environment, audio levels are not consistent across the project nor are the audio levels at optimum settings. These audio files may still be used and brought to maximum levels by normalizing them to an average level across the median plane. Two approaches to normalizing are used—normalize to peak values of XdB or normalize to an average RMS value. Use a normalization of an average RMS value if you wish to match the apparent overall loudness of a sound file. The Normalize to Value selects the volume to which the sound file will be normalized. As an example, when using peaks, if the peak level is –10dB and the Normalize to setting is set to –3dB, a constant boost of 7dB will be applied to the entire file.

When using RMS levels, normalizing to 0dB means boosting the signal so that it has the same apparent loudness as a 0dB square wave. This process usually creates a file that is very loud and often clipped or distorted. Normalizing to values between –12dB and -6dB is recommended.

Normalizing on a peak value allows for more dynamic interplay in the audio file. The file is scanned for its maximum peak value, which is then raised to –.03dB. This process applies equally weighted amplitude across the audio file. Most normalizing functions allow for the introduction of dynamic compression at any stage in the normalization process. Using this tool is advisable as it prevents clipping at all stages, while allowing the normalize tool to bring audio up to maximum levels. This is especially desirable when the sampling frequency or bit rate of audio will be changing. Audio files should always be maximized before converting the format.

After the file has had the extreme low and high frequencies removed, been equalized to the desired sound, and normalized, the file is ready for encoding/compression for streaming formats.

If the file is an audio-only file, it is a simple matter to encode to REAL, Microsoft media, or QuickTime formats using the tools built directly into your audio application or using third-party tools. Be aware of the ability to insert command markers or instructional markers into the audio or video file. These command markers can display copyright information, authoring information, HTML redirections, and much more. If the processed audio file is part of a video file, it is an equally simple process to encode the video file for streaming. Reducing the audio content and maximizing the audio volume both make for more encoding bandwidth for the video portion of the file and provide a more efficient use of available bandwidth. These benefits are especially useful when dealing with low-speed connections, such as dial-up service.

Until bandwidth and connections bring broadband to every home and business in the world, and even after that point for purposes of bandwidth and storage, content creators/providers need to learn every trick in the book and invent some new ones in order to keep media files appearing and sounding the best that they can. Audio is generally an afterthought in the video creation/editing world, although that is rapidly changing. Experiment a bit, listen closely, and you'll be surprised how great audio can really help out a less-than-great visual presentation. Don't forget metadata can be a great tool for audio-only delivery, as well as a video delivery over the web.

Delivery

Encoding is not much of a challenge if the techniques mentioned earlier are employed in production and editing stages. Vegas, however, offers a number of choices for the encoding/output side of media.

9.12   Normalizing a file to maximize volume.

An exceptionally valuable tool found in Vegas is the ability to encode portions of the timeline for preview, rather than rendering out entire files, encoding, and if dissatisfied, repeating the entire process. Vegas is one of the only tools available today that can encode directly from the timeline, complete with metadata insertions. This Preview from Timeline tool is valuable in that producers are able to see exactly what their media will look like when viewed from the web, directly in the media player of their choice.

Open the Streaming Project on the accompanying DVD.

The project file already has three sections of metadata embedded: two text instruction lines and one URL locater line. When viewed in the media player, the text data shows up at the bottom of the screen (in the Windows-Media Player, select VIEW | NOW PLAYING TOOLS | CAPTIONS). Place the cursor on the timeline at the first marker, labeled Insert Command Here. Press C, and a command dialog box will pop up. In the Command dialog box, use the menu and select Text. In the parameter box, type the words, *Then I go and spoil it all by saying something stupid*.

Select a small section of media on the timeline over the top of the section containing at least one metadata flag. This section will be highlighted in gray (or blue if looping [Q] is enabled). Open the TOOLS | PREVIEW IN PLAYER dialog (Ctrl+Shift+M). In the dialog, choose Windows-Media V9 (*.wmv) for the codec and select 256 Kbps for the streaming bandwidth. Click the Custom button, and in the audio attributes, choose the 48 Kbps, 44 KHz Mono (A/V) CBR setting. Click the Video tab, and in the Format window, choose Windows-Media Video 9.

Now click the Summary tab and note the text boxes that may be filled out. This data is embedded with the file and shows up in the player on the client (viewer) side when the file is streaming. This dialog also provides a great means of data management for later use, as information about the file can be embedded in the file for database searches. Be aware that the last information entered in this dialog carries to the next time the tool is opened, so be certain to check this dialog with each stream.

Click OK in the Custom Template dialog and click OK in the Preview in Player dialog. Vegas will begin to render the file as a WMV file. After the file has rendered, Vegas will automatically

---

What Is Metadata?

Metadata is what makes streaming reach out and touch someone. Metadata is embedded information in a streaming file that opens secondary browser windows, directs viewers to web pages, provides lyrics or text information to a song or informational media piece, provides advertising opportunities, all from a streaming file. The author of the streaming file places the metadata markers on the timeline, and viewers have a more in-depth experience as a result. Vegas has many metadata authoin tolsfound in the Command key (C).

9.13   Metadata may include song lyrics as displayed text.

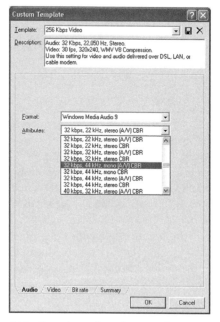

9.14 Streaming audio attributes may be set to user preferences.

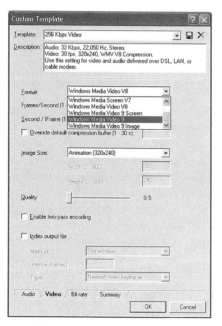

9.15 Select the video codec and other attributes in this dialog.

call on the Windows-Media Player to open and play the file. If the Captions option is enabled in Windows-Media Player, you'll see the captions on the bottom of the Windows-Media Player screen. This will show only the selected portions of the timeline. In addition, only a temp file has been written for the streaming file. A full render will still need o be completed for a final output file.

 Tip

Preview in Player is a powerful tool. Use it to identify trouble spots in the streaming media by previewing high motion/intense color areas. This process helps you determine how the video should be handled. Prerendering trouble spots at various frame rates before rendering a streaming file often helps make high-motion media look more polished. Tight cropping while following motion often helps as well, as it reduces background imagery.

Importing a Spreadsheet

Vegas has the ability to import a scripted spreadsheet. This asset is very important for the content creator who has concerns about complying with Rule 508 Assistive Technology laws. For any government-funded streaming endeavor, these laws almost always must be complied with. Colleges, training facilities, hospitals, corporate environments, and federally subsidized businesses, among others, must comply with these laws.

Vegas' streaming toolset enables closed caption-text to be embedded in the video or audio stream for hearing-impaired viewers. To do this, start by creating a four-column, tab-delimited spreadsheet in your spreadsheet application of choice and continue the process as follows:

1. In the first column cells, type 00:00:00:00.

2. In each of the second column of cells, type the word *text* to specify the command format.

3. In the third column, type the text messages that you wish to be seen, for example, *When I was 17*.

4. In the fourth column, type marker information that you can use to identify the caption information. For example, they might be called *cap 1* or *line 1* in the cell.

5. In the last row of cells, leave the third column empty, which will clear the last caption text from the screen of the media player.

6. Select all information on the spreadsheet, or press Ctrl+A in Microsoft Excel. Copy all information.

7. In Vegas, select VIEW | EDIT DETAILS | SHOW | COMMANDS. Right-click in the gray box in the upper-left corner and choose Paste. Vegas will paste the spreadsheet information into the Edit Details window.

8. In the Edit Details window, click the first column, which will sort the captions by line number as named in step 4. Position the cursor where you wish the first caption to occur. Select the first row in the Edit Details window and play the video/audio file by pressing the Spacebar. Press Ctrl+K to drop a marker for the first caption. Repeat for all subsequent captions. Caption markers can be dropped on the fly and moved on the timeline by clicking and holding on the markerand then dragging to the desired position.

 *Tip*_____

Be sure Captioning is enabled in Windows-Media Player by selecting VIEW | NOW PLAYING | CAPTIONS. Otherwise captions will not be previewable nor can they be seen in the playback of a rendered file.

After all edits have been made, all metadata inserted, screen markers completed, and various points in the timeline checked for quality, the file is ready to be rendered. Open the FILE | RENDER AS dialog, select the format of media you wish to stream, the bit rate at which to stream, and any summary information you wish to appear. If custom selections, such as variable bit rate (VBR) streaming or custom audio settings, are needed, click the Custom button. This action opens the same dialog shown during the Preview in Player exercise.

The Audio tab opens by default. As mentioned earlier, audio should be kept in mono to provide greater bandwidth for video. The Video tab is next on the menu tabs; settings can be adjusted according to need. Experiment with settings that best suit your requirements.

When you select various bit rates in the Bit rate tab, the file rendered by Vegas will be a multiple bit rate (MBR) file. If only one bit rate is selected (the default), the file is rendered as a constant bit rate or variable bit rate (CBR/VBR) file. Viewers also generally receive a more stable stream with CBR instead of MBR files.

The Summary tab allows for information, such as copyright information and author information, to be embedded with the file. This information shows up in the information bar of a REAL, Windows, or QuickTime media player, and in most third-party media players as well. Other than re-rendering the file, this information is difficult to remove and is a starting point in the concern for digital rights management (DRM).

After the custom selections/setups have been accomplished, you may wish to save the template settings for future use. A menu is available at the top of the Custom Templates dialog. Clicking the cursor in this menu allows you to rename the template, and clicking in the Description field allows you to create a new description of the template. After defining the name and description of the new template, click the icon that resembles a floppy disk, which saves the template for future use. After the template has been saved, the final render can take place.

Click OK in the Custom Templates dialog, which closes. Define where you want the final rendered file to be saved/rendered to and click the Save button. The render begins. After the render is complete, Vegas provides an option to open the folder in which the rendered file was stored. If you do not wish to see the Open Folder dialog in the future, you can use the check box that Vegas provides to disable this pop-up screen in the future.

The finished file is now ready to be uploaded to a website and streamed. Bear in mind that with REAL and QuickTime media, unique streaming server software is required for streaming, as opposed to download-and-play files. REAL's new Helix server is capable of serving all three stream formats, in addition to many other formats in the streaming world. A non-commercial free version with a very limited number of streams is available at www.real.com.

Don't be afraid to use streaming media for more than streaming over the Internet. It's a great tool for delivering high-quality media on a CD to a potential client. With the ability to burn a high-definition file to a CD and to include a player-installer on the CD for the client, this tool is very powerful in creating workflows between client and editor, while not taking inordinate amounts of time to show the client what the video project looks like.

9.16 Checking multiple bit rates creates a multiple bit rate (MBR) file.

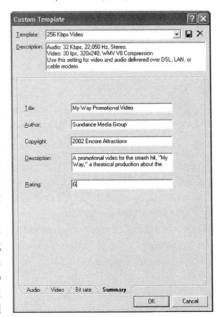

9.17 Use the Summary tab to embed copyright, author, and other information that can be seen in the stream/media player.

DVD Architect

Setting Up a DVD Project

DVD Architect 3 (DVDA) is an extension of the Vegas 6 NLE system. Until now, authoring a DVD has been a fairly complex and expensive undertaking; however, with DVDA, Sony has taken DVD authoring to a new level.

In keeping with the format-agnostic/resolution-independent attributes in Vegas, DVDA also allows nearly any format of media to be placed on the workspace. DVDA encodes files directly from the workspace, saving render time and helping prevent bad DVD burns because of errors in the editing process. Additionally, DVDA is capable of creating a DVD slideshow as a drag-and-drop process, having motion backgrounds, motion buttons, and motion submenus and menus. All aspects of the DVD can be previewed before burning the DVD.

> ✊ *Tip*
>
> DVD Architect 3.0 has the ability to burn dual-layer disks, or 8.7 GB DVD9 disks. This is important for being able to burn longer videos in a higher quality format, without having to sacrifice quality for lower bitrates required by the smaller 4.7GB DVD 5. Additionally, DVD Architect 3 offers the ability to master DLT for mastering on tape, to be delivered to a replicator. Most replicators today, can take a DVD 9 as a master.

10.1 DVD Architect is a powerful yet simple application. With a little bit of time invested in learning this application, professional, dynamic, and exciting menus may be built quickly.

Menu Flow in DVD Architect 3

Menu flow is a critical component to having a clear message in the DVD content. This aspect should be planned out before inserting media into the DVD project. With a weak flow, viewers of the DVD can easily be confused. It's usually helpful to create a workflow chart on paper before starting the layout of a DVD project, much like the flow chart shown in Figure 10.1.

Giving advance thought to layouts also helps build comprehensive menus as to how they should be laid out in DVDA, saving unnecessary steps in the authoring process. Compiling all media to one folder or having a project folder is helpful so that all media is accounted for in the authoring process.

DVD Architect

DVD Architect has undergone substantial improvements from previous versions. End actions, rollover effects, dockable windows, (including dual monitor support) higher resolutions, Flash file import, external monitor preview, and more are all part of the DVD Architect 3.0 software package.

 Tip_____

Additionally, one of the great features in DVD Architect is the ability to apply image controls to the media after you've imported it. Suppose that you've imported graphics, and when you compare those graphics to the media you've rendered out in Vegas, the color, contrast, or other aspects aren't quite matching up. In the past, users would have to go back to their graphics application and modify the images. DVD Architect allows the modification of certain attributes of the graphic. DVD Architect allows users to adjust the Brightness, Contrast, Contrast Center, Colorization, Alpha, and Crop.

10.2 Beneath the Explorer tab, you'll find the Backgrounds, Themes, and Buttons tabs. Use these to access prebuilt assets for your project.

10.3. Using these buttons, media found in the Explorer may be previewed prior to being added to the project. Enabling Auto-preview is great for one-click previewing of media.

A Whole New Blueprint!

For those familiar with earlier versions of DVD Architect, when the latest version of the application is first opened, the appearance is similar but much more mature. First off, you'll notice that the workspace has grown tremendously, with several new windows. While the Preview window is in the same location, and the hierarchy appears to be the same, there is a lot more going on under the hood than meets the initial view.

To the left of the screen, you'll find the Project Overview window. This window provides a tree-view of the entire project, giving immediate visual access to what assets are in the project, what is linked to where, and a clear understanding of what is happening in the project. In fact, this Project Overview window can be used to assemble the entire project. Assets may be dragged directly to this window and linked later.

Directly beneath the Project Overview window is the Explorer that functions just as the Explorer in Vegas (and Windows) operates. Here is where you'll access all your assets for the project. Just like Vegas, the Explorer window contains three additional tabs that provide rapid access to Buttons, Backgrounds, and Themes. These are prebuilt assets for you to work with if you'd prefer to not build menus by hand.

In the Explorer toolbar, you'll find the typical buttons for navigating up, refreshing the contents, adding a new folder, deleting media, and adding to favorites. What is different about this Explorer view are the media preview buttons.

The Start Preview button, just as its name implies, begins playback of any file selected in the Explorer. The Stop Preview button will stop playback of the selected file. Enabling the Auto Preview button will auto-start any file selected in the Explorer view. This is a handy function, as it alleviates the need to manually start playback of a file. To stop playback of a file that was auto-started, either press the spacebar, or move the cursor to the Stop playback button and click it. You can also stop playback by clicking anywhere in the workspace, with the exception of the Explorer. (Clicking another file in the Explorer window will begin playback of that file.)

If the default view is loaded in DVD Architect, the timeline view is to the right of the Explorer and assets tabs. The timeline in DVD Architect behaves similar to the timeline in Vegas. Here is where you'll drop chapter markers, mark in/out points, insert audio tracks, and add subtitles to the project.

Directly above the timeline is the Properties view/window. Here is where you'll set the properties of buttons, colors, end actions, and graphics found in the project. Beneath this window is the Compilation window. This is where you'll access slide shows or musical compilations created in DVD Architect.

Last but certainly not least, is the center of the workspace, where the Preview window is located. Here is where you'll build the project, preview all links, view the behaviors of the DVD, and preview the entire project before burning it to DVD when you are finished putting it all together.

Setting Up DVD Architect

One of the first great features of DVD Architect is that you can dock/undock windows to live where you'd like them to live. If you save the project, the windows will open up exactly as you left them when you last saved the project and closed DVD Architect.

Docking windows are great on small monitor screens like a laptop, and even better on dual monitor setups where windows may be docked on the second monitor, freeing up the workspace of clutter and allowing all windows to be visible at once.

To dock or undock a window, click on the left side of the window on the docking handle.

Depending on whether the window is docked or not, the handle will be found on the upper left corner of the window, or at the top right side of the window. Windows may be dragged over top of each other, creating tabbed accesses to each window. This is very useful in a small monitor workspace such as most laptop monitors. Of course, this is of great benefit to users with dual monitors, allowing docked windows to live on a different computer monitor than the main workspace is in.

Windows may also be left floating independently in the workspace, just as Vegas allows. Just the same with Vegas, hold the Ctrl key while moving a dock over another window to prevent the window being moved from docking with the window beneath it.

If you find that you've somehow gotten windows docked into undesirable areas and can't get them back to where you'd like them, simply hold Ctrl+Shift while the application is loading. Just as it will do with Vegas, this will reset all windows to their docking location.

10.4. Grab this handle to drag the docking window into or out of a docking area.

When the File>New option is selected, a dialog opens, asking about the type of project you wish to create. In this dialog, it will optimize the workflow, depending on what you'd like to accomplish. One tip that is valuable from this dialog, is the ability to create a continuously looping movie that never ends. This is great for museum displays or point of purchase displays where a video requires unattended, continuous playback.

Open this dialog from the File>New menu option and select Single Movie from the dialog. This opens the Explorer window, where you'll navigate to the movie you want to be contained in the DVD project. Open this video, and it will be inserted to the workspace.

In the Properties window, open the End Actions category by clicking on the + symbol next to the End Action description. This may already be open.

In the End Action dialog, specify the End Action Command to be a link. Next, to link to the single play video, click on the Destination box, and choose the name of the single play video you wish to repeat. This will tell the DVD player to link back to the start of the video that just completed. This will loop endlessly when set up in this manner.

It's also possible to have the single movie loop back to a chapter point rather than the beginning of the movie. This would be useful if a bumper video was used to introduce the movie but you don't want viewers seeing this bumper each time the movie restarts. To have the end action link back to a chapter, select the Destination Chapter box,

10.5   Use the End Actions option to link the video back to its own beginning, thus creating an endlessly looping video.

and in the dropdown menu, select the chapter that you'd like to link back to. If no chapter marker is present, then the link will not be able to return to a chapter point. See below for information on inserting chapter points and markers. (Chapter markers may also be inserted in Vegas as part of the rendered MPEG file or elementary stream.)

A tip for creating and endlessly looping video: It may be jarring going from the end of a video to the beginning if the end and beginning are dissimilar. Consider finishing the video with media similar to media found at the beginning, even if it means fading to a static image and then starting the video with the same static image. This will prevent the end of the movie from jarring the viewer when it loops back to the beginning. This is also a good way to avoid the jarring repeat of a menu selection when a settop player cannotseamlessly loop an audio selection.

 Tip_____

In the Menu/General tab, try selecting the Reduce Interlace Flicker if your project has interlace artifacts. This is useful if you use high-resolution graphics to create menus.

From the Top Down

Starting with the top of the application, let's look at what's under the various menu options. Most of the application has keyboard shortcuts, it's very useful to learn these shortcuts, as it will help speed your use of the application and authoring DVDs.

Under the File menu option, find the standard New, (Ctrl+N) Save, (Ctrl+S) and Save As. In the Save as dialog, you can not only save the projec to a new file name, you can also save the project with all media to be transported to another computer system or save for a replication house.

10.6   In the Save As dialog, you can save the project for local use, save the project with media for transport to another computer with DVD Architect installed, or save project with all media and theme media to be edited on another computer that has DVD Architect installed.

Also under the File menu option is the Burn DVD instruction which may also be accessed via the toolbar.

Optimize DVD is a very important menu selection. In the Optimize DVD dialog, you'll set the project's default bitrate, determine the audio format (AC3, PCM, or AC3 5.1 surround), determine whether the project is PAL or NTSC formatted, and fit the entire project to a disc regardless of what the bitrate might be.

Fit to Disc is a great tool, as it will fit all media to the disc size specified in the Burn DVD dialog. Further, Optimize DVD will show you what is going to be recompressed as an asset, regardless of whether it's audio, MPEG video, or AVI video format. Any MPEG file

10.7   In this dialog, you can force all media to fit within the DVD size limits.

that isn't too large for the disc and is compliant with the DVD spec will not be recompressed unless the Fit to disc option is selected, and the media exceed the disc capacity. Another option is to select a lower bitrate in the Recompress settings dialog. This is exactly what the Fit to Disc option will do, except it will optimize to the best bitrate it can based on estimated disc size.

> DVD Architect will only recompress or encode media with a variable bitrate (VBR). DVD Architect does not encode with a constant bitrate (CBR). If a constant bitrate is desired, files should be encoded in Vegas prior to import to DVD Architect. DVD Architect also does not offer 2-Pass encoding for VBR that Vegas offers.

10.8. In this dialog the project settings are set. The default setting is NTSC/720x480 with AC3 stereo audio. In this dialog you also may input information relating to Title, Artist, Engineer, and other comments.

10.9 Use the Edit menu to reach specific tasks in DVD Architect. However, most of the Edit tasks may be accessed via shortcuts or toolbar commands.

The only other option to fit media that is too large for the disc is to reduce the number of files you are placing on the disc if you prefer to not reduce the bitrate or use the Fit to Disc option.

Any file displayed in the Optimize DVD window that contains a green check mark next to it is compliant and will fit on the disc. Any file with the bright yellow icon containing an exclamation point will require recompression to be placed on the final DVD. Any video file that is not MPEG will require recompression/ or compression. Any audio file that is not PCM or AC3 will require recompression.

The Get Media from the Web option allows access to Sony proprietary media for your use in the DVD project. You must be connected to the Internet and a registered user of DVD Architect 3.0 to access this media. You'll find DVD backgrounds, music for menus, and more on the Sony Get Media site, accessible via this menu option.

In the Properties Wwindow and menu selection, you'll set up the project properties. This is where frame rate and project size are determined, such as NTSC/PAL, widescreen, standard aspect, and other resolutions and display sizes.

If you set property information to your personal preferences, you may check the "start all new projects with these settings" check box, and DVD Architect will default to these settings each time you open the application. Of course, they may be modified at any time for special or unusual projects. This option is great for non-NTSC users.

Once the default settings for the project are determined, click the Apply button, and the new project defaults will be set and remembered by DVD Architect.

Next on the menu bar are the Edit menu items. In addtion to the commonly found Undo (CRTL+Z) and Redo (Shift+Ctrl+Z) there are the standard Cut (Ctrl+X) Copy, (Ctrl+C) and Paste. (Ctrl+V) These functions work exactly the same as they function in Vegas and most

Windows applications. The Select All function (Ctrl+A) selects all assets in the active window, allowing them to be globally moved, deleted, copied, or pasted.

The Set Background Media menu selection will open a file explorer dialog box when chosen from the Edit menu list. This allows you to locate a background video or still image file. DVD Architect will accept .wmv, .mpg, .avi, .mov video files, and most still image formats are also accepted. If a .psd file from Photoshop is inserted as a background menu image, the layers are merged into one image.

Media intended for use as a menu background may be changed at any time, either via this menu option, by choosing a background file if the layers aren't properly named. Later in this chapter, we'll talk about importing .psd files in the Project Properties window, by dragging a file to the currently displayed menu page, or by dragging a file to the background timeline window.

> Any time the Backgrounds tab is active, an image may be dragged from the library to the workspace, inserting a new background.

The Reapply Theme layout option is next in the Edit dropdown menu. Selecting this option will cause all information contained in the project to revert to the default theme layout regardless of how the project might be laid out in the Preview window. It will not change the assets however, so if you've used a different background image than what was originally contained in a theme that was chosen, or if you've modified buttons that were part of the original theme contents, DVD Architect will not change the background image or button frames to the theme default when this option is selected.

The Page Order and Object Order options, which can also be selected from right-clicking objects and selecting ordering options from the submenu, will allow for objects or pages to be brought forward or backwards in the project.

The Editing tool selection allows the selection tool (Ctrl+D) or the size tool to be selected. (There is no shortcut for the size editing tool.) These tool selections may also be made in the Preview window, located in the upper-left corner just above the alignment tools.

Editing text options may be accessed in the Edit window, but a better workflow is to select text on the workspace and press the F2 button or select the Edit Text button in the Text menu bar. Text may also be right-clicked and the Edit Text option chosen from the dropdown menu that will appear.

The Undo All option will undo all edits, additions, or deletions from a project going back to when the project was first opened. This is similar to the Revert command in some NLE systems. This is very useful for building a template project, saving the template project, and wanting to revert back to a blank template layout to start another project that might contain different assets while maintaining the same appearance, layout, and actions of the previous project.

In the View menu, you'll determine what windows are visible and what windows are hidden. This is also one location you can access previews, toolbars, and overlays.

Turning on and off the toolbar menu will show and hide the main toolbar at the top of the DVD Architect workspace. All functions found on the toolbar may also be accessed via keyboard shortcuts, but you might find it more efficient to use the toolbar until you feel proficient with

> Most of the functions of the View menu are accessible via keyboard shortcuts. Once you're familiar with the shortcuts, it's generally more efficient to use the keyboard shortcuts.

the keyboard shortcuts. Similarly, the Status bar found at the bottom of the workspace may also be shown and hidden. The Status bar provides constant feedback relating to actions being taken in the authoring process. Until you are very familiar with the DVD Architect workflow, it's a good idea to leave the Status bar visible.

Selecting the Preview option will open up the Project Preview where you can see exactly how the work in progress or finished DVD will end up, complete with the remote control functions. This may also be accessed via the Preview button found on the toolbar, or via the F9 button on your keyboard.

Choose Focus to Workspace (Alt+0) to focus editing tasks to the workspace.

10.10 The View menu contains several options allowing you to change how DVD Architect 3.0 appears; what windows are visible; grid safe area and button masks; and the order of objects in the project. Most of these options are available via shortcut keystrokes.

The next nine options show and hide various windows in DVD Architect. The workspace is the only window that may not be closed or hidden.

Alt+1 shows/hides the editing toolbar.

Alt+2 shows/hides the Text toolbar.

Alt+3 shows/hides the Explorer window.

Alt+4 shows/hides the Themes window.

Alt+5 shows/hides the Buttons window.

Alt+6 shows/hides the Backgrounds window.

Alt+7 shows/hides the Compilation window.

Alt+8 shows/hides the Properties window.

Alt+9 shows/hides the Timeline window.

Ctrl+Alt+1 shows/hides the Project Overview window. Of all windows in the project, this one is generally considered the most important as it always shows assets contained in the project, what they're linked to, or not linked to.

The Insert Menu may be used to insert all media types into the timeline or Project window. Most of these functions are accessible via toolbars, right clicks, or drag-and-dropping media to the workspace.

Inserting text to a project may be accomplished in the View menu, or by pressing Ctrl+T. This will open a text box where you can insert titles, names of files, or links to other menus, graphics, music, or video files.

10.11 The insert menu is one of several methods that may be used to insert media, text, or graphics to the timelinet.

10.12 Right-clicking the menu will open this sub-menu, where there are several options for editing or inserting media to the project.

There is no shortcut key to insert graphics. By selecting View>Graphics, graphics may be selected from the Explorer dialog. Graphics may also be dragged from the main Explorer window and dropped on the workspace. Be aware that graphics dragged directly from the Explorer window and dropped on to the workspace may become the background graphic for the project. Dragging a file from the Explorer to the Project Overview window first, and then dropping on the workspace, will create a dead link button that may be linked later on.

Submenus may be inserted by choosing the Insert>Submenu option, by right-clicking on the workspace and choosing Insert Submenu from the dropdown menu, or by using the Ctrl+M shortcut key. Double clicking the new submenu button will open the new submenu, ready for editing and inserting new assets.

Pressing Ctrl+L will insert a picture compilation/ slideshow button into the project, or you can access the Insert>Picture Compilation option from this menu option. Right-clicking the workspace and choosing Insert Picture Compilation accomplishes the same task. Double-click the new link/button to open the Compilation window on the right side of the DVD Architect application. By clicking on the Compilation tab to the right side of the application, images may be dragged individually or as groupings to this window. The order in which they appear in the Compilation window is the same order in which images will be viewed in the DVD playback.

Music compilations may be created as well, by selecting Insert>Music Compilations from the Insert Menu. This same function may be accessed with the Ctrl+L shortcut or by right-clicking the workspace and choosing Insert Music Compilation from the submenu that appears.

Music compilations are also great for putting together albums of music, with each musical selection having a graphic or video displayed during the playback. If a video is used as a background during a music compilation's playback, the video length will play, regardless of the length of the music dropped into the compilation. In other words, if the song is three minutes in length and

Music compilations may also be created as video compilations. With the first version of DVD Architect, this was a great workaround for the lack of end actions (which DVD Architect 3.0 now offers) where a new video should play following the end of another video. However, there may be circumstances where videos should play as a group, and rather than assigning buttons or end actions to a specific series of videos, users might find it easier to simply drag and drop video files to the Music Compilation window. Of course, these compilations will not have button access to each individual video; they'll merely be a slideshow-like display of videos playing in order.

the video is two minutes in length, the video will not repeat. The playback screen will simply appear blank. If the song is three minutes in length and the video is four minutes in length, the video will quit playback at the end of the song and move onto the next song or combination of song, video, and graphic. Viewers of the project may use their chapter buttons to move from song to song in the project.

Choosing Insert Media will open a dialog box, allowing virtually any sort of media to be dropped into the project. When the dialog box opens, search for the media you wish to drop into the project, select it, and press Open. You can search for specific file types by changing the dropdown box search parameter from All Valid Media to the specific type of media that you wish to use.

Insert Page will insert a new page, complete with a back-button link to the page that was active just prior to inserting the new page. New pages may also be inserted by right-clicking the work-space and selecting Insert Page from the submenu that opens up. The new page will be shown in the Project Overview at the left of the screen and is ready for rediting and insertion of titles, links, or media.

The arrow on the workspace signifies a link to the previous page.

A page may also be deleted from the project by right-clicking the page and selecting Delete Page or by deleting it from the Project Overview window.

The Scene Selection Menu option will insert a new page complete with links to scenes. When this is selected, a Scene Selection dialog box will open, requesting a name for the page, and the number of links you wish to have inserted to the page. When this information is filled in, a new page opens, and any chapters existing in the file linked to the Scene Selection button will show up in this page.

If a video link is not selected in the work-space, the Scene Selection option is grayed out, as there is no video to seek scenes within. If the video being linked to contains fewer chapters, markers, or scenes than the number of scenes called for in the Scene Selection dialog the new page will accommodate only the number of scenes found in the video being linked to. Therefore, if you specify six scenes in the dialog, but the video

10.13   In this dialog, you'll specify the name of the page, and the number of links you wish to have the scene selection menu create.

DVD Architect can identify markers dropped in the video stream from Vegas, or can identify scene markers inserted in the DVD Architect timeline window. When these scenes are identified and a Scene Selection Menu inserted, DVD Architect 3.0 will automatically create links to each scene.

only has three scenes or chapter markers, then only three scene and chapter links will be displayed.

Next in the menu options is the Insert Back Button. This will create a link to the previous page as shown in the Project Overview tree. Back buttons are automatically inserted when a submenu page is generated. However, if a new page is created separately, or if you inadvertently delete the Back button, then this is how you may replace the missing button.

Buttons that navigate to the next or previous pages may also be inserted from this menu option. If a Next button is inserted and there is no menu following the menu that the Next button has been inserted to, the button will do nothing.

Finally, an Empty button may be inserted as a place holder, or to be linked to later. Using Empty buttons in a menu template is a good way to create a consistent template that needs to have information linked to the button later. To link an Empty button to media, click the button properties in the Project Properties window at the right of the workspace. Expand the Action menu items in the Project Properties window, and in the Destination dropdown list, select the file that you wish the Empty button to link to. An Empty button may be linked to another menu, a chapter point, a video, or any other form of media.

Grid settings may be determined in the Options menu. Select this option via the Options menu or the keyboard shortcut Ctrl+Shift+G. A dialog opens that allows you to set your grid preferences as to color, size, and grid spacing. If you enable the Snap To settings, the grid will automatically snap all buttons or text links to the grid. This is a useful tool, but may also become frustrating if you forget it's enabled and are trying to freely place graphics, buttons, or text links.

Snapping may be enabled or disabled in the Options menu, or the shortcut key F8 may be used. Snapping is used to snap text or image buttons to the grid settings. This aids in assuring that all items are aligned to grid points that you've brought the graphic or text to.

You can force snapping to the gridlines by using the Snap to Grid option. The grid may be turned on or off in the View menu or by using Ctrl+F8. Snapping to Objects rather than a boundary line is possible as well, by using the Options>Snap to Objects (Shift+F8). This may allow greater creative freedom, depending on how you'd like the project display to appear.

Snapping to Safe Areas will snap objects or text to the safe area boundaries. Regardless of the safe area settings it's strongly recommended that you preview the project on an external monitor to be certain that the safe areas on your monitor are accurate. It's always better to err on the side of being too safe rather than being too close to

10.14: The options menu is used to help you author more efficiently.

safe areas, as less expensive monitors often mask more than 10 percent of the entire screen area. Always check menus on an external monitor if the project is being delivered to unknown display destinations.

Simulating an Aspect Ratio is recommended for preview as well, particularly if an external monitor isn't present or available. Widescreen letterboxing will be added as needed. This will also demonstrate where menu items may be taken out of aspect, depending on masks used, or text placement.

10.15 In this dialog, you'll set grid preferences.

Using an External Monitor

A terrific feature of DVD Architect is the ability to preview the project on an external monitor, including motion menus and animated buttons.

The external monitor option refers to a broadcast monitor of either PAL or NTSC format. The entire project may be previewed externally to give you a close approximation of what the DVD will look like when burned. It's not an exact approximation, as the menus, text, and animated buttons have not been compressed for burning. It's entirely possible that menu information may be slightly pixelated when compared to the finished DVD quality.

To connect an external monitor to the system, you'll need an OHCI card such as those available from ADS, Canopus ADVC 1394, SIIG, and Unibrain. You cannot use a proprietary card such as those offered by Matrox or Pinnacle.

The OHCI card is connected to a camera or video converter. The camera or video converter will take the digital information sent from the Fire Wire card or port and convert it to an analog video signal that your external monitor can read.

With everything connected, go to the Options/External Monitor option. Once this is selected, video will be ported to the external monitor and may be previewed with full motion. Be aware that with some system configurations, jerky playback may be observed on an external monitor. As of this writing (build 74), it appeared that slower systems with IRQ sharing had this issue. Sony has said that this will be fixed in future releases. Be sure that no background applications are running during preview, paying particular attention to shutting down virus protection and any network admin functions that are not pertinent to running the system. If you are running an NLE at the same time as DVD Architect and the NLE is using external preview, it's also possible that DVD Architect will not be able to access the resource. If DVD Architect cannot access the external monitor, you may find it necessary to close the NLE. This issue rarely exists within the Vegas 5/DVD Architect workflow.

10.16 Converters such as the Canopus ADVC 100 will convert digital video to analog so that it may be previewed on an external monitor.

Preview (F9) may be accomplished at various quality levels. Depending on menu content, compression, speed of CPU, and system load, you may need to reduce the preview quality. In the Preview window, reduce the preview quality by selecting the drop down menu in the upper-right corner. This works similarly to the Preview Quality output in Vegas where reducing resolution will allow for greater framerate playback. If your system is top-notch and very fast, you may be able to preview all media at Production Quality/Best resolution.

Next in the Options menu is the Customize Toolbar function. You can insert or delete tools from the toolbar in DVD Architect the same way you accomplish this in Vegas. This feature allows you to have the tools you need and use available to you on the toolbar and allows you to remove the tools you don't need or use, saving space on the toolbar and reducing the number of icons that you are constantly viewing. A clean workspace means faster editing and authoring.

10.17 If your playback is stuttering or jerky, try using this option to reduce resolution in the preview process. This is particularly useful when previewing to an external monitor.

Renaming Title clips etc in the media pool, you can have a bin of just titles, etc. One caveat is that when moving bins from project to project/instance to instance, title renames and subclip renames don't move across from project to project.

You should note six tabs in the Preferences window. The first tab is the General Preferences tab. There are several check boxes checked by default from the Sony engineers. These are checked for good reason, and generally should be left enabled as they came when you installed DVD Architect 3.0. Some users may find that automatically naming markers or displaying filenames in the timeline window has value. Personally, I prefer seeing file names always, as occasionally I'll have several similar files, and viewing thumbnails won't quickly let me know what files I'm using.

In the Video Device window, select the OHCI card from the dropdown menu. If more than one card is installed, select the card connected to the converter device. Set the external preview format to NTSC or PAL, depending on where you live and to what format you are authoring. Notice that this is where widescreen and standard aspect ratios are chosen for the preview as well.

In the Editing window, set the safe area and action area margins. The defaults of 10 percent and 20 percent are very conservative, so keeping these at this setting is generally the safest thing to do.

10.18 In this dialog, you can select which tools will be accessed in the toolbar. This is a great way to have DVD Architect work exactly as you'd like it to function without having lots of extra icons on the workspace or toolbar.

10.19 In the Preferences dialog, you'll instruct DVD Architect how to behave when you provide input to specific tasks.

10.20 This is the Editing Preferences setting dialog

Set the Selected items color here. This is great for those times when the selected items are of the same color as the background and you can't easily see what is selected in the workspace. The default color is half-transparent white.

You may also change the number of undos available. By default, this is set to 1,000 undos. It's often a good idea to reduce this number for best results in previewing a file, as each undo/redo level occupies memory. Setting an undo level at a value of say, 50 is a little more reasonable.

In the Display window, you can determine saturation and color amount found in icons. Icons may be viewed as primarily grayscale, or viewed with vivid color, depending on personal pref-

10.21 The Display window is used to set the preferred color saturation and tint of toolbar icons.

10.22 Set the behaviors of the Remote Control rewind and fast forward features in this preference.

erences. For those authoring and editing in darker rooms, you may want to reduce color saturation to ease eye strain.

In the Preview tab, you can set how fast the fast forward and rewind functions operate. Setting this too fast on slower, older systems may result in system crashes. Be aware of this if you are working with a system slower than a PIII 1 GB processor or if the system has less than 256 MB of RAM.

In the Burning window, you'll determine the sort of feedback that DVD Architect provides for you during the authoring stage, such as how much space your project will occupy on the burned DVD. You'll also determine the DVD size that you'll be working with.

Finally in this window, you'll also determine the working directory. For best results, determine a working directory that is not on the same drive as your application or boot drive information. In other words, choose a drive that is not your C: drive, which is the default application drive in most systems. Set both your Temporary and Prepare drive locations to a drive other than the C: drive.

10.23 Preferences for burning the disc are found in the Burning tab.

Hey, Look Me Over! The Project Overview Window

This window is very important to the DVD authoring process as it always shows what assets are included in the burning process. If you have an asset in this window that is not linked, it will show you what that asset is. The asset, linked or not, will be burned to the DVD, taking up space, so it's important that the asset is linked, or no one will ever see or hear it.

This is but one of the uses of the Project Overview window. While everyone has their own workflow, one good method of working is to load all the desired assets into the Project Overview window by dragging items from the Explorer into this window.

All non-linked assets will appear in the lower portion of the Project Overview window.

The Project Overview window will show linked assets similar to how the Windows Explorer displays files, folders, and contents, in that it's a tree-down view of the overall project. This provides a quick view of how everything comes together.

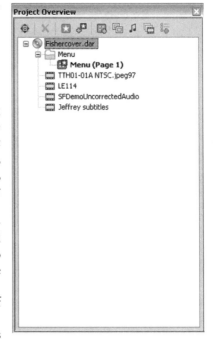

10.24 Notice that none of the files are currently linked to anything in the project. A menu has yet to be built that these assets will link to.

If you are just getting started with DVD authoring, or are new to DVD Architect, here is a workflow you might find beneficial.

Drag and drop all media to be contained in the DVD to the Project Overview window.

A blank menu was created when the application was opened, so now media may be dragged to the workspace. Drag a video file to the workspace. A text and graphic button has been created by dragging the file to the workspace.

If the file does not contain chapter points imported from Vegas, double-click the file and it will open in the timeline view. Notice that the workspace now shows the first frame of the video contained in the file dragged to the workspace.

In the Track view, place the cursor where you'd like to insert a chapter point and press M for Marker. Give the marker a name that will allow you to identify the chapter point later on. Viewers will eventually see this chapter name, so name it accordingly.

Repeat step 4 until you've got chapter points identified throughout the project.

Notice in the Project Overview window that the file you've just inserted chapter markers to is identified as a linked menu item.

Click the Menu 1/Page 1 icon in the Project Overview and you'll be back to the menu page containing the video link.

If you'd like to insert a scene selection menu to go along with the Play-all behavior of the button first dragged to the workspace, then right-click the button associated with the entire file. Choose Insert Sub Menu from the menu that opens on right-click.

A new menu page has opened up. Notice that all the chapter points you just created (or were imported from Vegas) are now part of the sub menu that you just created. DVD Architect auto-creates the submenu and chapter points based on the markers you inserted to the video.

Press F9 or click Preview DVD to view how this button and submenu button will function on the DVD. In the Preview window, click the button linked to the full-length video, and you'll see

10.25. Chapter markers and subtitles may be created in the Track View.

it begin to play. Click Stop on the Preview remote control. Click the Back button on the remote control and it will return you to the main menu page. Now click the Scene Selection button on the menu. Notice that the menu that opens is the submenu you specified. Click any of the submenu links, and DVD Architect will begin playback from that chapter point.

Now that you've gotten the menu structures set up, you probably want to set a First Play, or DVD Start video or still. This is the first thing viewers will see when the DVD is inserted into the player. Often times, this is a copyright reminder or studio logo.

To create the DVD Start item, drag the video or still to the Project overview window as an asset if it's not there already. Right-click the file and select Set DVD Start from the submenu. The DVD Start video does not have to be linked to any button or end action. It lives on the DVD by itself. It may contain audio or not, and audio may be inserted to the DVD Start asset in the Track View window at any time prior to the DVD burning.

The DVD Start asset will be displayed with a small star next to the Start item. In the Overview window, you'll always be able to see what's going to play in what order, which is another reason it's a good idea to keep this window open.

This simple workflow will get you rapidly started in DVD Architect, but there is a lot more that you can do with DVD Architect.

Inserting a Background

DVD Architect will allow for static background images or animated background images. Backgrounds may be inserted in a few different ways.

The easiest way to insert a background is to right-click any menu and choose Set Background Media. When the Explorer dialog opens, navigate to the file chosen for background media and click Open. The file will now be inserted to the background of the project. If the file inserted to the background of the project does not match the aspect ratio of the project properties, it's

10.26   The star next to the video asset indicates this is the first playing video asset on the DVD.

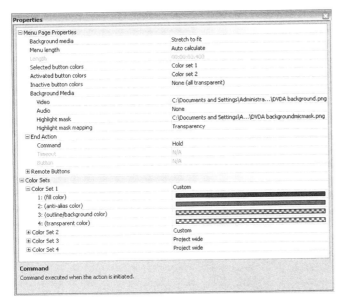

10.27 Use this drop-down menu to zoom, stretch, or letterbox background images that don't meet the aspect ratio of the project.

an easy task to fix the background image so that it stretches, letterboxes, or zooms to fill the background area.

In the Project Properties window, you'll note in the upper-right corner that there is a Background Media field. In this field, the background image may be letterboxed, leaving black lines above and below the image, display dependent on the original image size. If you choose the Stretch to Fit option, the background image will be distorted but will fill the entire background area. The next option is to Zoom to Fit. With the Zoom to Fit option, the image will not be distorted but rather zoomed in to the closest border of the image so that the image fills the screen while retaining its correct aspect ratio.

Properties Window

Notice in the Project Properties window that it will shift focus depending on whether a menu or link is selected in the project. When a menu is selected, the Properties page displays everything related to the menu, and when an object is selected, the properties displays all things relevant to that object.

Looking at the Menu Properties, notice that there is a Menu Length option. In this dialog, you can set the predetermined length of a menu or allow DVD Architect to calculate the length of the menu based on either the length of a background audio file or a background video file. If you specify the length of the menu, it's quite possible that animated or video buttons will exceed the length of the menu and therefore will allow the background audio or video of a menu to go silent or dark (or both) while the animated button plays on. Therefore, always be sure of your menu

Tip

You can now import Photoshop layered files into Sony DVD Architect 3. The layers must follow a specific naming convention, consult DVD Architect Help for more information on how to name each layer.

At the time of this writing, some pre-built templates from third parties such as Pixel Pops, would not correctly read, due to errors in the naming conventions. Be sure to check this prior to purchasing third-party template tools.

length. I typically create my background menu videos in Vegas, using ACID loops to create the background audio. Vegas provides me with the length, if I need to specify the length. However, when audio and video are of equal length, DVD Architect detects this and automatically sets itself to the length of the background media.

In DVD Architect 3.0, you can hold the Ctrl key while adjusting any slider, providing you with very fine control of parameter values.

Using the Color Sets in Vegas, users can create colors for inactive, active, and selected buttons, indicating to viewers which buttons they are selecting. Three color states may be selected, and you'll find the color selections in the lower portion of the Menu Properties page. We'll look at those in a moment.

Select different colors for the three states. Color 1, Color 2, and Color 3 may all be set up to be unique. Set one color for the Selected button, one for the Activated button, and one color set for the Inactive button. A fourth color may be specified, but it is by default a transparent color set in DVD Architect. Modify this to your desire.

The color sets will define how masks are filled when active, inactive, or selected.

The four styles in the colorsets are defined as follows:

Fill Color: The selection in this color field will determine the color of highlight masks and subtitle text.

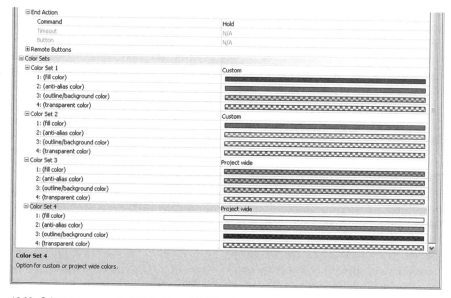

10.28 Colorsets are new to DVD Architect 3.0. This allows the inactive, selected, and active buttons to have three color states.

Anti-Alias Color: This color selection smooths the transition between subtitle text and highlight masks. It should be similar to the fill color and the background colors. Experiment with this colorset to best blend subtitles and highlight masks.

Background/Outline Color: shows the outline of a text button or highlight graphic, and subtitle text.

Transparent Color: This almost sounds like an oxymoron, a 'transparent color.' This color is used to select/determine the transparent areas of subtitle text and menu button highlights.

Below the Color Set designations, the Background Video and Audio fields are found. This is another location where the background video or image may be determined. Clicking in this field will allow you to browse through files to locate the file you want to insert as a background video. If a background audio file is to be used, the file may be selected in the Background Audio field. Audio may also be inserted in by right-clicking the workspace and choosing the Insert Background Media. You may insert .wma, .MP3, .mov, .wav, .AC3, .pca, and .ogg files as background audio. Audio files that are not PCM/wav or AC3 will be converted to PCM or AC3 format when the DVD is burned, depending on the preference settings at the time of burning the DVD. AC3 should nearly always be the first choice, as it provides very good audio quality while being small in size, leaving more room on the disc for video files.

Highlight Masks

In DVD Architect, you can now highlight masks, indicating a color change when a menu item is selected. You'll determine the highlight masking used in the Menu Properties window, just beneath the Background Audio field. Highlight masking involves using a graphics editor such as Photoshop or PhotoImpact. You can also create these graphics in Vegas, but it's somewhat easier to use a graphics editor with layer support.

Subtitling

Subtitling is one of the new additions to DVDArchitect 2.0, allowing DVDs authored in DVD Architect 3.0 to be Rule-508 compliant in addition to offering other language subtitles or subtitle information for the hearing-impaired. Up to 32 subtitle tracks may be inserted into a DVD project. Subtitles can be inserted into DVD Architect via two different methods. The first method is done directly in DVD Architect, using the track view.

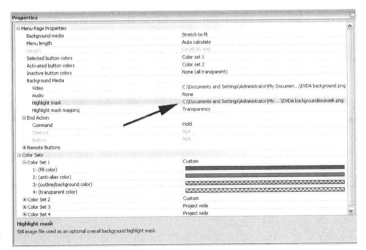

10.29 Insert highlight masking in the DVD Architect workspace in this menu field.

10.30 Click the Add Subtitle Track button to insert a subtitle track, allowing subtitles to be displayed within the DVD preview area.

Double-click any video file contained in the DVD Architect project. This will load the video into the timeline window. Click the Add Subtitle Track button to insert a subtitle track to the project. This will create a new track that will contain text cues to be displayed at predetermined times, within the Preview window. Viewers of the DVD will be able to turn on and off the subtitles with their remote controls.

In the subtitle track, position the cursor where the subtitle should occur. Press the T key to insert subtitle information. You can also right-click in the subtitle window and choose Insert Subtitle Text Event from the submenu. The text event will initially show as blank text.

10.31 Text will show as blocks of information when inserted to the subtitle text view.

In the Preview Window, a line labeled TEXT will be displayed. Click this word and either press the F2 key or right-click and select Edit Text from the sub menu. Input or edit the subtitle that is to appear at that moment. The finished subtitle will appear in the text block in the track view.

Finish all subtitles in this manner.

Subtitles may be given name designations such as English, French, or Spanish, by clicking the Track Language dropdown menu. Typical languages appear in the drop down, by selecting Choose Language, less common languages such as Twi, Persian, Punjabi, or Hebrew may be chosen as language designators.

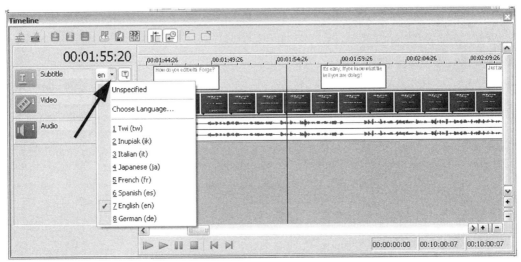

10.32 By selecting the Choose Languages, several different languages may be chosen to display in the DVD player.

This is the first method of inserting subtitles. The second method may be a little easier for some users, particularly those editing video in Vegas.

To export regions from Vegas to be used as subtitles, first open the project in Vegas. Create the region in which the subtitle is to appear by dragging the cursor under the audio or video, creating a selection. With the selection highlighted in blue or gray, depending on whether looping is enabled or disabled in Vegas, press the R key to create a region. In the region naming field that

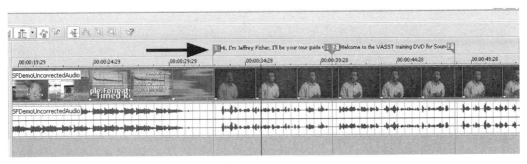

10.33 In Vegas, regions may be created that contain subtitles. Those regions, complete with subtitles, will be recognized by DVD Architect.

opens, type the text that is to appear as the subtitle in DVD Architect. Repeat this process until all subtitle text has been created. Save your work.

Now go to Tools>Scripting>Export Regions as Subtitles. This will export a .sub file that may be saved to a location where you'll be able to find it later, while working in DVD Architect. You can also export this region as a .txt file to send to a translator to create a script for language voiceover, or simply to keep as a text log of the dialog found in your video. To export as a text file, simply choose TEXT (.txt) from the dropdown menu in the Export Regions dialog.

Open DVD Architect, import the file to the Project window or Project Overview window and double-click to load the file into the Track view window.

In the timeline window, insert a subtitle track by either right-clicking the track header and selecting Insert Subtitle Track or by pressing the subtitle button found in the timeline window toolbar.

Now press the Import Subtitle button and browse to where you stored the subtitle information file. It will be imported, and all subtitles will show up in the Subtitle window, already completed for you. If you had DVD Architect opened while you created the subtitle, be sure to press the Refresh button in the DVD Architect Explorer window or the subtitle file may not be shown for import.

Subtitles may be edited for length in the track view window. I recommend that text sections be fairly zoomed so that very exact edits may be created. By clicking on the Expand Window button found on each DVD Architect window, the window will be expanded as large as the screen will allow. You can zoom further in by pressing the up and down arrows in DVD Architect just as you do in Vegas for a tighter view.

Placing the cursor at the edge of a subtitle track will create an icon or cursor that is the same as it is in Vegas, indicating that the text event may be increased or decreased in length. If increasing or decreasing length should have an effect on text events taking place downstream or later in the project, rippling, just like rippling in Vegas, may be used to insert or subtract time throughout the project, maintaining relative time between subtitles. To ripple a text event, grab the edge of the event to be made longer or shorter and drag to the desired length. All text events will either move to make room, or move to fill the empty space, while maintaining relative time between

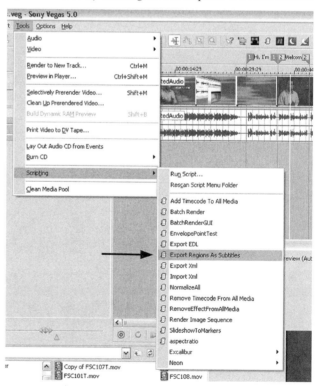

10.34 You may also export .txt files to send to a translator or log as a .txt script file for later use.

text events. If you prefer not to ripple text events, disable rippling by pressing the Auto-Ripple button in the track view timeline.

10.35 Disable Auto-ripple if you want to lengthen or shorten subtitle events without affecting the relative time of other subtitle events in the project.

Changing Fonts and Sizes

By default, DVD Architect uses 14-point Arial as the subtitle text. But what if you don't want this font or point size? Changing it out is quite easy.

Click on the subtitle text in the workspace. The Text toolbar will light up, allowing you to change the text size, font, and placement. Colors may be changed in the Subtitle Properties window, based on one of the four color sets that may be determined for the overall project.

If you change your mind about subtitle properties after you've inserted all subtitles, it's still easy to make changes. First, select all subtitles in the track view by holding Ctrl while clicking on them. You can also select the first subtitle, hold Shift, and click on the last subtitle to select all events. Set the font, size, and location of subtitles to where and how you'd like them to appear with the subtitles selected. Now right-click the subtitles and choose Apply Formatting to Selected Events from the submenu. This will cause all subtitles to take on the properties you just determined. You may also apply this same formatting to other text event or subtitle tracks by selecting the events, modifying them, and then selecting other subtitle tracks. Then right-click the subtitles and choose Apply Formatting to Selected Tracks. This will then apply the formatting to all selected tracks. If you have 32 subtitle tracks in the project, this single step will save hours of editing subtitle formatting.

Secondary Audio Tracks

The DVD specification allows up to eight tracks of audio to be contained in a DVD. DVD Architect supports this specification, and therefore, up to eight individual tracks of audio may be part of the project. These tracks of audio may contain director's comments, perhaps a music-only version of the film, or a version of the film with no music, alternate language tracks, parody dialog, minus versions that contain no M&E (Music and Effects), and so forth. You can be very imaginative with multiple audio tracks.

Audio tracks should be of the same length as the video project's original track. DVD Architect will not permit multiple files to be inserted into a single audio track. The audio track must be more or less synced to the video. Therefore assemble secondary audio tracks in Vegas, so that they are correctly relative to the picture being seen. If you have multiple tracks of audio in Vegas and need to output only one track for use in DVD Architect, solo the single audio track in Vegas and render the single track to a .wav or .AC3 file format to be imported into Vegas.

DVD Architect will also allow you to import audio directly from an .avi file.

To create a sub-audio track, click in the track view window header to make that window active. Then press Ctrl+Q to insert a new audio track. (This is the same shortcut as in Vegas to create a new audio track.)

> You can also right-click in the track view window and choose Insert Audio Track, or press the Add Audio Track button seen in the upper-left corner of the track view.

In the DVD Architect Explorer window, browse for and locate the audio file(s) to be inserted as additional audio tracks. Remember that if the new audio track was created while DVD Architect was open, the Explorer window will need to be refreshed in order to see the new audio file.

Files may be dragged from the Explorer window to the new audio track in the track view. In the new audio track, language specifications may be inserted as part of the descriptor for the track, which will be displayed on a set-top DVD player. DVD Architect only has language specifications, therefore if a director's commentary or other non-language-related track is inserted, leave the language type unspecified. When you choose a language for an audio track, DVD Architect remembers the language chosen and adds it to the list of languages first seen in the initial drop-down menu.

In the audio tracks seen in the track view, there is a small icon that looks like an audio speaker. This icon is used to activate a track. When a track is activated, it becomes the default audio track heard when a viewer puts the DVD in a set-top or computer DVD player. Only one track may be active, otherwise viewers would hear more than one track of audio simultaneously and become confused.

Select the icon to activate the audio track that should be heard as the primary audio track when the DVD is inserted. Viewers will access the other audio tracks via the language button on their

> The Timeline view will allow you to exchange audio or video files at will. This is also where you might include a 5.1 audio file along with the stereo version. AC3 files may be draggged straight into the Timeline audio tracks.

remote control of the DVD player whether it is software or hardware-based. During Preview of the project in the Preview window, use the Audio button found on the DVD Architect software remote in the Preview window to access other audio tracks.

Audio tracks may be deleted from the project at any time by selecting the audio track and pressing Delete or by right-clicking the track and choosing Delete.

In DVD Architect 3, you can import/author with multiple angles, too. This is very useful for training videos, or product specific video projects. Consult the DVD Architect help files for more information.

Editing in DVD Architect

DVD Architect is not intended as a video editing application, but it does have some options for editing what parts of a video project that viewers will see.

Sometimes a little too much black was left at the beginning or end of a video project, or perhaps there is a section that you don't want the viewer to see for whatever reason. DVD Architect has tools that allow you to skip past or ignore certain sections of a video stream.

Create a menu and insert a video to the menu. Double-click the video link to load the video into the track view. In this view, notice that there are yellow triangles at the beginning and end points of the video, similar to the In and Out point markers seen in the Vegas Trimmer tool. These triangles are the same in DVD Architect as they are in Vegas, In and Out points. These points may be moved to create new beginning and ending points in the video project. As previously mentioned, these In Out points are most useful for removing extra black at the head of a video file.

Be sure to use Quantize to Frames when inserting new In and Out points in the video stream. Otherwise, it's possible to insert In and Out points in the middle of a frame rather than on a frame edge, and this could create a black chapter point, beginning, or end, or cause other glitches in the playback of the file when it begins.

10.36 By using In and Out points in the timeline window, buttons may be linked to any point in the video stream, setting different start and end points in how the DVD is seen. I recommend you leave Quantize to Frames enabled to ensure that the file is not linked to or cut on a half frame.

Masks, Masking, and Masked Images

DVD Architect allows for the creation and implementation of masks that will provide a viewer with feedback as to what button is active, what button they've selected, and what video or slide-show they are clicking on. This is very useful and intelligent and affords DVD authors tremendous latitude in creating DVDs for commercial sale. DVD menus are only going to become more creative and artistic in coming years, and DVD Architect offers great tools to make authoring easier for non-graphic artists and folks like me who are more visually capable than consciously considering a layout. I like to look at what I'm doing and work from the inspiration of what I've just edited, rather than planning out my structure beforehand.

You'll need to understand a few things about buttons in DVD Architect.

First, there is the Active Button. This is the button that is currently highlighted but has not been selected.

Then there is the Selected Button, which is the button that has just been selected, and then there are the Inactive Buttons, which are buttons that are neither selected nor active. Each of these button types may have a mask associated with it. The mask may be the same or different for each button, depending on your creative desires and processing.

Open the DVD Architect demo file on the DVD in this book, entitled "Fishercover.dar." Notice how there are three highlighted images on the workspace. If you do not see them, go to View>Workspace Overlays>Show Button Masks. (Ctrl+B) This will cause the three highlight images to light up.

> Did you know that you can open a rendered project's original media in the Sony application it was created in? If you rendered your media from Sony Vegas, Sound Forge, or ACID, simply right click the file in the Project Properties window, and select Edit Source Project. This will open the project media in whatever application it was authored in. Make your edits to the media, and render back to the same filename. Any changes will be updated in DVD Architect.

10.37   Vegas may be used as a graphics editor to create either motion or stills for a DVD menu with masks.

To create overlay masks in DVD Architect, you'll need a photo editor, or you can also create masks in Vegas. Using Adobe Photoshop or Ulead PhotoImpact (or any other image editor) may prove easier, depending on your skills in Vegas. At some point, you'll want to use a photo editor to create specific or clean masks.

To create highlight masks to DVD Architect, you need two components: the background image and the highlight mask image. You'll want to have the background image or still of the background video in order to make highlight masks in either Vegas or your graphics editor.

In Vegas, you can create masks very easily using multiple tracks, alpha channels, and exporting stills. Open the Fishercover.veg to get an understanding of how this works.

Create a number of blank tracks. In the bottommost track, insert the video or still that should serve as the background for the DVD menu. You can insert titles or whatever you'd like. Now, in the upper tracks, place the graphic shape that you'd like to have act as a mask or selection indicator in the DVD menu. The graphic shape can be created from any image, but keep in mind that this graphic will not contain details nor gradients of colors. This graphic should also be transparent away from the actual mask with no background color, you could easily use a Chromakey filter or secondary color corrector to create the mask area. The graphic will be filled with whatever color is selected in a color set in DVD Architect. Colorset One is the typical choice for this, but it is entirely up to the user.

Place the graphic where it is near the text or button image. It's going to be part of a blank button, so it may not overlap with any button space, because if it does, then a portion of the masked image will be visible when it should not be. For example, if the graphic assigned to button one is too close to button two's link space, when button two is rolled over, part of button one's image mask will be visible.

After all graphic and mask images are in place, mute the background image so that it is not visible. In the Vegas Preview window, set the preview quality to BEST/FULL. Now click the Save Snapshot to File button, and save this image in the .png file format. You've now got a .png file with a transparency or alpha channel. This will become your overlay mask in DVD Architect.

One of the most powerful features in DVD Architect 3.0, is the ability to import .psd files from Adobe Photoshop or other graphic editing apps, while keeping the layers intact to be used as buttons in the overall project. Navigate to a menu, right click, and choose "Submenu from file" or select Insert from the tool bar, and slide down to Submenu from file. (There is no keyboard shortcut)To add links to the buttons, click the button, and click the "Actions" option in the Button Properties window. In the Command box, choose the Link option. In the Destination field, browse to the asset you'd like to link to. This will link the button to the asset. Remember the title must be part of the project properties prior to a button being linked to it. Also be aware of how to properly name layers to meet the DVD Architect specification. Buttons may only be named with the following characteristics: button-01-thumbnail, button-01-thumbnailmask button-01-frame. The number indicates the button layer order. If you do not use these naming conventions, DVD Architect will not recognize the layers correctly, and will not import the image. You will find explicit details in the DVD Architect Help guide that cannot be improved upon in this book.

> The steps to creating a highlight mask in a photo editor are the same as in Vegas, except that you'll use layers rather than tracks to lay the mask image in place for the final .png file export and save.

10.38 Here is where you'll be setting the background image or video and using a .png mask as a highlight mask or graphic.

In DVD Architect, open the Menu Page Properties. In this series of input fields you'll select the background image and the .png file you just created in Vegas.

In the Background Media>Video, select the image or video you used in Vegas to create the highlight mask. In the Background Media>Highlight Mask field, browse to the .png file created in Vegas and select it as the highlight mask. In the Highlight Mask Mapping, select Transparency, Intensity, or Color Channel. If you select Transparency, the highlight mask will be filled with the color specified for the selected button colors. If you choose Intensity, a blend of colors in the selected colorset will create the colors of the highlight mask. Select colors carefully and preview often to be sure colors blend well. If you select Color Channel, then the color in the selected color set will determine the fill color of the highlight mask.

To make the mask highlight work correctly, it must be connected to the button or text that it serves. To make this work, insert an empty button by choosing Insert>Empty button. Choose Select Graphic Only as the button type.

10.39 In the left side of this image, you can see how the empty button does not completely cover the highlight mask. On the right side, you can see how this button will show up in the finished DVD.

To see the active buttons and selected buttons interacting with the highlight masks you've created, use the Remote Control buttons in DVD Architect to see how these work, or the up or down arrows on your keyboard. DVD Architect will not show a mouse rollover that some DVD authoring tools display, so you will not see rollovers taking place without using the Remote or the arrow keys.

Size the Empty Button boundary so that it covers the button that you created in Vegas or in your graphics editor. Stretch the boundary so that it covers not only the button but the highlight area as well.

Place Empty buttons around each button area, being certain that it entirely encompasses the highlight mask.

Masks may also be used as button shapes, similar to the frames seen in the button library. Create buttons in a graphic editor, or in Vegas, that contain transparent centers, and these may be brought into DVD Architect as button masks.

To experiment with how this feature functions, drag a video to the workspace. A button is automatically created in the workspace. In the Button Properties window to the right (default layout) expand the Graphics fields by pressing the + key. In this set of

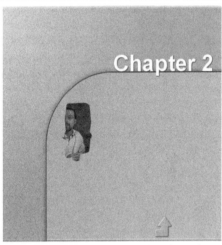

10.40 DVD Architect will allow masks to be used over buttons, providing unique shapes for buttons.

fields, you'll find a field labeled Mask. Click on this dialog and browse for the mask you've created in Vegas or in your graphic editor. Select this mask and watch how DVD Architect can have moving video inside your mask shape.

The new Bezier Masking feature found in Vegas 5 can be excellent for extracting image sections from Vegas and creating button masks. Use this feature to extract a transparent image, leaving the center of the mask transparent so it allows a graphic or video to show through in DVD Architect 3.

Building Compilations

Music and Picture compilations are easy and fast to build with DVD Architect. Picture compilations may be accompanied by sound if desired. Music compilations may be accompanied with an image of an album cover or video screen as well. Compilations is just a large word for slide show.

Creating compilations of pictures with audio is amazingly simple. Right-click the workspace and choose Insert Picture compilation. (Ctrl+L). This will open the compilation window.

Using the Browser or Explorer, browse to the images you wish to be used in the compilation. Insert them as a group or individually by dragging them from the Explorer to the Compilation window.

The images will show in the order they appear in the Compilation window. Image order may be rearranged by dragging them up or down in the Compilation window to set their order of appearance.

If images do not entirely fill the preview screen area, you have three options:

- Zoom image to fit. This will crop out portions of the image, as the image zooms to fit without modifying the aspect attributes of the image.

- Stretch image to fit. This will stretch the image horizontally or vertically so that it will properly fit the aspect ratio and display area. This will distort the image.

- Letterbox. This will create letterboxes or pillar boxes to allow the entire image to be seen. Letterboxes or pillar boxes are black bars found either above or below an image or to the sides of an image, masking the unseen portions of the screen.

10.41 Here is where you drag images files to create a compilation in DVD Architect. The Audio Compilation window functions in the same manner.

Images may also be rotated. For example, a vertically focused image may be rotated to place it correctly as a horizontal image format. Press the Rotate Image Clockwise and counter-clockwise buttons, found at the bottom of the Compilation window.

To insert an audio file to accompany the compilation, locate the audio file to accompany the slide show. Drag it to the track view.

The compilation by default will play for the default length of each image in the compilation of five seconds. Each slide may be given its own individual duration by typing in a new display time in the lower-right side of the Compilation window.

10.42 Notice that each image in the track view contains a marker, showing where it will change to the subsequent image in the compilation. These markers may not be moved, but by right-clicking and choosing Go To, or by double-clicking the marker, the slide relating to that marker will be displayed.

The picture compilation may be timed to match the length of the audio associated with the compilation by clicking the Fit Compilation to Audio button at the lower-right side of the Compilation window. This will auto-adjust the length that each image is displayed. When this option is selected, individual image times are invalidated, as each image will be displayed for whatever length of time is required by matching the compilation length to the length of the audio track.

Subtitles may be added to a compilation in the same manner as described previously in this chapter, and up to eight audio tracks may be inserted into any compilation. Simply create new audio tracks, give them language names if desired, and set the active track.

Creating a Music compilation is the same as creating an image compilation. Pressing Ctrl+K or right-clicking in the workspace and selecting Insert Music Compilation will create a new button. Choose the button preference of Image and Text, Text Only, or Image Only. Double-click this button, and the Music Compilation window opens. Drag audio files (or video files) to this compilation window.

If you'd like to have a still image display during the play of the Music Compilation, drag an image from the Explorer to the music track that the image should be associated with. The image will display as a static image during playback of the audio file. This is great for showing an album cover during playback of a particular song, or a graphic depicting what's being described in a dialog track. Video may be used in the compilation as well, creating somewhat of a video playlist. Subtitles may be added to a music compilation.

> Music and Image compilations may be given their own end actions, transporting the viewer of the DVD to wherever you'd like them to be sent to following the viewing of the compilation. While in the Compilation window, choose the Properties tab. Here you'll find the End Action options. Choose the Command Link, and then in the Action field, choose where you'd like the viewer to be transported to, following their viewing of the compilation. In this same dialog, you'll find the ability to enable and disable remote control functions for the user, preventing them from exiting a menu item, chapter, or having access to additional audio channels.

Remote Control Actions

DVD Architect allows you to control how the viewer's remote control will interact with the DVD being viewed. For example, you may specify a forced play within a scene or video.

In the Menu Properties window, click the Remote Control + symbol to expand the dialogs or fields. Here you will find a variety of options to enable or disable navigation properties of a scene or chapter's playback. This is excellent for forcing a view of a copyright video, for example.

Protecting Your Media

Regional limitations can be set to prevent DVD's from being played back in various regions, By using the Region Coding found in the Project Properties, you can choose where your DVD may be played. Additionally, DVD Architect 3 allows copy protection in the form of CSS encryption and Macrovision® flags insertion. However, Regional coding, CSS Encryption, and Macrovision flagging cannot be used on a burned DVD. You must author to DLT and submit the DLT to a

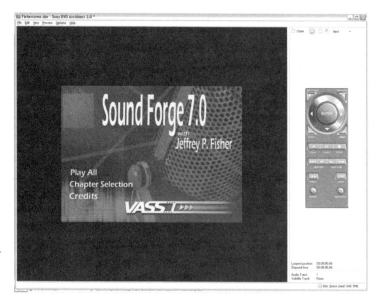

10.43 In this window, you'll
        preview the entire DVD,
        checking links, viewing back-
        grounds, subtitle tracks, and
        audio tracks.

replication facility that is licensed by Macrovision to use their encryption tools. Access these tools via the Burn DVD/Write Master option.

One of the most fun new features found in DVD Architect 3.0 is the ability to control button navigation. (Insert "navigation" image) This allows DVD authors to control how buttons on the DVD player remote control will jump from link to link, video to video.

Previewing the DVD

In the Preview Window, the entire DVD may be previewed either on the computer monitor or on an external monitor. Press F9 to open the Preview window, or choose the Preview DVD button from the toolbar. This opens the Preview window

Use the remote to navigate the DVD just as if you were holding a physical remote, checking all aspects of the project. Be sure to check languages and subtitles by pressing the audio and subtitle buttons. In this Preview window, you can also check one last time for safe areas, being sure that all buttons, titles, and links are within safe areas. Select the Safe Areas button in the upper-right corner of the Preview window. Still shots may be extracted here as well, using the Copy to Clipboard command. The still may be pasted to an Explorer or to a graphics editor for further use.

Next to the Copy to Clipboard button, you'll find an output resolution dropdown. The setting of this menu item does not have any impact on the quality of the final output of the DVD

 *Tip*_____

Get familiar with the F9 function to preview your video. Previewing the video, using the remote control, will always give you a clear idea of how your DVD is going to navigate

but may reduce the load on the CPU in the event that you cannot preview DVDs with full framerate. Reduce the resolution if you find that your system is choking or slowing down too much. Generally, the resolution should be set to High.

We discussed external monitor preview earlier, so to reiterate, if you have the required hardware, you only need click the External Monitor button in the Preview window to send video via FireWire to the external monitor. I highly recommend that you check projects on an external monitor to be sure that all aspects are safe and that colors appear externally the way you'd like them to appear.

Close the Preview window to return to DVD Architect's workspace.

10.44 In the File>Save As dialog, you can save all media to an external drive, DVD, or other portable format, complete with themes. This allows archiving of projects, sharing of projects, and aids in the portability of projects from desktop to laptop.

Transporting a Project

In DVD Architect, you can now save a project much as you can in Vegas, where all media and assets are saved and packaged together, allowing the entire project to be sent via FTP, stored on a portable drive, or saved on a network. This will allow any computer with DVD Architect to open the project intact, exactly as it was stored on the original system.

Go to File>Save As and choose the method in which you'd like to copy and store the information. By default, the copy method is Normal, which means that nothing is copied. By selecting Copy User Media with project means that everything will be copied except any theme information from a DVD Architect theme. This method assumes that the second computer will have the DVD Architect themes or any custom themes already installed on it. The next method is to save everything, including the themes. Both are found in the Save As dropdown menu.

The Final Burn

Burning the DVD is the culmination of all the prep work you've done in Vegas and DVD Architect, and if all edits, renders, and authoring have gone according to plan, you're probably excited to see the media come off the computer, onto the DVD, and

10.45 Here, you'll prep the DVD and discover any pre-burning issues.

end up in your set -top player to share with family, friends, co-workers, your boss, or on the shelves of your local Blockbuster store.

Burning can be a simple or frustrating process, depending on hardware, media choices, and the project itself. If you've encoded the MPEG files from Vegas, you already have an idea of how much media you have. While a DVD will hold 4.7 GB of information, some of the space is required for DVD overhead and menu information, so keep those numbers in consideration. A DVD5, or 4.7 GB DVD, can hold approximately 90 minutes of video information, but the content of the media will ultimadetermine the bitrate at which the media is encoded. The default standard in DVD Architect is 8 Mbps maximum, and 6Mbps average. DVD Architect supports only VBR, or Variable Bitrate encoding. If you want a constant bitrate, encode your video in Vegas. In fact, most of the time it's beneficial to encode all assets prior to importing them to DVD Architect.

10.46 Vegas has specific rendering templates available for DVD Architect.

DVD Architect has tools to assist in bringing the media to a size that will fit on a finished DVD, in the event that you run into a challenge.

Press the Make DVD button. This will open the Burn dialog. Here, you'll prep the DVD and optimize it for burning. Press the Prepare DVD button, and DVD Architect will display where any problems in the project might be found.

Click the Optimize button. This will open a dialog that will display any files that are not compliant with the DVD standard in terms of encoding size, file format, and audio stream.

The yellow caution signs indicate which files will require recompression .

Notice in the dialog, there is a Fit to Disc button. This will take all assets regardless of size and fit them to the disc. This could result in the loss of quality, depending on the size of the media.

Once you are aware of what DVD Architect will be doing to the media, if anything, you can either proceed, or drop the files back into Vegas for further editing. If you wish to proceed, press the Next button. This opens a Prepare Folder dialog. Here, you should determine where the prepared file should be stored. For best results, specify a folder on a drive that is not the boot drive or same drive that DVD Architect is installed on. Click the Finish button, and then sit back, relax, and DVD Architect will do the rest.

Of course, prepping the files first in Vegas is always the best practice.

In Vegas, render MPEG files using the DVD Architect presets, and specify a file name and location you can find easily. Render audio to an AC3 format using the same file name (only the extension should be different) and DVD Architect will automatically seek and connect the AC3 audio file with the MPEG video file of the same name.

Mixing File Formats in DVD Architect

DVD Architect will allow for mixed media formats in the audio stream. Both PCM and AC3 files may be part of the final output and playback structure of the DVD. This is a fairly unique feature, as most DVD authoring applications will only permit one format or another.

If the DVD contains high-quality music files, such as a promotional for a music group or other high quality audio is necessary or preferred, this is a valuable option. However, this will use much more space on the DVD than if AC3 audio is used. PCM is an uncompressed format, and while it does have a somewhat higher quality than AC3, disc size must be a constant consideration. DVD Architect will reduce quality of video to make room for the PCM file format if the Fit to Disc option is used and files are too large to easily accommodate the PCM file format.

To access the PCM format choice, click the Make DVD button. This will open the illustrated dialog.

Choose the Prepare DVD or the Prepare and Burn DVD button, and then select Optimize. This dialog will open. In this dialog, you'll be able to

10.47 In this dialog, you'll determine the final settings of the finished DVD.

10.48 In this dialog, you may choose recompression settings for video or audio, if you wish to not use the DVD Architect 3 defaults.

select an individual audio or video file, and choose the parameters to be set for each individual component of the project. Select PCM if you wish to have the file be different than the default project setting of AC3. You can also instruct the entire project to be PCM format audio.

In this same dialog, the settings for video compression and recompression may also be set if you are choosing to do your encoding inside of DVD Architect rather than inside of Vegas.

You're going to love the Smart Prepare found in DVD Architect 3. This allows you to re-encode only the changed segments of any existing project. Access this feature after you've prepared a DVD to burn, by clicking the Advanced button in the burn dialog. Simply check the box for Smart Prepare (enabled by default). This prevents DVD Architect from having to re-encode any unchanged media. After you've made your changes, use the prepare option again, but this time, choose the "Use Previously Prepared Project" as your project. DVD Architect will inspect the file, and make any necessary changes.

Working with 24p Media in DVD Architect

If you're using the MainConcept MPEG-2 encoder in Vegas, use the DVD Architect NTSC video stream or DVD Architect 24p NTSC video stream template to render your video stream. (You'll need to render your audio stream separately according to the parameters listed in the AC-3 audio or PCM audio headings.) The MPEG-2 files are not recompressed, and AVI files are compressed at the correct rate when selecting the 24p template. Previews of 24p media are correct in DVDA and are previewable with either AC-3 or PCM audio. If you wish the final product to be progressive scan, use the 24p template without pulldown. Adding pulldown will interlace your image. If the project will be displayed on anything but a computer or progressive scan television or projector, the television, projector, or other display device will interlace the image at display. This occasionally can lead to display problems, or lesser quality display than desired.

24p files allow for up to 20 percent greater disc efficiency, as the files are smaller. 1080i and 720p support coupled with 24p makes for an awesome picture quality when encoded to MPEG-2. 24p also renders nearly three times as fast as 210.97 interlaced (60i) video. However, at the time of this writing, no settop DVD player is capable of playing back the 720p or 1080p stream from the deck; these are for computer playback only.

Be certain to check the Allow Pulldown Removal check box in the DVD Architect General Preferences if you are working with 24p files.

One exceptional benefit to DVD Architect is the ability to include extra files and media. For example, if you have created an informational disk for your company finances, you could include an Excel or other financial file on the DVD as an "Extra." Or, perhaps you'd like to deliver Extra information in the form of a completely contained website (which cannot be accessed from the DVD menus) that might be opened from the Windows Explorer. To access this option, open File/Properties (ALT+Enter). In the Properties dialog, choose the "Extras" option, and browse to the file/folder you'd like to include. That's it! Be sure to consider the size of the included files along with determining bitrate for your project.

Inserting an AC-3 Audio File

DVDA supports 5.1 surround and Stereo AC-3 audio file formats. Files can be encoded to AC-3 in Vegas as a separate audio file that is a companion to video files. Audio is imported as a separate file format in DVDA. The video file is rendered as an AVI or MPEG in Vegas, and the audio is rendered separately in Vegas as an AC-3 file format. If video is rendered as an MPEG video/

audio file in an NLE application, such as Vegas, the audio is rendered as an MPEG Audio format. DVDA requires that this audio be re-encoded as AC-3 or as a PCM audio file. It is recommended that files encoded outside of DVDA be encoded without audio, as an elementary stream. The extension associated with the elementary stream is .M2V, or MPEG-2/video. Audio should be rendered as an AC-3 in the editing application when rendering elementary streams

When you insert video into a DVDA project, the video is imported to DVDA by dragging the video to the workspace, and the accompanying audio is replaced by the AC-3 file in the Media Properties menu. Double-click the media file to navigate to the Media Properties menu.

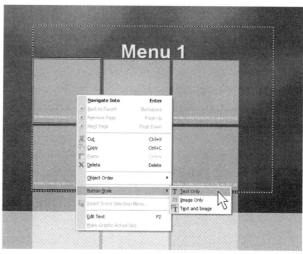

10.49 Text-only links to audio files can be created quickly by dragging several audio files to the workspace and selecting Text-only from the Object Properties drop-down menu. AC3, .wav, QuickTime, MP3, and other formats may all be dragged to the workspace and linked as audio..

10.50 You can instruct DVD Architect to auto-link AC3 and video files of the same name if they are stored in the same folder. This is a great time saver and may prevent you from accidentally using the wrong audio file or having to recompress a .wav file.

 Tip

When audio and video-only files are of the same name and in the same root directory, DVDA automatically opens the AC-3 audio file when the related video-only file is opened. This attribute can be selected by visiting the OPTIONS | PREFERENCES | GENERAL dialog and checking the "Automatically link similar audio and video files" check box

Audio files encoded at bit rates higher than 448 Kbps are not recognized by DVDA, as the DVD standard does not allow for bit rates higher than 448 Kbs.

 Tip_____

Remember to check button locations to ensure that buttons and linked text are inside the safe viewing zone.

Regional limitations can be set to prevent DVD's from being played back in various regions, By using the Region Coding found in the Project Properties, you can choose where your DVD may be played. Additionally, DVD Architect 3 allows copy protection in the form of CSS encryption and Macrovision® flags insertion. However, Regional coding, CSS Encryption, and Macrovision flagging cannot be used on a burned DVD. You must author to DLT and submit the DLT to a replication facility that is licensed by Macrovision to use their encryption tools. Access these tools via the Burn DVD/Write Master option.

 Tip_____

PAL DVD authors should be aware that AC-3 5.1 surround files might not play in all PAL-format DVD players This issue predominantly affects older players. If a warning appears in your project when it is time to burn the DVD, and authors are certain that DVDs will only be played in compliant PAL DVD players or NTSC DVD players, this warning may be ignored. Otherwise, PAL DVD authors should use LPCM (WAV) files at 48KB/16bit settings.

Determining Bit Rates

With DVDA, determining bit rates is not necessary as DVDA figures the bit rate for you based on the project. If this figure is to be overridden, however, the formula is 600 divided by project minutes. (This is a good rule of thumb for the total bit rate in Mbps of a 4.7GB disc. Note that the rule of thumb is only relative to 4.7GB discs.) The reason it works is the following:

4.7GB x (1 min / 60 sec) x (8 bits $\prod$ 1 B) = 624 Mbps x min

As an example, for a 90-minute project, 600 / 90 = a bit rate of 6.6 Mbps.

Also, the bit rate of AC-3 stereo can range from 0.064 Mbps to 0.448 Mbps depending on how it was encoded. Dolby's recommended bit rate for stereo is 0.192 Mbps and for surround is 0.384 Mbps. That's the bit rate at which DVDA encodes AC-3 audio.

 Tip_____

DVDA provides an option that is enabled by default that uses bi-cubic stretching during the render process. This feature increases render time while ensuringthe finest possible quality of video. Turning this feature off in the OPTIONS | PREFERENCES | GENERAL dialog speeds the render process but does not ensure the highest quality render.

Output and Export

Last Steps with Vegas

Vegas is unique in that it is currently the only end-to-end NLE or digital audio workstation (DAW). Vegas contains tools for output to every web format, CD/VCD format, serial digital interface (SDI), high-definition broadcast quality, and multiple audio format. Vegas is formidable. No wonder it's the choice of many large encoding and finishing houses!

As mentioned previously, Vegas started life as an audio-only tool. As a result, the audio features in Vegas are what first brought attention to the application years ago. Development for audio has continued, and Vegas is currently one of the most open-ended output DAW systems in existence on any platform.

Output Formats

After a mix is completed, it needs to be output in a format that others can hear or distribute or that a replicator can work with.

Open a multitrack mix in Vegas. Assuming all parts of the mix are satisfactory, the multichannel mix needs to be mixed to a two-track mix that can be put on a CD and prepped for distribution. This process is called the mixdown. Mixing down multiple tracks is the next-to-last step in the finishing process.

To mix the multichannel mix to a two-track mix, select FILE | RENDER AS and render the mix to a Stereo WAV mix.

When rendering the multiple tracks to a final two-track mix, be certain that if any buses were used they all point to the master output. This issue only occurs if multichannel hardware has been used, with outputs assigned to other devices.

If the project has been recorded at any sample rate other than 16 bit, 44.1 KHz, the mixdown process is not where the sample rate should be dithered to 44.1. Keep files in their higher resolution state where applicable. They'll be dithered to a 16/44.1 state later in the process.

11.1   Rendering multitrack to a two-track mix, ready to be mastered.

After this process has been performed with each song, or multichannel audio project, the multiple two-track mixes are ready to be mastered. Vegas has excellent mastering tools—tools that have been used to master/produce my Grammy-winning and Grammy-nominated recordings.

Mastering

The mastering process is not to be taken lightly. This stage is the final one before sending the master disc to a replicator. It is generally advisable to do the mastering in a familiar room, using familiar monitors. It's rarely a good idea to master on the same monitors that were used in the mixing stage, as it is entirely possible for monitors to mask or enhance problems in a mix. The entire point of mastering is to discover anomalies or errors in a mix and to bring all cuts of a project to a state of consistency so that regardless of sequencing, tracks compliment each other and flow comfortably from one cut to another. Mix on a different set of speakers if possible. Move to a different room, if possible. If nothing else, check the mastered mix multiple times on different stereo systems to assure a consistent and balanced master. In one studio years ago, we installed an FM transmitter that was fed by our master tape deck. We then went out to the car in the parking lot and listened to the mix over an FM receiver. To this day, all mixes at Sundance Media Group are checked on an old Craig boom box, a standard home stereo system, and a high-end car audio system before being sent off for replication.

Mastering is not mixing. Mixing is blending several channels of audio together, placing elements in different portions of the sound field while using EQ, reverb, delay, and other tools to create a sense of depth and space. An analogy might be that mixing is like baking a cake, whereas mastering is the decorating part that pretties things up.

Mixing is an entire book in itself, so this section covers mastering only. See Chapter 6 for more information on mixing.

Mastering is taking the 2-channel, 4-channel, 5.1, 7.1, and 16.1 final mix and finishing it for the audio space/delivery mechanism. The primary preparation is making sure that all audio is of maximized level, in phase, properly faded in/out, with all hum, pops, and noises removed, proper compression applied where/if needed, relative level adjustment between cuts of audio matched, and other tweaks applied to give the audio that final sparkle. Mastering is rarely done in the same room as the audio mix was done in, as a different set of speakers in a different environment tells the tale when poor audio practices, sneaky noise, or other anomalies are present but were not heard in the original recording environment. Mastering is also generally done by a mastering engineer, rather than by the engineer who mixed the audio. A fresh set of ears is invaluable at this point, even if it's just a friend with good ears who can make comments on how something sounds.

If you'll be mastering for surround 5.1 or 7.1, be certain that you have a high-quality audio tool, such as the Echo Audio Layla, Mona, M-Audio Delta Series, or a similar tool. A low-quality audio card will create problems in any instance at this point. Higher-quality cards allow for synchronous playback of multiple channels of audio, whereas a low-end sound card with surround ability will have slur and phase issues in most instances. Worse still, many low-end audio cards induce noise into the audio path. (With Microsoft's Windows-Media 9, you'll need a surround-capable card in order to prep audio for the new codec/delivery tools.) Remember, this stage is the last stage in preparing your audio for the world to hear. If you've worked hard to have a mix, video, or other project that sounds great, you'll want to put your best foot forward, especially when presenting the product for sale or broadcast.

11.3   Echo Audio Layla (back view).

11.2   Delta 1011.

Meters are critical to this endeavor. Vegas has two meter display spaces: one is the master and the other is for buses/auxes. For this section, we're only concerned with the master volume meters. Notice the small lock icon on the master meters. This locks right and left together, so that both channels are identical. They may be unlocked by clicking the icon.

Ideally, during the mix process, the audio was mixed to a level not exceeding 0dB and not less than -6dB at peaks, which are the loudest points in the audio mix. Audio that is too quiet won't be heard well over the television or stereo system on which the video is played or on which the CD is played. In addition, in the event of poor playback equipment, audio that is too quiet can cause any noise associated with the poor playback equipment to shine through, making your finished product sound unfinished or of poor quality.

Many ways exist to bring up audio levels in the digital world. One is to apply a simple volume adjustment. In Vegas, volume can be increased by 12dB at the track slider and decreased infinitely until to the point of no volume whatsoever. Vegas' track pane setting for volume is 0dB, at which point there is no increase or decrease in the volume of the audio.

Another means of raising volume is to normalize the audio levels. Normalizing in Vegas instructs the application to search the various peak levels of the audio information and set the loudest point to a prespecified level. To normalize in Vegas, right-click the audio file and select PROPERTIES | NORMALIZE. This step can also be done by selecting EDIT | SWTCHES | NORMALIZE from the Vegas menu bar.

Change the Normalize Default Level in the OPTIONS | PREFERENCES | AUDIO dialog. Normalize defaults to -.1dB in Vegas.

11.4   Disable locks on master faders if separate control of right/left channels is necessary.

Yet another method to bring audio to the maximum level is to use a maximizing tool, such as Sony's Wave Hammer or the industry favorite, WAVES Ultramaximizer. Maximizers are fantastic for bringing audio to an optimum level without distortion. These are usually applied last in the chain however.

11.5 WAVES Ultramaximizer plug-
in is great for mastering output levels.

11.6 All audio cuts on separate tracks provide the greatest control.

During mastering, effects, such as delay and reverb, are rarely applied. These are more mix tools than master tools. However, EQ, compression, and audio wideners are all commonly applied. Filters/processes can be applied either at a track-level or at an event-level in Vegas. Generally, it is best to apply filters at the track-level, only for purposes of maintaining consistency and clear processing paths.

To begin the mastering process, place all audio to be included in the final output on the time-line in the desired order. This process can be done either with each event on its own track or each event on the same track. It makes no difference other than catering to individual workflow preferences. (Leave exactly two seconds of blank space at the head of the first track, if the audio will be burned to a Redbook/duplicatable CD.) Vegas can auto-insert these two seconds as well, which is defined in the OPTIONS | PREFERENCES | EDITING dialog. Audio CDs have specific areas for specific info, such as in the first 46mm of the CD, where the lead-in occurs. Lead-in is where indexing, table of contents, data information, logical block address (LBA), and length of track information is stored. If anything more or less than two seconds is defined at the head of the CD, Vegas will give an error message indicating that the error must be repaired.

11.7   Set default time between tracks at 2.00 seconds in the OPTIONS | PREFERENCES | EDITING dialog.

11.8   Ozone contains tools specifically for video editors and voice over artists, as well as being very musical and warm.

Listen to the timbre/tonal differences between pieces of audio. Perhaps one has more or less bass than another, or more high-end or less mid-range information. This might be desirable or it might not be. The first part of the process is to determine how to make each event complement the next, without appearing to have jumps in bass, midrange, treble, volume, or pan/right-left information. The transition from one event to the next should be fairly seamless, regardless of whether it's musical or not.

To add EQ to an event at the event level, select TOOLS | AUDIO | APPLY NON-REALTIME EFFECTS, choose an EQ, and click Add. Graphic or parametric choices are available and depend predominantly on the engineer's requirements. Graphic EQs are broader in terms of frequency adjustability, and parametric EQs allow for specific frequency controls.

Here is where plug-ins really shine. While Vegas does come with a selection of audio plug-ins, many third-party plug-ins are available. For instance, the WAVES Q series or Renaissance plug-in tools are very natural, yet powerful tools. They are very musical and have great control.

Ultrafunk also has some great plug-ins available as well, and their EQs are very musical and warm-sounding. Apply EQ sparingly and lean more toward smoothing out harshness, rather than attempting to fix a problem with the overall EQ from the mix. If the track requires a tremendous amount of EQ at this point, it's probably a good idea to revisit the mix. If the master file is audio from a video file, pay attention to the weaknesses in EQ and compensate in future times with better mic techniques and attention to room acoustics.

Applying a touch of bass at the 150 Hz setting will add punch to the mix, while adding any frequencies below 90 Hz will most likely enhance any low-end rumble or noise. It's generally a good idea to roll these lower frequencies off with an EQ, using the high-pass filter setting. Adding 1 to 3dB of gain in the higher ranges, 8 KHz to 12 KHz, will give a little sparkle to the overall mix, but again, too much can create resonant frequencies that are painful to the ear and difficult to control. Watch for harshness in the 1 KHz to 2 KHz regions. When working with audio recorded in a large reflective room, such as a warehouse, bathroom, or conference room, pay close attention to the frequencies around the 500 Hz point. This combination often creates a boomy sound in the audio and should be compensated for or removed if overt and noticeable to the average listener.

Listen to the applied filter and determine if the sound is to satisfaction. If so, then move on to the next event. Notice that when the non–real-time plug-in is applied, a new file is written for the event. Track-level mastering/processing becomes valuable at this point, as real-time effects can be applied without writing a new file. To apply filters/processing at the track-level, open the track filter/processing dialog by clicking the FX Filter button found on the Track Control pane. The dialog box will show a noise gate, compressor, and EQ already in place, with check marks showing that the processors are selected. There is also a Plug-In Chain button in the upper-right corner, which allows you to insert other real-time effects and processes. Click this button to add a real-time effect, from the Cakewalk, Sony, WAVES, Ultrafunk, iZotope, or other DX plug-in. Keep in mind that this effect will affect every piece of audio on the track, which is why placing each piece of audio on its own track is a good idea for the mastering process.

When all audio is finished, it is ready to be output. To output to an MP3 format file, select FILE | RENDER AS, and choose MP3 from the Save As Type drop-down menu. The file will be rendered as an MP3 file. Using this same method, Vegas can output AIFF, Ogg Vorbis, or Windows-Media Audio files.

11.9 The Plug-in Chain switch/button in the Vegas plug-in chooser.

Burning to a Master CD

With all tracks processed to satisfaction, all levels checked, compression at correct settings per cut, and a master compression or EQ setting for the overall project (if it needs a master compressor or EQ), the project is nearly ready to be burned to a CD. Track indexes must be inserted so that listeners have track numbers to skip around to. This process is quite easy in Vegas; just double-click each audio event/track event and press N for a new index point. If subindexes/chapter markers are required, use Shift+N to insert subindex markers. Index points can also be laid out automatically in Vegas 6. Select TOOL | LAY OUT AUDIO CD FROM EVENTS. Vegas will inspect events on the timeline and auto-create index markers. However, if events overlap, Vegas will not see the-individual beginning/end of events and therefore not assign a track index marker. Check each event beginning to ensure it has a track index marker if this is desired. Auto-layout can also be achieved by right-clicking the Marker toolbar, visible only when at east one marker is on the timeline.

11.10 The Burn Disc-at-Once Audio CD dialog offers speed, testing, and performance options.

11.11 Vegas is capable of automatically creating track indexes for audio CDs.

With markers inserted to indicate track indexes, Vegas is ready to burn a CD. Vegas is capable of Disc-at-Once (DAO) CD burns or Track-at-Once (TAO) CD burns. If a Redbook Master is required for duplicating, Disc-at-Once is the only option. Redbook standards do not support TAO-burned discs. (Redook is a mastering/duplicating standard.)

 *Tip*_____

All CDs have errors, which is a fact of digital media creation regardless of the authoring application used. However, errors can be minimized. CDs destined for a duplicator will contain fewer errors when burned at lower burn speeds. Although errors cannot usually be heard, they are seen by replicating equipment in most professional duplication houses. Minimize burn errors by burning CDs at the 1x speeds where possible.

Audio CDs have specific areas for specific information, such as the lead-in in the first 46mm of the CD. For burning a Redbook-compliant CD, there must be exactly two seconds of dead space/silence before the beginning of the first track. Some burners will allow more than two seconds but all require not less than two seconds of blank space. Up to 99 tracks are allowed on a Redbook-compliant CD.

Track-at-Once CDs

11.12 Track-at-Once (TAO) burns are efficient for getting a session burned to disc for referencing the session's work.

TAO CDs can be burned from Vegas. TAO burns are handy for capturing tracks as they are mixed for reference purposes or when merely getting the audio to a CD is necessary.

To burn a TAO, have the track/cut to be burned to a disc on the timeline and select TOOLS | BURN DISC | TRACK AT ONCE. Select the burn speed and burn device, and finish.

In TAO mode, Vegas can also burn a region to a disc from the timeline. Select the Burn Loop Region Only check box. This option is useful for authoring Sony's ACID loops, for sending an advanced digital recording (ADR) loop section out, or for burning a section of a track that needs to be reviewed without cutting and pasting sections of the track.

Mastering Audio for Video

Mastering for video broadcast is different from mastering for audio CD or DVD. Broadcast standards require deep bass and ultra highs to be rolled off or they'll be chopped off at the limiter/compression stage at the broadcast facility. It's better to have control over the amount of cut off and roll off at the editing/mastering stage than to be unhappy about processing during the broadcast stage. While no set standard exists for audio roll off in the NTSC or PAL broadcast world, the average is an −18dB per octave roll off at 80 Hz and a −9dB per octave roll off starting at 12 KHz in most houses. Going beyond these ranges almost ensures that you'll have frequencies cut off and compressed at broadcast. DVD and CD playback allow for almost any levels of audio, so long as levels don't exceed 0dBfs. (See Chapter 5 to refresh yourself on the differences between analog and digital zero.)

Using Compression in Vegas for Video

Audio for video should not have a dynamic range of greater than 20dB. Generally, a dynamic range of less than 15dB is preferable, depending on the content or attitude of the video and the desired effects. A scary visual might call for a 20dB dynamic range, going from sublime to extreme to elaborate a particular shot, but in the general norm, dynamic ranges for video should be fairly limited.

Vegas comes with a good compressor. Here again, however, is where a third-party tool can really shine. The Ozone compressor from iZotope has a very warm and broad sound, as they use analog emulation in their application. The maximizer, stereo widener, and compressor alone are worth the price of admission with this tool.

Ozone has to be the sexiest-looking plug-in around, worthy of a Hollywood appearance. Sonic-Timeworks Compressor is also fantastic, with a warm sound, soft or hard compression, and a great look and ease of use, too, as are the WAVES, Ultrafunk, and Cakewalk plug-ins.

Compression must be used sparingly at the mastering point; generally settings of less than 3:1 are used at the mastering stage, as audio should have been compressed in the mix stage if the mix process was done to standards. Compression is applied to smooth out dynamic range. If desired, a compressor can bring quiet passages up to a nominal level, while reducing loud passages to a manageable point. Compression is used to get maximum levels while maintaining control over distortion and output levels.

A compression tool can be used at this stage as well when only one or two frequencies are causing the audio to go beyond rational norms. A dynamics compressor, which is a compressor that works only on specific frequencies, is invaluable at this point. Troublesome frequencies can be specified, and the amount of compression of those specific frequencies can be controlled. This option helps smooth out sibilant or plosive sounds from a poor interview mic or helps take down the overdriving pulse of a train that might be in the background of a wide shot mic'd with a handheld or shotgun.

11.13 TC Works have great plug-ins, and they are quite reasonably priced. These tools will tremendously improve the quality of your audio whether for audio production or audio for video.

11.14 A dynamics compressor is excellent in the finishing stages to suppress irritating frequencies, particularly from background sounds interfering with primary dialog or primary audio information.

To tune a compressor, listen to the audio closely and notice the peaks and valleys in the spoken word or music. These can be watched at the same time as being listened to. Notice how the peaks seem to jump out and how the valleys need special attention to be heard.

The space between these peaks and valleys is dynamic range. Too much dynamic range creates fatigue on the ear and creates a sense of overdriven sound, even though the audio might be clean. It's a quick way to tire out viewers.

Using Equalizers

A touch of EQ may be added at the final stage as well to bring the overall product to a consistent EQ attitude. The addition of EQ at this last stage, however, should be very minimal and only used to balance out inconsistencies that might arise or to create a final personality in the mix. Most professionals, however, do not add a final EQ as the proper EQ will have been applied during the initial stages of mastering. Keep in mind, there have been two previous opportunities to add EQ to each event/track in the mixing and mastering processes, and it's usually a mistake to apply much EQ to a final master stage. Often, EQs are mistakenly used here to compensate for error in the initial master, mix, or recording stage. If EQ is used in the finishing/mastering stages for video, it should be sparing and applied as an overall mix setting.

Dithering Audio in Vegas

Dither is valuable when audio is going to be printed to a CD, and the original recording was at a sampling rate higher than 44.1 KHz or at a bit rate of other than 16 bit. Of course, this is valuable when working with audio for video as well, rather than simply truncating bits in the sample rate change. This process is not the same as resampling but is part of the resampling process. Sony has a dithering plug-in, and a demo of the iZotope Ozone plug-in is on the DVD in this book.

The dithering plug-in should be applied to the master bus in order to ensure that the last audio process is dither.

Sony's dithering plug-in is Type triangular and the noise shape high pass contour should be similar to the Ozone Type 2, simple shape. The Ozone Type 1 is rectangular; Type 2 is triangular. Triangular is recommended regardless of which dither you're using, and high-pass shaping is good in both plug-ins. For more advanced noise shaping, the Clear shape for acoustic stuff is highly recommended. It's not as aggressively shaped as the psychoacoustic shapes. The Clear shape sounds natural, but it still has less perceived noise than a simple high-pass shape.

Fade in/out will be the most noticeable applications of dithering. Highlight the last part of a fade, turn it up fairly loud, and compare right when the audio fades into the noise floor. With the in/out check boxes on plug-ins, it's pretty easy to A/B. No dither (just truncation) will make the end of the note fade sound like a buzz, harmonic distortion, or metallic. It will most likely have a zipper sound before it fades out completely. Add dither and get a smoother tail but more noise. Add dither and some noise shaping, such as the Sony or Ozone Type 2, Clear shape, and you'll get a smooth tail but less noise on the fade. (iZotope has excellent information on dithering on their website at www.izotope.com. There's also a dithering guide from iZotope on the DVD found in this book.)

Rendering Options in Vegas

Vegas is amazingly flexible when it comes to outputting video whether to tape, CD, DVD, the Internet, or a hard drive. AVIs, QuickTime, Windows-Media, REAL media, MPEG-1, MPEG-2, MPEG-4, and any other codec installed on the computer can be used for output. (See Chapter 10 for information on outputting streaming media files.)

Vegas has the option of either rendering an entire project or merely doing a print to tape. The difference is that with a print to tape, Vegas temp-renders sections of the project that require recompression. These sections are written as multiple AVI files. A full render writes an entirely new file as one long file. Either method works as well as the other, and the choices are up to the user's workflow and time constraints. A video that needs to be moved off the hard drive and back to tape quickly might be best handled as a print to tape. For final archiving or for multiple file-type outputs, a full render is recommended. If the same media will be output to Windows-Media, QuickTime, REAL, and DVD, all of these processes will go much faster if working from an AVI file, rather than from a project file.

Save the file before rendering, just as a precaution. Writing long video files is taxing on a hard drive and processor, and some older systems cannot handle multiple drives getting very hot and will shut down.

11.15 The Render As dialog box provides a choice for the destination of the rendered file. Notice the new Network Rendering option for Vegas 6.

Rendering to an AVI

Select FILE | RENDER AS to render to an AVI format file. In the Render As dialog box, click the Custom button.

In the Project tab of the Custom Template dialog, select Best. This option will slow down the rendering time slightly, yet ensures that the best rendering options will take place. Under the Video tab, the "Create an OpenDML compatible file" check box may be unchecked. Unchecking this option will prevent users from rendering a file larger than 2GB. You might need to uncheck this box to be compatible with some third-party applications. Leave this box checked if the file contains alpha channels that will need to be accessed later in another editing session.

For a standard AVI file to be printed to tape using the Vegas Capture tool, leave the settings under the Audio tab, including the codec and aspect settings, at their default positions for a successful print to tape. The video must be 720x 480 for an NTSC-DV print to tape and 720 x 576 for a PAL-DV print to tape, and audio must be 48 KHz/16 bit. Otherwise, the camera, converter, or whatever is being used to get the video to a DV tape will not be capable of accepting the media.

To print to tape without rendering the entire project, select TOOLS | PRINT VIDEO TO DV TAPE. This option opens a series of dialogs that mkesur te project is prepped correctly to print.

11.16 First dialog box in the print to tape process. Be sure you have the entire region selected if leaving the Render Loop Region box checked.

11.17 Second dialog box in the print to tape process. Here is where color bars and test tones are chosen.

Clicking Next in the first dialog leads to the second dialog. In the second dialog, test tones and color bars can be specified. Color bars are standard SMPTE color bars, and the test tone is a 1 KHz test tone, output at -20dB. Color bars can be substituted for any test pattern by using the choices in the menu in this second dialog. These bars and tones are necessary, even required by most replication houses and broadcast houses. If this is a print to tape for personal use or to a VHS tape deck, the tones/bars are not required.

Click Next in the second dialog; a third box is displayed. This box asks whether you want automatic control of a tape machine or manual control. Automatic control will start printing

The tones in previous versions of Vegas were at -12dB.

Vegas 6 has output tones in alignment with the new Advanced Television Standards Committee (ATSC) output standards (www.atsc.org). If any products are calibrated to the old output standard, recalibration will be necessary.

to tape after a series of prerenders are finished wherein all recompressed media on the timeline is written to a temp file. This option should be selected when long prerendering times are anticipated. This option is useful for the overnight renderer, or for those users who edit during the day or evening and then render and print to tape late at night while all the world is sleeping.

11.18 Vegas warns users if the render process appears to be a lengthy task.

Manual tape control is useful for DV decks that cannot be controlled by the computer or for printing to an analog tape deck, such as a VHS or Beta deck. Selecting the manual option still allows users to walk away from the computer during renders, as Vegas gives a countdown option to printing manually.

11.19 The rendering progress window indicates how long a render will take.

After this selection is made, click the Finish button. Vegas then does one of two things:

- Vegas will start to print to tape immediately if no prerenders are left to complete, or if there are very few prerenders, it will complete those and begin the printing or countdown process.

- Vegas will give a warning that more than 80 percent of the project must be rendered and will ask if you wish to proceed. In either event, instruct Vegas to complete the process.

Click OK from the warning, unless a standard render is determined to be more time-efficient.

After Vegas has completed the render process, if automatic control was selected in the Print to Tape dialogs, Vegas will start the DV machine automatically and print the project to tape with

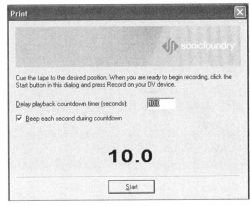

11.20 Vegas allows users to define the length of a countdown.

no further input/involvement from the user. In a situation in which manual control has been selected in the Print to Tape dialog, Vegas will prerender the recompressed sections and then wait for a click in a countdown box. Vegas will then count down from ten, providing a beep at each second, until it reaches three seconds. It will then start to print to tape. To effectively use this manual feature, allow Vegas to count down and, when the counter reaches three and no more beeps are heard, click Record on the tape machine. These steps usually provide enough leader time for various tape machines to get up to speed and begin the recording process.

Exporting Events to Third-party Applications

Sometimes it is necessary to export video events from Vegas to use in a third-party application, such as Adobe After Effects or Pinnacle Commotion. When exporting, files should be exported at the best possible resolution, and choices are therefore limited. If files are exported from Vegas using the standard NTSC-DV settings, most third-party applications can read the files, but until Sony opens their codec up to other applications to use, those third-party applications can't write back to the Sony codec. Using the Microsoft codec really isn't a solution either, as it limits quality output too much. Therefore, an uncompressed codec is the answer.

In the FILE | RENDER AS | CUSTOM dialog, an uncompressed setting can be chosen. Understand that using this output method will exponentially increase render times.

Be certain to uncheck the "Create an OpenDML compatible file" option. Most third-party applications cannot read these file types yet.

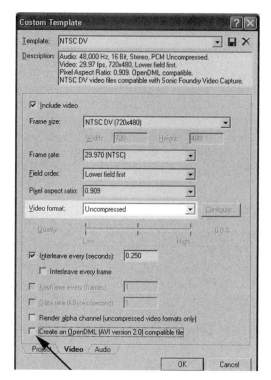

11.21 Select Uncompressed in the Video tab in the rendering options. This option also allows the uncompressed file to retain an alpha channel, should one exist or have been created in the editing process.

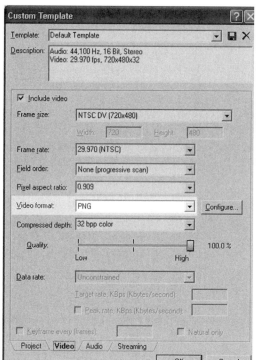

11.22 Rendering to a PNG/QuickTime format is a high-quality output method for exporting to a third-party application.

Another option is to use QuickTime for output, with its numerous options. A few users of Vegas have found great success using the PNG codec as an output option that both Vegas and most third-party applications can read. The PNG format is a lossless compression format that keeps file sizes more manageable and render times slightly faster than using a standard uncompressed output.

To render to the QuickTime format and its various codecs, select the part of the file or event that requires export. Select FILE | RENDER AS, choose QuickTime/.mov from the Save As menu. Click the Custom button. In the General tab, select Best. In the Video tab under the Video Format menu, select PNG. Adjust the quality slider to 100 percent.

Animators and rotoscope artists often require Targa files (TGA) for their editing applications. Render to QuickTime format, select the Video tab, and select FORMAT | TGA. Set the frame rate, pixel aspect, and frame size in their menus according to the requirements of the importing application.

If audio is part of the export and sync is important, move to the Audio tab and change the default output sample rate to 48 KHz/16 bit, rather than 44.1/16 that QuickTime asks for.

Files exported and imported in these formats will be clean and without quality loss. Using any codec or compressed format between applications runs a risk of loss of quality, so experiment with various outputs to discover what is best for each particular situation. Upsampling/downsampling is a foolish thing to do, as video always loses some information in the up/downsample. Some applications upsample imported DV as 4:2:2 or 4:4:4. Use caution and check files carefully for color accuracy when upsampling or downsampling between images.

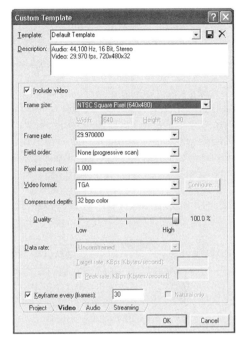

11.23 Render a Targa file by using the QuickTime option in the Render As dialog. The QuickTime authoring tools must be installed on the system to access this menu.

EDLs and Vegas

One of the perceived weak points in Vegas is the lack of OMF, AAF, and EDL support. Before saying anything else, I'll comment that Vegas is a finishing tool. It's designed to be used as a start-to-finish solution.

11.24 Select the MPEG format you wish to work with from the Save As Type drop-down menu.

That said, Vegas now provides scripting tools for CMX 3600-style EDL export that will support standard editing functions. Several steps must be taken to have accurate EDL value.

First, make sure your tapes are clearly and cleanly labeled, as the third-party application will likely require recapturing of the media on the tape. Most applications will not be able to read the timecode from Vidcap.

Second, edit the media as a cuts-only project. Most systems will not be able to read wipes and color correction. Set your project up as a drop-frame project rather than non-drop frame.

Third, use the Tools>Scripting>Export EDL feature. This will generate an EDL to be provided to whoever will be using the edits to finish their final project.

On the audio side, there are those times that something must be imported or exported from ProTools, AVID, SAW, SadIE, and other applications. Perhaps someone is sending you a file generated in another application and you want to use their EDL information in Vegas, or perhaps you prefer to work in Vegas but your coworker prefers another application. This used to be a problem. However, there is now a new product available from Cui-Bono Software that will convert most any format of EDL to another format of EDL. This company, based in Germany, has perceived the difficulties of all the various studio formats out there and has created a killer product that works for more than just Vegas users, since this is an industrywide issue.

EDL Convert Pro is a great application that no professional studio should be without. It's capable of dealing with fades, markers, and in and out points and is basically just a series of clicks. EDL Convert Pro will examine the project settings of the original EDL and set up the conversion based around those settings. You only need to alter these settings if you are taking the EDL to a project that has different settings, but in most instances, you'll use the default properties.

This tool will work in most any format you can imagine, converting Vegas files to or from Samplitude/Sequoia, Auditon/Cool Edit Pro, SAW, Wavelab, SADiE3 & 4, Sonic Studio, Discreet

11.25 This tool will allow you to convert most any audio EDL to a format that Vegas can read, or format that Vegas files can be read in.

edit, AES31, OpenTL, OMFI formats. If you are working with a SONAR user, you'll use the OMFI format to import and export for Vegas.

Check out the demo on the DVD in the back of this book or visit the Cui-Bono website: http://www.cuibono-soft.com/Products/products.html.

Outputting Other than AVI Files

Vegas has output capability for nearly every output format, including MPEG-1 and MPEG-2.

While Vegas does a reasonable job of outputting MPEG-1, the primary MPEG format output focus is on MPEG-2, which is used for DVD encoding and authoring. The primary benefit of an MPEG-1 file is that although it's an old codec and not of top quality, MPE-1 files do indeed play on just about any player in the world.

*Tip*_____

If working with DVD Architect to author DVDs, rendering to an MPEG file is not necessary at this time. DVD Architect works with multiple file formats, and users of Vegas+DVD might find it in their best workflow interest to work with AVI files or native file formats until the project is ready to burn. Vegas 4 provides a render template for DVD Architect in the render settings, while DVD Architect has similar encoding qualities to Vegas 6. See Chapter 10 for more information.

MPEG Rendering Improvements

Vegas 6 has an excellent MPEG rendering process that provides options for two-pass encoding, among other new features. Two-pass encoding allows the encoder to scan the media in the project, allocating bits for which sections need more attention in the encoding process as opposed to single-pass encoding, which merely encodes what is put into the encoder.

Two-pass encoding is much slower than single-pass encoding, but for high-motion or highcontrast video projects, it's well worth the end result.

To use the two-pass encoding process after you've edited your video, go to File>Render>MPEG2 and press the Custom button in the render dialog. Then select the Video tab.

In this dialog, you'll see several options. To access the two-pass encoding, you'll need to select the VBR (variable bit rate) radio button. Notice the check box for two-pass encoding. Check this box, and set the rest of the encoding parameters to desired settings.

In the two-pass encoding process, Vegas will first scan the project and write a log file containing information about what's in the project media, noting what's found in the project media. It then begins the scanning process again, encoding the media based on information contained in the log file. Static media, media that contains little movement, or little contrast will not substantially benefit from two-pass encoding. It's a good idea to render short sections of your project to see if there is a discernable difference between the two-pass or single-pass process of encoding. In most instances, there should not be a large difference from one to the other. If your project contains a lot of still images, remember to set the video rendering quality to Best. This will lengthen the render time, but will providea cleaner encode quality.

MPEG-2 file types are fairly ubiquitous, and it is the file format of choice for DVD. Vegas uses the MainConcept codec to encode files to the MPEG format, although the Sony version of the MainConcept codec should not be confused with other applications using this codec. Each group of software engineers from the various NLE manufacturers have written individual interfaces to the codec.

To render to MPEG codecs, select FILE | RENDER AS and choose MPEG-1 or 2 from the Save As Type drop-down menu. Selecting MPEG-1 renders an MPEG-1 format video that can be placed on a CD or on the web for download. Selecting the MPEG-2 option renders the MPEG-2 file for use on CD or for sending to a DVD authoring application. (When using Vegas with DVD Architect, files are not required to render to MPEG until DVD Architect prepares the media for the DVD burn.) Audio files in the MPEG-2 format are rendered to an MPEG-2 audio format.

MPEG files can be rendered as progressive scan or as interlaced files. MPEG files should be rendered to a progressive scan output for best appearance if the targeted display is a computer screen or progressive scan television. If the file will predominantly be played on television sets, leave the file interlaced. If the primary target is for computer viewing, set the file format as progressive scan. In the event that a progressive scan file is displayed on a television that does not have progressive scan settings, the television or output device will interlace the video. The settings for progressive scan/interlaced are found under the Custom button in the Render As dialog box.

The bit rate (encoding depth) can be selected in the Custom dialog as well. This option is found in the Video tab. Bit rate for standard DVDs should be 8 Mbps variable bit rate (VBR). Using VBR allows the encoder to determine the quality of frames based on motion in the various frames.

Some DVD authoring applications require separate video and audio streams. Vegas can output separate streams to meet these requirements. To output separate video/audio streams, select the FILE | RENDER AS | MPEG-2 | CUSTOM | SYSTEM

11.26 Bit rate can be selected in the CUSTOM | VIDEO tab.

11.28 Create separate audio/video streams for DVD authoring applications that require separate streams.

tab. Place a check mark in the "Save as separate elementary streams" box in this dialog. Vegas will create two separate files: one labeled m2v for the video stream and one labeled mpa for the audio stream. Import these two streams into the DVD authoring application.

Unless you are exceptionally well informed about MPEG encoding functions, you shouldn't change anything else in the MPEG output settings. For more MPEG setting information, see the Sony MPEG white paper on the DVD included with this book.

Outputting an AC-3 Format File

One of the features of Vegas is the ability to output AC-3 audio files. AC-3 is a compression scheme devised and overseen by Dolby Laboratories (www.dolby.com). AC-3 can be output in stereo or 5.1 channel formats. The primary benefit of AC-3 is that it allows for audio to be compressed, leaving more space for video on a DVD. AC-3 audio delivers high-quality audio in an encoded format that most consumer and computer DVD players can decode. This option gives viewers the best possible audio experience.

To output AC-3 files, select FILE | RENDER AS and select AC-3 from the menu. Vegas will ignore the video file and render the audio as a stereo or 5.1 audio file, depending on project settings. If the project is a stereo project, audio will be rendered as a stereo/two-channel AC-3 file. If the project is a 5.1 surround project, the AC-3 file will render as a 5.1 file.

For most purposes, the AC-3 presets in Vegas are designed to function as they are built. Experienced AC-3 encoders, however, might find some of the menu options quite valuable for creating a better listening experience. Changing AC-3 settings could possibly create an invalid render in the output file, so experiment on projects that are not time-critical.

11.28 Stereo or 5.1 surround, Vegas offers a number of choices for output formatting.

👍 *Tip*

Create a custom template for AC3 files by setting the Dialog Normalization to -31dB, and setting the Preprocessing Film setting to None. This will cause the AC3 file to more closely approximate the audio heard during the monitoring process.

Creating a VCD/SVCD

Burning a super video compact disc (SVCD) or video compact disc (VCD) is a one-step process in Vegas, with or without a rendered project. VCD is only capable of reading an MPEG-1 file. SVCD is capable of reading several file formats.

With a project on the timeline, rendered or not, select TOOLS | BURN CD | VIDEO CD. This selection will open a dialog that allows either a non-rendered project or a previously rendered project to be specified.

If the project has not been rendered to an MPEG-1 format file, Vegas will render to this format automatically when it is instructed to burn a VCD. The new file will need to be named, which will be the name/title that appears in the header file of the burned CD when it is complete. Vegas will indicate the required amount of disc space that the finished render will use. If the file size exceeds the amount of disc space, Vegas will indicate this before the burn.

The menu choices in the VCD dialog are few, as the VCD spec is very narrow. The only options are to burn an NTSC CD or a PAL CD.

Burning an SVCD is a much more open option. QuickTime, REAL, Windows-Media, AVI, MPEG-1, and MPEG-2 are all SVCD-capable formats. To burn the SVCD, the project does not need to be rendered separately from SVCD authoring. The file will require rendering in its final format; this can be done directly from the SVCD burn dialog. Select TOOLS | BURN CD | MULTIMEDIA CD.

In the dialog that opens, select the destination for the final render. Then select the file format to which the SVCD file will be rendered. Select a file template based on the file type chosen. NTSC and PAL variants are available for AVI and MPEG file formats.

As with all other render formats, a loop region can be defined as the only area to be rendered.

Defining a loop region allows you to select a smaller area of a larger file to be rendered without splitting, copying and pasting, or rendering new sections.

11.29 Select the "Use an existing file" check box and browse to locate and burn a previously rendered MPEG-1 file to create a VCD if the project is finished.

11.30 Menu options include playing video inside a web page and including a player/installer with the SVCD

11.31 The vieo can be played inside a company web page or inside any form of HTML document.

If including a player/installer on the disc to be distributed, be sure that the executable file (EXE) is the extension seen on the file. Players can be found at www.microsoft.com, www. quicktime.com, www.real.com, or at several third-party player sites. For any distribution other than personal/internal distribution, a license is required from the appropriate owner of the player software.

11.32 Viewers of the file who do not have an appropriate player will receive this message complete with links to download-able installers.

11.33 When the disc has been burned, a successful burn message is displayed.

Additional Rendering Options

Vegas has additional rendering options available, giving users a wide variety of choices. As an example, a loop region can be defined on the timeline by creating a selection and pressing Q, which will turn on the Looping tool. In the Render As dialog, rendering only a loop region is an option that is valuable when only selections need to be rendered out.

Another option is to stretch the video to fill the screen. This option prevents black bars from being added to the top, bottom, or sides of a video render that is of a different aspect ratio than the project. Check this box in the RenderAs options if you want to stretch to fill the aspect ratio.

11.34 Defining a loop region for rendering allows select sections to be rendered for output or export.

11.35 Pillar Boxed rendered for RGB output/Windows Media.

11.36   Stretched image, using the Stretch to Fill Screen option.

Network Rendering

A favorite, fantastic, and powerful feature in Vegas that everyone will be excited about is network rendering. Sometimes this is referred to as "render farming" because processors from multiple computers are used to render a project, or rather, pieces of the project are "farmed out" to other locations to "grow" the final project file.

If you're a typical computer geek, you likely have more than one machine and will have a network of some sort installed in your office or home. Vegas can now take advantage of all the processors on your network, saving hours of rendering time. This allows you to keep working on a project in Vegas while rendering is taking place in the background, over the network, with very little load on the host machine.

It's as though each computer on the system is taking part in the render and the host machine (where your editing version of Vegas is installed) assembles all the small rendered sections from the various computers into one finished file. The host machine decides which computers on the network receive which portions of a file for rendering. Vegas uses two different types of workload distribution for network rendering. The first is non-distributed network rendering, which behaves much like a single rendering machine. This format is best used for streaming or other encoded renders requiring multiple bitrates. Using this type of rendering distribution instructs one assigned computer to complete the entire rendering process on a file. In non-distributed rendering choices, multiple files may be queued up for rendering as single files on each machine. However, projects may not be broken down so that portions of a file are rendered on various machines.

Non-distributed renders are also best for audio-only projects, as Vegas renders video first in a rendering process.

> Vegas sets render tasks in either Distributed or Non-Distributed assignments. Use Distributed rendering for DV and uncompressed file types for fastest rendering results. Each machine on the network will render small portions of the timeline and the host machine assembles the small pieces into one finished file.
>
> Non-Distributed rendering is best for encoding to .mpg, multiple bitrate, or audio-only render tasks. This uses one machine per finished file, with no portions being rendered separately, and no portions being assembled or stitched together to form a complete file. (MPEG, AC3, and MP3 files cannot be rendered on a client-only license of Vegas.)

Distributed rendering causes Vegas to send out small packets or portions of a timeline to be rendered over various machines on the network. The host, or parent machine, then assembles all of the various rendered portions in to one large, finished file. This is best for .mpg or .avi file formats to be rendered quickly.

> If you intend on using this feature regularly, you should find it beneficial to set up a "File Server" on which all files for projects are stored. Not only will this allow for multiple users or machines to access the same files easily, it will also allow for a fast and simple set up for the Network Render feature.

Setting Up the Rendering Network (Render Farming)

The components of a render farm are critical to the system functioning correctly. Without all components set up, render farming will not work.

You need:

- A minimum of two computers, each with at least 256 MB of RAM. More RAM is advised. At least one machine must have a full version of Vegas 6 installed, and other machines must either have full versions or render-client-only versions of Vegas installed on them.

- A switched network. A wired hub will not work; go purchase a switch. They cost slightly more money, but they're necessary, as a switch will not determine workflow speed like a hub will.

- A wired 100Mbps network. Using a wireless network, sexy as they are, simply will not function for this. There is too much data that needs to pass through the network. If you have a gigabit network, it's all the better for rendering speed.

- Shared folders to hold the veg file, all media, and all assets to the project to be rendered over the network. All folders must have permissions set to read, write, delete, and create files on the network.

Rendering Clients

The machines used for rendering that are not the host machine, are known as clients. Each client machine must have either a full version of Vegas installed, or a render-client version of Vegas installed on it. Render-client licenses are available from Sony, the cost of which was not determined at the time of this writing. MPEG, AC3, and MP3 file formats cannot be rendered on render-client-only machines due to the way files are stitched together, so if you plan on rendering a number of these licensed file formats, you'll do best to purchase full versions of Vegas for each client machine. (Just prior to printing of this book, Sony announced that rendering these file types over a network, see Sony's website for more information.

Install the software on the client machines.

On the rendering-client machines, start the rendering service. It may take a moment to load, as the application is going to search for any machines connected to the network prior to displaying the user interface. This application will determine how the network renders your project files. You'll need to be logged into each machine to be used on the network prior to rendering. Start the VegSrv50.exe application. You can create an icon on the desktop for this. Simply browse from the Desktop shortcuts menu to the C:\Program Files\Sony\Vegas 6 folder and locate this file, and an icon will be created on the desktop. When you run the application, an icon will appear in the system tray. This may also be used to determine how a network render will function.

You do not need to start the rendering service for each rendering job, but as mentioned previously, you'll need to be logged on to each client prior to rendering. Once logged on, if the client or host machine sees a project, it will automatically be ready to start working for you.

In the Rendering Services application, you should see each machine logged onto the network that is able to be used as a client machine. Click the Renderers tab to select which machines will be used to render the project.

Depending on your network configuration, you may need to modify TCP settings on the host machine. This is rarely necessary, however, some systems may require it. If you are unsure of what to do, consult an IT person in your company, or call an IT specialist to help you set up the rendering network.

The following steps may be necessary for some systems:

1. Exit the Vegas Network Render Service application if it is running.

2. Open the NetRenderService.config file in a text editor such as Notepad. This file is located at C:\Program Files\Sony\Vegas 6.

3. Edit the <channel ref="tcp" port="53704" /> tag in the file to reflect the port you want to use.

4. Save the modified file information.

5. Relaunch the Vegas Network Render Service.

You'll need to know the name of each computer on the network in order to assign and access it from within the Vegas Network Render Service. To locate the name of each computer on the network, right click the My Computer icon on the desktop or in the application menu and choose

Properties. Choose the Computer Name tab, and the computer's full name will be displayed. You can copy and paste this name into the Renderers tab of the Network Render Service dialog to connect the client machine to the host machine.

To connect the client machines to the host machine, select the Renderers tab. In the Host dialog box, input either the IP address or computer name you wish to add to the render service. Press Enter and the Render Service application will then communicate with the client machine. If the machines communicate successfully, the Render Services application will show "ready" in the Status box. If the two machines fail to communicate, a "Failed to add" dialog will open up. If this error occurs, double-check the IP address or name of the client machine you are attempting to connect to, and try again. Be sure you are logged on to the client machine. If the client machine is in a room far from your host machine, log on to the client machine and use Ctrl+Alt+Delete to lock the machine while communicating with the client machine via the host machine.

To set up a distributed network render:

1. Save the project.

2. From the File menu, select Render As.

3. Use the Render As dialog to determine the file type and location where you want to save your finished project file. The location of the finished file must be in a shared folder.

4. Select the Render using networked computers check box in the Render As dialog, and click the Save button. The Network Render dialog will be displayed.

5. Select the Distribute Rendering Among Peers check box in the Network Render dialog.

6. From the Stitch Host dropdown list, choose the computer you want to use to assemble the rendered segments. If you are planning to be working on the host machine during network rendering, it's advisable to select another machine as the Stitch Host for best results during the editing-while-rendering process.

7. Choose a file format for your rendered segments.

8. Select the Use Final Render Template check box if you want to render segments using the format you chose for your final output in the Render As dialog.

9. Use this option when you're working with DV or uncompressed files. In this case, using the rendering template for rendered segments makes the final stitching process fast because the segments are copied and assembled without being re-encoded.

11. Clear the Use Final Render Template check box and choose settings from the "Save as Type" and Template dropdown lists if you want to render segments using a format other than your final output format. You can create your own templates for final output, and these custom templates often come in handy.

Use this option when you're rendering to a format that uses temporal compression, such as MPEG, QuickTime, RealMedia, or Windows Media. Rendering segments as uncompressed or DV AVI files allows transitions and composited tracks to be rendered in a high-quality format. When the segments are stitched, the project is re-encoded using the format you chose for your final output in the Render As dialog.

At the time of this writing, AC3, MPEG 2, and MP3 rendering were not supported over the network because of recompression issues. Due to the method in which these file types are created, segments may not be stitched together without recompressing the file, causing a loss in quality.

11. Click OK to start rendering. The segments of the project will begin rendering on the various machines as instructed in the Network Rendering Services application dialog.

For non-distributed network rendering:

1. Save the project.

2. If you want to render only a portion of the project, create a time selection that includes the segment to be rendered.

3. From the File menu, choose Render As.

4. Use the Render As dialog to choose the file type and output location where you want to save the finished file. The location of the output file must be in a shared folder.

5. Select the "Render loop region" only check box in the Render As dialog if you want to render the selected portion of your project.

6. Select the "Render using Networked Computers" check box in the Render As dialog, and then click Save. The Network Render dialog wil be displayed.

7. From the Render Host drop-down list, choose URL or location of the renderer you want to use to render your project.

8. Click OK to start rendering.

9. To add a project to the queue, open the project and repeat above instructions.

You can select a different render client for each project or time selection if you want to render the files at the same time on separate machines. If you choose the same client, the rendering jobs will be queued to run sequentially on that machine.

Monitoring Rendering Progress

You can monitor the progress of a project render by right-clicking the Network Services icon found in the system tray and choosing Show from the submenu. The Rendering Services dialog will open and show rendering progress on the system. Details or a summary may be viewed by selecting Detail or Summary from the Progress dropdown menu.

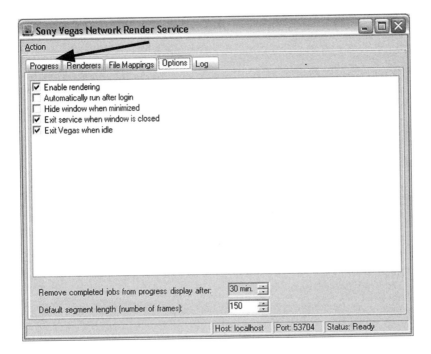

11.37   Monitor Network renders from the Render Services application.

File Mapping

File mapping tells render clients where to locate media assets used in a project. When you import media assets from a local disk, the file paths saved in your project are usually valid only on the local machine. This can be the case even if the media resides in a shared folder. Generated media needs and contains no such location information.

Use the File Mappings tab to map local folders to universal paths.

1.   Right-click the icon in your system tray and choose Show from the menu to display the Sony Vegas Network Render Service window.

2.   Select the File Mappings tab. The tab displays a list of local folders and their universal paths.

3.   Click on a blank row in the table.

4.   In the Local box, type the path to the local folder (c:\media, for example).

5.   In the Universal box, type the UNC path or mapped drive letter to the folder. An example might read similar to (\\project file \media\ in the Universal box.

Do not place media in a root directory. Network rendering will not be able to locate it and the render will not complete.

If you get a Failed To Initialize Network error:

1. Open a DOS window.

2. From the Start menu, choose Run to display the Run dialog.

3. In the Open box, type CMD.

4. Click OK. A DOS window will be displayed.

5. Type ipconfig at the command prompt.

6. Your Windows IP Configuration information is displayed. Note the Connection-specific DNS suffix setting in the display.

7. Update your machine's DNS suffix:

6. Right-click My Computer on your desktop and choose Properties from the shortcut menu (or press the Windows key + Pause) to open the System Properties dialog.

7. Select the Computer Name tab.

8. Click the Change button to display the Computer Name Changes dialog.

9. Click the More button to display the DNS Suffix and NetBIOS Computer Name dialog.

11. In the Primary DNS suffix of this computer box, type the DNS suffix you recorded in step 2.

11. Click OK to close all dialogs and restart your system.

Keep in mind that your End User License Agreement does not permit running Vegas on more than one machine at a time, so you'll need to choose a machine on the network that will be used for network rendering, that you won't be editing with. One system needs to be loaded with the client-only version of Vegas. Additional licenses may be purchased from Sony on its website.

Additional Functions of the Network Rendering Application

The Network Rendering application has several options that you can specify to make the rendering process as efficient as you'd like it to be. For example, the local host may be used as a rendering machine or not. You make that choice.

To access these choices, right click the Network Rendering icon in the system tray and choose Show from the submenu that is displayed. This will open the dialog.

At the time of this writing, the Network Rendering feature is still undergoing testing and writing. Please check the Sony Media Software website for updated information.

Network Rendering Options:

Enable Rendering	Select this check box if you want the computer you are working with (local) to be available as a rendering machine.
Automatically run after login	Enable this feature if you want to start the service automatically after logging in to Windows.
Exit Service when window cleared,	Select this check box if you want to keep the service running after closing the window. If the check box is is closed cleared the service is minimized and found in the the system tray when you exit. Leave this checked in most instances.
Exit Vegas When Idle	Select this check box if you want to close the instance of Vegas software that is launched by the network render service when no jobs are set up to be rendered. If the check box is cleared, the application continues running until you close it or exit the service.
Remove Completed Jobs from Display After:	Choose a setting to indicate how long jobs should be maintained on the Progress tab of the Sony Vegas Network Render Service window. The default is one hour, lengths as short as 5 minutes may be specified.
Default Segment lengths	Choose a setting to indicate the number of frames per segment when using distributed rendering. Adjusting this value can increase performance slightly depending on the complexity of the project and the speed of the rendering clients. If the setting yields more than 90 segments for a rendering job, the segment length for that job is automatically increased to limit the number of segments.

High-Definition Video

Vegas also brings the ability to edit and output high-definition media in 720p, 1080i, and 1080p formats. Currently, Vegas does not have the ability to capture high-definition media, so any hardware card used for the capture of high definition will require the use of any capture utility associated with the hardware card. At the time of this writing, Black Magic Design was nearly ready to release a 10-bit high-definition video card that is compatible with Vegas. Black Magic also has announced an SD (Standard Definition) video card to support Vegas. These cards were no available at the time of this writing. Visit www.decklink.com for more information.

11.38 Project Properties in Vegas include high definition settings.

24p has some very significant benefits and support in Vegas. Transitions, titles, and filters are optimized in Vegas for 24p. Vegas also has specific support for the new Panasonic DVX100 camera and cameras with similar features. Vegas auto-detects 2-3 and 2-3-3-2 pulldown at capture and previews and prints to tape in the 24p format when using the Panasonic DVX100 camera. The 2-3 and 2-3-3-2 pulldowns are performed on the fly in Vegas with no additional hardware required. Vegas also allows for preview on external monitors at 24p.

On the output side, Vegas can output a still image sequence up to 2048 ¥ 2048, is capable of outputting 1080i or 720p at the 24p frame rate, and can print to tape at 24p as well. Windows-Media 9 has support for 24p/HD, and streaming file sizes are smaller at 24p than at 29.97. 24p also offers up to 25 percent additional disk-space savings on a DVD.

Given that 24p renders twice as fast as 60i (standard NTSC frame rate) and that 24p offers a look closer to film, this format will continue to grow.

Vegas edits and prints media at 720p with frame rates of up to 60 fps, at resolutions of 1080p with frame rates of 24 fps and 29.97 fps, and at 1080i with frame rates of 60 fps (29.97 interlaced). With the output capability of 24 fps/progressive scan, video shot with the newer 24p will stay in their native format with no pulldown.

When working with high-definition media, full frame rate playback is very difficult to achieve because of the load on the processor. Be aware that playback at full frame rate is unlikely on all but the fastest systems. On a Pentium 3 with 1.8 GHz processor with 1GB of RAM, the best playback achieved was less than 15 fps. Rendering to RAM allows for full motion playback; however, for most circumstances, a different workflow may appeal to most users.

With Vegas' ability to recapture media via the Project Media or to work with originally captured media, try to capture using a dual-stream card where possible, so that a low-resolution/com-

When working with high-definition media, current IDE drive speeds will prove to be unsatisfactory for most users. SCSI drives/RAIDS with a 320-controlle crd are considered good starting points for most high-definition editing practices.

11.39 Rendering/output settings include high-definition capability in Vegas.

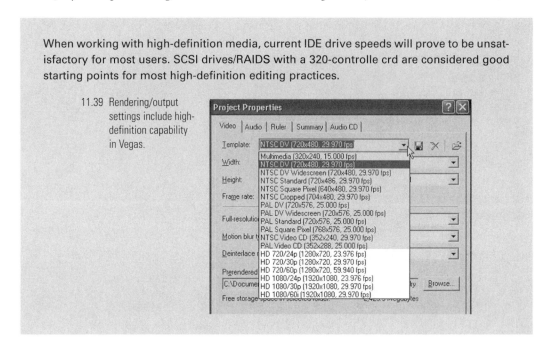

pressed capture takes place at the same time as the high-definition media is being captured. Most high-definition cards allow for this to take place. Edit on the timeline using the lower-resolution media and replace media with the high-definition video in the Project Media when you finish editing. This process will allow editing to take place with full motion and full resolution without taxing the processor as heavily as native high-definition media. Rendering to a RAID, the media can then either be printed to tape using a high-definition card, capture tool, and high-definition tape machine, or using the RAID delivered to a service bureau for final print and replication for distribution. This is a form of offline/online editing but can be done natively with Vegas as both a rough cutting and finishing tool. By using the Super Sampling Envelope tool, even DV can be effectively upsampled to HD output. Bear in mind that render times will be fairly slow on longer projects. Up-sampling from resolutions of 720 x 480 to 1920 x 1080 will more than double the resolution of DV.

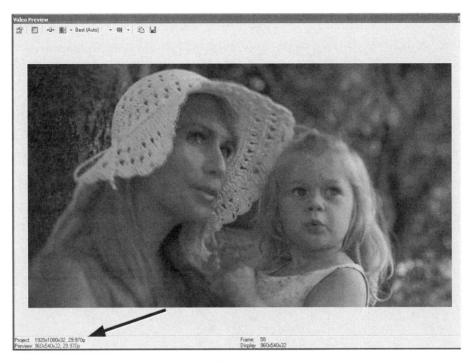

11.40 This high-definition footage from Artbeats fills most of a standard monitor even at three-quarter size (Artbeats Family Lifestyles HD library).

4:2:2 MPEG Capability:

Vegas is also capable of rendering broadcast streams for delivery to a media server in a broadcast facility such as a Telestream or Matrox videoserver. This functionality is not for the typical Vegas user but designed exclusively for professional broadcast delivery formats. 4:2:2 broadcast streams have a delivery data rate of up to 80Mbs, compared to a DVD delivery data rate of up to 15Mbps. Most DVDs are at a substantially lower bitrate, but the spec allows for a higher than the currently used delivery bitrate .

The 4:2:2 format provides for greater luma and chroma information in the stream, allowing for higher quality video broadcast display instead of the standard 4:2:0 delivery of consumer-oriented DVD MPEG delivery.

While it might be tempting to render to this format, there is nothing to be gained by the end user, unless it's as an archival format. No set-top player can play back files at this datarate. If you intend to deliver an MPEG-encoded project for broadcast, check with the broadcast house in advance to learn what datarate they'd like to see the project come in at.

New Codecs

In Vegas, there is a new 4:2:2 YUV codec. This is of great benefit to those rendering files to archive or for multi delivery. Faster than rendering uncompressed, and enabling better image quality than 4:2:2 media, this is great for those doing SD-based (Standard Definition) projects as well.

11.41 Sony has created a 4:2:2 YTUV codec, found in Vegas 6.

Where this is of value to DV editors is when a project needs to be archived or delivered in multiple formats. Render the project to the 4:2:2 YUV codec, and then use the new .avi file to render MPEG, streaming media, and any other secondary format. Using this as an intermediary codec serves no value if delivering to a final MPEG format, for instance. Encoding MPEG from the timeline is always a best proposition if MPEG is the only delivery format.

When DV is dropped on the Vegas timeline, the video is already compressed at 4:1:1. When color correction, transitions, and other changes to the media are applied, Vegas upsamples those changes to 4:4:4, or uncompressed media in these processes. The uncompressed sections then become compressed when the final file is rendered. Rendering to 4:2:2 keeps the new media at a higher quality than the 4:1:1 render. However, when media is rendered from the timeline to MPEG, it's rendered at 4:2:0, creating yet a third transcode in the process of rendering. Therefore, if you are rendering any sort of project to a single delivery format, it's always best to render to that format directly from the timeline, saving transcodes and time. However, if there are multiple delivery formats required, it's a good idea to render to either uncompressed or to the higher quality 4:2:2 format to input to a batch encoder, assuring that the original source file is of the highest quality available depending on allotment of time in the final rendering process.

There is no benefit of rendering 4:1:1 DV project files to 4:2:2, and then rendering the 4:2:2 to MPEG, unless again, the final source files will be delivered in some format other than DV, and in one or more other delivery formats. If you were to render to 4:2:2, then convert that to 4:1:1 again for print to DV tape, information is actually lost in the process due to transcoding.

Rendering to the 4:2:2 YUV codec is slower than rendering to the 4:1:1 Sony codec, as one might expect.

Scripting

Vegas has a feature that is terrific for users needing customized output and processing options. This feature uses JavaScript to define these behaviors. Vegas can literally be instructed to render several file types, to batch process, to match aspect ratios, even to build a video at random with random transitions from media in the Project Media! Scripts basically provide an open-ended function for Vegas users to implement code in order to instruct Vegas to provide unique behaviors.

To use scripting, you'll need to have the Microsoft .NET framework installed. The .NET framework can be downloaded at no cost from Microsoft. Visit `http://www.microsoft.com/net/` to order a CD or download the framework.

Many scripts are available on the Sony website, as well as on the VASST website `http://www.vasst.com`. Writing scripts is a challenge for those not familiar with Visual Basic or JavaScript authoring. You can write scripts with any plain text editor, even Notepad. The Microsoft developer's website (msdn.microsoft.com) probably has the most authoritative reference for the .NET scripting languages, but other tutorials are available on the web. In addition, several bok on JScript .NET and Visual Basic .NET are available from Amazon.com and other bookstores.

11.42 Access the scripts by seleccting TOOLS | SCRIPTING | RUN SCRIPT.

Here is a sample .js script that opens ten tracks with blank events on them:

```
* Sample script that script creates 10 tracks each containing 10
 * events. No media is assigned to the events.
 *
 * Revision Date: Feb. 04, 2004.
 **/

import Sony.Vegas;
import System.Windows.Forms;

var trackCount = 10;
var eventCount = 10;
var eventLength = new Timecode(10000); // 10 seconds

var mediaType = MediaType.Audio;

var track, trackEvent;
var i, j;
var startTime;

for (i = 0; i < trackCount; i++) {

    // create a track
    if (mediaType == MediaType.Audio)
        track = new AudioTrack(i, "Audio " + (i+1));
    else
        track = new VideoTrack(i, "Video " + (i+1));

    // add the track
    Vegas.Project.Tracks.Add(track);

    startTime = new Timecode();
    for (j = 0; j < eventCount; j++) {

        // create an event
        if (mediaType == MediaType.Audio)
            trackEvent = new AudioEvent(startTime, eventLength, "Audio Event "
+ (j+1));
        else
            trackEvent = new VideoEvent(startTime, eventLength, "Video Event "
+ (j+1));

        // add the event to the track
        track.Events.Add(trackEvent);

        // increment the start time
        startTime += eventLength;
    }

    // toggle the media type
    if (mediaType == MediaType.Audio)
        mediaType = MediaType.Video;
    else
        mediaType = MediaType.Audio;
```

Running scripts can also appear to be intimidating, when in truth, running scripts is quite straightforward. After locating/downloading scripts, place them in a directory. The default location for scripts in Vegas 6 is C:\Program Files\Sony\Vegas 6.0\Script Menu. To run a script, select TOOLS | SCRIPTING | RUN SCRIPT, which will open a browse dialog box. Browse to where the .vb or .js scripts are stored. After adding scripts to the folder, go to Tools|Scripting|Rescan Script Menu Folder. This will place scripts in the Tools|Scripting dropdown menu. This will save time in not needing to search out scripts in other folders.

Select the script you wish to run, which will start the script. Scripts are like trading cards that are available from many Vegas users, and a small cottage industry has sprung from this concept of having an open engine. Batch Render Pro, Neon, Tsunami, and Excalibur are all for-purchase tools that take advantage of scripting operations, potentially saving users inestimable time, depending on the sort of workflow used. It's easy to become dependent on scripts, as they can perform many mundane tasks with one button. And with keymapping, you can map scripts to any button you'd like, making Vegas a totally personal system. At the time of this writing, over 100 scripts were available, and can be found at www.vasst.com/login.htm site.

Scripts will continue to add to the power of Vegas and offer users a tremendous number of options.

One aspect of scripting that creates exceptional ease of use is to create a button on the toolbar for the script. This option allows rapid access to commonly run scripts. Up to ten scripts may be

If you have Vegas 4 and want to import scripts from Vegas 4 into Vegas 6, you'll need to edit the line in the script text that calls for SonicFoundry.Vegas to Sony.Vegas. Otherwise the scripts will not function correctly.

associated with ten buttons on the toolbar.

To place a button/script on the toolbar, double-click the toolbar, which will open the Customize Toolbar dialog. Select a script button to add to the toolbar. In Figure 11.46, Script 3 is selected to be placed in the toolbar. This step places a button on the toolbar that can be associated with a script by pressing Ctrl+Shift+3 or by clicking the Script button. Vegas will open a browser window that allows you to select a specific script to be assigned to that button.

Another method of assigning a script to a toolbar button is to select TOOLS | SCRIPTING | SET SCRIPT and choose the script number to which you wish to assign a script. This action will open

11.43 The script used in this instance locates in and out timecodes for all files on the timeline, lists their running time/length, and saves them as an HTML file.

11.44 The Batching script renders multiple forms of Windows-media from one timeline and one action.

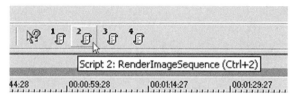

11.45 Assign a script to a button on the toolbare in Customize Toolbars.

the Browse Scripts window as well, from which a script can be assigned to a script number. This same script number can be associated with a button by following the steps outlined earlier.

11.46 Select scripts for use in the Script browser.

11.47 Buttons can be created on the toolbar for scripts.

Using Vegas with DVD-Architect

To use Vegas with DVD Architect, render the project as either an MPEG-2 or as an AVI file. If the project is to be 5.1 at final output, render the file as an MPEG-2 file. Insert markers in the file for chapter points if desired. DVDA will recognize these markers as chapter points and will insert them as such if instructed to do so in DVDA.

Audio that is to be associated with the MPEG file, regardless of whether it is stereo or mono, should be rendered as an AC-3 file. DVDA will automatically convert stereo audio to an AC-3 file during the DVDA render/burn process. (See Chapter 10 for more information.) Audio in a 5.1 channel project file will not be embedded in the MPEG file in any form. (See the previous sections in this chapter on creating AC-3 audio for DVD Architect.)

Files that are rendered as 24p files will not be transcoded/recompressed in DVDA; they will stay in their native format. This feature allows 20 percent more video media to be placed on the DVD, which can be monitored/previewed in DVDA as well. Export of 24p NTSC MPEG-2 for DVD Architect is also supported as an output format in Vegas. Bear in mind that to view 24P media on an external monitor, the frames will have to have pulldown added, creating a 60i or 50i video stream that the external monitor can comprehend.

The best workflow I've found for rendering files for MPEG 2 and AC3 files while leaving the system unattended is to use the Batch Render script found in Vegas 6. Go to Tools>Scripting>Batch Render and run the script. An interface will open, looking like the one you see here.

In this interface, expand the MainConcept MPEG option. In this subset, select the format of MPEG you wish to use. Do not simply check the MPEG tick box without expanding. During beta testing, I did this for a project containing 11 regions as I hadn't expanded the subset.

It rendered all night, and the next morning, I had 209 files! Nineteen templates rendered for all 11 regions, and it created a mess. I've accidentally done this for AC3 as well. If you check only the file format, Vegas will render a version of the file for each template setup in your preferences. Expanding the subsets allows you to select the specific format you'd like files rendered to.

For standard export to DVD Architect, choose the DVD Architect NTSC or PAL video stream and tick the box next to that subset option. Contract the MPEG set, and choose the AC3 subset. Select either the Stereo DVD or 5.1 Surround DVD check box, depending on the project type. Let the project render, and when it's finished, you'll have both file types of the same name, stored in the same folder. DVD Architect 2 will locate the audio with the video, and you'll be set. This batch script is great for rendering to .avi, .mpg, and streaming media while you're gone for the night or out to lunch. Long projects don't need as much babysitting.

24p HDCAM/DVCA Workflow for the Independent Filmmaker

by Dave Hill, Sony Pictures Digital

Overview

With the rapid and continued adoption of Sony HDCAM as the acquisition format of choice for the independent filmmaker, many people have asked how they could use Sony Vegas software as an editing tool for 24p HDCAM production.

Sony Vegas 6 delivers many exciting new features, including cost-effective tools for 24p HDCAM editing using DVCAM proxies.

12.1   The 24p/XPRI workflow.

With Vegas 6 you can:

1.   Connect Vegas 6 to a Sony JH-3 HDCAM deck and capture frame-accurate DVCAM downconverts over i-link. You can also make DV/DVCAM dubs from your HDCAM masters and capture using your DV deck or camcorder.

463

2. Remove 2–3 pulldown from the downconverted 60i DV clips.

3. Retain original 24p HDCAM timecode in the DVCAM downconverted video files.

4. Cut your project in a 24p Vegas timeline with perfect frame accuracy.

5. Create finished audio tracks in a 24p Vegas timeline.

6. Create finished HD composites and video fx, and export as 24p uncompressed .avi.

7. Export a frame-accurate 24p EDL for final finishing in Sony XPRI or other 24p HD editing systems. Finished audio and HD composites can be used natively in the finishing system, and HDCAM source clips will be recaptured as needed by the finishing system.

8. Even if you are not immediately delivering a 24p HDCAM master or doing a film-out, you can use this process to create extremely high-quality 24p DVDs, DVCAM or other SD masters, as well as 24fps web video.

24p HDCAM Acquisition

Sony offers an extensive line of HDCAM cameras and decks, many of which are also available for rental.

HDCAM information can be found at http://bssc.sel.sony.com/Professional/webapp/SubCateg ory?m=0&p=2&sp=19&sm=0&s=&cpos

Setting Up a 24p Vegas Project

In order to ensure frame-accurate edits as well as a time-accurate soundtrack, you need to set up your Vegas project correctly before editing.

Set the trimmer time format to "SMPTE Film Sync IVTC (23.976 fps, video)." This allows you to set in/out marks in the trimmer using the original 24p source timecode. Timecode will still be properly tracked even if you do not set the trimmer time format to "SMPTE Film Sync IVTC (23.976 fps, video)."

Confirm that "Quantize to frames" is on. Keep this on for all video editing. You can turn this off for fine-tuning the audio but

12.2   Set the project to NTSC DV 24p (or NTSC DV 24p Widescreen if the project is 16:9)

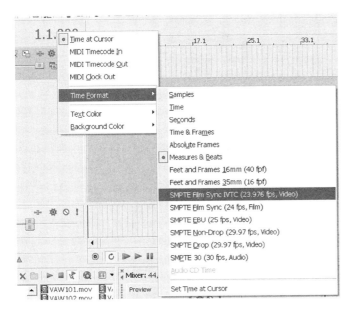

12.3 Set the project time format to "SMPTE Film Sync IVTC (23.976 fps, video)"

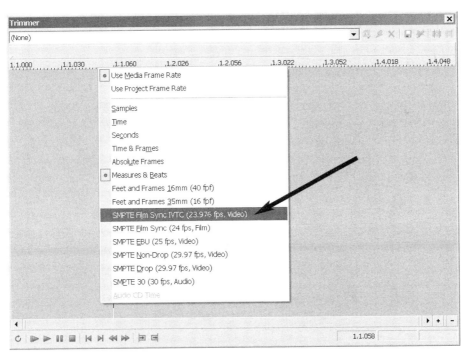

12.4 Set the Trimmer window to 23.976 so that you are trimming at the project and media frame rates.

remember to turn it back on when editing video.

Additional Capture Notes

You are now ready to capture your downconverted footage. It is recommended that you use the Sony Vegas capture tool for capturing your downconverted DV footage directly from the JH-3 deck or from DV/DVCAM dubs. Other capture tools may or may not work correctly and have not been tested.

As always, proper tape naming and clip naming is essential during the logging/capturing stage. You will need a reference back to the original master tapes, and failure to name the tape correctly at capture time can result in time-consuming and expensive searching at the online facility.

It is not recommended that you capture across scene breaks in the the original HDCAM tape. This may result in improper timecode or pulldown removal inside Vegas. For best results, log each scene in the Vegas capture tool, then batch capture.

12.5   Enable "Quantize to Frames" from the Options menu.

12.6

Remove 2-3 Pulldown from the Downconverted 60i DV Clips

Once you have captured your downconverted DV clips in Vegas, you will need to remove the pulldown that is inserted by the HDCAM deck when creating 60i (29.97 interlaced) DV from 24p HDCAM original footage.

Load the captured clips into the Vegas Project Media (this happens automatically when you launch the capture application from within Vegas). In the Vegas Project Media, select all of the downconverted clips, then right-click and choose "File format properties." The dialog box below will appear. Check the "Enable 2-3 pull-down" option, then choose OK.

If the JH-3 downconvert options were set properly (see section "Capturing 24p HDCAM footage as 24p DV using the Sony JH-3 deck") the starting frame offset for all clips will be zero, pulldown will correctly removed, and timecode will be tracked correctly.

The pulldown flag will be stamped into the DV file, so you can open these files in any Vegas 6 or later project and it will be interpreted as a 24p DV clip. There is no need to close and reopen Vegas after setting the pulldown flag (above).

You can confirm that the footage has been flagged as 24p by checking the media properties for the DV clip. Format should be "DV (removing 2-3 pulldown)" as below:

If you are working from a film transfer or multi-generation dub, you can still convert the DV clip to 24p DV, but you may have to manually set the starting frame value (starting frame offset value, 0-4). This may require some trial and error to find the correct starting frame.

12.7 Enable 2-3 pulldown in the Project Media.

12.8 Verify that pulldown is being removed.

Editing with 24p DV Video Files

Vegas 4 shipped with many 24p DV editing features, and they are described at http://mediasoftware.sonypictures.com/support/productinfo/24p.pdf. If you followed all the steps above and are not planning on an HDCAM online session, you can edit your project and make a great-looking 24p DVD, create SD masters or web video with no additional steps beyond the normal editing process.

24p Timecode

If you are planning on an HDCAM online session at some point (or need an EDL or XML project data export for any subsequent process), it is a good idea to confirm proper timecode handling before proceeding. The easiest way to this is to add the "Sony Timecode" filter to one or more of your 24p DV files.

In the Vegas 6 Project Media, select a 24p DV file, choose media FX, select "Sony timecode," and choose the "SMPTE Film IVTC (23.976 fps)" preset.

NOTE: This must be done at the media level, from the Project Media and nowhere else.

If you chose to burn in timecode during the downconvert process, your video will look like Figure 12.10.

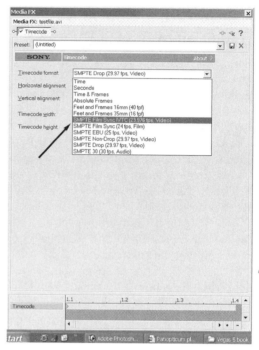

12.9   Insert the Sony Timecode filter to track time. Insert it in the Project Media to reflect the T/C from the media rather than the timeline.

12.10

After applying the "Sony timecode" filter with the "SMPTE Film IVTC (23.976 fps)" preset, your video should look like Figure 12.12. Importantly, note that the "ORG" timecode burned onto the frame matches the timecode displayed by the "Sony timecode" filter.

12.11

A script could be used to apply or remove this filter with the "SMPTE Film IVTC (23.976 fps)" preset to all items in the Project Media. Using Notepad, you can modify the scripts "Add Timecode To All Media.js" and "Remove Timecode To All Media.js." Scripts can be found in :\Program Files\Sony\Vegas 6.0\Script Menu. In either script, change:

```
var presetName = "SMPTE Drop (29.97 fps)";
to
var presetName = SMPTE Film IVTC (23.976 fps)";
Save the script with a new name containing the .js extension.
```

Create Finished Audio Tracks in a 24p Vegas Timeline

If you are creating finished audio tracks for use in your final HD online session, you are strongly encouraged to check with the post facility for exact format requirements. Most facilities can accept 16/48 PCM .wav files for use in HDCAM sessions, which can be rendered from Vegas 6 using following settings:

12.12   Set the project to NTSC DV 24p (or NTSC DV 24p Widescreen if the project is 16:9)

If you are cutting in a 24p Vegas timeline and doing a 24p HDCAM online, you will not need to worry about time-stretching your audio during the online session if your render out .wav files as above from a 24p Vegas timeline.

If you need to convert to Vegas 6 audio tracks to OMF, the following tool is recommended: http://www.cuibono-soft.com/Store/EDL_Convert_Pro_v3/edl_convert_pro_v3.html.

Create Finished Composites and Video fx, and Export as 24p HD Uncompressed .avi

If you are creating finished composites or graphics for use in your final HD online session, you are strongly encouraged to check with the post facility for exact format requirements. Most facilities can accept uncompressed 24p HD .avi files for use in HDCAM sessions, which can be rendered from Vegas 6 using following settings:

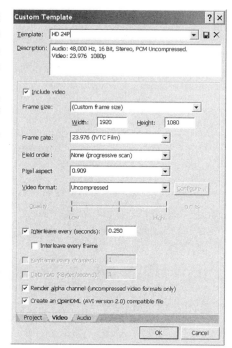

12.13   Use this render setting to output 24P HD avi files.

12.14 Use the EDL Export script to export a CMX 3600 list.

Exporting a 24p EDL

You have picture lock, the soundtrack is complete, and you are now ready to export your EDL. Choose Tools>Scripting>Export EDL, and save the file with the .edl extension.

You are strongly advised to send the EDL to your post house prior to arriving at the online session. They can verify the EDL, note any errors, and adjustments can be made prior to the actual online session.

24p EDLs created in Vegas 6 have been tested with Sony XPRI. Cuts and dissolves work correctly with one video track and two audio tracks in all tests. Speed changes, wipes, and other project data will not be exported with the EDL. Recommended practice for HDCAM online using Sony XPRI is:

Render mixed audio tracks from your Vegas project, for import into finishing system (Sony XPRI).

Render HD uncompressed graphics and video fx from your Vegas project, for import into finishing system (Sony XPRI).

Export 1 EDL per video track, for import into finishing system (Sony XPRI).

XML project interchange between Vegas 6 and Sony XPRI will be demonstrated at NAB 2004.

24p DVDs

You can make 24p DVDs from a 24p Vegas 6 timeline. See the Vegas 6 documentation for more information.

Exporting the Project to DV

You can render your 24p timeline as NTSC or PAL DV. See Chapter 8 for additional information.

Index

PRODUCING 24P VIDEO
JOHN SKIDGEL

Take an introductory "crash course" in 24p video production, ideal for students and filmmakers. Field techniques include real-world setups (close-up, medium shot, wide shot) presented as demonstrations or tutorials. Case studies present profiles of people producing 24p projects. The companion DVD includes tutorial projects plus templates and checklists for production planning.

$54.95, full-color softcover with DVD, 256 pages, ISBN 1-57820-263-9

VIDEO SHOOTER
STORYTELLING WITH DV, HD AND HDV CAMERAS
BARRY BRAVERMAN

Create a compelling visual story for any project with this engaging guide. Industry veteran Barry Braverman draws on over 20 years of experience, including work on *National Geographic* specials, to illustrate the complete range of skills required to capture great images. Key topics include equipment selection, set-up, camera operation, shooting techniques, lighting, and audio.

$44.95, full-color softcover with DVD, 240 pages, ISBN 1-57820-289-2

THE WEDDING VIDEO HANDBOOK
HOW TO SUCCEED IN THE WEDDING VIDEO BUSINESS
KIRK BARBER

Thrive in the wedding video industry with this savvy guide. *The Wedding Video Handbook* explains everything a wedding videographer needs to know—from business to production. Topics include secrets for getting clients, selecting the proper equipment, and tips on capturing special wedding moments despite difficult filming conditions.

$34.95, softcover with DVD, 280 pages, ISBN 1-57820-281-7

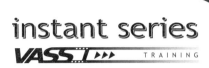

instant series

Visual, step-by-step instruction for getting up to speed. The Instant series is designed to efficiently deliver the essential skills readers need to get the job done. All of the books feature detailed screen shots and step-by-step directions that present the complete range of pertinent functions as well as professional techniques for polish and efficient workflow. Launched in 1997, VASST (www.vasst.com) is the training arm of the Sundance Media Group offering Video, Audio, Surround, and Streaming Training.

Audience Level: Novice to Intermediate

INSTANT DIGITAL AUDIO
DOUGLAS SPOTTED EAGLE

Quickly master digital audio principles and techniques, from recording and production to postproduction, with this guide for the non-audio specialist. The author walks you through selecting the right hardware and software, and shows you how to use it with straightforward explanations and screenshots.

Available December 2005

$24.95, softcover, 224 pages, ISBN 1-57820-276-0

INSTANT SURROUND SOUND
JEFFERY P. FISHER

Unravel the mysteries of multi-channel audio processing for musical and visual environments. This comprehensive resource teaches techniques for mixing, and encoding for surround sound. It is packed with tips and tricks that help the reader to avoid the most common (and uncommon) pitfalls.

$24.95, softcover, 191 pages, ISBN 1-57820-246-9

INSTANT ACID
JOHN ROFRANO & IACOBUS

Learn everything you need to know about Sony ACID software in an instant. This complete guide, designed as both a tutorial and quick reference, covers recording, adding effects, mixing, and burning the final project, as well as interfacing with nonlinear video editing systems. The authors include personal tips and workflow habits to help you become productive quickly.

$24.95, softcover with DVD, 256 pages, ISBN 1-57820-266-3

CMP*Books*
www.cmpbooks.com

What's on the DVD

The DVD accompanying this book is packed with information, files, and samples to help you learn more about Vegas and make better media more efficiently.

Nearly 1000 ACID loops
Over 60 video files
Raw HDV/m2t files
Full-Resolution XDCAM footage
Over 50 stock stills
More than 50 various demo software and free software files relating to Sony Vegas and video
12 motion backgrounds for use in DVD Architect
Over 120 veg/project files
24 Additional bonus chapters
Copyright registration forms
Location release forms
Minor releases
Shooting releases
Work for Hire Agreement
16 Themes for Vegas
Test tone media for calibrating equipment
8 Video training files